The Search for Criminal Man

The Dangerous Offender Project

JUSTICE

John P. Conrad and Simon Dinitz
Project Co-Directors
The Academy for Contemporary Problems

In Fear of Each Other   John P. Conrad and Simon Dinitz
The Law and the Dangerous Criminal   Linda Sleffel
The Search for Criminal Man   Ysabel Rennie
The Violent Few   Donna Martin Hamparian, Richard Schuster, Simon Dinitz, and John P. Conrad
Restraining the Wicked   Stephan W. Van Dine, John P. Conrad, and Simon Dinitz
The Career of the Dangerous Criminal   John P. Conrad, Simon Dinitz, and Stuart A. Miller
Out of Circulation: The Dangerous Offender in Prison   Simon Dinitz, John P. Conrad, Israel Barak, and Robert Freeman
Felons in Court   Winifred Lyday, John P. Conrad, and Simon Dinitz
The Dangerous and the Endangered   John P. Conrad

Cover: Cuneiform characters for the word *Justice*, the emblem of the Dangerous Offender Project.

The Search for Criminal Man

A Conceptual History of the Dangerous Offender

Ysabel Rennie

Lexington Books
D.C. Heath and Company
Lexington, Massachusetts
Toronto

Library of Congress Cataloging in Publication Data

Rennie, Ysabel Fisk, 1918-
   The search for criminal man.

   Bibliography: p.
   Includes index.
   1. Crime and criminals—History. 2. Criminal psychology—History. I. Title.
HV6045.R46   364.3'2   77-3109
ISBN 0-669-01480-x

Second printing, March 1980.

Published simultaneously in Canada.

Printed in the United States of America.

International Standard Book Number: 0-669-01480-x

Library of Congress Catalog Card Number: 77-3109

Contents

Foreword

An essential element of a well-designed research program is a survey of the literature bearing on the problem under investigation. Knowing that a vast literature directed at the understanding of crime had been created by philosophers, jurists, biologists, and social scientists, Dr. Dinitz and I brought Mrs. Rennie into our group to produce an annotated bibliography. Clearly, if we were to undertake the empirical studies to which the Dangerous Offender Project was committed, the review of the contributions to the literature of dangerousness from Hammurabi to the present time would be beyond our powers. Mrs. Rennie is a trained historian. She was willing to take a respite of this kind from an activist role in the cause of penal reform. All we expected was a classified inventory of the principal works that seemed relevant to the problem, with such comments on the content as seemed appropriate to her in guiding us to the use of references in the studies we intended to produce.

This volume is much more than we bargained for. A few weeks after starting her labors, she suggested that it might be possible for her to produce a full-scale book reviewing the course of ideas about dangerous offenders and the men, women, and children who are so designated. At the time we were apprehensive about the feasibility of such an undertaking; two years later we see it published with proud amazement.

In his *Structure of Scientific Revolutions*, Thomas Kuhn accustomed the historian of science to the idea of the paradigm that disciplines scientific thought until it exhausts its usefulness in solving the puzzles nature poses to man.[a] Once a paradigm has been replaced by a more serviceable concept of science, it goes to the attic, there to moulder forever as an archival relic. Kuhn was writing primarily of the natural sciences, and his conceptualization has led many to conclude that the social sciences are preparadigmatic—awaiting the great unifying concepts that have made possible the triumphs of physics, biology, and astronomy.

I doubt that this is generally true of the social sciences. Our paradigms lack the elegance that Darwin and Einstein, for example, contributed to their disciplines. But if there have been no spectacular conceptual shifts that have changed the whole course of social science, the world can never be the same as it was before the labors of Marx, Freud, Weber, and Keynes. We are unlikely to go back to their predecessors for ideological nourishment.

As Mrs. Rennie shows, notions in the guise of paradigms rotate across the stage in criminology with cyclical regularity. No idea is ever so discredited that it cannot be refurbished into a new vernacular to captivate a public that is understandably dissatisfied with what is being done about crime. Confident that

---

[a]Thomas S. Kuhn, *The Structure of Scientific Revolutions* (Chicago: The University of Chicago Press, 1962).

change will bring about success, this public is unduly susceptible to the attractions of novelty, even if under the new paint there creaks the rusty machinery of an old model that has served its day.

The beginning of knowledge is classification. To search for Criminal Man is to imply that there is something unifying about crime. That is natural enough. The law has a limited armory to use in its confrontation with criminals of every description, and we rely on the law to control and diminish their depredations. *De minimis non curat lex*: Fine distinctions between defendants in the dock are not responsive to the law's blunt instruments. So the rational man of the economist has replaced the anxious man of the psychoanalyst, and now we hear that although the law cannot cure the criminal of the disease that made him a predator, it can assume that if he is sufficiently punished, he will come to his senses and behave properly. We used to be Freudians; now Bentham reigns again. This succession of old favorites on the stage of criminology will doubtless continue until the problem of crime is seen as consisting of many problems, linked together in most cases by no more than the violation of the laws that citizens have to observe if they are to survive.

In spite of its ironies, it is a tragic history that Mrs. Rennie relates. There are luminous ideas and eccentric perversities from some of the greatest minds of Western thought as well as nasty fallacies contributed by intellectual buffoons and worse. What stands out is the misery that human beings can inflict on each other with the best of intentions. Surely none of the cardinal sins of theology has the potential for evil that is contained in a bad idea. In this book Mrs. Rennie has contributed toward stamping out the infamy of slovenly thought about Criminal Man. In doing so, she may have led us part way toward a good idea—a durable paradigm for thought, research, and action to relieve us of some of the dangers we impose on each other.

John P. Conrad

Acknowledgments

I should like to express my appreciation to John Conrad and Simon Dinitz of the Academy for Contemporary Problems for the opportunity to study the extensive and often fascinating literature on dangerousness and criminality, as part of the academy's Dangerous Offender Project, and for the unfailing support and constructive criticism they gave me during the two years this book was in preparation.

A number of persons both inside and outside the project were helpful in their criticism. I should like to mention especially Dr. Ian Gregory of the Ohio State University Department of Psychiatry for his comments on the psychiatric chapters, Dr. Harold Goldman of the Wayne State University Department of Pharmacology for his comments in the area of psychopharmacology, and Linda Sleffel for her invaluable advice on the legal literature dealing with the mentally disordered and psychopathic offenders. It should be mentioned that in addition to their overall direction of the project, Dr. Dinitz was particularly helpful in guiding me through the enormous sociological literature in the field, and John Conrad watched over my English with the punctiliousness of a Fowler. I am grateful to all these kind friends and colleagues for the time they devoted to my work, even though they have not always agreed with my conclusions.

These acknowledgments would be especially remiss were I not to mention the weeks and months that Jean Gregory devoted to tracking down the journal literature in such disparate fields as criminology, psychiatry, psychology, anthropology, genetics, and the law—labor she performed without recompense, out of a combination of personal friendship and intellectual curiosity. She shortened my labors by a good six months, and I can never thank her enough.

Finally, to Sherry Flannery and her diligent assistants, Lois Gaber and Gail Williams, my gratitude for deciphering my hieroglyphic manuscript and turning it into something even those who run may read.

This work was undertaken with a grant from the Lilly Endowment of Indianapolis, to whose generosity the whole Dangerous Offender Project is deeply indebted.

Ysabel Rennie
Columbus, Ohio
15 August 1977

Introduction

The criminal fascinates even as he repels us. Like Cain, he is not his brother's keeper. Like the serpent, he tempts us to guilty knowledge and disobedience. He is to men what Lucifer was to the angels, the eternal outcast and rebel, challenging all the assumptions of the moral order and risking heaven to do so. We are dismayed by his often dark and bloody deeds, and we run from him when the sun goes down, leaving the streets of our central cities dark and deserted. But even as we escape in terror, we seek him out in our imagination, as though he held locked within him some dirty secret of our own. He is after all a brother, acting out the primitive part in us that we struggle to keep dark. He is hated for being too much like us; he is envied for his freedom and the blessed gift of unrepentance.

When he was ninety-nine years old, Joseph "The Yellow Kid" Weill was interviewed about his life as a swindler. "It was so fascinating," he replied. "I didn't have time to regret my activities. There was so much happiness and joy in swindling." Willie Sutton, who called himself "the last of the old-time gentleman robbers," wondered whether someone can be born with a criminal mind. "Because even as a little boy, when all the other little boys were playing baseball, I was thinking about robbery." He called himself "a true professional thief. A professional thief is a man who wakes up every morning thinking about committing a crime the same way another man gets up and goes to his job."[1] Al Capone prided himself on his patriotism and claimed to have made his money by supplying a popular demand. "Don't get the idea that I'm one of those goddam radicals . . . " he said. "My rackets are run on strictly American lines, and they're going to stay that way. . . . The American system of ours, call it Americanism, call it Capitalism, call it what you like, gives each and every one of us a great opportunity if we only seize it with both hands and make the most of it."[2]

In a way this book is a study of those who seized the great opportunities and how their contemporaries saw them. It began as a search of the literature, not on the criminal as such, but on the "dangerous offender," a term much favored by contemporary criminologists. I wanted to find out exactly what was meant by this concept, which has found its way into legislation, as well as into the Model Penal Code of the American Law Institute and the Model Sentencing Act of the National Council on Crime and Delinquency. What is the difference between a *dangerous* offender and any other kind? Willie Sutton, the gentleman bank robber who boasted of never using violence: Was he a "dangerous offender"? Was Al Capone, who claimed that he was only seizing his opportunities? Are people "dangerous offenders" when they dump poisonous waste into our lakes and rivers? Is there some difference between an ordinary criminal and a "dangerous offender," and if so, should the law treat one differently from the other?

In the popular mind, the "dangerous offender" is the armed robber, mugger, rapist, murderer; the alien *mafioso*; the shadowy figure we call the "psychopath," although we are not certain what we mean by this. He is the madman locked in the University of Texas tower who shoots at passersby; he is the Boston Strangler. The more violent, and above all, the more *unmotivated* his act, the more dangerous we find him. But individuals attempting to draw up model penal codes or legislate a special punishment for the dangerous find it hard to do. The trap they fall into is tautology: They define a dangerous offender as one who poses a danger. Thus the Ohio Revised Code (2929.01B) says that " 'dangerous offender' means a person who has committed an offense, whose history, character and condition reveal a substantial risk that he will be a danger to others, and whose conduct has been characterized by a pattern of repetitive, compulsive, or aggressive behavior with heedless indifference to the consequences." A "substantial risk," it says further, is "a strong possibility, as contrasted with a remote possibility, that a certain result may occur." This formulation, which dates from 1974, is better than most, but it is circular, and it also begs the question, what is a "substantial risk"?

The Model Penal Code of the American Law Institute (ALI), in an older definition (1962), says that a dangerous person may be sentenced to an extended term of imprisonment if he is (1) a persistent offender over twenty-one who has previously been convicted of two felonies or one felony and two misdemeanors committed when he was older than juvenile court age; or (2) a professional criminal whose commitment is necessary for public protection, is over twenty-one, and who "has knowingly devoted himself to criminal activity as a major source of livelihood," or has "substantial incomes or resources not explained to be derived from a source other than criminal activity"; or (3) "a dangerous, mentally abnormal person" whose long-term commitment is necessary to protect the public. There must be a psychiatric finding that his mental condition is gravely abnormal; that his criminal conduct has been characterized by a pattern of repetitive or compulsive or persistently aggressive behavior "with heedless indifference to consequences"; and that his condition makes him "a serious danger to others." Or, finally, (4) "the defendant is a multiple offender whose criminality was so extensive that a sentence of imprisonment for an extended term is warranted."[3]

The ALI's model statute is a veritable omnium gatherum, including past behavior, repetitiveness, professional criminality, unexplained resources, mental abnormality, aggressiveness, compulsivity and "heedless indifference to consequences" in a single, all-encompassing embrace. It deals with dangerousness not so much by definition as by a catalogue of antisocial behavior.

The Model Sentencing Act of the National Council on Crime and Delinquency (1972) defines a dangerous offender as someone who "(a) inflicted or attempted to inflict serious bodily harm, or (b) seriously endangered the life or safety of another and was previously convicted of one or more felonies not related to the instant crime . . . ", *and* who is (c) "suffering from a severe mental or emotional disorder indicating a propensity toward continuing dangerous criminal activity."[4] Note that qualification c is required before the offender is officially defined as dangerous. But how can a sane man not be dangerous who has committed previous felonies, endangered life and safety, and attempted to inflict serious bodily harm?

Many statutes attempting to define dangerousness are purely circular. The U.S. Organized Crime Control Act of 1970 says that a defendant is dangerous if a longer period of confinement "is required for the protection of the public." The New York State Criminal Procedure Law, sect. 730:10 (1971) defines a "dangerous incapacitated person" as "an incapacitated person who is so mentally ill or mentally defective that his presence in an institution run by the Department of Mental Hygiene is dangerous to the safety of other patients therein, the staff of the institution, or the community." The only thing about these statutes, model and actual, is the difficulty involved in defining dangerousness. Are we dealing with harm past or harm to come? The term implies *potentiality*; yet as David Levine has pointed out, the popular definition refers more to the heinousness of an anticipated act than to the probability of its occurrence. Thus its function in everyday speech is based on ambiguity: Once we know precisely the risk involved and the nature of the harm effected, he says, we use words like "violent" or "habitual."[5]

The psychiatrists, too, have attempted to define "dangerousness," but from within the head of the offender, so to speak. In their article, "The Diagnosis and Treatment of Dangerousness," Harry Kozol, Richard Boucher, and Ralph Garofalo have this to say:

We conceive the *dangerous* person as one who has actually inflicted or attempted to inflict serious physical injury on another person; harbors anger, hostility, and resentment; enjoys witnessing or inflicting suffering; lacks altruistic and compassionate concern for others; sees himself as a victim rather than an aggressor; resents or rejects authority; is primarily concerned with his own satisfaction and with the relief of his own discomfort; is intolerant of frustration or delay of satisfaction; lacks control of his own impulses; has immature attitudes toward social responsibility; lacks insight into his own psychological structure; and distorts his perception of reality in accordance with his own wishes and needs.

The essence of dangerousness appears to be a paucity of feeling-concern for others. The offender is generally unaware that his behavior inflicts suffering on others. The potential for injuring another is compounded when this lack of concern is coupled with anger.

... No one is totally primitive—concerned only with the immediate satisfaction of limited goals—or totally mature—maintaining judicious control of all impulses. The dangerous potential may be fixed and habitual, episodic, or sporadic. People cannot be divided into the dangerous and the non-dangerous—the bad guys and the good guys. The spectrum is wide, with the extremely dangerous at one end and the absolutely non-dangerous at the other.[6]

But if dangerousness is a point along a spectrum, where is the point to be found? There is a certain relativity in our perceptions. This was borne home to me when a prisoner of my acquaintance chided his mother for calling one of his fellow convicts "dangerous." To put this discussion in perspective, the speaker was a convicted bank robber with a long list of prior violent offenses, and the individual whose dangerousness was being discussed was a man who boasted of having killed eleven people, including a prison guard. When the bank robber's mother asked him why such a dangerous inmate was allowed in the general visiting room, her son replied, "He ain't dangerous, Mama, he just likes to stab people."

Thus the answer to the question, "Who is dangerous?" may well depend on who is answering: It may also depend on *when* this question is asked. This study concerns first the way different people of different classes and political ideologies have thought about "dangerousness," not only in the twentieth century but also in times past, and in what ways and for what reasons that thinking has changed. This will require not only a historical summary of ideas about crime but also an analysis of the matrices—cultural, theological, social, economic, and legal—in which they were formed. We shall see the development of the law as it responds to the ideology of the time and the evolution of punishment in Continental and English practice.

A second broad area of concern is causation. Why are some people dangerous? Is it something in *them*, or is it something in the organization of society, that creates a "dangerous offender"? Exploration of these questions will involve causative theories from the ancient dictum that "poverty is the mother of crime" through the many etiological concepts that have sought to explain the presence of criminals in our midst: atavism, constitutional inferiority, differential association, alcoholism, social disorganization, familial influences, climate, geography, heredity, genetics, and so forth. It will also entail an examination, not only of the views of sociologists, geneticists, physiologists, pharmacologists, and mental health professionals, but of the logic-tight compartments into which their theories are divided. What do we really know about the etiology of crime? How much of what we "know" is science, how much dogma, how much pure conjecture? To what extent do our theories of causality depend on the mythos of our times?

Another subject to be considered is the treatment of criminals, including both punishment and rehabilitation. In dealing with someone who has committed a crime, are we giving him his just deserts and hence looking backwards to the offense, or are we interested in social defense and thus looking forward to his future and to the safety of society? Rehabilitative strategies will be surveyed and discussed: psychotherapy, behavior modification, psychoactive drugs, psychosurgery, and so forth. We will consider not only whether a proposed treatment is efficacious, but also whether it is ethical, and we will look at the moral and constitutional issues involved in such notions as "informed consent" and "right to treatment." Are we ever justified in tampering with the human personality in the name of a higher social good? If so, when, under what circumstances, and with what safeguards?

No single study could begin to do justice to these issues. The best I can hope for is to clarify the tangle of ideation, prejudice, unexamined assumptions, and economic self-interest that has always underlain our concepts of criminality. Today we are not only the prisoners of a time and place: In this field we are dealing with no single discipline or science, but rather, with a multitude of them, each with its own canons and received wisdom.

Difficult though it is to cope with one orthodoxy, it is far worse to cope with half a dozen. Gunnar Myrdal, the Swedish economist and Nobel laureate, once warned his fellow economists about the dangers of received wisdom. "Those adhering to the dominant body form an establishment," he wrote:

their writings enjoy prestige; they quote each other and usually nobody else, least of all rebels. . . . Thus they tend to create around themselves a space often amounting to an isolation, and not only toward other social science disciplines. . . . What gives status in the academic world and opens up positions in the research and teaching institutions of our craft and also opportunities for being called upon to advise governments, organizations, and businesses, is to work within the set pattern and to demonstrate acumen and inventiveness by embroidering upon it. To these even materially important rewards should be added the force of tradition. It has been said that no vested interests are stronger than those rooted in ingrained thoughtways and preconceptions.

All knowledge—like all ignorance—tends to be opportunistic, when not critically scrutinized. It is inherent in the nature of an establishment that it protects itself forcefully against that type of critical scrutiny by ignoring as long as possible criticism from outside its narrow group.[7]

In this case the problem is compounded by the number of disciplines involved: medicine, law, psychiatry, psychology, sociology, and the various administrative and police sciences that deal with the living, as opposed to the theoretical, offender. To the observer, they seem to struggle over criminology like dogs over a bone.

The present study can claim the neutrality of its author's ignorance. It is the work of an outsider, trained not in criminology, but in history. In middle life, I had the opportunity to know many a "dangerous offender" in person. It was only after a considerable acquaintance with them that I began a belated search of the literature in the field. I will declare my preconceptions, for they are the baggage I carry with me in this study: first, a belief, with Santayana, that those who cannot remember the past are condemned to repeat it; and second, that "the dangerous offender" as a concept and the dangerous offenders I have known in the flesh are not necessarily the same thing. "Dangerous offender" is a protean concept, changing its color and shape to suit the fears, interests, needs, and prejudices of a society. It is an *idea*, not a person. So is the concept we borrowed from Lombroso, of the criminal—a bipedal primate somewhere above the apes and below the Hottentots.

Writers, like ideas, are captives of their time and place, and it is only fair to confess my biases. I wear the blinders of my religious faith (Christian), my political faith (democratic), my country (the United States), and my era (the late twentieth century). A search through old books and discarded theories can be at once both orienting and disorienting. One thing I have learned from it is the truth of Ellen Glasgow's observation, "No idea is so antiquated that it was not once modern. No idea is so modern that it will not some day be antiquated."[8] And, one might add, in penology no idea is so old but what it can be dusted off and sold as brand new merchandise. The historical memory is very short.

This study deals with two related concepts, because there is no way to separate them. One is the idea of Criminal Man, which derives from the Italian positivists. The other is the idea of the Dangerous Offender, which is also a positivist concept. What do these ideas mean? Where did they come from? How have they affected the way we deal with the flesh-and-blood malefactors crowding our courts and jails? Are we so blinded by theories that we cannot deal with the reality of crime? These are important questions. Searching for the answers has taught me some humility. There is very little in this field that has not at some time been tried and found wanting, forgotten for a generation or two, and then revived as the answer to the crime problem. In no other area has a history of practical failure provided a surer guarantee of ideological immortality.

This work will first examine the concept of dangerousness. As Theodore Sarbin has pointed out, the word *danger* derives from the Latin *dominium*, the power of a lord to dispose of, or to harm. It denotes relative power and esteem in a social hierarchy, he says, and it is not the same concept as violence: "Violence denotes action; danger denotes a relationship." The antecedents to violence are not necessarily the antecedents to danger.[9] This is a difficult notion to grasp. We are so used to thinking of the predatory poor as dangerous and the predatory wealthy as the pillars of law and order—they *write* the laws, after all—that we must, so to speak, stand on our heads to view this idea as our ancestors once must have. How did *dominium*, the power of the mighty to rob and injure the humble, become the *danger* that the humble might rob and injure the mighty? Clearly, at one time the threat was perceived as coming from above. To understand the metamorphosis of language, one must know the history of the idea—not only whom do we consider dangerous today, but whom did we consider dangerous in other times and other places? It would be possible to cite many countries and epochs: I have limited myself to the Christian era and to the experiences of Europe, England, and especially the United States, because this is the material with which I have the most acquaintance. I think also it will do much to illumine Sarbin's notion of "danger" as derived from power relationships. It is often easier to see the anomalies of past behavior than to be as wise about our own.

Some of this material will strike the reader as incredible. How could our ancestors have been so ignorant, so barbarous, so blind to realities? Let me commend something I once heard Etienne Gilson say. The French philosopher was lecturing an audience on the ideas of the twelfth century and paused to admonish: "Remember. In looking at past periods, we should not judge them on the basis of *what they don't know yet,* but on the basis of where they are in comparison to those who went before."[10] It is a good thought to bear in mind. In criminology, hypotheses abound; but most of the field lies in the area of "what we don't know yet."

This book deals with many theories of crime, often mutually contradictory, but almost all deeply held. Like *Pinafore*'s Ralph Rackstraw, they are "a living ganglion of irreconcilable antagonisms." For the bewildered reader seeking to judge among them, I commend the thought that was expressed by a very old gentleman who was the last living survivor of a celibate religious colony at Zoar, Ohio. "So many religions in the world," he said, rocking gently in his chair. "They can't all be right. But they could all be wrong."[11]

**Part I
The Dangerous Classes and
the Law: Crime and
Punishment in Historical
Perspective**

1 The Dangerous Classes

In 1838, as was their annual custom, the French Académie des Sciences Morales et Politiques announced a contest on a question of absorbing public interest: "To seek, by actual observation, in Paris or any other great city, which elements of the population, by their vices, their ignorance and their poverty, constitute a dangerous class; and to indicate the means by which the Administration, the wealthy, those in comfortable circumstances, and intelligent and hard-working laborers might improve that dangerous and depraved class."[1]

The winning entry in this contest was submitted by H.A. Frégier, Bureau Chief of the prefecture of the Seine. Published in 1840, it was titled *The Dangerous Classes of the Population in the Great Cities, and the Means of Making Them Better*. No one smiled at the concept of "the dangerous classes," any more than anyone today would smile at mention of the "dangerous offender": These classes were too well known and too widely feared to evoke amusement. True, said Frégier, there was also an educated dangerous class of wealthy, vicious idlers; but penal law, with its responsibility to protect society, should direct its attention less to the "vicious classes" than to "those who, joining to vice the depravity of destitution, are justly suspected of living at society's expense. The vicious man who is rich, or comfortably well-off, and who wastes his surplus, or even part of his capital, in blameworthy pleasures, inspires pity and distrust, but not fear; he does not become dangerous until he is without either the means of existence or the desire to work. . . ."[2]

Both the concept behind the academy's competition and the two-volume work Frégier submitted on this absorbing topic embody some of the oldest, as well as the most contemporary, postulates on the nature, etiology, and management of violent crime. There lurks in the great cities of the world, it says, a dangerous underclass that embraces both the working (virtuous) and the idle (vicious) poor. Although this underclass may share a common moral depravity with many of the well-to-do, it is worse to be poor and vicious than rich and vicious. No one fears the idle wastrel who may squander capital on top of income: What we do fear is the hungry man with a dagger who, lurking in the squalid alleys of our cities, would cut our throats for a pocketful of change.

And yet—and yet, surely—these wretches, with "their vices, their ignorance and their poverty" *can* be improved through the determined efforts of "the Administration, the wealthy, those in comfortable circumstances, and intelligent and hard-working laborers." Just how this was to be done was to be the subject of many treatises by nineteenth- and twentieth-century reformers. Charles

3

Loring Brace, in his work of a generation later, *The Dangerous Classes of New York* (1872), suggested that "the cheapest and most efficacious way of dealing with the 'Dangerous Classes' of large cities is not to punish them, but to prevent their growth; to so throw the influences of education and discipline and religion about the abandoned and destitute youth of our large towns; to so change their material circumstances, and draw them under the influence of the moral and fortunate classes, that they shall grow up as useful producers and members of society, able and inclined to aid it in its progress. In the view of this book, the class of a large city most dangerous to its prosperity, its morals and its political life, are the ignorant, destitute, untrained, and abandoned youth: the outcast street-children grown up to be voters, to be the implements of demagogues, the 'feeders' of the criminals, and the sources of domestic outbreaks and violations of law. If the narrative shall lead the citizens of other large towns to inaugurate comprehensive and organized movements for the improvement of their 'Dangerous Classes,' my object will be fully attained."[3]

Here again is an idea, which we still embrace today, although with diminished optimism, that if we bring the lower classes "under the influence of the moral and fortunate classes" (i.e., of their betters, namely, ourselves), they will grow up to be "useful producers and members of society." This may be denominated the contagion theory of social betterment: It is the reverse of the contagion theory of criminal behavior, and it is much less well documented.

The concept that the poor are more dangerous than the rich and hence, *eo ipso*, more criminal, is a very old one. Cassiodorus[a] is credited with the dictum that "poverty is the mother of crime," and through the centuries wits and scholars have rung their changes on this theme. Holbach: "If wealth is the mother of vices, poverty is the mother of crimes."[4] La Bruyère: "If poverty is the mother of crimes, want of sense is the father of them."[5] And so forth. Perhaps, then, this very ancient and perseverant notion is as good a point of departure as any for our discussion.

To the rich, the poor have always been dangerous. The criminals in the Roman mines and galleys or nailed to crosses at the Esquiline Gate were not patricians; they were revolted slaves, or the *humiliores*, the pauper rabble who swarmed to the great cities from an impoverished countryside. If a Roman gentleman committed any crime but treason, the worst punishment he would likely suffer would be banishment or loss of property and civil rights.[6] For what might be called their White Toga criminals, the Romans, like us, had a system of differential justice.

And so has every age. In modern times as in ancient, the poor and dangerous are seen as dangerous, while the rich and dangerous are simply rich. Sarbin's observation that "danger" is derived from *dominium*, or lordship, and denotes a relationship between those with power and those without it, can be illustrated in

[a]Flavius Magnus Aurelius Cassiodorus (A.D. 490-575), who served under Theodoric when the Ostrogoths ruled Italy.

every period of history. In medieval England, for example, the criminal law was much concerned with "strangers" (Statute of Winchester, 1285), beggars (1331 and the centuries following), and escaped servants, laborers, and artificers [craftsmen] (1349). Yet, as David Hume observed, "The barons, by their confederacies with those of their own order, and by supporting and defending their retainers in every iniquity, were the chief abettors of robbers, murderers, and ruffians of all kinds, and no law could be executed against those criminals."[7]

The means by which the upper classes exempted themselves from punishment is in itself an absorbing chapter of legal history. In England it began as a right called "benefit of clergy," which in the early Middle Ages permitted a cleric accused of a crime to be tried in an ecclesiastical court. The privilege was soon extended to anyone who could read or write. The accused was permitted to make an oath of his innocence, after which twelve compurgators swore they believed him; then witnesses (for the defense only) were examined. Under this happy system the accused was almost always acquitted. If not, he was "degraded or put to penance," and branded on the brawn of his left thumb.[8]

There was a curious duality in the English law, not only toward upper- and lower-class criminals, but also toward crimes of violence and those against property. Till late in the seventeenth century the most violent crimes against the person were treated as misdemeanors, punishable usually by fines. This attitude had its origins in ancient custom. Before the Norman conquest such crimes were considered torts, and the laws set forth with the utmost minuteness and particularity the compensation to be paid, but no one considered them a violation of the moral law. If you did damage to another person, you paid for the damages, and that was all. As Sir James Fitzjames Stephen commented, "The extraordinary lenity of the English criminal law towards the most atrocious acts of personal violence forms a remarkable contrast to its extraordinary severity with regard to offenses against property."[9] It is possible that the reason for this lenity was that the feudal classes were themselves given to acts of violence, whereas the crimes they feared were theft and robbery by the lower classes.

It is impossible to understand the criminal law outside its social and economic context. For nearly four hundred years, from the thirteenth through the sixteenth centuries, the English criminal law was obsessed with vagrants and beggars, who were viewed as a great danger to society. The first groups of wanderers were those who fled from feudal service after the Black Death of 1348. Much legislation concerns these vagabonds, who were seeking better wages and employment in the towns and cities. People were forbidden under pain of imprisonment to give them alms "so that thereby they may be compelled to labour for their necessary living."[10] The law imposed fines on the mayor and bailiff of any town "who refused to deliver up a labourer, servant or artificer" who had run away from service. These latter were to be branded on the forehead with the letter F "in token of falsity."[11]

It was no doubt true that "robberies, murther, burnings and theft be more often used than they have been heretofore," as the Statute of Winchester (1285) put it. But it was also characteristic of criminal law that it dealt with symptoms. Brush was ordered cleared from the highways; town gates were to be closed at sunset; if any "stranger" passed by the country in the night, he was to be arrested.[12] Said Hume of the reign of Edward II (1307-1327), "The disorder of the times from foreign wars and intestine dissensions, but above all, the cruel famine which obliged the nobility to dismiss many of their retainers, increased the number of robbers in the kingdom, and no place was secure from their incursions. They met in troops like armies, and overran the country."[13]

With the breakdown of feudalism and the rise of the wool trade, conditions grew worse. Where once serfs had left the land to escape service, they were now evicted by their landlords to make room for sheep. The common lands of the villages, which under feudal tenure belonged to everyone, were now claimed by the landlords, under concepts of ownership derived from Roman law. The result was that thousands of people were driven from their homes; whole villages were abandoned, and, as one statute put it, "a marvellous multitude of the people of this realm be not able to provide meat, drink, and clothes necessary for themselves, their wives, and children, but be so discouraged with misery and poverty that they fall daily to theft, robbery, and other inconvenience, or pitifully die for hunger and cold."[14]

In the reign of Henry VIII there was now a large class of penniless vagrants, roaming the countryside. Sir Thomas More called them "poor, silly, wretched souls, men, women, husbands, wives, fatherless children, widows, woeful mothers, with their young babes, and their whole household small in substance and much in number. . . . What can they do," he asked, "but steal and then justly, God wot, be hanged, or else go about a-begging? . . . . What other things do you do, than make thieves and then punish them?"[15] And, indeed, the law punished them most grievously. It provided that whoever was found begging should be taken to the "next market-town, or other place most convenient, and be there tied to the end of a cart naked, till his body be bloody by reason of such whipping." For a second offense, he was to be scourged for two days, put in the stocks, and have his ear cut off. The reason for this severity, as the statute explained, was that "idleness, root and mother of all vices" had given rise to "continual thefts, murders, and other offenses and great enormities, to the high displeasure of God, the unquietation and damage of the king's people, and to the marvellous disturbance of the common weal."[16]

Thus the victims of misfortune were doubly punished. Having been turned from their homes and robbed of their livelihoods, they were deemed too dangerous to be at large. During Henry's reign, not only were countless multitudes scourged but some 72,000 major and minor thieves were hanged. Under his daughter Elizabeth vagabonds were strung up in rows, as many as three and four hundred at a time.[17] Said Georg Rusche and Otto Kirchheimer, "the system acted as a kind of artificial earthquake or famine in destroying those whom the upper classes considered unfit for society."[18]

An Act for the Punishment of Rogues, Vagabonds and Sturdy Beggars, 39 Elizabeth c. 4 (1597-1598), lists the following dangerous types: "all persons calling themselves scholars going about begging; all seafaring men pretending losses of their ships and goods on the sea; all idle persons going about either begging or using any subtle craft or unlawful games and plays, or feigning to have knowledge in physiognomy, palmistry, or other like crafty science, or pretending that they can tell destinies, fortunes, or such other fantastical imaginations; all fencers, bearwards [bear keepers], common players, and minstrels; all jugglers, tinkers, pedlers, and petty chapmen; all wandering persons and common labourers, able in body, and refusing to work for the wages commonly given; all persons delivered out of gaols that beg for their fees or travel begging; all persons that wander abroad begging, pretending losses by fire or otherwise; and all persons pretending themselves to be Egyptians [i.e., gypsies]." All such persons "shall be taken, adjudged, and deemed rogues, vagabonds, and sturdy beggars, and shall sustain such pain and punishment as by this Act is in that behalf appointed." In the same year, 43 Elizabeth c. 3 includes men claiming to be soldiers and mariners who "do continually assemble themselves, weaponed, in the highways, and elsewhere, in troops, to the great terror and astonishment of her Majesty's true subjects. And many heinous outrages, robberies, and horrible murders are daily committed by these dissolute persons."[19]

Although the Enclosure Movement was responsible for much of the vagabondage and mendicancy in the fifteenth and sixteenth centuries, there were other factors at work. The end of the Hundred Years' War with France saw the demobilization of thousands of soldiers. Some years later, the closing of the monasteries under Henry VIII abolished the only eleemosynary institutions in England. Many of the same problems afflicted France also. Indeed, the efforts of Paris and other French towns to deal with the wandering poor sound like nothing so much as translations of the parliamentary statutes. There were the same "whereases"; the same efforts to keep the poor in their own villages; the same injunctions against beggary or almsgiving; the same lists of rogues, vagabonds, and sturdy beggars.

In fourteenth-century France great companies of unpaid soldiers roamed and pillaged. In the fifteenth, there came also thousands of gypsies from the provinces of the Byzantine Empire, which had been devastated by the Turks. The opening of seven new universities in the fifteenth century created a host of unemployed "clercs," or university graduates without clerical posts, who begged, stole, told fortunes, and counterfeited for a living. And there were wandering groups of so-called pilgrims, known as Coquillards, who had their own king and their own special ways of making a living: Some were cutpurses, some card sharps, some con men, some assassins. Among them were many university scholars, including the famous poet, François Villon. "This should not astonish anyone," said Christian Paultre: "The frightful poverty which had desolated France for so many years had singularly debased the level of morality, and for many people, all means of livelihood were good."[20]

For a long time considered no more than nuisances, wanderers had by the sixteenth century come to be viewed as dangerous. Various expedients were tried: imprisonment on bread and water; flogging; branding; cutting off the ears. Some were sent to the galleys, some chained and put to work building town fortifications. Jean Bodin (1577) thought that "there is no way to cleanse Republics of this excrement but to send them to war, which is like a purgative and necessary method to drive out the corrupt humors from the universal body of the Republic."[21]

The numbers involved were truly astonishing. One writer estimates that there were eighty thousand beggars in Paris in the early fifteenth century,[22] and the numbers were much greater in the sixteenth, when a succession of bad harvests and the closing of parish poorhouses sent thousands drifting to the cities in search of work. So desperate did the towns become that in Troyes an *estrapade* was erected in the middle of the wheat market. This was an instrument of torture in which the condemned was hoisted, hands tied, to the top of a pole, then allowed to fall with sufficient force to break his arms and legs.[23]

If such punishment was inflicted on beggars, it can be imagined what happened to thieves and other felons. Speaking of punishments in Europe, Rusche and Kirchheimer said that "the most morbid imagination today can hardly picture the variety of tortures inflicted. We read about executions by knife, ax, and sword, heads being knocked off with a plank or cut through with a plough, people being buried alive, left to starve in a dungeon, or having nails hammered through their heads, eyes, shoulders, and knees, strangulation and throttling, drowning and bleeding to death, evisceration, drawing and quartering, torture on the wheel, torture with red-hot tongs, strips being cut from the skin, the body being torn to pieces or sawed through with iron or wooden instruments, burning at the stake, and many other elaborate forms of cruelty." As the authors observed, when Hieronymus Bosch, Peter Breughel, and Matthias Grünewald depicted the torture of martyrs, they were recording the public's everyday experience with criminal justice.[24] Yet it was a kind of justice that such religious leaders as Martin Luther applauded. Mere execution was not punishment enough, Luther thought. Rulers should pursue, beat, strangle, hang, burn, and torture, for "the hand that holds the sword and strangles is no longer a human hand, but the hand of God."[25]

Even in Luther's perfervid imagination, however, God would not have looked on benignly while gentlemen were subjected to wheel, rack, or red-hot tongs. The general differentiation between classes in the sixteenth century made assessment of fines or corporal punishment dependent, simply, on ability to pay. "Thus while those who had enough money to pay were able to buy exemption from punishment," said Rusche and Kirchheimer, "offenders without means (and they made up the great majority in these hard times) were powerless to save themselves from the harsh treatment to which they were liable.... The poorer the masses became, the harsher the punishments in order to deter them from crime."[26]

England tried every way it knew to contain the crime engendered by vagrancy: transportation overseas (The Vagrancy Act of 1597); houses of correction (beginning with Bridewell in 1553,[27] and spreading to every county); and the multiplication of capital offenses, which in the eighteenth century, with the Second Enclosure Movement under way, reached staggering proportions. In England, as late as 1688, no more than about fifty offenses carried the death penalty; after that, their number soared. In the reign of George II, thirty-three new capital offenses were created; sixty-three were added during the first half-century of George III's reign. Thus from the Restoration to the death of George III in 1820, the number of capital offenses had increased by about one hundred ninety. As Sir Samuel Romilly remarked, "there is probably no country in the world in which so many and so great a variety of human actions are punishable with loss of life as in England."[28]

When Romilly tried to persuade Parliament to repeal the law providing that criminals should not only be hanged but publicly disembowelled and quartered, he was accused of being not so much soft-hearted as soft-headed. Clearly, he did not understand that, as Sir James Stephen was later to explain, "The object of the criminal law is to overcome evil with evil."[29] It was an objective that eluded the best minds. While punishments multiplied, so too did crimes, a phenomenon that puzzled and disturbed people no less in earlier centuries than in our own. It was as though the more harshly they legislated, the more prevalent crime became. Sir Thomas More was not the last observer to see the economic nexus. Said Jean-Jacques Rousseau in his *Discourse upon the Origin and Foundations of Inequality* (1755): "The first man, who, having enclosed a piece of ground, took it into his head to say, 'This is mine,' and found people simple enough to believe him, was the true founder of civil society. What crimes, wars, and murders, what miseries and horrors would have been spared the human race had someone torn up the stakes or filled the ditch, and cried to his fellows: 'Beware of heeding this imposter; you are lost if you forget that the fruits belong to all, and the ground itself to no one!' "[30]

Holbach, writing in 1773, said that "a bad government has its own negligence or its own injustice to blame for the great number of malefactors.... When a state is badly governed and wealth is too unequally divided, so that millions of men lack the necessaries of life, while a small number of citizens are surfeited with luxuries, there we commonly see a great number of criminals, whose number punishments do not diminish.... The man who has no share in the wealth of the state is not held to society by any bond."[31]

J.P. Brissot de Warville saw society divided into two classes, "the first, consisting of citizens with property, living in idleness; the second and more numerous class composed of the mass of the people, to whom the right to exist has been sold dear, and who are degraded and condemned to perpetual toil. To confirm this new right of property, the most cruel punishments have been pronounced upon all those who disturb or attack it. The breach of this right is called theft; and see how far we are from nature! The thief in the state of nature is the rich man, the man who has superfluity; in society the thief is he who robs this rich man." A man is not born an enemy to society, said Brissot de Warville. It is circumstances like poverty or misfortune that give him that title: "He does not disturb the general tranquility until he has lost his own."[32]

What we observe in this history is two parallel but entirely separate ways of thinking about crime. One is causative and answers the questions: Where does violence come from? Is it something in the nature of man, or is it rooted in society? Are our "dangerous offenders" merely the dispossessed—victims, in Rousseau's words, of that "first man, who, having enclosed a piece of ground, took it into his head to say, 'This is mine' "? or are they somehow different from the rest of us—inferior, twisted beings, an atavistic throwback to the primitives who, surviving among us, are condemned by their inferiority to attack our lives, our safety, and our institutions?

The other kind of question is, what do we do about these people? This should logically depend on our views of causation; but in fact, throughout history the criminal law has been enclosed in a logic-tight compartment where that issue plays no part. Thus on the one hand we have philosophers, sociologists, and theoreticians of many different disciplines asking why, and on the other, legislators answering quite independently the question, what do we do?

For thousands of years their response was to make punishments more dreadful, as though hungry, homeless, and starving people could somehow be terrorized into submission. The idea, certainly, was general deterrence: This was the reason for the revolting spectacles, the hangings, burnings, and crucifixions. But it is undeniable that in all recorded history, nobody hit upon a formula for extirpation of crime, however apt they became in the extirpation of criminals. That we are in the twentieth century no closer to a solution than we were in the second says something, I think, about who makes the laws, and the purposes the laws really serve. They express our indignation, certainly; they vent our wrath on "the enemies of society"; but at the same time laws to protect life, liberty, and property are drawn in such a way as to ensure that those who write the laws suffer as little as possible from their sanctions. That is why the prisons, the stocks, and the gallows have from time immemorial been filled with the losers of society—not the rich and vicious, but the poor and vicious—those the Académie des Sciences Morales called "that dangerous and depraved class."

2 Changing Concepts of Crime and Punishment

It is possible that legislated punishment would have continued exponentially growing ever more frightful as cities filled and crimes multiplied—although one is hard put to imagine what expedients might have topped the tortures of the past. However, the great and growing middle class of the eighteenth century was increasingly dissatisfied with the criminal law as it existed on the Continent. England had had its Magna Charta, its Bill of Rights, its Glorious Revolution to establish the ineluctable privileges and immunities of the king's subjects. On the Continent, however, law was uncertain, ill-defined, and arbitrary. There were crimes against religion (heresy, witchcraft, atheism); crimes against the state, including the publication of critical writings; and "crown and judges exercised arbitrary powers to convict and punish for acts not legally defined as crimes at all."[1] In a number of kingdoms and principalities, the monarch could issue what the French called *lettres de cachet.* Under them, persons were imprisoned on the flimsiest pretexts, to gratify private pique or revenge, and asserting no grounds whatever. The *lettre de cachet* was to monarchies of the eighteenth century what the midnight knock on the door is to dictatorships of the twentieth. Almost anyone could be imprisoned as *potentially* dangerous, a fate reserved in twentieth century America for the mentally ill.

Today we think we know who is dangerous. So, of course, did our ancestors, though their views occasionally surprise us. For two hundred years after Christ, for example, his followers were considered so dangerous to the peace and welfare of the Roman State that the most frightful punishments could with impunity be visited upon them. The excuse was the Christians' refusal to sacrifice to Roman deities, a very dangerous offense, in the popular view. "If the Empire had been afflicted by any recent calamity, by a plague, a famine, or an unsuccessful war," said Edward Gibbon; "if the Tiber had, or if the Nile had not, risen beyond its banks; if the earth had shaken, or if the temperate order of the seasons had been interrupted, the superstitious pagans were convinced that the crimes and the impiety of the Christians . . . had at length provoked the Divine justice."[2] For the unfortunate Christians it was dangerous to be so dangerous. Nero chose to blame them for the fire that in the tenth year of his reign destroyed Rome. A multitude were seized. According to Tacitus, "some were nailed on crosses; others sewn up in the skins of wild beasts, and exposed to the fury of dogs; others, again, smeared over with combustible materials, were used as torches to illuminate the darkness of the night." The Roman historian agreed that "the guilt of the Christians deserved indeed the most exemplary punish-

11

ment"; but he felt that there had been what we should today call a lack of due process in the way they were punished—"that those unhappy wretches were sacrificed, not so much to the public welfare as to the cruelty of a jealous tyrant."[3] No one, including Tacitus, however, doubted that they constituted a dangerous class.

Probably no class of dangerous persons was more grievously abused than those accused in the late middle ages and Renaissance of witchcraft. These were not isolated individuals but rather scores, even hundreds at a time, most of them women. In their famous *Malleus Maleficarum*, or *Hammer of Witches* (1486), Heinrich Krämer and Jacob Sprenger, two Dominican inquisitors from Upper Germany, asked themselves, why *women*? and answered their own query by saying "that there are three things in nature, the Tongue, an Ecclesiastic, and a Woman, which know no moderation in goodness or vice." Just how dangerous these witches were was explained by the authors: They "raise hailstorms and hurtful tempests and lightnings; cause sterility in men and animals; offer to devils, or otherwise kill, the children whom they do not devour. . . . They can also, before the eyes of their parents, and when no one is in sight, throw into the water children walking by the water side; they make horses go mad under their riders; they can transport themselves from place to place through the air, either in body or imagination; they can affect Judges and Magistrates so that they cannot hurt them . . . they can at times strike whom they will with lightning, and even kill some men and animals; they can make of no effect the generative desires, and even the power of copulation, cause abortion, kill infants in the mother's womb by a mere exterior touch; they can at times bewitch men and animals with a mere look, without touching them, and cause death; they dedicate their own children to devils. . . ."[4]

During this period many contemporary observers looked on witchcraft as the greatest single threat to Christian civilization. The numbers prosecuted for this offense were truly astonishing. In the fourteenth century there were mass burnings in Provence, the Alpine regions, and Spain. The following century saw mass trials and executions in Rome (1424), Heidelberg (1446), Cologne (1456), Como (1485), and Metz (1488). Various writers have come up with estimates of the numbers killed; they run from fifty thousand to as high as a million. The truth is that nobody knows the total numbers, but contemporary observers saw witchcraft and the prosecution for it as involving great masses of people. It also involved very little due process for reasons that Jean Bodin explained in his *De la démonomanie des sorciers* (1580): "Those too who let the witches escape, or who do not punish them with the utmost rigor, may rest assured that they will be abandoned by God to the mercy of the witches. And the country which shall tolerate this will be scourged with pestilences, famines and wars; and those which shall take vengeance on the witches will be blessed by him and will make his anger to cease. Therefore it is that one accused of being a witch ought never to be fully acquitted and set free unless the calumny of the accuser is clearer than the sun, inasmuch as the proof of such crimes is so obscure and so difficult that not one witch in a million would be accused or punished if the procedure were governed by the ordinary rules."[5]

It is extraordinary today to consider the numbers of distinguished persons who believed witches were dangerous offenders. Pope Innocent VIII issued a bull against witchcraft (*Summis desiderantes*, 1484). Luther and Calvin condemned it. King James I of England made a scholarly study and wrote a dissertation on it. And in fact, theological notions of danger, including the danger of witchcraft, persisted through the Wars of Religion and down to the eighteenth century. To the Inquisition, heretics were dangerous, to Protestants, Catholics, to the New Englanders, witches, to believers of all persuasions, freethinkers and atheists. But in the eighteenth century, after the witchcraft madness and the ferocity of the Religious Wars, the climate of opinion began gradually to change. The new ideas first made themselves felt in Paris among a group of freethinkers who called themselves *philosophes*. It became fashionable to question all kinds of ortho-doxies, said Carl Becker, though "rather too much after the manner of those who are but half emancipated from the 'superstitions' they scorn." Of the *philosophes* he remarked that "they had put off the fear of God, but maintained a respectful attitude toward the Deity. . . . They courageously discussed atheism, but not before the servants."[6]

Intellectual doubts, once admitted, spread from the salons of Paris to the bookshops and thence to the literate of all classes. When the nonconformists, political and religious, became also the people of wealth and education, it began to seem intolerable that the criminal law should pursue and punish them for their opinions. The same thing, of course, had happened in the fourth century, when Constantine announced his conversion and Christians gained control of the Roman Empire. There had been then a sudden redefinition of the "dangerous classes," and with it a reconsideration of the scope and direction of the criminal law.

In the eighteenth century thinkers once again asked themselves, who is really dangerous? And the answer was, of course, that those people are dangerous who are dangerous to *us*—those who threaten our lives and property. Forget the freethinkers and the heretics: The criminal law has quite enough to do to keep up with thieves, highwaymen, brigands, and assassins. Then, as now, crime flourished, and thoughtful minds were much more concerned by the failure of the law to deter criminals than by its failure to stamp out nonconformity.

Why, they wondered, was crime so prevalent? It could not be for lack of sufficient punishment: As crimes had multiplied, so had the ferocity of the sanctions. So what, then, was the matter? Why were criminals not deterred? One of the earliest thinkers to look at this question was Charles Louis de Secondat, Baron de la Brède et de Montesquieu, whose work *On the Spirit of the Laws* was published in 1748. In his sixth book Montesquieu argued that harsh punishments were simply not the best means of managing human beings. "If you examine the cause for laxness," he wrote, "you will see that it comes from the impunity for crimes, not from the moderation of the penalties." As for those countries "where men are only contained by cruel punishments, be sure that that comes in great part from the violence of the government, which has employed such punishments for venial offenses." He concluded, "It is essential that punishments be in harmony with one another, because it is essential that one avoid a great crime rather than a lesser one—that which injures society more, rather than that which offends it less."[7]

In the multiplication of sanctions that had occurred since the Renaissance, more and more crimes had become capital crimes so that, as the old saw had it, the criminal might as well be hanged for a sheep as a lamb. When a man can be hanged for destroying a fishpond or cutting down a cherry tree, how do you deter him from committing murder? This problem was quite evident in England, where judges and juries were increasingly unwilling to convict anyone who faced the gallows: "The persons, lay and official, who administered the criminal law, invented and indulged in practices which almost nullified the capital penalty in most non-clergable felonies," says Jerome Hall. "Juries, judges, prosecutors, and complainants collaborated. The juries returned verdicts which were palpably not findings of fact but such deliberate misstatements of facts as would have been punished by attaint a half century earlier. . . . By the middle of the eighteenth century the practice of returning fictitious verdicts was so widespread that it was generally recognized as a typical feature of English Administration of criminal justice."[8]

A contemporary French observer laid this practice not so much to compassion as to concern "lest the effect of example should be weakened by the frequency of executions. . . . They are indifferent whether among the really guilty such be convicted or acquitted. So much the worse for him against whom the proofs are too evident, so much the better for the other in whose favor there may exist some faint doubt; they look upon the former as singled out by a sort of fatality to serve as an example to the people, and inspire them with a wholesome terror of the vengeance of the law; the other as a wretch whose chastisement heaven has reserved in the other world."[9]

"There may be some exaggeration in this," admitted the Victorian scholar Sir James Fitzjames Stephen, "but the sentiment here described is not altogether unlike the practical result to be expected from the maxim, '*Timor in omnes poena in paucos,*' a sentiment not unnatural when the practice and the theory of the law differed so widely as they did sixty years ago. It was natural that a convicted prisoner should be looked upon as a victim, chosen more or less by chance, when the whole law was in such a state that public sentiment would not permit of its being carried even proximately into effect."[10] Just how much chance was involved can be seen from the few available statistics. In 1818, 13,567 persons were tried for nonclergable offenses (that is, those exempt from benefit of clergy) which were, in theory at least, capital offenses but did not in this case include crimes of violence or murder. Of these 13,567, 8,958 were convicted, 1,254 sentenced to death, and 97 executed.[11] Leon Radzinowicz has called this system "suspended terror."[12]

In debate in the House of Commons, February 9, 1810, Sir Samuel Romilly pointed out that in the middle of the eighteenth century, when there were far fewer capital crimes, from 50 to 75 percent of offenders capitally convicted had been executed; now, with the multiplication of capital offenses on the statute books, the percentage had dropped to between 10 and 15. "The sole object of human punishment, as has often been said, but can hardly be too often repeated, is the prevention of crime; and to this end, they operate principally by terror of example." This does not work, however, when legal punishment is seldom exacted; this is no more than a "lottery of justice." Certainty of punishment is more important than its severity. "So evident is the truth of that maxim," he told Parliament, "that if it were possible that punishment as the consequence of guilt, could be reduced to an absolute certainty, a very slight penalty would be sufficient to prevent almost every species of crime, except those which arise from sudden gusts of ungovernable passion."[13]

The whole question of "sanctions" (meaning both punishment *and* reward) was an absorbing one to the eighteenth and early nineteenth centuries. The father of what came to be known as the Classical School of Criminal Law was Cesare Bonesana, Marquis of Beccaria. In 1764 Beccaria, then only twenty-six and barely out of law school, published in Leghorn, Italy, a slim volume entitled *An Essay on Crimes and Punishments.* It appeared anonymously because the young author, a Milanese whose territory was then under the rule of Austria, feared reprisals if his authorship were known. Quite the opposite occurred. Beccaria was lionized; his slender volume was translated into all the languages of Europe. It was read as avidly by the Austrian Emperor Joseph II as by Sir William Blackstone, then a lecturer on the English law whose lecture notes would soon be published as Blackstone's *Commentaries on the Laws of England.* Seldom has a single work had so galvanizing an effect on the legal thinking of an age as did Beccaria's essay.

Beccaria demolished the corrupt and arbitrary system of jurisprudence then existing in Europe; but this was only his starting point. "His unique achievement," said Leon Radzinowicz, "was to express, in the most coherent and concentrated form, that whole new conception of criminal justice emerging from the ideas of the enlightenment and the growing force of liberalism. . . . *Dei delitti e delle pene* was the manifesto of the liberal approach to criminal law, its rallying cry and its plan of campaign."[14]

Basing the legitimacy of criminal sanctions on the social contract, Beccaria called laws "the conditions under which men, naturally independent, united themselves in society. Weary of living in a continual state of war, and of enjoying a liberty which became of little value, from the uncertainty of its duration, they sacrificed one part of it, to enjoy the rest in peace and security." This they deposited with the sovereign as lawful administrator. "But it was not sufficient only to establish this deposit; it was also necessary to defend it from the usurpation of each individual, who will always endeavour to take away from the mass, not only his own portion, but to encroach on that of others."[15]

The authority of making laws rests with the legislator, "who represents the whole of society, united by the social compact. No magistrate then (as he is one of the society) can, with justice, inflict on any other member of the same society, punishment that is not ordained by the laws." And Beccaria had little use for the spirit, as opposed to the letter, of the law; it made justice dependent on the judge's good or bad logic, his good or bad digestion, the rank and condition of the accused, and whether the criminal has influence with the magistrate. "The disorders that may arise from a rigorous observance of the letter of penal laws, are not to be compared with those produced by the interpretation of them." To adopt the common maxim, "*the spirit of the laws is to be considered,*" said Beccaria, "is to give way to the torrent of opinions."[16]

Developing the suggestion of Montesquieu, Becarria said that there ought to be a fixed proportion between crimes and punishments. The most serious offenses, he thought, are those that tend to the dissolution of society, such as high treason. Next come those destructive of individual security. Attempts "against the life and liberty of a citizen are crimes of the highest nature. Under this head we comprehend not only assassinations, and robberies, committed by the populace, but by grandees and magistrates; whose example acts with more force, and at a greater distance, destroying the ideas of justice and duty among the subjects, and substituting that of the right of the strongest, equally dangerous to those who exercise it, and to those who suffer."[17] The smallest crime, deserving of the least punishment, is the smallest possible injustice done to a private member of society. "If there were an exact and universal scale of crimes and punishments, we should there have a common measure of the degree of liberty and slavery, humanity and cruelty of different nations."[18] As it is, "ideas of virtue and vice, of a good or a bad citizen, change with the revolution of age; not in proportion to the alteration of circumstances, and consequently conformable to the common good; but in proportion to the passions and errors by which the different law-givers were successively influenced."[19]

Legislators, said Beccaria, should have in view only one end: "*the greatest happiness of the greatest number.*" He agreed with Montesquieu that every punishment that does not arise from absolute necessity is tyrannical. "Observe that by *justice* I understand nothing more, than that bond, which is necessary to keep the interest of individuals united; without which, men would return to their original state of barbarity. All punishments, which exceed the necessity of preserving this bond, are in their nature unjust."[20]

He agreed with Montesquieu that crimes are much more effectually prevented by the *certainty* than by the *severity* of punishment, "for it is the nature of mankind to be terrified at the reproach of the smallest inevitable evil, whilst hope, the best gift of heaven, hath the power of dispelling the apprehension of a greater. . . ." To illustrate this, he imagined the reasoning of a robber or assassin: " 'What are these laws, that I am bound to respect, which make so great a difference between me and the rich man? He refuses me the farthing I ask 'of him, and excuses himself, by bidding me have recourse to labour with which he is unacquainted. Who made these laws? The rich and the great, who never deigned to visit the miserable hut of the poor; who have never seen him dividing a piece of mouldy bread; amidst the cries of his famished children and the tears of his wife. Let us break those ties, fatal to the greatest part of mankind, and only useful to a few indolent tyrants. Let us attack injustice at its source. I will return to my natural state of independence. I shall live free and happy on the fruits of my courage and industry. A day of pain and repentance may come, but it will be short; and for an hour of grief I shall enjoy years of pleasure and liberty. King of a small number, as determined as myself, I will correct the mistakes of fortune; and I shall see those tyrants grow pale and tremble at the sight of him, whom, with insulting pride, they would not suffer to rank with their dogs and horses.' "[21]

Punishment might be necessary, said Beccaria, but it is an evil nonetheless. Therefore, it should exceed the reward expected from the crime, but it should not be unduly severe. "All severity beyond this is superfluous, and therefore tyrannical." Capital punishment was not authorized by any right arising from the social contract. "Did any one ever give to others the right of taking away his life? Is it possible, that in the smallest portions of the liberty of each sacrificed to the good of the public, can be contained the greatest of all good, life?" To be just, a punishment should have only that degree of severity that is sufficient to deter others. Capital punishment is pernicious to society, from the example of barbarity it affords. "Is it not absurd," he asked, "that the laws, which detest and punish homicide, should, in order to prevent murder, publicly commit murder themselves?"[22]

And he concluded with this theorem: *"That a punishment may not be an act of violence, of one, or of many against a private member of society, it should be public, immediate and necessary; the least possible in the case given; proportioned to the crime, and determined by the laws."*[23]

Perhaps never in history has a work on criminal justice achieved the kind of celebrity that Beccaria's did. The philosophes embraced him: Voltaire wrote a chapter-by-chapter commentary; the learned academies set up prize essay competitions in which Robespierre and Marat were among the prizewinners. Beccaria was quoted by the French attorney-general in an address on "The Administration of Criminal Justice." The Berne Society awarded him its gold medal of honor. Catherine the Great invited him to Saint Petersburg to codify the Russian criminal law (he did not go). Even the Austrian government, whose tyranny had made him so fearful that he had published his little work anonymously, created a special university chair for him in Milan. Beccaria was, in short, published everywhere, read everywhere, and admired, not only by the greatest minds of his generation, but also by the princes and ministers who could put his theories into practice.

He was a classic example of a thinker who had found the right moment. His was the age of Enlightenment. Yet seldom in human history had there been a wider gulf between the ideas of a generation and its practices, especially in criminal law, whose barbarity would have shamed the Dark Ages. It was a law that had responded to violence with violence, without diminishing either crime or disorder. Worse, perhaps, from the point of view of the influential classes, it operated almost entirely by whim, injuring not only the dangerous and criminal elements of society but also the responsible ones as well. Crimes were neither defined in advance nor punished with justice or proportionality. Beccaria expressed the resentment of an educated urban class, tired of the tyranny of church and state. His ideas would find their expression in the American Bill of Rights, the Declaration of the Rights of Man, and the French Constitution of 1790; a hundred years later, his influence over European legal theory would be at its zenith.

3 The Ends of Punishment: A Classical View

We have thus far observed that both ideas of dangerousness and the laws we fashion to deal with it are specific to a time, a place, and a pattern of popular beliefs—what might be called the mythos of a society. The eighteenth century marked a turning point in the secularization of the criminal law. For many centuries sanctions had found their origin in God or in the king, who ruled by Divine Right. Now the idea of a social contract had taken hold. The power of the temporal magistrate to inflict coercive penalties, said Sir William Blackstone (1765), is

by the consent of individuals, who in forming societies, did either tacitly or expressly invest the sovereign power with the right of making laws, and of enforcing obedience to them. . . . The lawfulness, therefore, of punishing such criminals is founded upon this principle, that the law by which they suffer was made by their own consent; it is a part of the original contract into which they entered when first they engaged in society; it was calculated for, and has long contributed to their own security.[1]

The great English jurist followed tradition in dividing offenses into two categories, the *mala prohibita*, forbidden by law, and those *mala in se*, or evil in themselves. It is interesting, in view of his acceptance of the social contract, that Blackstone still considered that the punishment for certain offenses was ordained by God, "as in the case of murder, by the precept delivered to Noah, their common ancestor and representative, 'whoso sheddeth man's blood, by man shall his blood be shed.' In other instances," he said, "they are inflicted after the *example* of the Creator, in his positive code of laws for the regulation of the Jewish Republic: as in the case of the crime against nature."

It is therefore the enormity, or dangerous tendency of the crime that alone can warrant any earthly legislature in putting him to death that commits it. It is not its frequency only, or the difficulty of otherwise preventing it, that will excuse our attempting to prevent it by a wanton effusion of human blood. For, though the end of punishment is to deter men from offending, it never can follow from thence, that it is lawful to deter them at any rate and by any means. . . .
  As to the *end* or final cause of human punishments. This is not by way of atonement or expiation for the crime committed; for that must be left to the just determination of the Supreme Being: but as a precaution against future offences of the same kind.[2]

Thus Blackstone, who had read and admired Beccaria, did not agree with him that the death penalty was beyond the just powers of civil society. The English

19

jurist thought that the right to impose capital punishment derived from God himself. Nothing else than the "enormity, or dangerous tendency" of the crime could otherwise justify so dreadful a remedy. He also manifestly believed in deterrence, but not "at any rate and by any means."

It is one of the oldest questions in criminal law, whether its purpose is retributive or deterrent. Sir James Fitzjames Stephen said that "The criminal law stands to the passion of revenge in much the same relation as marriage to the sexual appetite."[3] It is hard to disagree that what underlies the criminal law is often no more than revenge with a mask on. "In giving retribution *legal standing*," says Gerhard Mueller, "society does admittedly support an urge that is not very mature. Indeed, it is one of man's primeval urges. Yet it is so powerful within man that it would be more irrational to ignore than to admit its existence."[4]

But no society likes to appear as a tribe of vengeful primitives. Regardless of all the evidence to the contrary, sanctions have usually been justified as preventive in purpose. True, the criminal may be getting his just deserts. But "if we consider all human punishments in a large and extended view," said Blackstone, "we shall find them all rather calculated to prevent future crimes than to expiate the past." He divided punishments into three classes, "such as tend to the amendment of the offender himself, or to deprive him of any power to do future mischief, or to deter others by his example." Nowadays we should describe these purposes as rehabilitation, incapacitation, and deterrence. They all, said Blackstone, conduce to one and the same end, that of preventing future crimes.[5]

Blackstone was the last of the great theorists to call on heaven for his authority. Regardless of their respectful obeisance to the deity, the eighteenth-century philosophers were much less likely to invoke the God of Abraham in defense of their theories than to invoke, like Robespierre, the Goddess of Reason. Louis de Jaucourt, who wrote the article on punishment for Diderot's *Encyclopedia* (published 1751-1765), had this to say on the subject:

Punishment may be defined as *an evil, by threatening which the sovereign seeks to deter his subjects from breaking the law, and which, if they do break the law, he visits upon them, in just proportion to their offences, with a view of obtaining some future benefit, and—upon an ultimate analysis—to secure the safety and good order of the community. . . .*

Although, under the Law of Nature, punishment follows upon crime, it is clear that the sovereign ought never to inflict it unless someone will be benefited. To impose suffering upon anyone, simply because he has made another suffer, is an act of pure cruelty, condemned by Reason and Humanity. The object of punishment is to promote public peace and security. In punishment, Grotius observes, there must always be in view either the welfare of the culprit himself, or the interest of the victim, or the advantage of the community.

According to Jaucourt, the purposes of punishment were, first and foremost, "to secure the safety and good order of the community," and, second, "to correct the culprit, and to deprive him of any inclination to return to crime by proving to him that it does not pay a balance of tempting pleasure, but one of pain."[6]

In his remarks on crime for the same *Encyclopedia*, Jaucourt said, "The gravity of every crime may be judged by reference to its object, the intention and malice of the culprit, the damage done to society; and, of those three considerations, the importance of the first two ultimately depends upon their relevance to the last. Thus, the most enormous crimes are those which damage humanity at large; those which damage the state come next; and finally those which affect only individuals."[7]

Among the most influential eighteenth-century thinkers about crime was Jeremy Bentham, a contemporary of Beccaria, who in 1780 published *An Introduction to the Principles of Morals and Legislation*. Bentham was steeped in the ethos of his own period and particularly in the utilitarian ideas of the Scottish philosopher David Hume, who believed that human behavior is the product of environmental influences—that what we know is no more than the sum of what we experience. Said Bentham,

Nature has placed mankind under the governance of two sovereign masters, *pain* and *pleasure*. It is for them alone to point out what we ought to do, as well as to determine what we shall do. On the one hand the standard of right and wrong, on the other the chain of causes and effects, are fastened to their throne. They govern us in all we do, in all we say, in all we think: every effort we can make to throw off our subjection will serve but to demonstrate and confirm it.[8]

Bentham believed that morality is that which promotes "the greatest happiness of the greatest number," a phrase he borrowed from Beccaria and Joseph Priestley. "The business of government," he said, "is to promote the happiness of the society, by punishing and rewarding."[9] But "all punishment is mischief: all punishment in itself is evil. Upon the principle of utility . . . it ought only to be admitted in as far as it promises to exclude some greater evil." In a footnote he explains further,

The immediate principal end of punishment is to control action. This action is either that of the offender, or of others: that of the offender it controls by its influence, either on his will, in which case it is said to operate in the way of reformation; or on his physical power, in which case it is said to operate by *disablement*: that of others it can influence no otherwise than by its influence over their wills; in which case it is said to operate in the way of example.[10]

Again, Bentham, like Beccaria, is giving three reasons for punishment. Today we call these rehabilitation ("reformation"), incapacitation ("disablement"), and deterrence (influence over the wills of others, as Bentham put it). But what of vengeance? Bentham admitted that punishment of the offender gives happiness to the victim. "But no punishment ought to be allotted merely to this purpose, because (setting aside its effects in the way of control) no such pleasure is ever produced by punishment as can be equivalent to the pain."[11]

Jeremy Bentham, like all the utilitarians, operated on what has been called the "calculus of hedonism." Nowadays we should probably call him a behaviorist. He believed that men, by nature, avoid pain and pursue pleasure and that they can be controlled by the use of sanctions—punishments and rewards. But he had a curiously quantitative view: Sanctions to him were so many ounces (or pounds) of pain or pleasure, weighed in the scales of social utility.

Punishment, he said, should have four objectives: (1) to prevent all offenses, if possible; (2) but if a man must commit an offense, to induce him to commit a less rather than a more serious one. (3) When a man has resolved upon a particular offense, "to dispose him to do not more mischief than is necessary to his purpose," and (4) to prevent this mischief at as cheap a rate as possible. From these objectives he derived six rules:

1. The value of the punishment must not be less in any case than what is sufficient to outweigh that of the profit of the offence.
2. The greater the mischief of the offence, the greater is the expense which it may be worth while to be at, in the way of punishment.
3. Where two offences come in competition, the punishment for the greater offence must be sufficient to induce a man to prefer the less.
4. The punishment should be adjusted in such a manner to each particular offence, that for every part of the mischief there may be a motive to restrain the offender from giving birth to it.
5. The punishment ought in no case to be more than what is necessary to bring it into conformity with the rules here given.
6. That the quantity actually inflicted on each individual offender may correspond to the quantity intended for similar offenders in general, the several circumstances influencing sensibility ought always to be taken into account.[12]

To Bentham, law was not the familiar figure holding the scales of justice. She had taken off the blindfold and was actively scrutinizing the needle as each act was weighed, announcing: "This is heavier—this is *much* heavier than that was! It should be paid for accordingly."

Perhaps most remarkable about the Age of Reason was its faith in reason. It was a faith that, like most, was the more fiercely embraced as it proved difficult to confirm. To eighteenth century thinkers, the criminal was a rational being who could precisely calculate his chances of detection and the quantum of punishment and decide, "This crime is worth committing; that crime is not." If this were, indeed, the fact, then the calculus of hedonism could be as precisely plotted as the trajectory of the planets, making possible, for the first time, a rational system of criminal justice. In the view of the Enlightenment, this was, in fact, the case.

Bentham and Beccaria were the fathers of what has been called the Classical

School of jurisprudence. Based on liberalism, their doctrine was that the law should place no more restrictions on individual freedom than was needed to promote the welfare of society ("the greatest happiness of the greatest number"). Both offenses and punishments should be defined in advance and written into a criminal code that weighed the relative evils to be prohibited and provided punishments in proportion to the offense. Because of the hedonistic nature of man, penalties should be swift and sure, so as to create within the offender that association between the crime and its punishment without which the hedonistic calculus would fail. Punishment should always fit the *crime*, not the criminal. As Radzinowicz puts it, "the penologists of the liberal school would unite to proclaim that criminals should be punished strictly for what they have done under the criminal law in force, not for what they are or are likely to become."[13]

But classical jurisprudence was not merely theoretical: It was created out of the needs of a rising middle class and founded on the rock of experience. The new jurisprudence sought the protection of the law against the preferential treatment that had historically been granted to the nobility. What Beccaria and Bentham did was to make explicit and give a theoretical basis to this legal redress of grievances. They were not dealing with abstractions but with the everyday experiences of ordinary people who had felt themselves outraged by an arbitrary and unjust legal system. Just how theory interacted with experience may be seen in the reports that the various provinces of France sent to the Estates General on the eve of the revolution. These demanded, first, equality before the law; second, suppression of the discretionary power of judges; third, the abolition of crimes against religion and morals; fourth, publicity of procedure; fifth, right to counsel;[a] sixth, abolition of the compulsory oath the defendant must take; seventh, the duty of the court to state the grounds for judgment, and to declare them publicly; and eighth, trial by jury.[14]

In its Declaration of the Rights of Man, August 26, 1789, France's Constituent Assembly said that the aim of political society is "the preservation of the natural and inalienable rights of man" a phrase Lafayette, its chief author, may have borrowed from the American Declaration of Independence. Hence "the law has the right to prohibit only actions harmful to society." No person is to be interfered with on account of his opinions, even on the subject of religion, provided their expression does not disturb public order. (This ended prosecution for blasphemy, heresy, and witchcraft, and automatically redefined them as not dangerous.) "The law shall inflict only such punishments as are strictly and clearly necessary," it said further, adding, "no person shall be punished except by virtue of a law enacted and promulgated previous to the crime and applicable according to its terms."[15]

Five months later these concepts were written into law. The French criminal

---

[a]Even England did not provide full right to counsel in felony cases until the middle of the nineteenth century.

code of 1790 decreed in Article 1 "that offenses of the same nature shall be punished by the same kind of penalties, whatever be the rank and the station of the offender." This principle was incorporated into the Constitution of September 3, 1790,[16] and in 1791 the Constituent Assembly declared that "penalties should be proportioned to the crimes for which they are inflicted and . . . they are intended not merely to punish but to reform the culprit."[17] Most of these were ideas that Beccaria had first enunciated. Yet it would be less true to say he invented them than that he gave tongue to long-standing grievances and provided a remedy for them. What Beccaria suggested was a rationalistic, secular approach to crime and punishment. Even today—perhaps *especially* today—the order, clarity, and logic of his work and the works of Bentham are a pleasure to read. They take us into a world of classical thought, which, like the garden of Eden, we have irretrievably lost. Never again would we believe so firmly in the rationality of homo sapiens or the simplicity of the sanctions necessary to bring him to heel. Nevertheless, the age left its mark both in continental criminal law and in the American Constitution and Bill of Rights. European legislation is founded on classical theories of crime and punishment. Ours has in some respects diverged, in ways and for reasons that will be explained later. But the basic dogmas of classical theory remain the linchpins of both American and European criminal law: that man is a rational being; that he avoids pain and pursues pleasure; that the criminal law should impose such sanctions as will outweigh the rewards of crime; that sanctions should be announced in advance; that they should be proportional to the offense; that everyone should enjoy equal justice; and that what a man does, not what he thinks, is the proper ambit of the criminal law.

For thousands of years punishment had been implicitly (if not explicitly) retributive and hence backward looking in nature. Immanuel Kant gave voice to the idea of just deserts when he said that if a civil society should resolve to dissolve itself by consent of its members (as in people leaving an island), "the last murderer lying in the prison ought to be executed before the resolution was carried out. This ought to be done in order that every one may realize the desert of his deeds, and that bloodguiltiness may not remain upon the people; for otherwise they might all be regarded as participators in the murder as a public violation of Justice."[18]

Utilitarianism, on the other hand, was consciously and emphatically forward looking. It held that not the past but only the future should concern us. Retributive justice, says John Rawls, looks back to crime and the law: Utility looks forward to furthering the interests of society. If we ask the question, "Why was J. put in jail?," the retributive answer is, "Because he robbed a bank, was tried and convicted." But the utilitarian asks the question, "Why do people put other people in jail?," and for him the answer is, "To protect good people from bad people." In our society the judge looks back, but the ideal legislator looks forward. ". . . One's initial confusion disappears," says Rawls, "once one sees that these views apply to persons holding different offices with different duties, and situated differently with respect to the system of rules that make up the criminal law."[19] Anthony Quinton puts it this way: retributivism answers the question "When (logically) *can* we punish?" Utilitarianism answers the question, "When (morally) *may* or *ought* we to punish?"[20] It is the responsibility of the judge to answer the first question, of the legislator to answer the second. But the laws we write depend ultimately on our view of the nature of man, and especially of criminal man, a view that in the nineteenth and twentieth centuries was to undergo a striking and revolutionary change.

4 Political Deviants as "Dangerous Offenders"

The classical theorists secularized the dangerous offender. He was no longer a sorcerer, a heretic, or an atheist. On the other hand, he might still be a political dissident—a republican (in a monarchical society), a communist (in an aristocratic or bourgeois society), or an anarchist (in any kind of society)—because it remained dangerous to challenge the legitimacy of power. By the eighteenth century the ecclesiastical establishments no longer exercised either power or *dominium*, and the law was merely reflecting that fact. Their decline in influence paralleled a decline in popular belief and in the importance of religion to Western society. People no longer took a Manichaean view of the struggle between light and darkness, good and evil. It was not so much that God had been demoted as that the devil had. A society that no longer believed in a tangible, candescent hell was unlikely to tremble at the thought of witches.

In this rational universe, danger now meant a challenge to the order of things—a threat to purse or person or to the secular government. Concepts of danger are ultimately based on fear that something will be taken from us. The revolutionary movements of the eighteenth and nineteenth centuries challenged both the legitimacy of established sovereignties and the immutable social and economic order and thus established whole new classes of dangerous offenders.

This is not a history of nineteenth-century Europe; nevertheless, a few examples might be in order. The French Revolution represented a triumph of the bourgeoisie; its influence was spread to the very borders of the Russian Empire by the arms of Napoleon, and the overthrow of Napoleon in turn brought about a reaction as Catholic Royalists paid off old scores. (Talleyrand said, "They have learned nothing and they have forgotten nothing.") During this "white terror," Republicans and Bonapartists were hunted down and imprisoned. Many joined underground secret societies, and there were insurrections and assassinations in France, Austria, and Italy. The middle-class Italian nationalists, who mourned Napoleon, organized revolutionary groups called the Carbonari. A wave of revolutions swept Europe in 1820; among its victims was the Duc de Berry, heir to the French throne. More serious revolts broke out in 1848. There were many currents at work in this turbulent century: nationalism; a revolt of the bourgeoisie against aristrocratic and reactionary regimes; a revolt of the working classes against both the bourgeoisie and the aristocracy; irridentism; and new revolutionary philosophies such as communism and anarchism that attracted fanatical followings and were viewed by the governments of the day as very dangerous indeed.

Political heretics now came to occupy somewhat the same place in the pantheon of criminality that had once been held by witches and heretics: They were suspected of being everywhere; they were detected by methods that owed as much to fear as to dispassionate observation; and they were relentlessly pursued and punished. Austrian police hunted down members of the Pan-Slavic underground, as well as Bohemian, Hungarian, Polish, and Italian patriots. Prussians and Russians persecuted Poles. Turks persecuted Greeks; the Papal State persecuted those who favored the unification of Italy.

Nor was nationalism the only issue. There was an interface between political and economic heresy that involved most of the great social movements of the nineteenth and twentieth centuries. The Industrial Revolution had brought with it a new threat to the established order in the form of workingmen's associations, which were at first viewed by all European governments as criminal conspiracies. The French Loi Le Chapelier of 1791 and the British Combination Acts of 1800 were examples of this, as were the many laws throughout the German principalities that made labor unions unlawful. From the point of view of many European governments, the unions were political heresies; led by radical intellectuals, the early associations reflected demands for universal suffrage, free education, and political equality, all of them anathema to the reactionary monarchies of nineteenth-century Europe. Later on the unions were to be active in all the great radical movements of the century: socialism, communism, and anarchism.

The great influence on the nineteenth-century labor movement, that of Karl Marx, began with the Communist League, a German workingmen's association, which Friedrich Engels described as "unavoidably a secret society,"[1] and which in the mid-nineteenth century had branches throughout Europe. At a congress of the league held in London in 1847, Marx and Engels were commissioned to prepare a party program. Published as *The Communist Manifesto*, it opened with the historic line, "A spectre is haunting Europe—the spectre of Communism. All the powers of old Europe have entered into a holy alliance to exorcize this spectre; Pope and Czar, Metternich and Guizot, French Radicals and German police-spies." Marx and Engels threw down the gauntlet to the governments of Europe, which they viewed as dominated by the bourgeoisie:

The history of all hitherto existing society is the history of class struggles.
　　Freeman and slave, patrician and plebian, lord and serf, guild-master and journeyman, in a word, oppressor and oppressed, stood in constant opposition to one another, carried on an uninterrupted, now hidden, now open fight, a fight that each time ended, either in a revolutionary re-constitution of society at large, or in the common ruin of the contending classes. . . .
　　The modern bourgeois society that has sprouted from the ruins of the old feudal society, has not done away with class antagonisms. It has but established new classes, new conditions of oppression, new forms of struggle in place of the old ones.
　　Our epoch, the epoch of the bourgeoisie, possesses, however, this distinctive

feature; it has simplified the class antagonisms. Society as a whole is more and more splitting up into two great hostile camps, into two great classes directly facing each other: Bourgeoisie and Proletariat.[2]

The challenge of this *Manifesto* did not go unnoticed. The manuscript (in German) was sent to the London printers a few weeks before the French revolution of February 1848; a French translation was brought out in Paris before the insurrection of June 1848. English, Danish, Russian, Armenian, and Polish editions followed. The defeat of the second insurrection, which Engels called "the first great battle between Proletariat and Bourgeoisie," led to a fierce repression of the Communist League. The Prussian police hunted out the central committee of the league, then located in Cologne; the members were arrested, tried in October 1852, and seven of them were sentenced to terms of imprisonment in a fortress.[3] The league was formally dissolved, but the *Manifesto* lived on to haunt that century and this. If a document could be labeled a "dangerous offender," the *Communist Manifesto*, the ultimate challenge to bourgeois power, would not escape hanging.

Marx's influence on the labor movement was to be enormous. But it was not communism but anarchism that would, by the end of the nineteenth century, pose the greatest threat to the dynasties of Europe. In its early theoretical stages anarchism was a rather mild, academic doctrine that favored the disappearance of political, social, and religious institutions. In 1840 one of its founding fathers, Pierre-Joseph Proudhon, had asked, in the title of a famous essay, "What Is Property?" and had given the answer, "property is theft." But it was Bakunin who raised anarchism from a dogma to a program. Building on the ideas of Proudhon, Bakunin rejected Marx's belief in the inevitable withering away of the state. He and his followers, who were eventually to capture the labor movements of Spain, Italy, and Russia, broke with social democracy—eschewed ties, in fact, with all political parties—and urged sabotage, violence, and assassination in the furtherance of their social objectives.

Thus political and economic heretics had replaced religious heretics as a danger, a challenge to *dominium.* Many of them were very dangerous indeed, none more so than the anarchists. In 1893 they exploded a bomb in the French Chamber of Deputies. In 1894 an Italian anarchist assassinated President Sadi Carnot of France. In 1898 another anarchist assassinated the Empress Elizabeth of Austria. In 1900 an attempt was made in Brussels on the Prince of Wales; in the same year King Umberto I of Italy was killed. In 1901 President McKinley also fell victim to an anarchist, Leon Czolgosz. And it was anarchists who in 1906 tried to blow up King Alfonso and Queen Victoria of Spain on their wedding day.

But there were other radical movements too which threatened the established order. In Russia the Narodnaya Volya (People's Will, or People's Freedom), after six prior unsuccessful attempts, managed in 1881 to assassinate the Tsar Alexander II. Their previous efforts had cost them twenty-one executions: This one led to the total extermination of the movement. According to Bertram Wolfe, the new Tsar replied by "multiplying the police, enlisting spies, closing the feeble liberal newspapers, purging the libraries, supervising professors and curricula, reducing the local self-government . . . prohibiting student organization . . . and in general tightening all the chains in the great prison house of people."[4]

The Russian government was to discover, however, that it is easier to proscribe than to control terror. The Narodnaya Volya was no sooner exterminated than it was resurrected by radical students, who, on the anniversary of Alexander II's assassination, in 1887 tried to kill Alexander III. Five of the conspirators were hanged, one of them being Alexander Ulyanov, Lenin's older brother. It was an event that would create a new danger to the established order; not only was Lenin ineradicably affected by this terrifying event but so was the brother of another conspirator, Bronislaw Pilsudski. Joseph Pilsudski, who testified at Bronislaw's trial, was one day to be dictator of a resurgent Polish nation.[a]

Russia provided an example of a class long considered dangerous, the university students. Students were not only involved in the assassination of Tsar Alexander II and the attempt on Alexander III but also assassinated the Russian minister of education (N.P. Bogolepov, 1901), the minister of the interior (D.S. Sipyaghin, 1902), the Premier and former interior minister (V.K. von Plehve, 1904), and the Grand Duke Sergei (1905). An interesting footnote to these events is that the students belonged to the Terror section of the Social Revolutionary party, a group of agrarian radicals who had so worried Plehve when he was minister of the interior that he had permitted the Okhrana (secret security police) to infiltrate the party. At the time of Plehve's and the grand duke's assassination, the Terror section of the Social Revolutionary party was headed by none other than a Moscow police agent, Yevno Azev. The Moscow police, therefore, were responsible for the death of their own government officials.[5]

Nor was the extraordinary role of police spies limited to this case. Okhrana agents headed up the chief labor unions, and one of them, Roman Malinovsky, so ingratiated himself with the exiled Lenin that he became the Bolshevik leader in the Russian Duma. Thus a police spy was the chief Bolshevik operative inside Russia. His role was not revealed until the police files fell into Communist hands after the Revolution.

Clearly, in so Byzantine a system it is not always easy to separate the good guys from the bad guys, or to put it another way, to know who, in fact, is a

[a]Bronislaw Pilsudski turned state's evidence and was spared. Joseph was revealed to have sent a message for the conspirators but was not punished for it. Lenin, however, never forgave the Tsarist government for what it had done to his brother. There are some who believe this hanging brought down the Russian Empire.

"dangerous offender." Was Azev "dangerous"—and if so, to whom? What about Malinovsky or the other *agents provocateurs*? They played their roles with such enthusiasm (and were perhaps so psychologically schizoid) that they furthered the very calamities they were hired to avert. When the Bolsheviks came to power, Malinovsky was put on trial. He defended himself with spirit, arguing that he had in fact served their cause well. But this former leader and comrade was redefined retrospectively as dangerous, taken out against the wall, and shot. So was the police chief who had employed him.[6]

It would be well here to consider once again the concept of Theodore Sarbin that "danger" is derived from *dominium*, lordship, and denotes relative power in a social organization. One thing that political terrorists have in common is their *powerlessness*. Martin Luther King was once quoted as saying that "riots are the language of the unheard." Terror is no less so. Wherever society has blocked the legitimate access to power, or to a redress of grievances, there is a danger of violence—a violence that will be defined by that society as criminal. The anarchist Georges Sorel, in his *Reflections on Violence*, makes this distinction between the violence of revolutionaries and that used by those in power to suppress them:

Sometimes the terms *force* and *violence* are used in speaking of acts of authority, sometimes in speaking of acts of revolt. It is obvious that the two cases give rise to very different consequences. I think it would be better to adopt a terminology which would give rise to no ambiguity, and that the term *violence* should be employed only for acts of revolt; we should say, therefore, that the object of force is to impose a certain social order in which the minority governs, while violence tends to the destruction of that order. The middle class have used force since the beginning of modern times, while the proletariat now reacts against the middle class and against the State by violence.[7]

Social revolutionaries have consistently justified their violence as an answer to the force of the state; governments have justified force as an answer to violence. A term frequently employed is "legitimate"; force by government is "legitimate," according to the particular definition of those in power. To nineteenth-century monarchists, "legitimate" meant rule by hereditary right. To Republicans, it meant rule according to law, or with established legal forms or requirements. Force is like a child, therefore—legitimate when lawfully begotten; but that leaves a lot of questions unanswered. To monarchists, republics were illegitimate, to republicans, monarchies; and to Communists, any government is illegitimate that is not the dictatorship of the proletariat.

This brings us to a real dilemma. If laws are written and crimes defined by those in power, is criminality in the eye of the beholder? Among those who have been seen as dangerous or potentially dangerous offenders have been Christians, slaves, vagabonds, strangers, gypsies, beggars, students, Catholics, Protestants, atheists, nationalists, demobilized soldiers and sailors, witches, Freemasons, labor leaders, and social revolutionaries. The truth is that most of these "dangerous offenders" have indeed been dangerous to *someone*. Protestants were dangerous to the Catholic church, papists to the English Protestant monarchy. Republicans were dangerous to monarchies. Communists were, and are, dangerous to republics. And nationalism was the force that brought down the Austro-Hungarian Empire. Thus among all those who have been defined by one society or another as "dangerous," only witches might reasonably be excluded. Even here, one could argue that to those who believe in witchcraft and imagine themselves under a malign spell, witches, too, are dangerous.

The criminal law is at once a creature of fact, and of what I call mythos, defined by Webster as "the pattern of beliefs expressing often symbolically the characteristic or prevalent attitude in a group or culture."[8] It is easy to see the unexamined philosophical, political, or religious assumptions of another age; it is hard, perhaps impossible, to see our own. We shake our head at a criminal law that concerns itself with witches. We smile when Blackstone justifies capital punishment "by the precept delivered to Noah" by God. Like that eminent eighteenth-century rationalist and man of letters, Bernard de Fontenelle, "we are under obligation to the ancients for having exhausted almost all the false theories that could be formed."[9] But the mythos of our own times, which shapes our thought and determines our institutions, remains, like the air we breathe, impalpable and unperceived.

The mythos of an age is what nourishes its criminal and civil law. It is when the two diverge—when our laws say one thing, and our beliefs another—that violence and terror become the rule, and law must be enforced by brute repression. This is what happened in the nineteenth century. The belief in the Divine Right of kings (and ordained hegemony of the feudal classes) had disappeared in the holocaust of the French Revolution. In the words of Carl Becker,

We can watch this enthusiasm, this passion for liberty and justice, for truth and humanity, rise and rise throughout the century until it becomes a delirium, until it culminates in some symbolical sense, in that half admirable, half pathetic spectacle of June 8, 1794, when Citizen Robespierre, with a bouquet in one hand and a torch in the other, inaugurated the new religion of humanity by lighting the conflagration that was to purge the world of ignorance, vice, and folly.[10]

Throughout the whole next century, this flame, like a fire in a coal mine, was to be smothered again and again by the autocracies of Europe: the Bourbons, the Hapsburgs, the Romanovs, and all the princelings and potentates whose secret police hunted, tortured, imprisoned, and executed their political heretics. Yet no sooner was the fire damped down in one place than it flared up in another. The criminal law can pursue the heretic (political or religious) and define him as dangerous. But unless opinion accepts the premises on which that law is founded—unless the mythos supports the policy—enforcement will be less a matter of justice than of war.

5 Crime and Determinism

In the main, however, criminal law concerns itself not with heresies (religious or political) but with the bread-and-butter crimes; and here, in the nineteenth century, the classical theorists were in splendid and visible ascendancy. The law is always traditional, conservative, and slow to change. It took hundreds of years to reach the point where secularism and rationalism could effect a great reform, but by the nineteenth century, they had. Never had criminal law seemed more what Sir Edward Coke once called "the perfection of reason." The new European legal codes reflected the ethos of the Age of Reason, even as the age itself was fading into history. Now a new spirit of scientific inquiry began to question many of its assumptions about the nature of man and society. The eighteenth-century classical theorists had seen man as a free agent, ruled by a beneficent natural law—"the regular and constant order of facts by which God rules the universe," as Volney called it; "the order which his wisdom presents to the sense and reason of men, to serve them as an equal and common rule of conduct, and to guide them, without distinction of race or sect, towards perfection and happiness."[1] Within this natural order but subordinate to it were the rules of conduct men legislate for themselves. Daniel Defoe had described laws as "buoys, set upon Dangerous Places under Water, to warn Mankind, that such Sands or Rocks are there, and the Language of them is, *Come here at your Peril.*"[2]

To such a view, man is rational and prudent, quite capable of navigating the shoals so long as he observes the markers; if he does not, he will sink—and he deserves to. The Enlightenment saw man as ruled not by Original Sin but by free will; the citizen had freely obligated himself to observe the social contract and to accept punishment if he infringed it. This was a model of justice based on legality, responsibility, and an objective conception of the criminal act: if you do this, you will suffer that. It did not ask any questions about the social order itself: Was it just? Do men commit crime because they want to or because they have to? Nor did it ask whether there is such a thing as free will or whether our actions are as inexorably determined as the orbit of the planets. Free will and determinism are like two ends of a seesaw: When one stands in high esteem, the other scrapes bottom. In the eighteenth century free will was in the ascendant. In the nineteenth the positions were to be reversed, and thoughtful men would again ask whether man is evil because he wills it or because he cannot help himself.

The great new tool in the study of crime was to be statistics. Until the mid-nineteenth century, "statistics" meant information about political states, especially demographic information such as births, deaths, and population, but including also exports, imports, arrests, and whatever else the country might choose to keep track of. What we should nowadays call theoretical statistics had its origins in such diverse fields as gambling, astronomy, and insurance. It was not until the late seventeenth and early eighteenth centuries that there had been the beginning of a calculus of probability. This remarkable delay has been attributed by M.G. Kendall to the philosophical and religious ideas that ruled the Western world. To the ancients, events were mysterious: No Being was in control of the universe. To the Christians, on the other hand, everything was ruled by divine purpose: In an ultimate sense, there was no such thing as chance. But with the beginnings of census statistics in the eighteenth century, it became possible to calculate life expectancies, and life insurance became an applied science that not only contributed an observable frequency distribution, with its associated calculus, but also contributed the concept of a population moving through time.[3]

With the collection of census, and later arrest, data, it became possible to apply the calculus of probability to crime. Is human behavior so predictable that we can calculate in advance those events we have always attributed to free will—the number of marriages, for example, or of divorces, or even of violent crimes? Mme de Staël, writing in 1796, suggested that it is. Although it is difficult to say what any one person is likely to do, when the number of cases is large, one can predict the outcome. "For example, it has been observed that in the canton of Berne the number of divorces is very much the same from one decade to the next, and there are cities in Italy where one can calculate exactly how many murders will be committed from year to year. Thus, events which depend on a multitude of diverse combinations have a periodic recurrence, a fixed proportion, when the observations result from a large number of chances."[4]

Within a generation, two statisticians, one in France and one in Belgium, were to establish this proposition beyond question. The Frenchman was a lawyer, André-Michel Guerry; the Belgian was an astronomer and mathematician, Lambert-Adolphe-Jacques Quételet. Their work—separately pursued—was made possible by the publication in France in 1827 of the first criminal statistics, *Le compte général de l'administration de la justice criminelle en France*. This work permitted a comparison of the incidence of crime with such factors as age, sex, poverty, geography, education, and race. It became plain from the data that some ancient ideas needed revision, notably that poverty is the mother of crime. "Several of the Departments of France condemned to be the poorest," Quételet observed, "are at the same time the most moral. Man is not driven to crime because he is poor, but more generally because he passes rapidly from a state of comfort to one of misery."[5] In other words, men do not commit crimes because of their condition of poverty but because of changes in that condition for the worse. The figures also showed that in the impoverished countryside, the incidence of crime was lower than in the more affluent cities.

Quételet called his study *Social Physics*; Guerry called his *Moral Statistics*. Said Guerry, "Moral statistical analysis does not deduce truths from each other, it does not seek to discover what ought to be; it states what is." And he criticized classical jurisprudence, "The time has gone by when we could claim to regulate society by laws established solely on metaphysical theories and a sort of ideal type which was thought to conform to absolute justice. Laws are not made for men in the abstract, for humanity in general, but for real men, placed in precisely determined conditions."[6]

Real men could be counted and measured; so could their height and weight, and such "moral statistics" as marriages, suicides, illegitimate births, and murders. To Guerry, these yielded "real men"; to Quételet, they yielded "the average man," a type no less abstract than the rational hedonist of classical theory, but one who has been enshrined as an ikon of the social scientists. *L'homme moyen*, or average man, was very real to Quételet, for he considered averages to be of the order of physical facts. He was no less interested in distributions of human attributes, and in 1844 Quételet was able to discover draft evasion in the French army by comparing the distribution of height of one hundred thousand French conscripts with his own observations of the distribution of heights. Quételet concluded that two thousand men had evaded service by shortening themselves to just below the minimum height.[7]

The Belgian mathematician's studies of criminality were based on data from the French court system, some seven to eight thousand cases a year, over a period of twelve years. "I have taken, for the same years, and for the city of Paris, the mortality of a period of ten years, and have found that, though my observations included a much larger number of persons, and these pertaining to a much more homogeneous population, the mortality of the capital proceeded with less regularity than the crimes of the kingdom, and that each age paid a more uniform and constant tribute to the jail than to the tomb."[8]

Quételet had proved what many observers, ancient and modern, had thought they discerned: that crimes are committed by young people. *"The propensity to crime increases quite rapidly toward adulthood,"* he said; *"it reaches a maximum and then decreases until the very end of life. This law appears to be constant. . . ."*[9] (By "law" Quételet meant the correlation between age and crime.) More important was his observation of regularity—one might almost say fatality—in the production of crime.

In every thing which relates to crimes, the same numbers are reproduced so constantly, that it becomes impossible to misapprehend it—even in respect to those crimes which seem perfectly beyond human foresight, such as murders committed in general at the close of quarrels, arising without a motive, and under other circumstances to all appearance the most fortuitous or accidental: nevertheless, experience proves that murders are committed annually, not only pretty nearly to the same extent, but even that the instruments employed are in the same proportions.[10]

This was a disconcerting discovery for a criminal justice system predicated on free will and holding the individual responsible for his behavior. Said Quételet:

... There is a *budget* which we pay with frightful regularity—it is that of prisons, dungeons, and scaffolds. ... We might even predict annually how many individuals will stain their hands with the blood of their fellow-men, how many will be forgers, how many will deal in poison, pretty nearly in the same way as we may foretell the annual births and deaths.
Society includes within itself the germs of all the crimes committed, and at the same time the necessary facilities for their development. It is the social state, in some measure, which prepares these crimes and the criminal is merely the instrument to execute them.[11]

Moral phenomena, he thought, observed on a great scale, resemble physical phenomena, and the greater the number of individuals observed, the more individual differences tend to disappear. The laws presiding over the development of man are the result of his organization, education, knowledge, wealth, institutions, local influences, "and an endless variety of other causes, always very difficult to discover, and some of which may probably never be made out." Societies can and do change, and can therefore effect changes in crime. The actions of man on society he called "secular perturbations."

Quételet came up with a concept he called *"the propensity to crime."* By this he meant the greater or less probability of men in similar circumstance committing a crime. The propensity to crime might be the same in France as in England, but because opportunity and means are different, there might be more crime in one country than the other. Among the factors he found to affect propensity to crime were:

1. The physical power and passions of men, whose propensity attains its maximum about the age of twenty-five.
2. Differences in sex: "there is only one woman before the courts to four men." Women prefer crimes against property to those against persons.
3. The seasons: There are more crimes against the person in summer, more property crimes in winter.
4. Climate appears to have some influence: In southern climes, there are more crimes against the person; in severe climates "which give rise to the greatest number of wants," there are more crimes against property.
5. Other things being equal, there are more crimes where a frequent mixture of people takes place: "those in which industry and trade collect many persons and things together, and possess the greatest activity" and "those where the inequality of fortune is most felt."
6. Professions influence crime: "Individuals of more independent professions are rather given to crimes against persons; and the labouring and domestic classes to crimes against property."

7. Education has less influence than had been supposed. "Moreover, moral instruction is very often confounded with instruction in reading and writing, alone, and which is more frequently an accessory instrument to crime."
8. Poverty also has less influence than had been thought. The poorest departments of France are at the same time the most moral. Changes in economic status are more important than the absolute level of poverty.
9. The higher one goes in the social scale, the lower the propensity to crime in women: "Descending to the lowest orders, the habits of both sexes resemble each other more and more."
10. "Of the 1129 murders committed in France, during the space of four years, 446 have been in consequence of quarrels and contentions in taverns; which would tend to show the fatal influence of the use of *strong drinks*."[1][2]

There are those who consider Quételet, not Auguste Comte, to be the father of sociology; he has just as good a claim to be the father of criminology. This was a science which in those days did not yet have a name but whose statistical observations would one day bring it into collision with the assumptions that underlie all criminal law. Indeed, the debate still rages whether crime is freely chosen by the malefactor, or whether, as Buckle insisted in his *History of Civilization*, "Society prepares the crime; the criminal commits it."[1][3]

Guerry and Quételet called into question the whole doctrine of moral responsibility that had derived from Roman and Christian law. If society is at fault, if it prepares the crimes for others to commit, and if the commission of those crimes is as predictable as the tides or seasons, then *where does guilt lie*? Here the enlightened nineteenth century had a magnificent new structure of criminal law, based on assumptions of individual responsibility and corrigibility, and suddenly its very premises were being challenged. If law had been one of the sciences, social or physical, such a blow might have forced a rethinking of its postulates. But the law is the most conservative of disciplines, particularly in the Anglo-Saxon countries where the legal structure, with its accretion of precedents, is like a stately ship full of barnacles. There was, in fact, no response to Quételet or to the many social scientists who were to follow him. The criminal law continued to assume that crime was freely chosen, that punishment would deter it, and that criminals were getting their just deserts. The social scientists, on the other hand, held, with Dickens' Mr. Bumble, that "if the law supposes *that*, it is a ass, a idiot."

Bread and Danger in the Nineteenth Century

If we can predict annually how many individuals will stain their hands with blood, how many will be forgers, how many poisoners; and if society contains within itself the germs of all the crimes committed and the facilities for their development (as Quételet put it), then what are the implications for social policy? Should we attempt to change the conditions that affect propensity to crime? Or should we consider society essentially unreformable and continue to act within the strictures of the criminal justice system, ignoring the actor and punishing the act? These were questions that would agitate the nineteenth century; they have continued, with unabated fury, down to the present time.

The two great intellectual currents in which nineteenth-century criminology would swim were the economic determinism of Karl Marx and the natural selection theories derived from Charles Darwin. A third great intellectual current, that of Freudian psychoanalysis, would not make itself fully felt in criminology until the twentieth century, and then for the most part only in the United States. Beccaria would not have found himself at home with any one of these; neither would the law, which Justice Holmes once called "the government of the living by the dead."[1]

It is interesting to conjecture what would have happened had the great reform in the criminal law come a hundred years later, after its premises of hedonism and rationality had foundered in the general shipwreck of ideas. As it was, eighteenth-century rationalism ruled the law while economic and biological determinism ruled the social sciences. Each operated within its own logic-tight compartment, and it was the law, not the social sciences, that would govern public policy.

This can be seen clearly when one compares the nineteenth-century literature on crime with the methods used to deal with it. An idea that was much to the fore was that of the "dangerous classes." The term appeared in many books, and in France, during the first half of the century, it was used interchangeably with "laboring classes" to indicate those who lived so close to economic disaster that a reversal of fortune or some lapse in moral integrity would send them out into the streets, dagger in hand, to deprive honest citizens of their money. During this century, also, the term "proletariat" was revived from the Latin *proletarius*, (from *proles*, progeny) which to the Romans had denoted a class so low in the social and economic order that its only function was to reproduce. In its revived usage, "proletariat" referred to the lowest economic class, the industrial workers who were without the means of production and sold their labor to live. The socialists attributed as many virtues to the "proletariat" as the well-to-do attributed vices to the "dangerous"; but they were, of course, essentially the same class.

There was during the first half of the century an almost overwhelming public awareness of the growth in population—not only of displaced country people thronging into the great cities, but of what was seen as a population explosion in the developed countries of the world. European population had risen from 140 million in 1750, to 187 million in 1800, to 266 million in 1850.[2] In 1798 the Reverend Thomas Malthus had published the first edition of his *Essay on the Principle of Population*. Written first as a pamphlet, it was expanded into book form in 1803 with the subtitle, *A View of Its Past and Present Effects on Human Happiness with an Inquiry into Our Prospects Respecting the Future Removal or Mitigation of the Evils which It Occasions*. Malthus' theory was comparatively simple, but it struck a chill into his readers: When population is unchecked, he said, it increases in a geometrical ratio, while food supply increases only in an arithmetical ratio; hence population tends to increase up to the level of mass starvation. There are two kinds of checks on population said Malthus—the positive checks such as famine or pestilence, which show up in the death rate; and the preventive checks such as abortion, infanticide, and birth control, which show up in the birth rate. Both checks are the consequences of lack of food, which is the ultimate check on population. In his second edition, Malthus added "moral restraint" to the preventive checks (by this he meant postponement of marriage and sexual abstinence).

To the alarmed bourgeois, it was the "dangerous classes" who, undeterred by moral restraint, were multiplying like animals in the dank cellars and airless garrets of the cities. This was a Malthusian nightmare come true, and it could be read in the statistics of prostitution, infanticide, suicide, and deaths from such plagues as smallpox and cholera, which took a greater toll from the poor than from the rich. Even a Socialist like Louis Blanc thought that overpopulation was a curse of the poor. "If one fact is incontrovertible," he wrote in *The Organization of Labor*, "it is that population grows faster in the poor class than in the rich class. . . . Births in Paris are only 1/32 of the population in the well-to-do-districts, and 1/26 in the others."[3]

Here then were the "dangerous classes" who, in the words of H.A. Frégier, joined "to vice the depravity of destitution." Crime was clearly the work of these hordes who, breeding to the Malthusian limits, were swarming from their alleys in the dark of the night to threaten the life and safety of their betters. "It served the interests and relieved the conscience of those at the top," says Leon Radzinowicz, "to look upon the dangerous classes as an independent category, detached from the prevailing social conditions. They were portrayed as a race apart, morally depraved and vicious, living by violating the fundamental law of orderly society, which was that a man should maintain himself by honest, steady work."[4]

Within two years of Frégier, however, another Academy essay winner, Eugène Buret, published a book *On the Misery of the Working Classes in England and France* (1840), in which he attributed criminality not to some inherent depravity of the lower classes, but to their poverty. "The lower classes . . . are little by little thrust back from the customs and laws of civilized life and reduced, by the sufferings and privations of poverty, to a state of barbarism. The poor are like those Saxon bands who, to escape the yoke of Norman conquest, hid their nomadic independence amongst the trees of forests; they are men outside society, outside the law, outlaws, and it is from their ranks all criminals come."[5]

Edouard Ducpetiaux, in his *Memoir on Pauperism in Flanders* (1850), called criminality "the inseparable companion of poverty. As the number of indigent persons increases, we see the number of crimes also increase. Hunger is a bad counselor. In the midst of crushing destitution, a man gradually loses the notion of justice and injustice, of good and bad; beset by needs that he cannot satisfy, he disregards the laws, and ends by recoiling from no attempt that appears capable of bettering his condition."[6]

No one dealt better with this theme than the great nineteenth-century novelists. Dickens had an unerring eye for the degradation of the poor, a subject that he had learned firsthand when his father was thrown into debtor's prison. In such works as *Oliver Twist* (1837-1839), he limns the criminal poor, the "dangerous classes" of Victorian London. Victor Hugo, with his great novel *Les Misérables* (The Wretched), shows both the degradation of poverty and its relationship to crime. Hugo called the poor "savages, yes; but the savages of civilization."[7] Balzac called them "this forgotten class . . . this pariah caste."[8]

Crime was one of the major themes in all writing on Paris from the Bourbon Restoration to the Second Empire. Says Louis Chevalier:

About no other city, even London, except for a few in our own time—Chicago between the two world wars, for example—has so much been written. . . . This writing has dwelled insistently on every aspect of crime, as if the proliferation of the criminal classes really was, over the years, one of the major facts of daily life in Paris, one of the main problems of city management, one of the principal matters of general concern, one of the essential forms of social malaise. No matter what groups we take, whether the bourgeois, apparently secure behind their triple bars and bolts, or the lower classes, menacing and menaced; no matter what trend we study in the events, whether social or political, however artificially divorced from such sordid considerations, this documentation and this weight of testimony loom on the threshold as we enter the Paris of the period and present us inescapably with a sanguinary preview of it.[9]

The streets of the city at night were like those of the Middle Ages, dark and deserted. The Vicomte de Launay, writing in 1843, said that Paris suffered from "nightly assaults, hold-ups, daring robberies. . . . Evening parties all end like the beginning of the fourth act of *Les Huguenots*, with the blessing of the daggers.

Friends and relatives are not allowed to go home without a regular arms inspection. . . ."[10]

But if crime was a terrifying reality for the upper classes, stark destitution was the reality of the poor. It is difficult, in these comparatively affluent times, to visualize just how close the urban proletariat once lived to absolute starvation. A bad harvest meant the difference between eating and literally dropping dead in the streets. "Near the Porte Saint-Martin," wrote Heinrich Heine on March 1, 1832, "a man as pale as death, and with a ghastly rattle in his throat, sprawled on the wet pavement. The passers-by gathered around him asserted that he was dying of hunger. But my companion assured me that the fellow died of hunger every day on one street or another; it was his living. . . . There is this particular point about this dying of hunger, that you would see several thousand people doing it every day if they were able to hold out longer. But the poor usually die after three days without food: they are buried one after the other, in silence; no one takes much notice."[11]

Victor Hugo describes the life of Jean Valjean in his great novel of crime and poverty, *Les Misérables*. Jean Valjean had broken a bakery window to steal a loaf of bread for his sister and her seven children, who were without food. Under the great classical criminal code of France, he was guilty of "burglary at night, in an inhabited house"; for this he was to spend nineteen years in the galleys.[a] Hugo describes the ex-convict at his moment of freedom when, brutalized and with a yellow passport describing him as "very dangerous," he is turned away from every house and inn.

Through the diseased perceptions of an incomplete nature and a smothered intelligence, he vaguely felt that a monstrous weight was over him. In that pallid and sullen shadow in which he crawled, whenever he turned his head and endeavoured to raise his eyes, he saw, with mingled rage and terror, forming, massing, and mounting up out of view above him with horrid escarpments, a kind of frightful accumulation of things, of laws, of prejudices, of men and of acts, the outlines of which escaped him, the weight of which appalled him, and which was no other than that prodigious pyramid that we call civilisation. . . . All this, laws, prejudices, acts, men, things, went and came above him, according to the complicated and mysterious movement that God impresses upon civilisation, marching over him and crushing him with an indescribably tranquil cruelty and inexorable indifference.[12]

To the poor of the great cities, the majesty of the law was a kind of judicial meatgrinder. Its logic and symmetry escaped them; all they knew was that it was controlled by awesome and distant figures—"here the jailer with his staff, here the gendarme with his sword, yonder the mitred archbishop; and on high, in a sort of blaze of glory, the emperor, crowned and resplendent." Hugo saw the poor drowning in this terrible "justice": "The sea is the inexorable night into

---

[a]Jean was sentenced to only five years for the "burglary." But for attempted escapes, he was given fourteen additional years.

which the penal law casts its victims. The sea is the measureless misery. The soul drifting in that sea may become a corpse. Who," asked Victor Hugo, "shall restore it to life?"[13]

However rational the criminal law, however beautifully designed, however proportional its penalties, in a society where you could plot the price of bread by the number of babies abandoned at the foundling hospital;[14] where, if the price rose above 12 or 13 sous, most of the working-class population was undernourished—in that society the law was only another millstone dragging the poor into the bottomless depths of misery and destitution. Buret described the realities of these "dangerous classes" and the "accursed districts in which they live":

... Wherever you go you will see men and women branded with the marks of vice and destitution, and half-naked children rotting in filth and stifling in airless, lightless dens. Here, in the very home of civilization, you will encounter thousands of men reduced by sheer besottedness to a life of savagery; here you will perceive destitution in a guise so horrible that it will fill you with disgust rather than pity and you will be tempted to regard it as the condign punishment for a crime.

Buret saw not only the pitiable condition of these outcasts, but also the danger they posed to civilized society: "Isolated from the nation, outlawed from the social and political community, along with their needs and miseries, they struggle to extricate themselves from this terrifying solitude and, like the barbarians to whom they have been compared, they are perhaps meditating invasion."[15]

Perhaps meditating invasion! This was the thought that struck a chill to the bourgeois hearts. For not only were the poor the conscripts in the great army of crime, theirs was the rage that toppled governments. In all the causes that brought about the French Revolution, none was so important as the price of bread. In June 1789, one month before the fall of the Bastille, when a Paris factory worker was living on effective daily earnings of 15 sous, a four-pound loaf of bread had risen to 14 1/2 sous, or *97 percent of his total income*. This left half a sous for everything else: rent, fuel, clothing, wine, vegetables, and oil.[16] Normally, a French worker of the eighteenth century had to spend only half his earnings on bread, but a bad harvest had meant sudden disaster to the populace. These crop failures recurred periodically throughout the nineteenth century, sending mobs—Hugo called them "savage legions"—howling into the streets.

Savage. We must explain this word. What was the aim of those bristling men who in the demiurgic days of revolutionary chaos, ragged, howling, wild, with tomahawk raised, and pike aloft, rushed over old overturned Paris? They desired the end of oppressions, the end of tyrannies, the end of the sword, labour for man, instruction for children, social gentleness for woman, liberty, equality, fraternity, bread for all, ideas for all. The Edenisation of the world, Progress; and this holy, good, gentle thing, progress, pushed to the wall and beside themselves, they demanded, terrible, half-naked, a club in their grasp, and a roar in their mouth.

These were the "savages of civilization." Hugo contrasted them in their wildness with the

other men, smiling, embroidered, gilded, beribboned, bestarred, in silk stockings, in white feathers, in yellow gloves, in varnished shoes, who, leaning upon a velvet table by the corner of a marble mantel, softly insist upon the maintenance and the preservation of the past, the middle ages, divine right, fanaticism, ignorance, slavery, the death penalty, and war, glorifying politely and in mild tones the sabre, the stake, and the scaffold. As for us, if we were compelled to choose between the barbarians of civilisation, and the civilisees of barbarism, we would choose the barbarians.[17]

But it was the "savages of civilization" who rattled the palace gates during the revolutions of 1789, 1830, and 1848. Contemporary bourgois accounts of the disturbances during the Restoration and the July Monarchy agreed with Frégier that "those who stir up popular seditions should be classified in the 'dangerous classes.'" This made them twice dangerous: dangerous to life and property as thieves, assassins, and brigands, and dangerous to governments as the troops of the revolution, when "they covered their hideous nakedness with hastily contrived blue cloaks and swarmed in the streets, already overburdened with the loot of the Royal Palace...."[18]

In a society where one bad harvest or one cold winter could mean the difference between living and dying, the Paris police followed the price of bread like an anxious doctor watching a patient's fever. "It is imperative to see that the price of bread does not go higher than 3 sous the pound," wrote the prefect of police in 1827. The price of 12 or 13 sous the four-pound loaf was a true physiological limit; above it lay hunger, crime, perhaps revolution. All during the early years of the July Monarchy (1830-1848), police reports were obsessed with the price of bread. When, in 1832, the price went to 16 sous and the government offered tickets for a 1-sous reduction in price, more than two hundred thousand people stormed the police stations and charity centers to seek this miserably inadequate assistance.[19]

Considering the social problems involved and the obsession of the times with criminality, it is not surprising that a number of statisticians began to look closely at the relationship between the crime rate and the price of bread. Georg von Mayr, making a study of crime and the price of rye in the Kingdom of Bavaria, concluded that in the period of 1835 to 1861, in Cis-Rhenish Bavaria, every half-groschen added to the price of grain called forth one more theft per one hundred thousand inhabitants.[20] A study by A. von Oettingen in Prussia, 1854-1859, showed that as the combined prices of wheat, rye, and potatoes fell, so did crimes against property; but crimes against morals and against persons increased. W. Starke also found a relationship between crime in Prussia and the coldness of the winters. (This was particularly true of the theft of wood.)[21] In England and Wales, a rise in grain prices seemed to be accompanied by a rise in property crimes and a decline in crimes of violence, and vice versa.[22]

Surveying many nineteenth-century studies of this type, Joseph Van Kan said, "Crimes against property find in large measure their indirect causality in bad economic conditions; their direct causality in acute need and even in more chronic misery.... Material well-being generally exalts the vital instincts, increases alcohol consumption, and therefore increases crimes against morals."[23]

What seems to have been happening, if one can judge from statistics which were not too reliable, was that when the winters were cold, requiring more money for fuel and clothing, and when bread was dear, property crimes increased. (In this period workmen normally spent about one-sixth of their total income on bread; in bad times, the proportion might be much higher.) On the other hand, when bread was cheap and winters warm, other disposable income increased. This led to a higher consumption of alcohol, and to an increase in tavern quarrels and in convictions for crimes of violence: murder, manslaughter, assault and battery. Good grape harvests, with cheap wine, had much the same effect: The German criminologist Gustav Aschaffenburg called them "detrimental to morality in general."

It is not the lack of the most necessary things, but the inability to give up habits acquired in times of prosperity, that makes the man prone to yield to temptation. And this danger of yielding is even greater if those who feel the pinch of poverty look on life's pleasures with immature eyes. The number of youthful offenders convicted of theft teaches us that.

To Aschaffenburg, poverty and distress were sources of crime in bad times, and alcohol was a source in good. "But the criminals who sit in the dock at these two times are not the same. Prosperity does not, as a rule at least, turn the man of dishonest ways into one who stabs and disturbs the peace, nor does the hero of the street turn to theft if he is in needy circumstances."[24]

Down to the present, all working people have lived close to the biological limits of starvation. This is why so many writers, beginning with Cassiodorus, have seen poverty as the mother of crime: Crime was often no more than a necessity for those who wanted to survive. It is no wonder that the criminal law, with its careful "calculus of hedonism," was like King Canute, waving back the sea. In the nineteenth century the "Iron Law of Wages" prevailed; the employer bargaining with his employee bargained with a terrible club. The great social reformers spoke with bitterness of the want that drove desperate men to war on society. Said Louis Blanc:

When a man who asks to live serving society is inevitably reduced to attacking it or dying, his apparent aggression is, in fact, no more than legitimate self-defense, and the society which strikes him down does not judge: it murders.... A manufacturer needs a worker: three present themselves. "How much for your work?" "Three francs; I have a wife and children." "Good. And you?" "Two francs and a half; I have no children, only a wife." "Wonderful. And you?" "Two francs will be enough; I am alone." "Then you get the job." Done: the deal is concluded. What will happen to the two workers who were shut out? They will, one hopes, resign themselves to dying of hunger. But if they go off to become robbers? Never fear, we have the police. Or assassins? We have the headsman. As for the luckiest of these three, his triumph is short-lived. Along comes a fourth laborer who is robust enough to fast one day out of two. The downward slope will go all the way to the bottom: another outcast, another recruit, perhaps, for the galleys![25]

7

Crime and Class Conflict: A Marxist View

The first half of the nineteenth century was a period of unparalleled misery, not only in Paris but in all the great industrial cities of Europe. Perhaps the greatest polemic ever written on the casualties of the Industrial Revolution was Friedrich Engels' *Condition of the Working Class in England*, which was published in Leipzig in 1845. Lorenz von Stein called it "beyond any question the best invective ever written in Germany against industrial society and its conditions, a partisan book like no other."[1] Its interest to us lies not only in its treatment of crime, but also in its author, who was the friend and collaborator of Karl Marx and one of the founding fathers of communism.

The nexus between crime and poverty, as we have seen, has been a recurring theme since Cassiodorus. With Engels, the connection was to be made explicit and given a theoretical framework. This German revolutionary was the son of a cotton manufacturer who had factories in Barmen, Engelskirchen, and Manchester, and himself became a partner in his father's business. Engels, in short, was a member of the very class whose "brutally selfish policy"[2] he was to attack with such ferocity. Yet from a very early age he had been impressed by the contrast between the pietistic Calvinism of the middle class and the misery of the poor. *The Condition of the Working Class in England* was written after a twenty-one-month stay in England, from 1842 to 1844; it appeared the year after his *Outlines of a Critique of Political Economy* (1844), and together with his speeches in Elberfeld (1845), provides the emergent outlines of a Marxist theory of crime.

What Engels saw in London and the other great cities was "the social war, the war of each against all. . . . People regard each other only as useful objects; each exploits the other, and the end of it all is that the stronger treads the weaker under foot, and that the powerful few, the capitalists, seize everything for themselves, while to the weak many, the poor, scarcely a bare existence remains."[3] Just what he means by a bare existence he makes plain as he describes the streets of London, "generally unpaved, rough, dirty, filled with vegetable and animal refuse, without sewers or gutters, but supplied with foul, stagnant pools, instead."[4] In London's rookery[a] of St. Giles:

The houses are occupied from cellar to garret, filthy within and without, and their appearance is such that no human being could possibly wish to live in them. But all this is nothing in comparison with the dwellings in the narrow

---

[a]Rookery: a crowded, dilapidated group of tenements.

47

courts and alleys between the streets, entered by covered passages between the houses, in which the filth and tottering ruin surpass all description. Scarcely a whole window-pane can be found, the walls are crumbling, door-posts and window-frames loose and broken, doors of old boards nailed together, or altogether wanting in this thieves' quarter, where no doors are needed, there being nothing to steal. Heaps of garbage and ashes lie in all directions, and the foul liquids emptied before the doors gather in stinking pools. Here live the poorest of the poor, the worst paid workers with thieves and the victims of prostitution . . . sinking daily deeper, losing daily more and more of their power to resist the demoralising influence of want, filth, and evil.[5]

Conditions were no better in the other "great towns." In Edinburgh, he said, quoting an unnamed English writer, "persons may step from the window of one house to that of the house opposite"; there, the excrement and refuse of fifty thousand people were nightly thrown into the gutters.[6] In Glasgow in the poorer lodging houses, ten, even twenty persons of both sexes and all ages slept promiscuously on the floor in different degrees of nakedness. Engels cited the observations of J.C. Symons, a government commissioner who had been sent to investigate the condition of the hand-weavers. "I did not believe until I visited the wynds[b] of Glasgow that so large an amount of filth, crime, misery, and disease existed in any civilised country."[7]

But Engels was not primarily interested in description, except to document his social theories. With respect to crime, he pointed out that the working man's "whole position and environment involves the strongest temptations to immorality. He is poor, life offers him no charm, almost every enjoyment is denied him, the penalties of the law have no further terrors for him; why should he restrain his desires, why leave to the rich the enjoyment of his birthright, why not seize a part of it for himself?"[8]

Engels showed by statistics that arrests for criminal offenses in England and Wales went from 4,605 in 1805 to 31,309 in 1842, a sevenfold increase in thirty-seven years. Today (1843) in England, he said, the proportion of crimes to the general population is 1:660. "These facts are certainly more than sufficient to bring anyone, even a bourgeois, to pause and reflect upon the consequences. . . . The enemies are dividing gradually into two great camps—the bourgeoisie on the one hand, the workers on the other. This war of each against all, of the bourgeoisie against the proletariat, need cause us no surprise, for it is only the logical sequel to the principle involved in free competition."[9] Social war, which began soon after the first industrial development, "is raging in England."

The earliest, crudest, and least fruitful form of this rebellion was that of crime. The working-man lived in poverty and want, and saw that others were better off than he. It was not clear to his mind why he, who did more for society than the rich idler, should be the one to suffer under these conditions. Want conquered

---

[b]Wynd: a very narrow street (Scottish).

his inherited respect for the sacredness of property, and he stole. We have seen how crime increased with the extension of manufacture; how the yearly number of arrests bore a constant relation to the number of bales of cotton annually consumed.

The workers soon realized that crime did not help matters. The criminal could protest against the existing order of society only singly, as one individual; the whole might of society was brought to bear upon each criminal, and crushed him with its immense superiority. Besides, theft was the most primitive form of protest, and for this reason, if for no other, it never became the universal expression of the public opinion of the working-men, however much they might approve of it in silence.[10]

In his *Critique of Political Economy* Engels explained the etiology of crime. Competition, he said, "sets capital against capital, labour against labour, landed property against landed property; and likewise, each of these elements against the other two. In the struggle, the stronger wins. . . ." Competition has "completed the reciprocal bondage in which men now hold themselves." He pointed out that "the extension of the factory system is followed everywhere by an increase in crime," that the number of crimes can be predicted year by year:

This regularity proves that crime, too, is governed by competition; that society creates a *demand* for crime which is met by a corresponding *supply*; that the gap created by the arrest, transportation or execution of a certain number is at once filled by others; just as every gap in population is at once filled by new arrivals; in other words, that crime presses on the means of punishment just as the people press on the means of employment.[11]

In a speech at Elberfeld, February 8, 1845, he fleshed out his theory of criminality and related it to what he called "a social war of all against all which inevitably in individual cases, notably among uneducated people, assumes a brutal, barbarously violent form—that of crime."

In order to protect itself against crime, against direct acts of violence, society requires an extensive, complicated system of administrative and judicial bodies which requires an immense labour force. In communist society . . . we eliminate the contradiction between the individual man and all others, we counterpose social peace to social war, we put the axe to the *root* of crime. . . . Crimes against property cease of their own accord where everyone receives what he needs to satisfy his natural and his spiritual urges, where social gradations and distinctions cease to exist.[12]

Thus Engels provided not only a diagnosis, but also a proposed cure for crime. He believed that the Industrial Revolution in England, the most advanced capitalist country of his time, had resulted in the formation of a new revolutionary class, the proletariat, whose position "is the real basis and point of departure of all social movements of the present because it is the highest and most unconcealed pinnacle of the social misery existing in our day." His long documentation of that misery "is absolutely necessary to provide solid ground for social theories . . . and to put an end to all sentimental dreams and fancies. . . ."[13] Others, including the utopian socialists, had described the suffering of the poor, but, as Lenin was to note, "Engels was the *first* to say that the proletariat is *not only* a suffering class; that it is, in fact, the disgraceful economic condition of the proletariat that drives it irresistibly forward and compels it to fight for its ultimate emancipation. And the fighting proletariat *will help itself.*"[14]

To Engels, crime was a form of revolt against the dreadful oppression of the industrial system; but it was too primitive, too unorganized to succeed against the apparatus of the state. Only a disciplined and organized working class could overcome class oppression and bring an end to the social war of which crime was the most savage expression. What a man has, Engels said, he does not have to steal.

In the 1840s Engels and Marx both foresaw an imminent uprising that would everywhere drive the bourgeoisie from power and bring the utopia of a classless society. In fact, the disturbance of 1848-1849, which swept the continent, came closer than any revolt before or since to the ideal of a world revolution. Virtually no capital escaped. Engels himself was so involved in the revolutionary movements in Germany that he was forced to flee to London, where he spent many years, first as an employee, then as a partner, in his father's Manchester cotton mill. It is always interesting to contemplate the revolutionary earning his bread as a capitalist; in Engels' case, he used his wealth to support that greatest of all communist theoreticians, Karl Marx, whose friend, editor, and financial angel he remained to the latter's dying day.

The high-water mark of world revolution was 1848. No series of events has in so brief a span shaken more governments, threatened the survival of more dynasties, or posed a greater challenge to the industrial and mercantile class of Europe—nor has any challenge proven more ephemeral. After 1849 the red tide seemed everywhere to recede, as England, Europe, and America underwent a period of unparalleled economic and political expansion. What remained to the Marxists during the next sixty-five years was a peaceful conquest of the continental labor movement and the acceptance in attenuated—one is almost tempted to say *un-Marxist*—form of their doctrine among the Social Democrats. "Suitable or not," says Alfred G. Meyer, "the merger of the ideology with the movement was a turning point because, with it, Marxism became a formal ideology, a guide to thought and action, a holy writ and catechism."[15]

In the next three-quarters of a century, many intellectuals would be tempted to apply Marxian analysis to the problem of crime. Everywhere the socialists taught (and believed) that equality of reward and the leveling of distinction between rich and poor would suppress all forms of antisocial activity. To them, capitalism was the provoking cause of, if not the complete justification for, crime. "Society is therefore the original offender. By producing unfortunates who can find no place at the feast of life—whom it thrusts from the brilliantly lighted banquet-table into the squalor of the gloomy street, it makes possible the existence of the malefactor."[16]

This thesis was embraced by such socialist theoreticians as Robert Owen[c] and August Bebel, as well as criminologists like W.A. Bonger, Achille Loria, Georg Rusche, and Otto Kircheimer; but, fortunately, or unfortunately, the course of history left it for many years untested. The same Social Democrats who embraced Marxian analysis eschewed revolutionary violence in the attainment of political power, and, until Lenin, the control of society remained firmly fixed where Marx had found it, in the hands of a triumphant bourgeoisie. Thus until November 1917 no one would be able either to confirm or to disprove the hypothesis that in a proletarian and classless society, crime, like the state, would wither away, and man attain once again to that primal innocence and moral perfection from which, in the Garden of Eden, he was tempted and fell.

[c]Owen, of course, was not a Marxist; but many non-Marxists also embraced the idea that communism would bring the abolition of crime. Said Raffaele Garofalo, *Criminology*, p. 143: "It is met with in the classic authors, whence it passed into the writings of Fénelon, was later adopted by Owen, and finally took its place in the doctrines of Bebel and the modern revolutionary socialists."

Some Reflections on Eighteen Hundred Years of Danger

We have come now to the middle of the nineteenth century, and it might be well to pause and reflect on the changing—and in some cases, unchanging—concepts of dangerousness that have marked the transitions from paganism to Christianity, from Christianity to secularism, and from feudalism (and later, mercantilism) to the urbanized world of the Industrial Revolution. A look at the record reveals some surprises. For example, during almost two millennia, from the persecutions of Nero to the scientific materialism that came to dominate Europe in the latter half of the last century, there seemed little conception of the "dangerous offender" as such—that is, of a single, uniquely threatening individual marked by some physiological or psychological stigma to prey upon his fellows.

There were dangerous people abroad, certainly. A robber armed with a stiletto was as frightening to the pedestrian in fifteenth-century London or Paris as one with a gun is to twentieth-century Detroit. But society thought of him less as an individual threat to his fellow man than as the representative of a *class* of dangerous people: wanderers, gypsies, unemployed scholars, demobilized seamen, or whatever. It did not occur to anyone to ask, "Why is so-and-so a criminal?" because Christians thought they knew the answer. All people are born sinners because of Original Sin, which the Anglican Articles of Religion (1553) defined as "the fault and corruption of the Nature of every man, that naturally is engendered of the offspring of Adam; whereby man is very far gone from original righteousness, and is of his own nature inclined to evil. . . ." (Article IX) A very popular doctrine, revived during the Protestant Reformation, was predestination—that certain persons were chosen by God "before the foundations of the world were laid" to be brought to everlasting salvation—a very comforting notion to the elect, but rather dismaying for those not chosen, since *they* were doomed to eternal damnation. As Article XVII put it, for "curious and carnal persons" to be under "the sentence of God's Predestination, is a most dangerous downfall, whereby the Devil doth thrust them either into desperation, or into wretchedness of most unclean living, no less perilous than desperation."[1]

They were dangerous, in short, because they had not been selected to be among the saved. This doctrine of predestination was one of the cornerstones of John Calvin's theology. Catholic dogma had asserted that Christ, by dying on the cross, had made possible the salvation of all men: Calvin maintained, on the contrary, that Christ's atoning death was offered for the elect alone. "He added to the gratuitous predestination of the elect the equally gratuitous and positive reprobation of the damned, to whom salvation is denied from all eternity without any fault on their part."[2]

To the Calvinists, the person who was damned was indeed dangerous because he had no hope of salvation, and no hope, even, of avoiding wickedness. True, outside of Scotland and Geneva, most Europeans were not Calvinists and did not subscribe to so extreme a theology; but all Christians believed in the doctrine of Original Sin, that "in Adam's fall we sinnèd all," as the old rhyme had it. The problem for the Christian was therefore not to explain evil, which was inherent in every man; the problem was only to control it. The Catholic church taught that although we are maimed by our sinful natures, we also have the power of free will; religion is one of the means of overcoming the Old Adam in us, by making men receptive to the Word, and through the Word, to the redeeming grace of God. ("For as in Adam all die," said St. Paul, "even so in Christ shall all be made alive.")[3] For those who did not get the word—the reprobates, scoundrels, and criminals—there were more tangible and effective expedients such as the whipping post, the chopping block, and the gallows.

Many a bourgeois Calvinist believed that the elect were foreordained, not only to salvation in the next life, but to affluence in this one. Thus poverty and wickedness become inextricably confused. Even among Catholics one can sense a terrified awareness of the poor, whose miseries aroused little sympathy but much apprehension. Because of the brutal exigencies of their lives, it was thought, these "dangerous classes" were subject to great temptation to prey on their fellow men; hence the criminal law was designed to terrify them into a respect for other people's property. The law did not apply such draconian measures to the rich. At first blush, this seems surprising, since the mighty, no less than the humble, were supposedly corrupted by Adam's Original Sin. However, the view of the criminal law seems to have been that because of the easier circumstances of their lives, the vicious rich were less subject to temptation and hence less dangerous than the vicious poor. Their offenses did not, and to this day *do* not, exact the same harsh penalties from the law—a net that has always and everywhere been woven to catch minnows and let the sharks swim free. (This becomes more understandable when one reflects that it is the great, and not the small, fish who design the net.)

An ascription of dangerousness has not, however, been limited to the lower classes. As we have seen, the state has throughout history recognized another kind of dangerousness in those who challenge its legitimacy. The challenge may be ideological; it may be purely political; it may be both. Joan of Arc was burned at the stake on a charge of heresy: she refused to abjure the voices which she claimed were from her saints, and which the Church said were from the devil. So the tragedy was played out at the theological level, even though the real question for her English inquisitors was not whether Saint Margaret or Saint Beelzebub was speaking, but what the message directed Joan to do. Anyone who could stiffen the spine of the dauphin, crown him king of France, and lead his victorious armies against the English occupation was clearly a *dangerous offender*—to the English, at any rate.

This brings us to a question that underlies all dangerousness: Who has reason to feel threatened? Dangerousness is not necessarily chimerical, but it *is* directed against some class, some government, some religion, or some person. Thieves are more dangerous to people with possessions, witches more dangerous to those who believe in spells. Cavaliers were a threat to Roundheads, Catholics to Protestants, anarchists to organized governments, Communists to the bourgeois state. Dangerousness is a perceived potential to do harm, and it is usually defined by the one who sees himself as the probable victim. If the potential victim controls the apparatus of the state, that dangerousness may be defined by statute; but dangerousness also exists outside the ambit of the law where there are racial and religious animosities that divide people and make them fearful. I once heard a young black professional tell a room full of whites: "I don't see danger the same way you do. For instance, if you are walking down the street late at night and meet a group of black teen-agers, your heart begins to pound, and your hands get clammy because you think they are *dangerous*. But *my* heart pounds when I walk into an all-white restaurant in a small town in Indiana, where I know every other man is a member of the Ku Klux Klan. To me, *those people are dangerous.*"

We asked the question once before, and it is appropriate to raise it again here: Does that mean that dangerousness is in the eye of the beholder? Are there, or are there not, some people who, because of the way their minds work, because of their uncertain tempers, because of some process of disease, or some degeneracy of body or spirit, are a threat to everyone? This question, until the mid-nineteenth century, had never been asked. The nearest anyone had come was the Calvinists, who believed some people were predestined from conception to "a most dangerous downfall." But this kind of determinism was not generally embraced, and after Beccaria and Bentham, the law assumed that each individual, having free will, was responsible for his own conduct. It was the business of wise legislators, they thought, to so structure the penalties that crime would be prudently and rationally avoided.

The classical jurists did not believe anyone was predestined to criminality. Even Engels, who thought the structure of an unjust society was the cause of crime, believed that under a more humane and egalitarian society this evil would disappear. Nevertheless, in the late nineteenth century there were forces abroad that would bring a revolution in the whole concept of dangerousness and raise, in a new and secular form, the Calvinistic view that some people are damned from the moment of conception—that dangerous criminals are born, and not made. What the forces were, and how they came to be applied to the nascent science of criminology, will be the subject of the next section.

**Part II
Science and the
Dangerous Offender**

9

The Ladder of Perfection

The nineteenth century in Europe and America was in every way a period of extraordinary development. Capital accumulated, industry grew, the world was explored to its farthest corners, and knowledge seemed to explode as old sciences were rejuvenated and new ones born. If nothing was any longer taken for granted, all, through the methodology of science, seemed knowable. Rudolf Virchow, the great German cellular pathologist, once told his father that his aim in life was "no less than a universal knowledge of nature from Godhead to stone."[1] He was twenty-one at the time, and such an ambitious program might be put down to the exuberance of youth. But Virchow was not unusual for his century. The whole movement that called itself "scientific materialism" believed that through the tireless and critical examination of facts, and the avoidance of irresponsible theorizing, all knowledge would eventually be knowable. Virchow insisted on the rule of causality, necessity, and law. Science begins with the history of material bodies; then it inquires into the mechanism of their development. "Knowledge," he said, "has no boundary other than ignorance. . . ."[2]

Auguste Comte, who is generally regarded as the father of sociology (having, in fact, invented the word), thought that every branch of human knowledge has to pass through three different stages of maturity. The first is the theological stage (opium puts people to sleep because God wills it). The second is the metaphysical stage (opium puts people to sleep because of a soporific principle). The third is the scientific, or *positive*, stage in which all phenomena are regarded as subject to natural laws that can be studied by observation and experimentation. In this stage the method by which opium puts people to sleep would be scientifically understood. Comte thought that different branches of knowledge reach the positive stage in logical order, beginning with those the most remote from human concerns, and ending with the social sciences. Therefore, the order of sciences is: astronomy (the first to achieve a positive stage of development), then physics, chemistry, physiology, and finally sociology, or as Quételet called it, "social physics." (Comte thought that psychology had not yet achieved positivism, being still in the metaphysical stage of development.)

"Positivism" was therefore another name for a scientific, empirical approach to knowledge. Everywhere, the methodology was applied in a tireless, painstaking examination of facts.[a] We see it in Darwin, spending twenty years study-

---

[a]On the other hand, George Canning (1770-1821), the British foreign secretary and prime minister, was once quoted as saying that nothing is so fallacious as facts, except figures.

ing and classifying his specimens before daring to publish *On the Origin of Species*. It was not his theory but his method that overwhelmed the opposition: Evolution was an old idea, which had been discussed for a hundred years, but until Darwin, nobody had demonstrated its mechanism. Similarly, Marx did not discover poverty or invent communism; he simply piled up evidence and devised a theory to explain everything. The new science of statistics, too, provided scholars with a vast array of data, including Guerry's "moral statistics." Ethnologists covered the globe, studying primitive tribes for a clue to modern man. Human beings were measured, drawn, observed by anthropometrists, and dissected by pathologists. Old bones were dug up: The 1860s were the time when Neanderthal man made his debut. For the scientist it was a dazzling time to be alive, and for none more so than for those who would understand the nature and character of man.

For centuries man had been seen as standing at the summit of the natural order—the *Scala naturae*, Chain of Being or Ladder of Perfection, which climbed from minerals and the lower forms of life to the higher vertebrates, and finally, at the top, homo sapiens. Said Joseph Addison (1712), "The whole chasm in Nature, from a Plant to a Man, is filled up with diverse kinds of Creatures, rising one over another by such a gentle and easy Ascent, that the little Transitions and Deviations from one Species to another are almost insensible."[3] This was not to say that all men thought "all men are created equal." On the contrary. Within the human species, as many scientists observed, there were imbeciles and savants, Hottentots and Englishmen, criminals and persons of high moral character. In other words, the Chain of Being did not stop with man but continued up through the various levels of savagery, mental retardation, and criminality until it peaked at the summit: modern, affluent, well-educated, and morally upright Caucasian man.

It became a subject of intense scientific interest to understand who got left behind, and why. George-Louis Leclerc, Comte de Buffon, in his forty-four volume *Natural History*, was the first to state a complete theory of biological evolution (1750-1788). Other eighteenth-century writers who speculated about evolution were the Scottish philosopher David Hume, who wondered about the survival of the fittest; the French philospher Denis Diderot, who set forth a doctrine of survival of the fittest and the development of species through long ages; the Swiss naturalist Charles Bonnet, who first used the term "evolution"; and the French botanist and geologist Lamarck, who created the most elaborate evolutionary doctrine of his time. Lamarck believed in the inheritance of acquired characteristics. He had the idea of "use inheritance," that use alters and heredity transmits new characters. (For example, the giraffe's neck got long from eating the tops of trees, and this characteristic was passed along to its posterity.)[4] This idea of use inheritance was still alive and well in the twentieth century in the theories of the Soviet plant geneticist Trofim Lysenko.

Both the old idea of a Chain of Being and the newer idea of evolution were hierarchical: There were lower and higher forms of life, and lower and higher forms of humanity, some not much above the apes, others, only a little lower than the angels. Furthermore, you could tell, *just by looking at them*, which men were of the higher and which of the lower order. Johann Kaspar Lavater, a physiognomist, purported to show, by many illustrations, that there is a "correspondence between the external and internal man, the visible superficies and invisible contents."[5] His plates, vividly drawn, appeared not only in texts on physiognomy but in psychiatric textbooks and in works on another new science of the late eighteenth and early nineteenth century, phrenology. (Phrenologists thought you could tell what was inside a man's mind by the bumps on his skull.) To the nineteenth-century anatomist and behavioral scientist then, skulls and faces became a veritable key to human behavior.

Franz Josef Gall, the founder of phrenology, was a lineal ascendent of those criminologists who believe that biology is the basis of dangerous conduct. It was one of his disciples Hubert Lauvergne who in 1844 published a study of convicts in the prison of Toulon in which he attributed their criminal instincts to the abnormal development of one part of their brain. Of assassins he said, "They possess marked protuberances and a peculiar face stamped by the seal of a brutal and impassible instinct. Their heads are large and receding with notable lateral protuberances, enormous jaws and masticatory muscles always in motion."[6] (One can only shudder at what Lauvergne would have thought of a classroom full of American second-graders, their mouths stuffed with chewing gum.) Carl Gustav Carus in his *Principles of a New and Scientific Craniology* (1840) said that delinquents are distinguished by a narrow forehead and an insufficient development of the occiput and by the length of the cranium. They are creatures who tend exclusively to a vegetative life and to the satisfaction of material wants; they are lacking in reason and willpower and are prone to offend.[7]

But why, if man is the summit of evolution (or of the Chain of Being), are some men so debased? Augustin-Benoit Morel, in his treatise on *The Physical, Intellectual, and Moral Degeneration of the Human Species* (1857), blamed it on a kind of retrogressive natural selection, a falling-away from the perfection of primitive man, owing to "the combination of the new conditions brought about by the original fall" (i.e., the Fall in the Garden of Eden). He traces the role of heredity in this gradual degeneration of the species. "The strange and unknown types which people our prisons," he said, "are not so strange and unknown to those who study the morbid varieties of the human species from the double point of view of the psychic and moral condition of the individuals that compose them. They personify the various degenerations of the species and the evil which produces them constitutes for modern society a greater danger than the barbaric invasion did for the old."[8]

Another view of the origins of criminality was set forth by Robert Chambers in his *Vestiges of the Natural History of Creation* (1844).[b] Primi-

[b]This work which, until Darwin, was the most sensationally successful book on evolution (ten editions in ten years) was published anonymously because Chambers feared the same kind of religious controversy that followed *On The Origin of Species.*

tive men—savages and criminals—are simply less advanced in the scale of evolution, *"representations of particular stages in the development of the highest or Caucasian type."* Cuvier and Newton "are but expansions of a clown, and the person emphatically called the wicked man, is one whose highest moral feelings are rudimental."

It may still be a puzzle to many, how beings should be born into the world whose organization is such that they unavoidably, even in a civilized country, become malefactors. Does God, it may be asked, make criminals? Does he fashion certain beings with a predestination to evil? He does not do so; and yet the criminal type of brain, as it is called, comes into existence in accordance with laws which the Deity has established.[9]

Chambers believed that successive generations of unfavorable environment lead to the development of "a mean type of brain." For example, slaves contract the habit of lying. What is habit in the parents becomes an inherent quality in the children. "And sometimes not one, but several generations, may be concerned in bringing up the result to a pitch which produces crimes." In unenlightened countries, criminals are treated severely.

But when order is generally triumphant, and reason allowed to hold sway, men begin to see the true case of criminals—namely, that while one large section are victims of erroneous social conditions, another are brought to error by tendencies which they are only unfortunate in having inherited from nature. Criminal jurisprudence then addresses itself less to the direct punishment than to the reformation and caretaking of those liable to its attention.[10]

The great evolutionary scheme of which we are but a part may seem harsh and difficult to reconcile with the idea of a Benevolent Deity, said Chambers. But we must remember that "the present system is but a part of a whole, a stage in a Great Progress. . . . Thinking of all the contingencies of this world as to be in time melted into or lost in some greater system, to which the present is only subsidiary, let us wait the end with patience, and be of good cheer."[11]

To anthropologists, the "great progress" showed itself clearly when one compared ancient man with modern, and primitive with civilized. The first Neanderthal skull cap was found in a small cave in Rhenish Prussia in 1856, and it was followed by other discoveries of primitive skulls that showed superciliary prominences and small and receding foreheads. The anthropologists decided that modern savages, and even modern criminals, were very like prehistoric man. Said J.W. Dawson, speaking of a recently discovered skeleton, "It may have belonged to one of those wild men, half-crazed, half-idiotic, cruel and strong, who are always more or less to be found living on the outskirts of barbarous tribes, and who now and then appear in civilized communities, to be consigned perhaps to the pentitentiary or the gallows."[12] Loren Eiseley said, "Neanderthal man is here quite close to being made one with those fallen, feral creatures who wander in the green forests of medieval romance."[13] More important for our purposes, he has become one with *homo criminalis*—an atavistic being, wild and deformed, who, on his evolutionary climb up the Ladder of Perfection, has somehow stumbled.

In 1859 Darwin published *On the Origin of Species by Means of Natural Selection, or the Preservation of Favoured Races in the Struggle for Life,* a work which, said Jacques Barzun, "was greater as an event than as a book." If it was, as many have said, the most important publication of the nineteenth century, this was "at least as much because of what it brought seething out of the European mind," said Barzun, "as because of what it put into it."[14] Evolution was not a new idea; it had been discussed for nearly a century. The concept of a struggle for existence and the survival of the fittest was well known; in his *Social Statics* (1851) Herbert Spencer had applied the doctrine to the development of mankind, showing how early man, "to the end that he may prepare the earth for its future inhabitants—his descendants . . . must possess a character fitting him to clear it of races endangering his life, and races occupying the space required by mankind. Hence he must have a desire to kill. . . . He must further be devoid of sympathy, or must have but the germ of it, for he would otherwise be incapacitated for his destructive office. In other words, he must be what we call a savage. . . ."[15]

By comparison with Spencer's writings, or even Chambers', Darwin's *Origin of Species* was mild, cautious, pedantic. It avoided any discussion of man. Darwin did not use the term "evolution," nor "survival of the fittest." He spent a great deal of time on pigeons, so much so that his publisher, John Murray, suggested he simply eliminate the rest of the book, and limit it to these animals, as "everybody is interested in pigeons." (Murray considered Darwin's theory of natural selection "as absurd as contemplating the fruitful union of a poker and a rabbit." The work, he thought, would not sell more than five hundred copies.)[16] Nevertheless, the book was so overwhelming in its scholarship and aroused such animus in religious circles that it created an international furore. The great debate had begun: Was man too descended from these lower forms? "Is man an ape or an angel?" asked Disraeli, in one of his most famous speeches. "I, my lord, am on the side of the angels."[17]

So the battle lines were drawn. Religious leaders denounced Darwin because he seemed to call into question the revealed Word of God, that heaven and earth had been created in six days, and that man came directly from the hand of his Maker. On the other hand, the positivists were only too eager to embrace the evolutionary religion, which seemed to buttress the many studies of primitive man, and to explain his laggard status on the Ladder of Perfection. It was now clear to scientists why "the brutal Hottentot" seemed to stand so close to the ape. Less culturally advanced members of the human race were living fossils: "The Mongol and the Negro are but human saurians who reached long ago . . . their full development, and are now moral fossils,"[18] as one writer put it. Another suggested that the missing link between the chimpanzee and the Negro was the idiot.[19]

That there was apparently a missing link—or, as Darwin said, a "rather wide gap ... between, say a Hottentot and an Orang"[20]—tempted all kinds of scientific speculation. There was a great interest in what were called "atavisms" or "reversions"—apparent throwbacks among modern man to more primitive evolutionary types. Darwin looked on "reversion—this power of calling back to life long-lost characters—as the most wonderful of all the attributes of inheritance."[21] The great German pathologist, Rudolf Virchow, saw in man certain bodily peculiarities of the lower animals, which he called "theromorphism."[22] Explorers reported that in the gloom of primeval forests they had seen individuals who "might as well pass for an Orang-Utan as a man": flat-nosed, long-armed, and black.[23] Asked one anthropologist in some alarm: "What will become of the unity of the human species, if we can prove that certain races are not a whit more intelligent than certain animals ... ?"[24]

It should be observed that even the most naive nineteenth-century theorists were empirical in their methodology. Franz Josef Gall was more than a quaint eccentric who plotted the human psyche from the contours of the skull; he was also a distinguished anatomist whose dissections of animal and human brains established for the first time the pathways between the brain and the nervous system. The ethnologists who thought they detected the natural inferiority of "lesser breeds without the law" were also indefatigable explorers; even at their most ethnocentric, they added vastly to the sum of human knowledge. Virchow may have believed in "theromorphism"; he was also the founder of cellular pathology. In short, these were distinguished figures in the history of modern science. Their methodology had taught them observation, a respect for the facts; but unfortunately, facts speak only the language that the hearer is prepared to understand, and as Darwin once observed, "the force of impressions generally depends on preconceived ideas."[25] Even the most conscientious scientist sees what his education, his culture, and the mythos of the times permit him to see. Those who see further are apt, like Galileo, to run afoul of the Inquisition, whatever its embodiment at the moment.

Herbert Spencer believed that "civilized man" had a larger skull and "a more complex or heterogeneous nervous system than the uncivilized man."[26] So did most European scientists, to whom the superiority of Caucasian man seemed self-evident. The French anatomist Paul Broca founded the *Société d'Anthropologie* in 1859, and many other groups dedicated to the measurement and understanding of man were organized. Unfortunately, what they saw was the supposed inferiority of other peoples. In the words of Jacques Barzun,

Combining with complete ignorance of genetics a Chinese reverence for the bones of the dead as indices of class and race, and a very superficial knowledge of European history, these men soon made racialism a source of international animus, class recrimination, and private *parti-pris*. Not content to measure skulls and outlaw the longheads (dolicocephalics) or the roundheads (brachycelphalics); not content to examine pigmentation and damn the yellow men for their racial backwardness . . . they discovered as well that individualists were one race and socialists another; that the poor and the rich, the burgher and the peasant, the nobles and the former serfs, all were races whose descendants, intermingled in the modern nation, were fighting a Darwinian struggle, a struggle which Broca had the honor of calling Social Selection.[27]

It was only a matter of time until someone would apply these methods and ideas—anthropometry, the study of skulls and faces, a belief in atavism, and the natural selection theories of the Darwinians—to the problems of crime and ask himself whether the thousands of beings who crowded the prisons were just people like everyone else, or were rather a special evolutionary type, stranded somewhere on the lower rungs of the Ladder of Perfection. It was also inevitable, given the nineteenth century, that this someone would be a scientist, a positivist, a tireless seeker after facts. And so it proved. His name was Cesare Lombroso; he was an Italian physician; and his Scuola Nuova, New, or Positivist, School, would mark the first "scientific" approach to the study of criminal man, and particularly to the study of that putative evolutionary throwback who would be dubbed "the born criminal."

10 The Positivist Revolution

In 1870 Cesare Lombroso was a professor of psychiatry at the University of Pavia. He had been carrying on researches in the prisons and asylums of Pavia upon cadavers and living persons, seeking to determine the differences between criminals and the insane, "without," as he explained later, "succeeding very well." One morning he was deputed to do a post-mortem on a famous bandit, when he suddenly noticed a long series of "atavistic anomalies, above all an enormous middle occipital fossa and a hypertrophy of the vermis analogous to those that are found in inferior vertebrates."[1]

This was not merely an idea, but a revelation. At the sight of that skull, I seemed to see all of a sudden, lighted up as a vast plain under a flaming sky, the problem of the nature of the criminal—an atavistic being who reproduces in his person the ferocious instincts of primitive humanity and the inferior animals. Thus were explained anatomically the enormous jaws, high cheek-bones, prominent superciliary arches, solitary lines in the palms, extreme size of the orbits, handle-shaped or sessile ears found in criminals, savages, and apes, insensibility to pain, extremely acute sight, tattooing, excessive idleness, love of orgies, and the irresistible craving for evil for its own sake, the desires not only to extinguish life in the victim, but to multilate the corpse, tear its flesh, and drink its blood.[2]

As Lombroso described it, this must have been very like the moment when, settling into his tub and watching his body displace water, Archimedes suddenly saw how to measure the purity of gold, or when the youthful Franz Josef Gall, looking at his fellow pupils, decided that those with the best memories had prominent eyes—an observation that led him to phrenology.[3] Of such gestalten are great discoveries born.

Lombroso's identification of atavistic man in the living criminal was a moment for which the entire nineteenth century had been preparing him. Yet the thirty-five-year-old physician was, as he himself complained, the product of a typical thirteenth-century education. Even though he was from a Venetian Jewish family, Lombroso was educated by Jesuits "—thrust back," he complained later, "into an environment of persistent medievalism" that was "so hateful to me that even now it visits me in dreams like a nightmare." The tone of the times was set by the Emperor Franz Josef—Austria at that time ruled Northern Italy— vho was reported to have said, "I want, not educated, but *obedient* subjects."[4]

Having been suckled on Saint Thomas, Lombroso was, however, weaned on evolution and anthropology. During his medical studies at the University of

Pavia, from which he got his medical degree in 1858, and at the University of Vienna, he became acquainted with, and was strongly influenced by, three contemporary intellectual currents: French positivism, German scientific materialism, and English evolutionism. He had also, as a psychiatrist, read the chief works in his field that dealt with the mentally disordered offender, including the type the twentieth century came to know as the "psychopath" or "sociopath."

Lombroso was very interested in comparing criminals with the insane; as a psychiatrist, he wondered whether there were differences or similarities—this was, of course, why he had been scouring the prisons and asylums, studying the living and the dead. He knew, from literature that went back to the seventeenth century, at least, that there were people who behaved in impulsive, strange, and criminal ways yet could not be called insane. In the common view, an insane person was one who suffered from distortion of the reasoning faculty. Yet various writers discussed another kind of mental illness that the nineteenth century variously denominated "mania without delirium" (Philippe Pinel), "instinctive monomania" (J.E.D. Esquirol), or "moral insanity" (J.C. Prichard). These "moral imbeciles" were quite rational, often intelligent, yet defective in a way that was incomprehensible to the alienists.

In his *Treatise on Insanity* (1806) Philippe Pinel described patients of this type who, though their reason seemed unimpaired, suffered from a perversion of the affections and moral feelings he called a *manie sans délire*.[5] In the same year, J.H. Cox described a patient who "to the casual observer might appear activated by a bad heart, but the experienced physician knows it is the head which is defective."[6] James C. Prichard (1835) described what he called "moral insanity," a term that was widely adopted from him. "This form of mental derangement," he said, "has been described as consisting in a morbid perversion of the feelings, affections, and active powers, without any illusion or erroneous conviction impressed upon the understanding: it sometimes co-exists with an apparently unimpaired state of the intellectual faculties." He continued,

In many instances the impulses or propensities to which the individual is subject, rather than his feelings or habitual temper and disposition, give the principal or the sole manifestations of insanity. . . . A propensity to theft is often a feature of moral insanity, and sometimes it is its leading if not the sole characteristic. . . . There is reason to believe that this species of insanity has been the real source of moral phenomena of an anomalous and unusual kind, and of certain perversions of natural inclination which excited the greatest disgust and abhorrence.[7]

Jean-Etienne-Dominique Esquirol, in his *Mental Maladies: A Treatise on Insanity*, described three kinds of mental illness. In one, reasoning is impaired; in a second, "affections and disposition are perverted." And

In a third class of cases, a lesion of the will exists. The patient is drawn away from his accustomed course, to the commission of acts, to which neither reason nor sentiment determine, which conscience rebukes, and which the will has no longer the power to restrain. The actions are involuntary, instinctive, irresistible. This is *monomania without delirium*, or *instinctive monomania*.

But, says Esquirol "in the moral insanity of this author [Prichard], in the *reasoning mania* of Pinel, in *mania without delirium*, the understanding is more or less affected. Were it not thus, the insane would permit themselves to be controlled by their understanding, and would discover that their views are false, and their actions, unusual and strange."[8]

Lombroso, after his moment of revelation with the bandit's skull, abjured the speculative psychiatry of the times, including the then fashionable arguments over free will, and pursued the study of criminals—and especially, this type of "moral imbecile"—in pathological anatomy. Something must be wrong, he felt, either with the brains, or the nervous system, or the evolutionary development of criminal man—or perhaps with all three. When Lombroso and his followers examined the bodies of prisoners and found a "theromorph,"[a] they asked themselves the following questions: (1) Is this peculiarity present in any of the authentic remains of prehistoric man, and if so, how frequently, compared to its frequency among criminals? (2) Is it met with in the lower races of man, and if so, how often? (3) Is it found in other species of the group of primates? (4) Is it found in animals lower than these in the scale of classification? (5) Is it found in human beings presenting congenital morbid anomalies; more especially, is it found in epileptics and idiots?[9] Lombroso thought he saw anatomical peculiarities in the brain, skull, skeleton, and viscera of his subjects, and his conclusion was daring:

At the sight of these strange anomalies, the problem of the nature and of the origin of the criminal seemed to be resolved; the characteristics of primitive men and of inferior animals must be reproduced in our times. Many facts seemed to confirm this hypothesis, above all, the psychology of the criminal; the frequency of tattooing and of professional slang; the passions as much more fleeting as they are more violent, and above all that of vengeance; the lack of foresight which resembles courage and courage which alternates with cowardice, and idleness which alternates with the passion for play and activity.[10]

Lombroso was not only daring, but dogged. He personally measured the skulls of three hundred eighty-three dead prisoners, and with the assistance of students, five thousand nine hundred five living ones.

The results of his studies were published in 1876 in *L'Uomo Delinquente* (*Criminal Man*), a book that almost overnight made Lombroso the most famous criminologist of his time. Criminals, he said, have "a physical insensibility like that which is encountered in some insane persons and especially in violent lunatics." They have dull olfactory, tactile, and taste senses. And "in general, in

---

[a]Theromorph: literally, a kind of Permian reptile that resembled a mammal. However, the criminal anthropologists used the term to mean a man who resembled a lower animal.

criminal man, the moral insensibility is as great as the physical insensibility; undoubtedly the one is the effect of the other. . . . The passions which make the heart of the normal man beat with the greatest force are very feeble in him. The first sentiment which is extinguished in these beings is that of pity for the suffering of another, and this happens just because they themselves are insensible to suffering."[11]

Criminals are vain, lascivious, lazy, and lacking in foresight, said Lombroso. The first characteristic of the born criminal is tattooing. Though tattooing is common in some of the "inferior classes," it is most common among criminals: "It may be said that, for these last, it constitutes on account of its frequency a specific and entirely new anatomico-legal chracteristic," the cause of which "is, in my opinion, atavism, or this other kind of historic atavism called tradition. Tattooing is in fact one of the essential characteristics of primitive man and of the man who is still living in a savage stage." In general, said Lombroso, "many criminals have outstanding ears, abundant hair, a sparse beard, enormous frontal sinuses and jaws, a square and projecting chin, broad cheekbones, frequent gestures, in fact a type resembling the Mongolian and sometimes the Negro."[12]

The man whom the alienists called a "moral imbecile" (and we call a "psychopath" or "sociopath") is often a born criminal, according to Lombroso. The English psychiatrist Henry Maudsley had said that "a person who has no moral sense is naturally well-fitted to become a criminal, and if his intellect is not strong enough to convince him that crime will not in the end succeed, and that it is, therefore, on the lowest grounds a folly, he is very likely to become one." Maudsley was a very distinguished alienist whose *Responsibility in Mental Disease* came out in 1874, while Lombroso was doing his initial studies: he gives perhaps the best description of the "moral imbecile" which had appeared to that time:

Notwithstanding prejudices to the contrary, there is a disorder of the mind, in which, without illusion, delusion, or hallucination, the symptoms are mainly exhibited in a perversion of those mental faculties which are usually called the active and moral powers—the feeling, affection, propensities, temper, habits, and conduct. The affective life of the individual is profoundly deranged, and his derangement shows itself in what he feels, desires, and does. He has no capacity of true moral feelings; all his impulses and desires, to which he yields without check, are egoistic; his conduct appears to be governed by immoral motives, which are cherished and obeyed without any evident desire to resist them. There is an amazing moral insensibility. The intelligence is often acute enough, being not affected otherwise than in being tainted by the morbid feeling under the influence of which the persons think and act; indeed, they often display an extraordinary ingenuity in explaining, excusing, or justifying their behaviour, exaggerating this, ignoring that, and so coloring the whole as to make themselves appear the victims of misrepresentation and persecution.[13]

Lombroso identified this "moral imbecile" with the born criminal in weight, skull, physiognomy, tactile insensibility, vascular reaction, and affectibility. He did not think every moral imbecile would necessarily become a criminal: External circumstances might help such a person overcome his criminal tendencies. However, "the perversion of the affective sphere, the hate, exaggerated and without motive, the absence or insufficiency of all restraint, the multiple hereditary tendencies, are the source of irresistible impulses in the moral imbecile as well as in the born criminal and epileptic."[14]

Through the many editions of his *Uomo Delinquente*, Lombroso was to change his views on the nature of the born criminal, concluding that both atavism *and* degeneracy might be at work. He also believed that epilepsy was a bond uniting "the moral imbecile and the born criminal in the same natural family"—that criminality is "an atavistic phenomenon which is provoked by morbid causes of which the fundamental manifestation is epilepsy." It is true, said Lombroso, that criminality could be provoked by other diseases [hysteria, alcoholism, paralysis, insanity, phrenasthenia (feeble-mindedness), etc.], but "it is epilepsy which gives to it, by its frequency, by its gravity, the most extended basis."

While all born criminals are epileptics, said Lombroso, all epileptics are not born criminals. "The perversion of the affective sphere, the hate, exaggerated and without motive, the absence or insufficiency of all restraint, the multiple hereditary tendencies, are the source of irresistible impulses in the moral imbecile as well as in the born criminal and epileptic." The criminal is "a savage and at the same time a sick man." He suffers from *both* arrested development and disease, making him at once atavistic and degenerate.[15] (Said Raffaele Garofalo dubiously, "It seems hardly possible to conceive our first parents as unhappy epileptics.")[16]

Garofalo, a senator and magistrate, was one of the two Italian criminologists whose names were for a generation associated with Lombroso's; it was Garofalo, in fact, who first used the word "criminology" to describe the scientific study of crime. The other name most often associated with Lombroso's was that of Enrico Ferri, a young lawyer who in 1878, at the age of twenty-one, wrote a thesis for his law degree at Bologna in which he formulated the idea that criminal law should *not* be based on the fictions of free will and moral responsibility.[17] Ferri was fascinated by *L'Uomo Delinquente* and sought out its author at the University of Turin, to which Lombroso had moved, and where he was now teaching in the medical school; the two men became lifelong friends and associates.

Although Lombroso was the dean and the acknowledged leader of the new Positivist School of criminology, Ferri and Garofalo differed with him on a number of points. Ferri, for example, thought that he gave undue importance to craniology and anthropometry and that in his first two editions, he tended to mix all criminals up in a single class. Said Ferri,

The only legitimate question which sociology can put to anthropology is this: "Is the criminal, and in what respects is he, a normal or an abnormal man? And if he is, or when he is, abnormal, whence is the abnormality derived? Is it congenital, or contracted, capable or incapable of rectification?" That is all; and yet it is sufficient to enable the student of crime to arrive at positive conclusions concerning the measures which society can take in order to defend itself against crime; whilst he can draw other conclusions from criminal statistics.

Ferri agreed with Lombroso that many habitual criminals showed a physical insensibility that could be recorded with instruments. Their two most marked psychological characteristics, he said, were moral insensibility and lack of foresight; they showed a lack of repugnance before committing an offense and a lack of remorse afterwards. "From this fundamental inferiority of sentiment there follows an inferiority of intelligence," said Ferri, "which, however, does not exclude certain forms of craftiness, though it tends to inability to foresee the consequences of crime. . . . Thus, the psychology of the criminal is summed up in a defective resistance to criminal tendencies and temptations, due to that ill-balanced impulsiveness which characterises children and savages."[18]

Ferri thought there were four kinds of criminals. First, there was the born criminal (delinquente nato), a term he suggested to Lombroso to describe his "theromorph." Then there were the criminal madman, the habitual or occasional criminal, and the criminal of passion. Ferri did not think it was enough for the law to decide guilt or innocence: "A criminal trial ought to retrace the path of the crime itself, passing backward from the criminal action (a violation of the law), in order to discover the criminal, and, in the psychological domain, to establish the determining motives and the anthropological type."[19]

Garofalo also divided criminals into four classes: murderers, violent criminals (criminals deficient in pity), property offenders (criminals deficient in probity), and sex criminals ("satyrs and cynics").[20] It was he who first came up with the idea of temibilità (fearsomeness or frightfulness), a term he invented to indicate the "active and constant perversity of the agent and the quantum of harm to be apprehended from him—or in other words, his capacity for crime." Ferri converted this to the related term of pericolosità, or dangerousness. The real question about criminals, the positivists said, was not their degree of guilt or the objective damage they had done in committing a crime, but the extent to which they posed a future danger to society. Thus positivism rejected both the Christian idea of moral responsibility and the classical idea that the punishment must be in direct ratio to the gravity of the crime.

" 'Moral responsibility'; 'penal proportion,' " said Garofalo: "these two postulates continue to form the keystone of criminal law, notwithstanding that science has demonstrated their inherent impossibility." When the criminal act is the result of a permanent pathologic condition or of a violent or irresistible impulse—in short, when we are dealing with a dangerous offender—what reason exists for abating social defense? "Are we not obliged to say that against the individual whose manifest total absence of free will makes him incapable of controlling himself or resisting his vicious impulses, society requires increased, instead of lessened, protection?"[21]

Garofalo thought that it was impossible to distinguish in the individual criminal which part of his criminal act was the effect of circumstances and which of free will. Even if we could,

We would still be without the history of his ancestors: we would still be unenlightened as to how far his tendencies may have been influenced by heredity or atavism. And even suppose that this knowledge could be acquired, how, again, are we to say what part has been played by psychic anomalies for which the man is not to blame, and what by anomalies due to the brain-structure, which only an autopsy can reveal?

The principle of relative or limited responsibility cannot therefore be applied to penal theory.[22]

Since it is impossible to know all the influences that may impinge on the criminal and therefore to judge the degree of his guilt, we should consign the ideas of free will and moral responsibility to the ashheap of religious and metaphysical ideas where they belong. Rather, let us approach the problem of crime from the positive—i.e., scientific and empirical—point of view. In looking at the criminal, we must measure "not the force of the criminal desire, but rather the strength of resistance to this impulse—in other words, the moral sense of the individual. Only by thus proceeding can we attain to the knowledge of what is to be feared from him. If this is possible, the problem is all but solved. Nothing more remains than to adapt the means of prevention to the agent's degree of constant perversity."[23]

The idea of classical jurisprudence was to make the punishment fit the crime; the idea of positivism is to make the punishment fit the criminal. "What we are aiming at is not to fix the quantum of suffering occasioned by the offense, on the basis of the value of what has been stolen, but to designate the repressive means which shall be exactly appropriate, that is to say, the obstacle capable of averting the danger."[24] Garofalo is not moved by the argument that to punish a man for being dangerous when he "is merely the victim of his own depraved organism is to do injury to justice."

Be it so: if the injury inflicted is necessary for the preservation of society, let abstract justice take such offense as it may. The entire world affords a continual spectacle of similar injustices. Men suffer because of mental and physical defects, because of an unfortunate situation in life, which they are without power to change. The child who is deficient in memory or attention will never receive good marks at school. However great a source of mortification he may find it, he will always remain at the foot of his class. For the clerk of small intelligence there is no hope of preferment; sooner or later he may expect his dismissal. Must we call these injustices? Is the law itself unjust, when it condemns the children to poverty because of the debts of the father? Is elegance unjust when it shrinks from squalor? Do we speak of injustice when an audience hisses from the stage a tenor who cannot sing?—when the populace hoots an incompetent general?[25]

Garofalo proposed the following punishment: for murderers, death. For violent criminals "instinctively disposed to bloodshed," and for habitual thieves who cannot adjust to a civilized environment, "transportation with abandonment"—i.e., to be carried to some distant part of the globe, and there marooned. Other habitual or professional thieves should be interned for life in an overseas penal colony. Recidivists who are not professional thieves, dangerous individuals belonging to the class of violent criminals, and sex criminals ("satyrs and cynics") should undergo indeterminate confinement. And finally, nondangerous violent criminals and nonrecidivist thieves with some means of support should be compelled to make compensation to their victims and to the state.[26]

True, it is difficult for a magistrate to weigh what is to him an unknown quantity—that is, the offender's ability to resist his criminal impulses. But he can, from "experimental data," estimate the probability of *future* danger:

Instead of advocating the infliction of a useless punishment proportioned to the hypothetical and indefinable quantity which represents the criminal's free will, we propose that he adapt to the case in hand the preventive means which it requires, keeping strictly within the limits of social necessity. Under this method, the criminal will undergo the punishment which has been merited, not by a doubtful faculty of his mind, but by all that which constitutes his personality, namely, his psychic organism, his instincts, and his character.[27]

That punishment is just, he said, which has the "single aim of disarming an enemy of society, when it is solely a means of *direct* and special *prevention*, when it is adapted to the *individuality* of the offender. . . . Such is the true justice," said Garofalo "—the justice by which is tempered the maxim 'Salus populi, suprema lex est,' the supreme law is the welfare of the people."[28]

Lombroso, Ferri, and Garofalo created a revolution in thinking about crime. It was their genius to combine evolutionism and scientific materialism with the utilitarian approach of Bentham and Beccaria. Like the classical theorists, the positivists felt that punishment should be no more nor less than what is necessary to prevent crime. They did not, however, believe either in free will or in the possibilities of behavior modification through punishment. To the Italian School, free will was simply a myth—a vestige of the theological and metaphysical stages through which the science of criminology had passed on its way to the third and positive stage of knowledge. And if there was no such thing as free will, then there could, of course, be no such thing as moral responsibility.

The positivists were concerned neither with guilt, nor the intention behind the crime, nor the seriousness of the offense—these questions, so central to classical jurisprudence, were simply beside the point. What concerned them was what Ferri called "the necessity for self-preservation, which applies to every individual and every social organism."[29] The punitive function becomes therefore "purely and simply a function of social defense."[30] Gustav Aschaffenburg, who was the father of German psychiatric criminology, put it this way:

More important than the right of the individual is the right of the totality; whoever injures it, must suffer in consequence. And, just as pity does not prevent our removing the insane from society, so too our course, as regards the socially dangerous, must be dictated by this point of view: the protection of our health, our honor, our property.[31]

The corollary of this view was revolutionary in its implication. It meant that someone who committed a very minor offense—or, indeed, no offense at all—might be removed from society for the rest of his life as a *measure of social defense.* The positivists were very pessimistic about the possibilities of changing criminals for the better—and no wonder, if the born criminal were indeed an evolutionary throwback to some predatory ancestor midway between the ape and the Hottentot. Even Lombroso, however, did not believe all criminals were born to be bad; and during the course of years, and under the influence of both friends and critics (Ferri was a socialist as well as a positivist), even Lombroso modified his views to include social and other components in the causes of criminal behavior. In fact, in his final formulation, he included every factor that had been considered in the etiology of crime: meteorology, geology, topography, race, population congestion, immigration, the press, food prices, alcohol, drugs, spoiled corn[b] (i.e., wheat), illiteracy, poor education, unemployment, poverty, illegitimacy, poor home environment, heredity, atavism, insanity, age, sex, aversion to work, psychopathy, availability of weapons, wars, bad government, prisons, and "epidemic ideals."[c,32] Nevertheless, Lombroso is best remembered for the theory that there is such a thing as a born criminal, that he represents evolutionary atavism, and that he can be recognized by the anomalies of his skull and face, a view that even in his own generation was widely ridiculed. Many criminologists disagreed with Lombroso, but for a generation, nobody was in a position to refute him—he and his students had, after all, amassed data on more than six thousand dead and living prisoners.

Then in 1913 another physician, Charles B. Goring (1870-1919), did a painstaking biometric examination of three thousand English convicts whose measurements were compared with a group of controls that included Oxford and Cambridge undergraduates, hospital inmates, and soldiers. He found the criminals somewhat shorter and lighter, on average, than his controls. But as for the measurement of skulls: "From a knowledge only of an undergraduate's cephalic measurement, a better judgment could be given as to whether he were studying at an English or Scottish university than a prediction could be made as to whether he would eventually become a university professor or a convicted felon."[33] Said Goring of Lombroso's theories:

---

[b]Lombroso made a lifelong study of pellagra, which he thought to be caused by spoiled wheat. His insistence on this view eventually cost him the fashionable medical practice he had enjoyed in Turin because it was considered an oblique attack on the landowning classes.
[c]By this he meant the ideological causes—social, political, religious—that led their supporters to commit crimes. Modern examples would be the Palestinian liberation movement or Irish republicanism in Belfast.

... Admitting the criminal does possess all the characters that have been attributed to him; admitting, even, that he is marked by a "dome-shaped" head, and by a face like a "bird of prey"; admitting that he is drunken, impulsive, obstinate, dirty, and without control—despite all this, we maintain that he is not an abnormal man. He may represent a selected class of normal man; many of his qualities may present extreme degrees from the normal average: yet the fact remains that, in the pattern of his mind and body, in his feelings, thoughts, desires, and recognition of right and wrong, and in his behaviour, however outrageous it may be, he exists by the same nature, and is moved by the same springs of action, that affected the conduct, and constitute the quality, of normal human beings.[d,34]

Lombroso's importance, however, lies not in his theory of atavism, but in the whole methodology that he and his followers introduced to the study of crime: an empirical approach, painstaking measurements, and a willingness to examine all the assumptions by which the criminal law had, until that time, been governed. No less important is the positivist approach to social policy, which abandons entirely the concept of just deserts. The only question for this school of criminology is, What policy best serves the social defense? All the other questions—retribution, deterrence, rehabilitation, proportionality of punishment—are at best metaphysical, and in any case, beside the point.

Positivism threw down the gauntlet to classical criminal law the moment it questioned the concept of free will—a concept that was anathema to the positivists. The classical view was well expressed by a draft penal code for the North German Federation when it said that "the right of the state not only to adopt measures of security against the criminal, but to punish him, rests on the general human opinion that *the mature and mentally sound man has sufficient will power to repress impulses to criminal acts, and to act in accordance with the general consciousness of right*" (emphasis added).[35] The positivists said, on the other hand, that free will was a metaphysical notion without substance or reality. Many criminals, because of biological defects, are born to be bad; when placed in unfavorable circumstances, they can no more escape their destiny than a fish can escape the water.

Since there is no such thing as free will, they averred, the usual legal questions such as responsibility or intent (*mens rea*) are beside the point. The real issue—and in fact, the only one—is *social defense.* Adolphe Prins discussed legal implications of this doctrine in his work *La défense sociale et les transformations du droit pénal* (1910). The idea of moral responsibility, he said, must be replaced in criminal law by the notion of the *dangerousness of the offender.* Sentences should be based, not on the immediate act for which the offender was on trial and not on the heinousness (or triviality) of the crime, but

---

[d]Harvard anthropologist Earnest A. Hooton in 1939 unleashed a strong attack on Goring, claiming he was prejudiced against Lombroso, that his work bristled with sophistries, and that he left the problem of the relation of the criminal's physique to his offense unresolved. (Hooton, *Crime and the Man*, pp. 16-19.)

solely on the *permanent state* of the offender. Never mind whether the punishment fits the crime: Does it fit the criminal?

Prins believed there were two categories of dangerous people: the mentally abnormal or mentally deficient and the recidivists or habitual offenders. He took the view that dangerousness is essentially a legal concept, as distinguished from diminished responsibility, which is a medical one. He believed that the protection of society must be maintained as long as the dangerousness persists.

Despite a divergence between the criminologists and the lawyers on the legitimacy and function of punishment, there was a convergence between the two on the management of dangerous offenders. The lawyers were unwilling to give up their doctrines of responsibility and proportionality, but there came to be a consensus on the segregation of incorrigibles, preferably by what the French called *rélégation*—"an additional penalty of a perpetual and colonial character" (in this case, banishment to French Guiana). The first genuine preventive measure to be given statutory form was the *rélégation* provided by the French statute of 1885, later copied by Portugal (1892) and Argentina (1903). In 1891 Belgium readopted the old idea of administrative internment, which made possible a tighter control of vagrancy. In New South Wales, Australia, the Habitual Criminals Act of 1905 introduced the idea of preventive detention into the British Empire; it was followed in England by the Prevention of Crime Act (1908).[36]

Just how well the new criminology had permeated the legal profession was manifest in the International Union of Penal Law, meeting at Berne in 1890. Said one of its resolutions, "There are malefactors for whom, in view of their physical and moral condition, the constant application of ordinary punishment is inadequate. In this class are specially included the hardened recidivists who ought to be considered as degenerate criminals or criminals by profession. Malefactors ought to be subjected, according to the degree of their degeneration, or of the danger which they threaten, to special measures, framed with the purpose of preventing them from inflicting them, and of mending them if possible."[37] The idea of "mending them," of course, was not part of positivist philosophy; neither Lombroso, Ferri, nor Garofalo expressed more than skepticism toward the regeneration of adult criminals. On the other hand, the acceptance of the idea that penalties should be proportionate to a criminal's dangerousness rather than to his offense was in complete agreement with the New School of criminology and with the doctrine derived from it that came to be known as "social defense." The question for classical jurisprudence had been, "How do we mete out justice?" The question for the new criminologists had become, "How do we protect society?" That the two questions have different answers was a dilemma for which the criminal law was not prepared, and with which today it is still struggling. What is involved is nothing less than the whole scale of values by which we weigh the rights of the individual against the rights of society, and strike a balance. As Raymond Saleilles put it,

In the life of society, as elsewhere, there are always risks to be run; one must learn how to accept them and to find wherein lies the least social risk. If through fear of crime men are deprived of liberty, where is the advantage? Society must guarantee not alone life and property, but also the means of enjoying them. If to secure life and property the chance is incurred of losing the possibility of enjoying them freely, the social risk incurred is quite as serious as that of the dangers that threaten us individually. Against the latter one may with proper caution come to protect himself; against the danger of an arbitrary authority in the hands of the State or the police, one is helpless.[38]

This is the nature of the problem that we face whenever we think of removing people from society with no concern for the question of guilt, for the nature of their offense, or for the intentions that motivated them. Who makes the decision for removal? Under what constraints? By what standards? With what safeguards? The questions remain, and as public debate shows, a hundred years after the Positivist Revolution, we are far from finding the answers.

11

The Jukes and the Kallikaks, or the Dangers of Being Ill-bred

By the last quarter of the nineteenth century, biological determinism was beginning a swift rise to ascendancy among the fashionable theories of criminal behavior. It was as if the gloomy predestinarianism of the Calvinists and the ancient doctrine of Original Sin, pushed out the front door by the Enlightenment, had somehow sneaked in the back, clad in new raiment and holding high the standards of modern scientific materialism. That is not to say that those who believed in the social etiology of crime had abandoned the field—least of all, the Marxists. They remained vocal; they too clothed themselves in scientific raiment and carried banners emblazoned with the names of such disciplines as economics and sociology. But in the battle for public attention, they were to have very hard going. To scholars and laymen alike, the biological sciences seemed somehow more positive, "hard," and, well, yes, *scientific* than the often muddy and ambiguous realities of the social scene.

Just as *The Origin of Species* was greater as an event than a book, and just as it was important "at least as much because of what it brought seething out of the European mind as because of what it put into it" (quoting Barzun), so also that extraordinary work by Richard Louis Dugdale, *The "Jukes": A Study in Crime, Pauperism, Disease and Heredity*, first published in 1877, was an event, not a book. What it brought seething to the surface of the European and American minds was some part of the collective unconscious that had always seen the dangerous classes as not only a physical, but a *biological* threat— philoprogenitive, promiscuous, and irresponsible. These were the people who, breeding like rats in their alleys and hovels, threatened, by sheer increase in numbers, to overwhelm the well-bred classes of society. Malthus, too, had tapped the same deep wells of apprehension.

It must be said at once that Dugdale was no scholar. Born in France of English parentage, but raised in America, he was not, like Lombroso, a man of science. Neither was he a legal scholar, nor a statistician. It is probable that he had heard of evolution, as had everybody on either side of the Atlantic who could read, and he was no doubt aware of the work of the ethnologists in their studies of primitive tribes—again, as any well-read man would be. But the perspective from which he worked was so different from that of the European jurists and scholars whom we have thus far discussed that he might be considered a pleasant aberration in the history of criminology were it not for one singular fact: There was no one of his generation, not even Lombroso, whose work had greater impact on the new sciences of eugenics and criminology, and no one who, with a single slender book, created a more enduring legend than did Dugdale with his study of "The Jukes."

It was the ethos of the times, the last quarter of the nineteenth century, which paved the way for an immediate acceptance of his *perceived* message. To an astonished and appalled public, if not to the more temperate author, that message seemed to be that criminals are not merely the victims of unfortunate circumstances, but a degenerate breed quite different from the rest of us. Furthermore, that difference is born and bred in them: The criminal is not simply one of our own who has gone astray, he is something depraved and subhuman. The perceived corollary, of course, was that nothing could be done about the dangerous classes but to prevent them from reproducing. It was a mere detail that Dugdale had not quite said that: being an American, and thus a believer in the perfectibility of man, he thought that, caught young enough, even a Juke could be saved from a life of crime. But as with any great new revolutionary message, the finer points of his work were lost. What came through instead was a dreadful lesson in dysgenics.

In July 1874 Richard Dugdale was deputed by the New York Prison Association, of which he was secretary, to visit and inspect thirteen county jails. In one jail in upstate New York he found six persons, under four family names, who turned out to be, in some degree, blood relations. One was awaiting trial for receiving stolen goods; the charges against the others included vagrancy, burglary, attempted rape, and assault with intent to kill. "These six persons belonged to a long lineage, reaching back to the early colonists," said Dugdale, "and had intermarried so slightly with the emigrant population of the old world that they may be called a strictly American family. They had lived in the same locality for generations, and were so despised by the reputable community that their family name *had come to be used generically as a term of reproach.*"[1] To this family, Dugdale, in his narrative, gave the name of "Juke," a name under which this clan has entered the folklore of the country as a synonym for depravity.

Dugdale at once made inquiry and found that "out of twenty-nine males, in ages ranging from fifteen to seventy-five, the immediate blood relations of these six persons, seventeen of them were criminals, or fifty-eight percent; while fifteen were convicted of some degree of offense, and received seventy-one years of sentence."[2] Their crimes included assault and battery, assault with intent to kill, murder, attempted rape, petit larceny, grand larceny, burglary, forgery, and cruelty to animals. "Impressed by this suggestive ratio," said Samuel Hopkins Adams—"as who would not be by thirty-two out of a possible twenty-nine?— Dugdale went sleuthing back through the generations. . . ."[3]

The earliest found ancestor of the unfortunate Jukes was one "Max," a descendant of early Dutch settlers, described as "a hunter and fisher, a hard drinker, jolly and companionable, averse to steady toil." Two of Max's sons married two out of six sisters, called "Juke" by the author. One of these sisters,

Ada Juke, was better, if somewhat mysteriously, known to the public as "Margaret, the mother of criminals." Margaret, or Ada, had one illegitimate son, progenitor of the criminal line. Ada's sister Effie, however, mothered the *pauper* branch of the Juke family. "It will be seen," said Dugdale, "that while the criminal branch shows thirty-five percent of outdoor relief, and twenty-one percent of alms-house paupers, with sixty percent of crime, the pauper branch shows sixty-one percent of out-door relief, thirty-eight percent of alms-house pauperism, and fifty-three percent of crime." (It was Dugdale's belief that "crime as compared to pauperism indicates vigor. . . . Criminal careers are more easily modified by environment, because crime, more especially contrived crime, is an index of capacity, and wherever capacity is found, there environment is most effective in producing modifications of career.")[4]

Dugdale found not only pauperism and crime among the Jukes, but also "harlotry," a term he used generically to include "all degrees of impudicity." Out of one hundred sixty-two marriageable Juke women, he said, eighty-four were "harlots." Thus "we find harlotry over twenty-nine times more frequent with the Juke women than in the average of the community." It is not clear what Dugdale meant by this, since "all degrees of impudicity" included those "who professionally sell themselves" as well as "those who have made lapses through imprudence or even passion," but who subsequently led reputable lives.[5]

Dugdale, and A.H. Estabrook,[6] who followed him a generation later, claimed to have traced some twelve hundred members of the Juke family. The fecklessness and criminality of this clan were always contrasted with the uprightness of the Jonathan Edwards descendants, who included presidents, governors, judges, teachers, and ministers. Generations of American school children were taught to shudder at the dangers of bad breeding, although the lesson was carelessly drawn: Dugdale never claimed that heredity was solely at fault in the case of the Jukes, and Jonathan Edwards, despite the eminence of his descendants, had some dubious ancestors himself, including a maternal grandmother divorced for adultery, a grandaunt who murdered her son, and a granduncle who murdered his own sister.[7]

What Dugdale claimed for his cautionary tale of "crime, pauperism, disease and heredity" was that "Where there is heredity of any characteristic, it would seem there is a tendency, and it might also be said, a certainty, to produce an environment for the next generation corresponding to that heredity, with the effect of perpetuating it. Where the environment changes in youth the characteristics of heredity may be measurably altered. Hence the importance of education." The brain cells, he thought, could be built up by training. "The all-important will does not usually reach its full growth till between the thirtieth to the thirty-third years. . . . We must therefore distinctly accept as an established educational axiom, that the moral nature—which really means the holding of the emotions and passions under the dominion of the judgment by the exercise of will—is the last developed of the elements of character, and, for this reason, is most modifiable by the nature of the environment."

This demonstrates that the natural process of the development of nerve tissue is a spontaneous and enormous force, capable of assisting in the work of reforming vicious and criminal lives. So long as there is growth, there can you produce change. Per contra, wherever you can change the environment so that the sensations, the experience, the habit of steady attention become automatic, you have at your disposal the means by which this will can be so developed, organized and made steady, that it can serve as a guide and as a restraint.[8]

Thus ultimately Dugdale's message, fittingly American, was one of hope. This was not, however, what came through to a mesmerized public, who looked at the unfolding pages of Juke genealogy, read the sordid story of their pauperism, harlotry, and crime, and concluded that not their environment, but their breeding, was at fault. The "infamous Juke family" was cited by Sir Francis Galton, the father of eugenics, in his *Inquiries into Human Faculty* (1883);[9] by Garofalo, in his textbook on *Criminology*;[10] and in virtually every study of criminality published for forty years after Dugdale. The influence of this work was incalculable, notwithstanding the fact that, as Samuel Hopkins Adams commented many years later, "The proper place of a Juke is not in criminology. It is in mythology."[11]

Modern criminologists have ridiculed Dugdale's methods and questioned the possibility of gathering so enormous a fund of information, including the greater or lesser "impudicity" of seven generations of drifters and ne'er-do-wells, scattered through the hills and hollows of upstate New York. Nevertheless, to call the Jukes a "myth" is not to dispose of them; myths often embody great truths. There are many Juke families in the United States, and doubtless elsewhere, with long records of criminality, pauperism, alcoholism, or insanity. It is as dangerous to dismiss the Jukes as a "myth" as it is to embrace them as a study in dysgenics. The real problem with the Jukes is that we don't really know the mechanism of the pathology involved: Perhaps Dugdale's guess was as good as any. That may be summed up as: Bad heredity tends to perpetuate bad environment, and bad environment, bad heredity, but even a Juke may, with difficulty, be salvaged.

What happened to the Jukes, however, was that they became a cautionary tale for the new science of eugenics, and they were joined a generation later by a family no less notorious in the annals of bad breeding, the "Kallikaks." Martin Kallikak, Sr., as every American school child will remember, was a Revolutionary War soldier of impeccable ancestry who met a feeble-minded girl at a tavern and fathered a feeble-minded son, Martin, Jr., otherwise known as "the Old Horror." From this unfortunate union, said Henry H. Goddard, the discoverer of the family, came 480 descendants,[a] of whom 143 were feeble-minded, 36

---

[a]Goddard wrote in 1912. There is no telling how many Kallikaks have been added since.

illegitimate, 33 "sexually immoral persons, mostly prostitutes," 24 confirmed alcoholics, 3 criminals, and 8 who kept "houses of ill fame." Said Goddard in his book, *The Kallikak Family: A Study in the Heredity of Feeble-Mindedness:*

We have here a family of good English blood of the middle class, settling upon the original land purchased from the proprietors of the state in Colonial times, and throughout four generations maintaining a reputation for honor and respectability of which they are justly proud. Then a scion of this family, in an unguarded moment, steps aside from the paths of rectitude and with the help of a feeble-minded girl, starts a line of mental defectives that is truly appalling. After this mistake, he returns to the traditions of his family, marries a woman of his own quality, and through her carries on a line of respectability equal to that of his ancestors.[12]

Here, indeed, was a lesson in dysgenics to give pause to any hero tempted to dally in a tavern. The Kallikaks, of course, were not criminals and not dangerous: On the contrary, Deborah Kallikak, whose photograph appears in Goddard's study, appeared to be a very pleasant young woman. (Goddard had found her in the Training School for Feeble-Minded Girls and Boys in Vineland, New Jersey, where he was director of the research laboratory, and had traced her ancestors back for six generations.) Nevertheless, if all feeble-minded are not criminals, it was Goddard's view that 50 percent of all criminals are feeble-minded. "One thing more," he said in another book, *The Criminal Imbecile.* "Careful studies have shown beyond the peradventure of doubt that at least two thirds of these mental defectives have inherited their defect; in other words, that they belong to strains of the human family whose intelligence lies below that which is required for the performance of their duties as citizens." That being so, the conclusion followed that to control crime, the feeble-minded should be prevented from propagating.[13] Justice Oliver Wendell Holmes put it more picturesquely when he said: "Three generations of imbeciles are enough."[14]

Goddard's research on the Kallikaks was undoubtedly more reliable than Dugdale's on the Jukes; his facts have never been seriously challenged, although no one any longer believes that criminals are predominantly feeble-minded. Nevertheless, the Kallikaks, like their criminal cousins the Jukes, have assumed an almost mythic quality in the popular imagination. The eugenic movement has come and gone; belief in the omnipotence of heredity has waxed and waned; but the Jukes and the Kallikaks, seemingly, go on forever.

12 Is Criminality Inherited?

With Dugdale and Goddard the debate was fairly launched: Are some individuals condemned by genetic inheritance to lives of pauperism, imbecility, and crime? The work of these two Americans seemed to show that in certain families biological degeneration indeed exists and that it is transmitted, like some ancient Greek curse, from generation to generation. Thus the Jukes and Kallikaks appeared to document the existence of degeneration; but whether atavism was also involved, or simply a kind of retrogressive natural selection—what Gabriel Tarde called *"sélection à rebours"*—and what the role of environment might be, were subjects that were to be hotly debated on both sides of the Atlantic.

Garofalo defended the theory of atavism, and he quoted from Walter Bagehot the description of our early ancestors who "had strong passions and weak reason; like savages, they preferred short spasms of greedy pleasure to mild and equable enjoyment; like savages, they could not postpone the present to the future; like savages, their ingrained sense of morality was, to say the best of it, rudimentary and defective."[1] "Are not these last the very characteristics which our analysis disclosed in criminals?" asked Garofalo.[2]

He admitted, however, that the resemblance between the instincts of savages and criminals falls short of establishing their identity. "The only conclusion which we are justified in forming," he said, "is that criminals have regressive characteristics—characteristics which indicate a degree of advancement lower than that of their neighbours."[3]

The French lawyer and sociologist, Gabriel Tarde (1843-1904), on the other hand, said that the criminal is a moral degenerate created by retrogressive selection. "The degenerate, whether moral or physical, is in general the result of heredity. We need but run back one or two steps in the line of descent to find the explanation of his anomalies. Hence it is a vain thing to pass over his parents and I know not how many other generations, in order to demand of his misty ancestors the secret of his perversities or deformities."[4]

The great biologist, Thomas Huxley, took still a different view. "In a large proportion of cases," he said, "crime and pauperism have nothing to do with heredity; but are the consequence, partly, of circumstances and, partly, of the possession of qualities, which, under different conditions of life, might have excited esteem and even admiration. It was a shrewd man of the world who, in discussing sewage problems, remarked that dirt is riches in the wrong place; and that sound aphorism has moral applications."[5] And the German Gustav Aschaffenburg concluded that it is impossible either to prove *or* to refute the theory that criminality is inherited: "The one fact that we can establish with certainty is, that the inheritance of the children of drunkards, insane persons, and epileptics consists of physical and mental inferiority."[6]

Havelock Ellis, an Englishman who is perhaps better known for his work on the psychology of sex than for his work in criminology, saw two factors in criminal heredity—the element of innate disposition and the element of social contagion. "Practically, it is not always possible to disentangle these two factors," he said; "a bad home will usually mean something bad in the heredity in the strict sense. Frequently the one element alone, whether the heredity or the contagion, is not sufficient to determine the child in the direction of crime."

The influence of heredity, even in the strict sense of the word, in the production of criminals, does not always lie in the passing on of developed proclivities. Sometimes a generation of criminals is merely one stage in the progressive degeneration of a family. Sometimes crime seems to be the method by which the degenerating organism seeks to escape from an insane taint in the parents.[7]

Ellis the eugenicist was prepared to go much further than Ellis the criminologist. It is not enough to deal with the living generation as we find it, he said: *we must learn to control the future.*

We must know what are those stocks that are unlikely to produce the worthy citizen of the future; we must know what are those stocks which deserve to be encouraged in breeding fine men and women; we must endeavour to educate the public conscience to feel and act in accordance with the knowledge thus attained. . . .

Those who uphold the ideals of eugenics are bound to proclaim the duty of all who are probably unfit to become the parents of a fine race to abstain from procreation, and, in effect, "make themselves eunuchs for the Kingdom of God's sake."[8]

Ellis was not prepared to castrate those who failed to "make themselves eunuchs for the Kingdom of God's sake," but he was prepared to support sterilization "short of actual castration," noting that this had already been introduced in Switzerland "with the consent of the law, the municipal authorities, and the patients themselves." He insisted, however, that it not be used as punishment and be done only with the consent of the patient.[9]

The eugenics movement, fathered by Sir Francis Galton, supported by people like Ellis, and armed with the horrendous evidence of "the Jukes," was prepared to do for the human race what the human race was doing for sheep and cattle: improving it through selective breeding. The argument of the eugenicists was cogent. We know, they said, that only by careful selective breeding can the finest domestic animals be produced. We do not allow our cattle and sheep to mate promiscuously. On the contrary, we carefully select the best stock and permit the inferior to die out. Yet human beings are allowed to breed promiscuously. Degenerates beget degenerates, idiots beget idiots, criminals beget criminals, and the human race, far from improving from generation to generation, bids fair to be swamped by its worst elements and revert to the bestiality from which it has so recently, with such effort, emerged.

Among such degenerates, the Americans thought, were families like "the Jukes," not to mention the immigrant hordes crowding American prisons, who doubtless represented inferior European stock. In the United States there was great pressure on the state and national legislatures to do something about immigrants and imbeciles, both. In the former case, it was thought that restrictions on the admission of "inferior stocks" was absolutely necessary to the salvation of the republic; in the latter case, sterilization was deemed the proper recourse. Accordingly, the federal government, in the Immigration Acts of 1921 and 1924, imposed immigration quotas that favored certain supposedly superior racial strains;[a] and state legislatures began to provide for the sterilization of the feeble-minded, in both instances under the firm conviction that not only mental retardation but crime was biological and hereditary in origin.

The contemporary thinking on this matter was nicely illustrated by the decision of Justice Holmes in *Buck* v. *Bell* (274 U.S. 200, 1927), one of the most widely quoted in all judicial literature. Virginia in 1924 had passed a statute permitting the sterilization of inmates in institutions for the feeble-minded. The statute was challenged in the courts and by 1927 had reached the Supreme Court of the United States. The plaintiff in the case, Carrie Buck, was the daughter of a feeble-minded mother and the mother of a feeble-minded child. Speaking for an almost unanimous court, Holmes upheld the right of Virginia to sterilize Carrie Buck even against her will. After reciting the facts in the case, he said:

We have seen more than once that the public welfare may call upon the best citizens for their lives. It would be strange if it could not call upon those who already sap the strength of the state for these lesser sacrifices, often not felt to be such by those concerned, in order to prevent our being swamped with incompetence. It is better for all the world, if instead of waiting to execute degenerate offspring for crime, or to let them starve for their imbecility, society can prevent those who are manifestly unfit from continuing their kind. The principle that sustains compulsory vaccination is broad enough to cover cutting the Fallopian tubes. . . . Three generations of imbeciles are enough.[10]

Max Lerner has commented that "there was a strain of social Darwinism" in Justice Holmes,[11] and so, indeed, there was. But the decision in *Buck* v. *Bell* encapsulated some of the most "scientific" theories of the age: that the human race, through dysgenics, was in danger of being overwhelmed; that criminals were biological "degenerates"; that there was an indissoluble nexus between

[a]In May 1921 Congress set immigration quotas at 3 percent of each nationality, according to the Census of 1910. In May 1924 it halved the quota and limited immigration to 2 percent of the Census of 1890, to reduce immigration from eastern and southern Europe. Owing to opposition, this law did not go into effect until 1929.

imbecility and crime, so that by stamping out the one, you could prevent the other. In this tacit biological determinism, we find Galton and Lombroso, Dugdale and Goddard. There is also, rather clearly expressed, a draconian view of "social defense." Said Holmes in his famous work *The Common Law*, "No society has ever admitted that it could not sacrifice individual welfare to its own existence. If conscripts are necessary for the army, it seizes them, and marches them, with bayonets in the rear, to death. . . . The law does undoubtedly treat the individual as a means to an end, and uses him as a tool to increase the general welfare at his own expense." Even if this course is wrong, "our criminal law follows it, and the theory of our criminal law must be shaped accordingly."[12]

Although Holmes here was really talking about the classical idea of deterrence—sacrificing the criminal to prevent others from committing crimes—it is clear from his writings that he was a student of positivism. "The Italians have begun to work upon the notion that the foundations of the law ought to be scientific," he said, "and if our civilization does not collapse, I feel pretty sure that the regiment or division that follows us will carry that flag."[13] He summarized in these words the biogenic-sociogenic arguments on the etiology of crime:

If the typical criminal is a degenerate, bound to swindle or to murder by as deep seated an organic necessity as that which makes the rattlesnake bite, it is idle to talk of deterring him by the classical method of imprisonment. He must be got rid of; he cannot be improved, or frightened out of his structural reaction. If, on the other hand, crime, like normal human conduct, is mainly a matter of imitation, punishment fairly may be expected to help to keep it out of fashion. The study of criminals has been thought by some well known men of science to sustain the former hypothesis. The statistics of the relative increase of crime in crowded places like large cities, where example has the greatest chance to work, and in less populated parts, where the contagion spreads more slowly, have been used with great force in favor of the latter view. But there is weighty authority for the belief that, however this may be, "not the nature of the crime, but the dangerousness of the criminal, constitutes the only reasonable legal criterion to guide the inevitable social reaction against the criminal."[14]

In *Buck* v. *Bell*, which became the ruling decision in American sterilization cases, can clearly be seen the influence of science and mythos on public policy—and how difficult it is, at any given stage in the development of human knowledge, to distinguish one from the other. As Holmes himself so well put it, "The felt necessities of the time, the prevalent moral and political theories, intuitions of public policy, avowed or unconscious, even the prejudices which judges share with their fellow-men, have had a good deal more to do than the syllogism in determining the rules by which men should be governed."[15]

In assigning criminality to imbeciles, Holmes was faithful to Goddard, whose works equating criminality and feeble-mindedness were published between 1914 and 1920. But unfortunately for this thesis, the army alpha and beta intelligence tests given to millions of American recruits in 1917-1918 showed that the general public was much less intelligent than Goddard had supposed; by his standards, nearly a third of the American Expeditionary Force were feeble-minded.[16] Carl Murchison, who was professionally connected with this American experience, went so far as to assert the superior intelligence of the *criminal*.[17] There have been all kinds of subsequent studies which, as psychometric testing got better, showed a declining proportion of feeble-minded among delinquent populations. Any remaining differences in intelligence between the prison population and those outside may reasonably be accounted for by the fact that the smarter the criminal, the less likely he is to be caught. The sterilization of Carrie Buck, while it might reduce the population of imbeciles, was not very likely to reduce crime. Even Goddard should have questioned the supposed correlation between delinquency and feeble-mindedness: Out of 480 Kallikaks, there were only three criminals. If the rest of us were as lawabiding as the Kallikaks, our police departments would have little to do.

Justice Holmes owed much of his thinking to the "Italians" as he called them, to Dugdale and Goddard, and to the Englishman Sir Francis Galton—in short, to the intellectual fathers of criminal anthropology, eugenics, and social defense. These were the movements of the day; they were international in scope, and for two generations their influence was to be felt wherever people considered the questions of criminal responsibility, prevention, deterrence, and retribution. But if, in Holmes' words, the typical criminal is like a rattlesnake, bound by organic necessity to injure his fellow men, "deterrence" becomes no more than an exercise in futility. And if he is thus bound by organic necessity, is the transmission hereditary?

A Munich psychiatrist, Johannes Lange, thought he had a way to answer this question. Sir Francis Galton, in 1876, had been the first to distinguish monozygotic (identical) and dizygotic (fraternal) twins, and he concluded that heredity had far greater influence on their development than did environment. (Galton once used the example of the cuckoo in arguing the case for heredity. The cuckoo, he pointed out, sings the same songs in all parts of the world, even though its eggs are laid in the nests of other birds.)[18]

It occurred to Lange, who was departmental director of the German Experimental Station for Psychiatry (Kaiser Wilhelm Institute) in Munich, that a comparison of identical and fraternal twins might yield the answer to the question: Are criminals born or made? Lange was assisted in his study by the Bavarian Ministry of Justice, which permitted access by his research assistants to all prisoners who were twins. They were also allowed to search among the psychopathic patients of the German Institute for Psychiatry for twins who had at one time been imprisoned. And at the Munich-Schwabing Hospital, of which he was physician-in-chief, Lange himself, while making his prescribed rounds, asked every twin he encountered for his criminal record. In each case, when Lange or his assistants encountered one twin who was a criminal, the other twin was checked out. Among thirteen pairs of identical twins, they found that in ten cases, where one twin was a criminal, the other was also. On the other hand, among seventeen fraternal twins, they found that this concordance existed in only two cases—that in the fifteen others, where one twin was a criminal, the other was *not*. Lange's study was published in 1929 under the title *Verbrechen als Schicksal* (*Crime as Destiny*). "*As far as crime is concerned*," he concluded "*monozygotic twins on the whole react in a definitely similar manner, dizygotic twins behave quite differently*.... As far as the *causes of crime are concerned, innate tendencies play a preponderant part*."[19]

Lange's little work created a sensation. In a *Harper's* article entitled "Scientific Calvinism," the English geneticist and biometrician J.B.S. Haldane said of the book, "It is only ninety-six pages in length, but it is quite conceivable that posterity will regard it as the most important book of this century." He described some of the cases discussed by Lange. One pair of identical twins became criminals even though they were separated as children. Another pair, separated somewhat later, both ran away from jobs at the same moment, even when living one hundred miles apart. Later, when even further separated, they both developed appendicitis on the same day.

These twins form only a sample. The odds are many millions to one that it is not wholly misleading. We may take it that in the course of a century similar data will have accumulated for thousands of pairs of twins. It will then be possible to say with certainty that at least eighty percent (or some such figure) of these moral decisions that land us in jail or otherwise are predetermined. ... Every educated person will be substantially a determinist in ethics as he now is in physics where individual atoms are not concerned.[20]

Since Lange, there have been a number of genetic studies of delinquency and crime, looking not only at the kind of concordance in the original work but also at the children of criminals adopted by noncriminal parents. The concordance studies have been undertaken in Holland (Legras 1932), the United States (Rosanoff 1934), Germany (Stumpfl 1936 and Kranz 1936), Finland (Borgstrom 1939), Japan (Yoshimasu 1957), Denmark (Christiansen 1968), and Norway (Dalgard and Kringlen 1976). All showed a higher criminal concordance between monozygotic twins than between dizygotic. The Danish study, however, although it showed a much higher concordance for identical than nonidentical twins, showed a lower criminal concordance between identical twins than did the other studies. Out of eighty-one identical twins studied, Karl O. Christiansen found twenty-seven pairs concordant and fifty-four pairs discordant. He himself attributed this to his more random sample and to the fact that in culling it, he had looked at six thousand pairs of twins born on the Danish islands between 1880 and 1910. Even Christiansen, however, found that the probability that one male monozygotic twin had been convicted if the other had been was better than 50 percent (0.527). With dizygotic males it was only 0.219.[21]

The least concordance and the smallest difference between identical and fraternal twins was found by the most recent study. Odd Steffen Dalgard and Einar Kringlen checked the names of all male twins born in Norway in 1921-1930 against the national crime register, and from this list winnowed 139 pairs of twins where one or both had been convicted. Using the strictest concept of crime—that is, excluding violations of military and motor vehicle laws, they found a concordance of 25.8 percent between monozygotic twins, and 14.9 percent between dizygotics, and they concluded that the difference was not statistically significant—that "if there does exist a genetic disposition to criminal behaviour, the disposition is a weak one." The authors felt that most of the observed difference between identical and nonidentical twins can be explained by the fact that identical twins are more often seen together, dressed alike, and treated alike. Furthermore, they are confused with each other because of the difficulty in telling them apart. "These findings lead us to conclude," said the authors, "that *the significance of hereditary factors in registered crime is non-existent.*"[22]

One of the difficulties in all twin studies relating to genetics, however, is that most twins are reared together, and genetic and environmental factors are difficult to disentangle. A new approach has been recently undertaken, to compare the criminal records of adopted children with the criminal records of their adoptive parents on the one hand, and their biological parents on the other. A register of all nonfamilial adoptions in Denmark in the years 1924-1947 has been established in Copenhagen by a group of American and Danish investigators. There have been 14,433 adoptions recorded, including information on the adoptee and his natural and adoptive parents. From this register, B. Hutchings and S.A. Mednick winnowed a group of 143 males adopted between 1927 and 1942, where the identity and police records of both the biological and adoptive fathers were known.

Hutchings and Mednick found that where neither the biological nor adoptive father was a criminal, 10.4 percent of the sons had criminal records. Where the biological father was not a criminal, but the adoptive father was, this figure rose to only 11.2 percent. But where *the biological father was a criminal*, and *the adoptive father was not*, the percent with criminal records rose to 21 percent. Of this finding, Mednick reported cautiously: "It seems to strongly favor a genetic-etiology assumption." In his view the many twin studies, combined with the adoption studies,[b] "support an hypothesis of the existence of genetic influence in the etiology of criminality."[23]

---

bIn addition to Hutchings and Mednick, there was a study of Danish psychopaths by Shulsinger (1972), and of female inmates of an Iowa reformatory who had given up their children for adoption (Crowe 1975), both of which also suggest genetic influences. See F. Shulsinger, "Psychopathy: heredity and environment," in *International J. Mental Health* 1 (1972):190-206, and R.R. Crowe, "An Adoptive Study of Psychopathy," in R.R. Fieve, D. Rosenthal, and H. Brill, eds., *Genetic Research in Psychiatry* (Baltimore: Johns Hopkins Press, 1975).

It is striking that with the rather consistent showing in all twin and adoption studies of a biological influence on criminality, their reception, outside of the medical profession, has nevertheless been so muted. In fact, there seems to be a marked tendency to explain these studies away. Where one generation embraced not only biological determinism but also the most ruthless eugenic measures, evidence of innate biological differences are today met with a disquiet which amounts to disparagement.

What happened between Lange (1929) and the most recent studies? In the nearly half century since, Haldane's prediction that every educated person would become a determinist has not materialized. Furthermore, the eugenics movement is dead, buried in the mass graves of Auschwitz, Dachau, and Buchenwald, along with the unnumbered millions whom Hitler selected for disposal—the Jews, the gypsies, and all those deemed by the Nazis to be of "inferior" human stock. The Third Reich, with its selective breeding of blond, Nordic, and heroic Germans and its zeal to exterminate what Hitler called the "mongrel races," was the ultimate eugenic experiment, and it dealt a fatal blow to the respectability of the movement. In the social sciences, particularly, it is no longer acceptable to ask whether one race is superior to another, whether the question is asked in terms of comparative intelligence quotients or crime rates; or to suggest that immigrants from northern Europe are more desirable than immigrants from southern Europe; or to seek out the Jukes and Kallikaks and propose their sterilization as a measure of social hygiene. The biological facts remain as they may be. What has changed is the degree of confidence we are prepared to bestow on the national state to be the husbandman of human genetics and select those among us who will be permitted to be at large, to survive, and to reproduce. We see ourselves now, not as the all-knowing stock breeder, but as the potential sheep.

This perspective has cast a long shadow over public policy and even research itself. Many scholars, particularly in the social sciences, are unwilling to undertake studies that would lay them open to the imputation of racism or to the suggestion that they view human behavior as biologically determined, and therefore, irremediable. The prevailing orthodoxy has changed. Thus it is possible that many genetic questions remain unanswered, not because they are unimportant, but because it is considered bad manners—and could be fatal to one's academic standing—to ask them.

13 Some Reflections on "Science" and the "Dangerous Offender"

Eric Sevareid once said that a way to go quietly mad is to think hard about the concept of eternity—another, to think hard about "progress."[1] The eighteenth century thought hard about "progress"; the nineteenth embraced it with enthusiasm and saw evidences of it everywhere, above all in that explosion of knowledge that kept educated people running harder and harder, just to keep up. Science, once so small and modest that anyone with a good library could know everything there was to know about it, was totally transformed. Disciplines multiplied and bred new disciplines; facts tumbled after facts, like water from an overflowing reservoir. Some day, scientists thought, when enough facts have been found, enough experiments performed, enough data analyzed, we would know everything.

The corollary was, of course, that facing any given problem, we could, by careful application of inductive methods, arrive at a solution. This was the view of the positivists. They gave their discipline a name—"criminology"; they marshalled facts from their own and such other disciplines as biology, genetics, and anthropology, and from these they generalized a concept of biological determinism,[a] ignoring the cautionary view that, in the words of Henri Poincaré, "every generalization is a hypothesis."[2] The Italian School perceived in nature what the earlier centuries had called "the Ladder of Perfection," rising through the plant and animal kingdoms by a natural progression from the simpler to the more complex forms of life; and to this hierarchical notion, they joined the nineteenth century doctrine of evolution, by which a species adapts or does not adapt to its environment, and either rises in the scale of evolution or stumbles, or, like the "born criminal," remains hopelessly stranded on a lower rung.

The science of criminology, which is only a hundred years old, has reflected in that period not only the explosion of knowledge but also the changing dogmas, the secret apprehensions, and the kaleidoscopic shift in perspective of a protean century. No sooner was one fact seemingly established than it was challenged by a hundred others. Bertrand Russell once said, "Science is what we know, and philosophy is what we don't know."[3] Actually, the case was less simple than that. Even while adding to the quantum of knowledge, science was so expanding our awareness of ignorance that as the century progressed, we seemed to know less and less each year. As President Wallace Sterling of

---

[a]They did not, of course, hold to this view *exclusively*, but Lombroso, Garofalo, and even the Socialist Ferri believed in the concept that for a large and important class of criminals, crime was biologically predetermined.

Stanford University once put it, "Total knowledge is increasing at such a rate that no matter how industrious and studious a person may be, his relative ignorance is always increasing."[4]

Not only the young science of criminology but many other sciences as well were learning the aptness of William James's observation that "the greatest enemy of any one of our truths may be the rest of our truths. Truths have once for all this desperate instinct of self-preservation and of desire to extinguish whatever contradicts them."[5] This will become more obvious as we consider next the social sciences' approach to criminology and the struggle between the biogenic and sociogenic schools as they sought to explain violence and criminality.

The history of science in the past hundred years has raised important questions of epistemology with which we are only now beginning to grapple. "Mythos," as we saw, is defined by Webster as "a pattern of beliefs expressing often symbolically the characteristic or prevalent attitudes in a group or culture." The same authority gives two definitions of science that are relevant to the present discussion: first, "possession of knowledge, as distinguished from ignorance or misunderstanding," and second, "knowledge attained through study or practice."[6] It must be clear to the reader who has followed the evidence thus far that it is much easier in theory than in practice to distinguish what is science from what is mythos. That which appeared in one generation to be bedrock knowledge, authoritative and incontrovertible, looks rather more to another generation like a blend of ignorance with self-delusion. All of us project outward what is within us; we also project the mythos of our times into those disciplines like biology, psychiatry, or genetics to which, collectively we give the title "science." This does not mean we know *nothing*, only that it is very difficult at any moment to know exactly what we do know.

The great nineteenth-century ichthyologist (and later president of Stanford), David Starr Jordan, once conducted a tour of the Norwegian fjords in which he lectured on the fishes and other fauna to a group of bemused tourists. There was one lady aboard ship who carried a collection of colored spectacles in her purse. As Dr. Jordan described some marine specimen, this lady would tiptoe to the rail and observe the water first through green glasses, then successively, through lenses tinted rose, yellow, and blue. She did the same with the scenery; she observed mountains, waterfalls, and meadows in the same fashion. Dr. Jordan afterwards complained, "She never once saw *anything* in its true colors."[7]

We are all of us, in a sense, like the tourist with the colored glasses. One generation seems to favor one shade of lenses, and the next, another. Thus the same scene may appear in one age to be roseate, in another, to be a dark brown; there are fashions in colored spectacles, as in everything else. The curious problem is that, unlike the lady with the tinted shades, most of us have no conception we are wearing them at all. We betray this blindness only when we introduce information with statements like "History proves . . . ," or "Science teaches us that. . . ." History can be as misleading as the Oracle at Delphi. As for science, it now and then lifts the curtain a bit and lets us rush into the darkness, crying, "I see! I see!", just before we stumble into the pit.

One can almost determine from the philosophy of an age how it will organize and interpret the facts of daily experience. Thus where Calvinism reigned in the seventeenth century, nobody considered either the causes of crime—wickedness and damnation were the causes, of course—or the possibilities of redemption through moral reformation. This was the age, you might say, of bilious green eyeglasses. In the eighteenth century the philosophers of the Enlightenment put on their rosiest spectacles and embraced progress and reform. In the nineteenth, determinism was once again in the ascendant. True, it wore secular garb and spoke of "science" rather than theology; but Haldane was right when he described it as "scientific Calvinism." To the biological determinist, the fate of the criminal was foreordained, and he could no more escape his destiny than could Calvin's sinner. Old ideologies, it seems, never die; they just fade away for a time and return in new raiment.

The real problem we face, whether as scientists or laymen, is to distinguish what is knowledge from what is ideology. It is very difficult for any age to know whether what it sees is really there or is rather a projection from the collective unconscious. Individual error and bias are easily emended, one's peers being only too happy to oblige. But a collective bias must wait for posterity to correct it, from a perspective that may be no less biased but stands at a different observation point in history.

One of the great sources of error in the evolutionary sciences of the nineteenth century was their naive ethnocentricity. True, man, no longer "a little lower than the angels," was demoted to the summit of the animal kingdom. But *Caucasian* man was as much higher than the Hottentot as the Hottentot was higher than the orangutan; and highest of all—at least to the Englishman—was the Englishman. As Barbara Wootton has observed, "Anthropological studies were born, not amongst the African tribesmen, or the Australian bush, but in the Reading Room of the British Museum. . . ."[8]

As we retrace our steps and look at the view that crime springs not from biology but from society, we must remember that the ideas of Karl Marx, which strongly affected this other viewpoint, were also born in the Reading Room of the British Museum. Lombroso thought his "born criminal" was an evolutionary atavism, and the Marxists, that he was the victim of society: There was as much ideology in the one view as in the other. The social determinists were and are not by any means all Marxists; but for a long time, in the nineteenth and twentieth centuries, it was the Marxists who kept the sociogenic view alive against the fiercely entrenched dogmas of criminal anthropology. There had, throughout history, been many to ring changes on the theme that "poverty is the mother of crime." But the Marxists went further; they saw crime as a legitimate struggle by the proletariat against class oppression, and as a part of the greater struggle that would one day see the overthrow of capitalism. On that day, they believed, crime would end in the millenium of a classless society.

The social determinists, like the biological determinists, would wrap themselves in the mantle of scientific materialism, invoke statistics and observation, and at the end, claim quite different conclusions. What these were and how they were arrived at will be the subject of the next section.

**Part III
Society and the Dangerous
Offender**

14 Darwinism, Socialism, and Crime: The Great Debate

The Marxists took a scornful view of criminal anthropology and particularly of the claim that crime was as much a product of biological as of social forces. From the time of Friedrich Engels, it had been a matter of dogma with them that crime had nothing to do with the supposed inferiority of one human to another but was rather the fruit of social and economic oppression. A corollary of this view was the assertion that with the emergence of a classless society would come, not only the withering away of the state but the withering away of criminality.

From the beginning, the socialists had seen Darwinism as a threat to their most cherished beliefs. Although Rudolf Virchow, the German cellular pathologist, once asserted that "Darwinism leads straight to socialism," this view was not shared by the socialists. Nor was it shared by the Darwinians, who thought their new science would mark the destruction of socialism. The great German biologist, Ernst Heinrich Haeckel,[a] saw three irreconcilable contradictions between socialism and Darwinism. (1) Socialism, he said, posits equality among men, while Darwinism demonstrates their diversity and explains the organic reason for it. (2) Darwinism teaches that in the struggle for existence, only a small minority wins; socialism, on the other hand, pretends that nobody need succumb. (3) The struggle for existence is an aristocratic process of selection: socialism is democratic and leveling.[1]

Most Marxists agreed with Haeckel, not with Virchow. To them, Darwinism was totally incompatible with what they called "scientific socialism." If men were not created equal, if they were not perfectible, if society was not the cause of inequality and misery and crime, then, indeed, was their faith vain. Accordingly, they attacked Darwinism as a noxious weed, wherever, and in whatever guise, it might appear. Positivism was the manifestation in criminology of the despised evolutionary doctrines, and after Lombroso's *Criminal Man,* followed by Ferri's *Education, Environment and Criminality,* the Italian Socialists moved to the attack.

The first polemic against criminal anthropology appeared in Milan in 1883 in a pamphlet by Filippo Turati entitled *Crime and the Social Question (Il delitto e la questione sociale).* Turati followed Engels in seeing the criminal as a

---

[a]Haeckel (1834-1919) was the first German advocate of organic evolution, and he formulated the biogenetic law that in the development of the individual animal, the stages through which the species has passed in the course of evolution are repeated ("ontogeny recapitulates phylogeny").

soldier in the class struggle, the never-ending war of the poor against the rich. For those who submitted to oppression, he had only words of scorn—"types of idiotic Christian resignation," he called them, "blessing the hand that smites them." He spoke witheringly of "the workman, who, selling his labor for a pitiful wage, causes the wages of others to fall." Where privilege dominates, he said, "every act of rebellion is a human fact to be studied with human sentiments; and even where it assumes the odious form of crime, it is a useful symptom since it points out the necessity of radical treatment."[2] This argument, which was little more than embroidery on Engels, roused Garofalo to the challenge that exponents of this theory "explain why it is that the poor no less than the rich are exposed to the depredations of the criminal. A strange revolt, this," he exclaimed, "in which attack is directed indifferently upon friends and enemies!"[3]

Turati, however, was directing his attack to Ferri, whose theory of crime he criticized. Ferri had said that there are three classes of factors in crime—the social, the natural, and the individual—and that there are five types of criminals: the insane, the born criminal, the criminal of passion, the habitual criminal, and the occasional criminal. Granted all that, said Turati, and even granting that the first three types would not be criminals except for individual factors, still, the crimes in which the individual element predominates amount at the most to 10 percent of all crimes. Most criminality is habitual or occasional, and is due, not to some putative biological inferiority, but to the social environment, with all its harshness and inequality.[4]

To this, Enrico Ferri made immediate reply in a work he titled *Socialism and Criminality* (*Socialismo e criminalità,* Turin 1883). Ferri argued that in attributing all evil and crime to society, socialists were overlooking the power and influence of individual factors. Even under a socialist regime, he said, there would still be a social environment and therefore a cause of crime. Ferri believed that with increasing social welfare, there would be more sex crimes and more violent crimes; furthermore, he argued, crimes against property would not disappear, since there would always be kleptomaniacs as well as people who were envious and lazy. Education is of no value in the war against crime; it is useless for those who are temperamentally evil, and it is superfluous for those who are good.[5]

Garofalo, too, attacked the socialist position, arguing that while it is true that the proletariat are exposed to privation, the Jean Valjeans of this world who steal a loaf of bread because their family is hungry are in fact extremely rare. The working class suffers not so much from the pangs of hunger, he said, as from their inability to procure the pleasures that others enjoy. "In the great cities, especially, is the cup of Tantalus thus perpetually at its lips." As we ascend the social scale, the wealth and position of each successive class dwarfs those of the class below:

He who is the owner of a million of capital envies his neighbor who enjoys a million of income: he is quite likely to entertain toward him the same feeling of cupidity which the tenant-farmer entertains toward the owner of the lands which he works. Now, just as this feeling of cupidity may impel the peasant to steal wood, it may impel the tenant-farmer to cheat his landlord, the cashier to falsify his accounts, the rich merchant to defraud his creditors, or the wealthy landowner to forge a will by which he hopes to add to his possessions. The sense of cupidity exists in all men in a greater or less degree. But what makes this sentiment capable of leading to crime is not the peculiar condition surrounding the individual, but his own psychic condition. In other words, there must be on his part a complete absence of the instinct of probity coupled with a disregard for his good reputation.

Garofalo thought this last point important because the desire to protect one's reputation "will often enable persons without an innate sense of probity to resist criminal temptations."[6]

A number of socialists, most of them Italian, now joined the argument about the social influences on crime. Perhaps the most erudite and sophisticated of these "scientific socialists" was Achille Loria (1857-1943), author of *The Economic Foundations of Society,* a book that greatly influenced (and somewhat rattled) Enrico Ferri. Loria was no vulgar polemicist but a scholar of impeccable credentials who was, in the words of one criminologist, "permeated with Marxian theories and saturated by a flood of scientific erudition."[7]

Loria preceded his discussion of crime with an analysis of ethics in a capitalistic society. "Ultimate ethics," he said, are based on the interests of the individual, while capitalistic morality is inspired exclusively by the interests of the dominant class. It is class interests alone that inspire moral sanctions and dictate the conduct of proprietors and workers; but their true character is hidden behind high-sounding phrases like "social welfare" and "collective utility." There is a double standard in our moral code, which allows pleasure and license to the rich and demands submission and obedience from the poor. Even John Stuart Mill recognized as much when in his great essay *On Liberty,* he wrote, "Whenever there is an ascendant class, a large proportion of the morality of the country emanates from its class interests and its feelings of class superiority. The morality between Spartans and Helots, between princes and subjects, between nobles and roturiers, between men and women, has been for the most part the creation of these class interests and feelings."[8]

The moral and economic coercion of the poor, said Loria, narrows their sphere of action, and the more limited their sphere of action, the more readily will the members of this class try to break through the barriers and break the laws that oppress them. The more rigorous the oppression, the more numerous these immoral acts. When "simple moral suasion" no longer suffices to keep the poor in line, "penalties that are substantial, and no longer merely imaginary" have to be imposed to preserve property. "Thus where morality is unable to hold human conduct within the orbit traced out by the necessities of capitalistic cohesion, a stronger and more definite connective institution—the law—steps in."[9]

Having disposed of ethics, Loria next proceeded to a discussion of the relationship between economics and crime. Economic conditions, he said, operate with equal force on the crime itself and on its punishment. One need not labor this point where property crimes are concerned; these clearly arise from economic conditions. But economic conditions also affect crimes against the person, as the latter are more common when living costs are low and there is general prosperity. Conservatives argue from this that such crimes are independent of economic conditions, but this is incorrect if greater earnings lead only to spendthrift behavior as so often happens when workers know their prosperity to be ephemeral. When wage increases are temporary, it becomes irrational for workers to employ them in a wise and prudent manner. On the other hand, if there were a lasting betterment of conditions among the poor, "this would have the inevitable result of raising the general standard of morality," and would in turn make it easier to resist "deleterious appetites." As for the criminality of the rich, we must bear in mind that economic conditions may also corrupt *them*—not through an excess of misery, but through a superabundance of wealth. "The criminality of the rich is, therefore, not so independent of the influence of the economic environment as one would think."[10]

Loria had little use for the criminal anthropologists and their "born criminals." A more independent look at the data will show, he said, that the physical characteristics of the so-called criminal type are not the product of nature or necessity but of economic causes that have operated long enough to bring about the degeneration of either the offender or his ancestors. Prolonged poverty, hard labor by pregnant women, malodorous and unhealthful dwellings, bad food, malnutrition, alcoholism, irregular employment, and fluctuating wages, all these are deeply degrading and can perfectly well reflect themselves in external characteristics and anomalies that lead to crime. In Lombroso's work:

The imperfection of the logical process is apparent, for it does not inquire into the causes that led to the asymmetrical skull and other anthropological peculiarities which [the criminal anthropologists] are content to regard as mysterious phenomena derived from some atavic [sic] reversion more mythical than the Indian Trimurti. The theory fails, in short, to recognise that these anthropological phenomena constitute simply the last detritus and external indications of a long erosive process worked out by economic conditions, mercilessly operating upon human life.[11]

Loria called crime "a morbid emanation of capitalistic conditions," and punishment no more than a means to consolidate and protect whatever may be the system of economic relationships in a society. "Thus, an agricultural state metes out its heaviest penalties to crimes against landed property, while a commercial state punishes most severely the crime of issuing false money." But whatever the system, the law always favors the rich. An Italian traveler had recently observed how theft and brigandage went unpunished among the Somali if committed on a scale large enough. "But when we notice what is going on round about us," said Loria, "honesty compels us to admit that, in the matter of legal morality, we Europeans are not much above the Somali."

To sum up. . . : the law is really derived from economic conditions, and it is only in the light of the latter that we are able to understand the genesis of legal sanctions, the history of the law, the real structure of its various institutions; the law is also a monopoly of wealth, and in the temple of Themis there is no place reserved for the labourer.[12]

Ferri was impressed and disturbed by Loria's arguments. He was also troubled by Haeckel's assertion that Darwinism and socialism are incompatible, for Ferri was a Darwinian who had also embraced socialism and would in 1898 become editor of the Socialist newspaper *Avanti.*[b] It was important to him, therefore, to prove "that Marx complements Darwin and Spencer" and that "together they form the great scientific trinity of the nineteenth century."[13] He made a public profession of his socialistic ideas on May Day, 1894. But he did not abandon his insistence on the multiple causes of criminality or on the importance of anthropological factors. As for the belief "that with socialism will disappear each and all forms of crime," he dismissed it as "sentimental idealism."[14]

To Haeckel's theory that Darwinism and socialism are incompatible, Ferri replied: (1) It is true that there are differences among men, but there is also an element of equality in that all *are* men. (2) The number of winners in the struggle for existence diminishes as one passes from the vegetable to the animal worlds, from the lowest to the highest steps of the zoologic scale. (3) In the struggle for existence, it is not the fittest who survive, but the most adaptable. What can be said of criminality under a socialistic régime is only this: "When poverty and the iniquitous disparity in economic conditions have disappeared, then, through the direct lack of the acute or chronic stimulus of hunger, through the beneficent and indirect influence of better nourishment and the absence of opportunities for abusive power and wealth," there will be a decided decrease in occasional crimes, but not in sexual ones. Even under a socialist régime, there will be those who are defeated in the struggle for existence: the weak, the infirm, the neurasthenics, the criminal, and the suicidal. Socialism, therefore, does not deny the Darwinian law, but it will put an end to the physical and moral poverty that are the primary causes of degeneration.[15]

Whether crime was born of society or of the individual was a debate that

[b]Ferri eventually followed another Italian Socialist and later (1912) editor of *Avanti,* Benito Mussolini, into the Fascist movement, and became a Fascist senator in 1929. He also worked under Mussolini in the revision of the Italian criminal code according to positivist principles but did not succeed in getting all his ideas adopted.

would absorb the fraternity of criminologists, whether they were men trained in law like Garofalo and Ferri and Gabriel Tarde, or professors of forensic medicine like Alexander Lacassagne, or sociologists like Achille Loria, or psychiatrists and anthropologists like Cesare Lombroso. In 1885 a hundred or so of them met in Rome at the First International Congress of Criminal Anthropology. The Frenchman Tarde described the group somewhat sniffily as "learned men more or less imbued with the new doctrines and who came from quite far away, even from Russia, to profess and to attest the propagation of their positivist belief." They spent much more time discussing biology than sociology, which moved Tarde to comment:

If the influence of religions, of governments, of education, of wealth, of social conditions, and of the period of history upon criminality had been discussed as were the influence of physiological heredity, of mental alienation, of epilepsy, of alcoholism, of age, of the temperature, and of the seasons, the socialists would have had a fine opportunity for showing that poverty and not cold or alcohol, is the cause of crimes, and for laying the responsibility for the offenders at the door of so-called honest society.[16]

It was in the course of discussion at this conference that the French physician Alexander Lacassagne made a comment that has been quoted ever since: "Every society has the criminals which it deserves."[17]

The Second International Congress was held four years later in Paris, and there a counterattack was launched, especially by the French criminologists, against the Lombrosians. Tarde described the Second Congress as "a brilliant affair. Much too large a place in it was usurped by the criticism of Lombroso's hypotheses; but we must not regret it after all, if, as the majority of the learned men who have followed these sciences have thought, the pretended criminal type emerged from it greatly crippled, or rather reduced to the condition of a phantom in the process of vanishing. A science which is being created should consider as a gain the loss of its chimeras." The 1889 meeting, which was dominated by the French, spent much more of its time on social causes and remedies than had the first one, and there was a move there to subsume criminal anthropology under either psychology or sociology.[18]

But although wounded, the positivists would not haul down their flags, and the debate would continue well into the twentieth century. In the meantime, there were other views of the nexus between crime and economics. What these were, and how they were received, will be considered in the next chapter.

15 Crime and Social Progress

The nineteenth century saw enormous progress in commerce and industry in England, France, Germany, and the United States. In Europe there was also an increase in crime that was commented on by many criminologists.[a] As we have seen, statisticians found apparent correlations between theft and the price of bread on the one hand, and violence and the price of wine on the other. These statistics gave rise to many speculations. Garofalo thought that they "conclusively prove that the oscillations in the always unstable economic equilibrium are not the real cause of criminality, but merely determine the form under which it manifests itself." The fluctuations he likened to the ocean tides: "The movement of the tides neither increases nor diminishes the volume of water; it is nothing more than the water alternately advancing and receding."[1]

A more interesting problem had to do with the secular increase in crime. Lombroso asked why, in every country in Europe, crime was increasing out of proportion to the growth of population. In France, from 1826 to 1837, one person was indicted per one hundred population: in 1868, one in fifty-five. In England, from 1805 to 1841, population rose 49 percent, crime, 600 percent. His answer was, "The progress of civilization, by endlessly multiplying needs and desires, and by encouraging sensuality through the accumulation of wealth, brings a flood of alcoholics and general paralytics [i.e., those suffering from tertiary syphilis] into the insane asylums, and crowds the prisons with offenders against property and against decency."[2]

But another and more interesting theory was advanced by certain writers—namely, that criminal activity is simply one form of economic activity and is therefore related to the expansion and progress of a society. Among the earliest to put forward this idea was the French penologist Charles Lucas. Press offenses, he pointed out, naturally increase with the growth of printing, as do bankruptcies and forgeries with the growth of commerce. What he was arguing, in effect, was that an increase in wealth gives a broader scope for crime. "We are

---

[a]In this period, there were no national crime statistics in the United States, but studies by twentieth-century scholars of police records in Boston, Buffalo, and other American cities suggest that from about 1830 to 1860 crime declined, then rose to a peak in the 1870s, and thereafter again declined until well into the twentieth century. See Roger Lane, "Urbanization and Criminal Violence in the 19th Century: Massachusetts as a Test Case," in Hugh Davis Graham and Ted Robert Gurr, *The History of Violence in America* (N.Y.: Praeger, 1969), pp. 470 *et seq.*; Roger Lane, "Crime and Criminal Statistics in 19th Century Massachusetts," *J. of Social History* (Winter 1968): 156 *et seq.*; and Elwin H. Powell, "Crime as a Function of Anomie," *J. Criminal Law, Criminology and Police Science* 57:2 (1966): 161 *et seq.*

not called upon to give especial credit to a poverty-stricken and ignorant people because of the small number of harmful acts occurring in their midst," he wrote in 1828. "This fact is due to the lack of occasion for inflicting harm; to nothing else than an animal-like ignorance. The greater number of such acts occurring among civilized people is merely the result of a larger development of human liberty."[3] Lucas saw civilization as primarily the progress of liberty; it increased the abuse, because it expanded the use, of freedom. Therefore, to assess the morality of a country, one had to compare the good uses of liberty to its evil uses.[4]

As is usual in such cases, this theory attracted its adherents and its critics. Giovanni Domenico Romagnosi, the Italian jurist and philosopher (1761-1835), thought the idea rather silly: "One might as well say that sin increases with progress in piety; that diseases multiply with the regular development of a sound body; that as men become more industrious and grow in mutual respect and friendliness, so increases the number of idle, vicious and criminal."[5] On the other hand, a number of writers thought this relationship between criminal and other kinds of activities was demonstrated by the statistics.

Among these was the Italian Filippo Poletti, who concluded from French statistics of 1826-1878 that while the crime index had risen from 100 to 254, social activities—in which he included exports, imports, the treasury balance, the value of property transmitted by inheritance, and the transfer of real property *inter vivos*—had increased threefold. Thus said Poletti, there was, in real terms, a diminution of criminality during this period. Poletti said that criminal activity develops in proportion to honest activity so long as the causes that produce the two remain constant. The time of this constancy he called the "criminal period." He believed that as we move from one period to another, the amount of criminality tends slowly and proportionately to diminish, "owing to the development of the intellectual faculties and the economic activities, as well as the general perfection of the power to resist crime."[6]

In his *La criminalité comparée* (1886), Gabriel Tarde said that Poletti's theory "consists in appraising criminality as one would judge the safety of a means of locomotion":

It would have us proceed exactly as we would to determine whether the modern railway passenger travels with a greater or less degree of safety than did his grandfather of, say, 1830, who made his journeys by stage-coach. Just as in the latter case we solve the problem not by comparing the number of travelers killed or injured under the two kinds of travel, respectively, but by ascertaining the number respectively killed or injured out of the whole number carried, so in the present case, this theory obliges us to proceed by saying, for example, that in 1830, for so many transactions likely to afford occasion for criminal breach of trust, there was one crime of this character prosecuted annually, while at the present time there is one such crime to a different number of transactions. Why not add, that in consequence of the greater facilities for social intercourse and the more dangerous allurements of urban life, the enormous increase of adultery witnessed of late years is in no way surprising, and is really proof of an actual improvement in feminine virtue?

Like Romagnosi, whose criticism was similarly picturesque, Tarde thought that this theory missed the point: "Nothing is gained by demonstrating that railways are the least dangerous mode of travel, or that gas is the least harmful means of illumination. The fact remains that a Frenchman of 1826 ran less risk of meeting death by accident of travel, less risk of being burned to death"—and, he might have added, less risk of being robbed or murdered—"than does his descendant of the present day."[7]

Poletti's view that criminality is only an aspect of the general economic system and is related to expansion and progress was generally and vehemently repudiated by his contemporaries. Garofalo cited statistics to show that in countries where the economic development was greater, such as France, the crime rate was in fact lower than in backward countries like Spain and Italy. In England, he said, crime was constantly decreasing in the face of a continuing growth in population, commerce, and industry.[8] And Enrico Ferri had little use for the attempt to measure crime against commerce. "How can we be sure," he asked, "that a six hundred percent increase of commerce represents proportionately three times as much as a two hundred percent increase in crime. . . ? To my mind, an increase of two percent in the number of crimes is something of much more vital import from the social standpoint than an increase of thirty percent in the exports of cotton and cattle."[9]

On the other hand, the French sociologist Emile Durkheim proposed a view of crime in his *Rules of Sociological Method* (1894) that rather paralleled Poletti's. Durkheim saw crime, not only as a sign of progress, but as a social necessity. Citing the statistic that from the beginning of the nineteenth century crime had increased in France by nearly 300 percent, he said, "There is, then, no phenomenon that presents more indisputably all the symptoms of normality, since it appears closely connected with the conditions of all collective life." That is not to say merely that it is inevitable but regrettable: "It is to affirm that it is a factor in public health, an integral part of all healthy societies."[10]

Crime he defined as "an act that offends certain very strong collective sentiments." Crime could only disappear if all the individual consciousnesses in a community agreed perfectly on what should be condemned and to what degree. But, in fact, there are always people who diverge from the "collective type," and among them, inevitably, are some with a criminal character. "Crime is, then, necessary; it is bound up with the fundamental conditions of all social life, and by that very fact it is useful, because these conditions of which it is a part are themselves indispensable to the normal evolution of morality and law." Durkheim thought that the moral conscience of a community should not be excessively rigid, "otherwise, no one would dare criticize it, and it would too easily congeal into an immutable form. To make progress, individual originality must be able to express itself. In order that the originality of the idealist whose dreams transcend his century may find expression, it is necessary that the originality of the criminal, who is below the level of his time, shall also be possible. One does not occur without the other."[11]

In Durkheim's view, the criminal is not "an unsociable being, a sort of parasitic element.... On the contrary, he plays a definite role in social life. Crime, for its part, must no longer be conceived as an evil that cannot be too much suppressed. There is no occasion for self-congratulation when the crime rate drops noticeably below the average level, for we may be certain that this apparent progress is associated with some social disorder." Assault cases, he said, never fall so low as in times of hunger.[12]

Arthur Cleveland Hall, the American sociologist, tended also to see crime as related to economic and social development. In his *Crime and Its Relation to Social Progress* (1902), he noted that definitions of criminality change as acts, formerly harmless or even beneficial, with the growing complexity of civilization, come to be viewed as antisocial.

Society's conflict with its criminal members, due to the enforcement of new social prohibitions, is one of the chief means by which humanity, in every age, has risen from a lower to a higher plane of civilization. ... For the amount of a nation's crime depends upon the degree of civilization attained, the rapidity of social evolution, necessarily calling into existence new forces of crime, and the general attitude of the people toward the criminal law, and especially the new laws, obedience being more difficult to obtain where individual liberty is customary and highly prized, and restraint consequently more irksome.[13]

It is not surprising that this view was repudiated by the positivists who, especially in Italy and the Anglo-Saxon countries, were very much in the ascendant at the time. Obviously, under such a view the dangerous offender is in danger of disappearing altogether, to be replaced by a remarkable new criminal, the spear carrier of social and economic progress. Yet Durkheim was at some pains to point out that, even if crime is normal, "it does not follow that the criminal is an individual normally constituted from the biological and psychological points of view." Crime may be normal, but it may also be at the same time painful, and even abhorrent. Yet, like pain, it plays a useful role in life, "for which reason it cannot be replaced."[14]

The view of crime as necessary to progress was no less distasteful to the Marxists. Crime to them was a symptom of social disease, no more normal than diabetes or cancer. The disappearance of the dangerous offender, not to mention the "born criminal," under such a concept of criminality was, of course, no concern of theirs; they did not believe people were born bad, feeling, rather, that if they became dangerous, it was for much the same reason that a dog becomes dangerous when he has been beaten and starved. But the thought of crime as an index to progress and prosperity or, worse yet, as necessary to the healthy functioning of society was abhorrent because it ran counter to their most cherished orthodoxy. To the Marxists, crime was like a fever thermometer that proclaimed the presence of disease in the body politic. In a healthy society there would be no crime, and there would be no criminals—dangerous or otherwise.

Finally, the adherents of classical jurisprudence, the men everywhere who made and administered the criminal laws, could not accept the notion that criminals were somehow doing society a favor by challenging its strictures. To do so, they would have to throw overboard every concept on which the law was premised. If laws were made to be challenged; if their injunctions not only could, but must, be regularly disobeyed; if crime is not pathological, but healthy, then why the legislatures, the courts, the police, the prisons, and the gallows? It was a dizzying thought—or it would have been, had anyone taken it seriously. But Durkheim and Poletti have been, if not repudiated, then simply ignored because their ideas were not useful to any of the prevailing orthodoxies, whether positivist, Marxist, or classical.

It is a very difficult thing to advance a theory that is convenient to none of the prevailing orthodoxies. It is rather like producing an illegitimate child: No one rushes forward to claim the infant. So it has proven to be with the idea that crime is a sign of, and necessary to, progress. The hypothesis would be an interesting one to test against the now-abundant statistics of world crime and commerce. Unfortunately, nobody stands to gain from proving it right, neither the biological determinists, the economic determinists, the sociologists, nor the criminal justice establishment. Under the circumstances, it is likely to remain a lonely but intriguing footnote in the history of criminological thought.

16 Economics and Criminality in the Twentieth Century

There have classically been three ways of looking at the economics of criminality. One, which is very ancient, is to see crime as an effect of poverty. A second view, which was formulated by writers of the nineteenth century, was that crime is related to affluence—either because it is another aspect of economic development (Lucas and Poletti) or because the example of wealth in the midst of misery tempts the poor to be dishonest (Garofalo's "cup of Tantalus" theory). The third view, that of the Marxists, embodied elements from both of these. But it was considerably more sophisticated, since it not only described the effects of economic conditions on criminality but also related these to the capitalist mode of production. Engels, Turati, and Loria all expressed the Marxist view. It was, however, a young Dutchman Willem Adriaan Bonger who wrote the classic exposition of Marxist theory as applied to crime.

While he was still a student, the University of Amsterdam held a concours on the topic: "A systematic and critical outline of the literature relating to the influence of economic conditions upon criminality." Bonger, then twenty-three, entered the competition but did not win. However, he used part of his monograph for a doctoral dissertation and later expanded it into a book, *Criminality and Economic Conditions,* which appeared in French in 1905.[a] The book was selected by the American Institute of Criminal Law and Criminology to be translated and published in its distinguished "Modern Criminal Science Series." In his preface to the American edition, Bonger said he was "fully convinced that my ideas about the etiology of crime will not be shared by a great many readers of the American edition." In this, of course, he was correct; American criminology of the time was largely positivist in character. By the end of the Depression, *Criminality and Economic Conditions* had become a minor classic, which Austin Turk has defined as "a book everyone knows about, a few have read, but hardly anyone ever uses." As Turk remarked in his introduction to the 1969 edition, *Criminality* had become a classic before its time.[1]

Bonger began by defining crime as "an act committed within a group of persons that form a social unit, and whose author is punished by the group (or

---

[a]There are two American editions, a complete translation published in 1916 under the sponsorship of the Institute of Criminal Law and Criminology and an abridged paperback edition published in 1969 by the Indiana University Press. The former contains Bonger's voluminous research in the literature of economics and crime and is invaluable to the student of this subject. The latter includes only Bonger's own analysis of the relationship of crime to capitalism, which is discussed in this chapter.

part of it) as such, or by organs designated for this purpose, and this by a penalty whose nature is considered to be more severe than that of moral disapprobation." This is the formal side of crime. But there is also a material side. "Is crime considered from a biological point of view an abnormal act? The answer to this, which is of the highest importance for the etiology of crime, must be negative. From a biological point of view almost all crimes must be ranked as *normal acts.*" (Emphasis mine.) The process that takes place in the brain of the law officer who kills a fleeing poacher is the identical process that goes on in the brain of the poacher who kills the pursuing officer. "It is only the social environment," said Bonger, "which classes the second act rather than the first as a crime." The same applies to assaults, where the police may club the strikers, or the strikers fight back. Again, it is the social circumstances which class self-defense as a crime, while police attack is considered lawful.[2]

Crime is an immoral act of a serious character. Acts are called immoral, said Bonger, when they are harmful to a group of persons united by the same interests. But as social structure changes, so do our ideas of what is immoral (and consequently of what is or is not criminal). Where society is divided into the ruling class and the ruled, the penal law is largely shaped by the former. True, most forbidden acts (homicide, rape, etc.) are prejudicial to both. However, unless an act injures the dominant class as well as the subject one, it is unlikely to be punished.

Why does the individual injure his social group—i.e., act egoistically? Most people, he said, believe in the innate selfishness of man, an egoism implied in the doctrine of Original Sin. Others, like Lombroso and his followers, think that egoism is natural but is gradually fading from human character as man evolves. Not so: What is really happening is that egoism is becoming less *violent* than it once was. The capitalist who locks out his workmen, thereby condemning them to hunger; the great speculator who forces thousands to pay more for necessities—these are no less egoistic than the robber baron of the Middle Ages. The difference is merely that the former attains his end without violence. Capitalism promotes egoism among the commercial and industrial classes, demoralizes the leisure class (by making it parasitical), and leads to the intellectual prostitution of the professional classes.[3]

Said Bonger, "The fluctuations of the mind of the person in whom the criminal idea is born may be compared with the oscillations of a balance; and it is upon sociology that must devolve the task of examining the forces which throw a weight on one side or the other. When the organization of society influences men in an altruistic way, there is then a considerable force which can prevent the balance from inclining towards the egoistic side." However, in our present society altruism is weak or nonexistent. We rely on the hope of reward (terrestrial or celestial) and the fear of being punished (by man or God) to keep people in line. "As believers themselves know very well, most men are not very responsive to divine rewards and punishments—heaven and hell are too far off."[4]

Enrico Ferri had asked how, if crime were the exclusive product of social environment, one could explain the fact that in the same social environment, and in identical circumstances of poverty, abandonment, and lack of education, 60 percent do not commit crimes, and of the other 40, 5 prefer suicide, 5 go mad, 5 become beggars or tramps not dangerous to society, while only 25 commit crimes. Said Ferri, "In every family in which there are several children, we find (in spite of identical surroundings and conditions of favourable kind, and suitable methods of training and education) individuals who differ intellectually from the cradle; we also find . . . the same individuals . . . differ from their cradle in physical and moral constitution."[5]

Bonger's answer was that men do indeed differ in moral qualities as they do in height, strength, weight, and intelligence. But, as Quételet proved, there is a regularity in the sense that people of average height predominate in number, and the very short and very tall form minorities.

The same thing must be true for men's moral qualities. . . . With the great majority the social sentiments would have only a moderate intensity, while there would be one small minority in which they would be weak, and another in which they would be very strong. . . . *The task that is incumbent upon us is to explain why individuals who, as a consequence of their innate qualities, run more danger than another of becoming criminals, actually do so.* He who is born with weak social instincts runs more *danger* of becoming a criminal. But the certainty that he will become such does not exist—that depends upon the environment. . . . Individual differences are of great importance for one who is studying an individual by himself, but . . . they do not belong to the domain of the etiology of criminality.[6]

Bonger distinguished four types of crimes: economic, sexual, political, and a heterogeneous category that he subsumed under crimes of vengeance. Economic crimes are undeniably influenced by unemployment. It is true that most vagrants and beggars, not knowing a trade, are worth little as workmen; but even if this were not so, there would still be no work for them because the demand for skilled labor would not increase. "*Vagrancy and mendicity would be no less extensive even if all the workers knew a trade and were equal in zeal and energy,*" he claimed.[7]

Willem Bonger did not believe that theft and analogous crimes had to be explained because he did not believe that honesty was innate. "No child can distinguish between mine and thine, it is only little by little that he gains this concept. On the contrary he has the tendency to monopolize everything that he desires (the prehensory instinct, Lafargue names it). It is just this instinct that must be combated to make a child honest. It would, therefore, be more correct to say that dishonesty is innate." There are three kinds of thefts: those committed from poverty, those committed from cupidity, and those committed by professionals. All are influenced by the capitalistic system, which excites cupidity by "beautiful displays" and "dazzling illuminations." "How can we expect a poor man to take care not to do a small injury to the rich for fear of causing them a little discomfort, when most rich people are insensible to the suffering which, without intermission, overwhelms the poor?" The very slight sensitivity to misfortune which, under a capitalistic system, people feel for each other "offers only a trifling counterpoise to the tendency to realize one's desires in a dishonest manner."[8]

Thus far his analysis does not differ markedly from that of his Marxist predecessors. Bonger's comments on violent crimes, like robberies, however, are more original. Such crimes, he said, are less common in advanced than in backward societies, which do not offer the same scope for larceny and fraud. Here Bonger took direct aim at the positivists and their "born criminal." If violence *were* of biological origin, he argued, there would be just as much of it in developed as in primitive societies. The fact that there is not proves that it is society, and not biology, which is the source of such crimes. All that has happened is that "with time, the number of persons who have a horror of violence has increased. Does this prove that men have become better, or simply that they feel a repugnance to the act only, not to its effect?" And he quotes Jean-Jacques Rousseau, who once asked: "If, in order to fall heir to the property of a rich mandarin living at the farthest confines of China, whom one had never seen or heard spoken of, it were enough to push a button to make him die, which of us would not push that button?"[b,9]

Next Bonger considered such rich men's crimes as fraudulent bankruptcies and the adulteration of food. From the point of view of the consumer, the adulteration of food is a very grave offense, he said.

This kind of crime must be the despair of those who seek for some biological anomaly of the criminal as the primary cause of crime, for here the anomaly forms almost the rule. Dr. Puibaraud, in his *Malfaiteurs de Profession,* rightly says: "The adulteration of food is carried on under our eyes, at our very doors, and we are so used to it that we say nothing. They put fuchsine[c] in our wine, margarine in our butter, chicory in our coffee, tallow in our chocolate, and we swallow it all in perfect good humor. What is the use of protesting? So things are, and 'business could not be carried on' if they gave us really pure food. So we swallow it all without gagging or moving a muscle. Provided we are not poisoned—too quickly—we profess ourselves satisfied."[10]

---

[b]That Rousseau was not far off the mark is illustrated by the Black Box experiment conducted in 1975-1976 by Dr. Paul Cameron, a psychologist and professor at the Fuller Theological Seminary in Pasadena, who interviewed 652 persons and asked them: "What is the least amount of money you would take to push a button to kill a person inside a black box (no one will ever know what you did)?" The people were divided into two groups, those who acknowledged having deliberately killed someone, as in military service, and those who had never killed or tried to do so. Of those who had killed before, 45 percent said they would murder for money, for an average price of $20,000. Of those who had never killed or tried to, 25 percent said they would do it, but their average asking price was $50,000. (*New York Times,* 14 October 1976, p. 55.) We do not, of course, know how much an eighteenth-century European might have expected to inherit from a "rich mandarin living at the farthest confines of China."

[c]Fuchsine: a bluish-red dye, produced by the oxidation of aniline and toluidines.

Bonger was equally indignant at the "great criminals," the manipulators, swindlers, and speculators: "What an ordinary criminal does in a small way, they do on a gigantic scale; while the former injures a single person, or only a few, the latter bring misfortune to great numbers." He did not employ the term "dangerous offender" for such malefactors, but clearly he considered them more dangerous than the ordinary unskilled criminal, because their crimes are on such a massive scale. In his eyes, the "great criminals," like their humbler brethren, are the fruits of capitalism. So, even, are sex criminals. Rape is more common among unmarried, widowed, and divorced men, and it is poverty that makes marriage impossible for the poor. Furthermore, he said, rapists come from the lowest strata of society, where, because of crowded living conditions, sexual life is at the animal level.[11]

In the end Willem Bonger emerged at almost the same point as Engels and Loria: a socialist society, he thought, "will not only remove the causes which now make men egoistic, but will awaken, on the contrary, a strong feeling of altruism." However, he did not claim that crime would wither away *completely*; "There will be crimes committed by pathological individuals, but this will come rather within the sphere of the physician than that of the judge."[12]

The Marxists were, of course, not alone in seeking an economic genesis for crime. Guerry and Quételet had applied the infant science of statistics to seek correlations between crime and the cost of food. Scholars like Poletti had sought to show a correlation between crime and economic development. In the United States there were a number of studies that sought to correlate crime with the business cycle or unemployment. In the nineteenth century, it will be remembered, various Europeans had suggested that crimes of violence increase during good times, and crimes against property during bad. In 1922 three American scholars, George R. Davies,[13] William F. Ogburn, and Dorothy S. Thomas[14] published studies which concluded that during most—not all—depressions the number of convictions rose above the normal trend lines, and in periods of prosperity it fell below. In 1927 Thomas did a study based on British data that found little correlation when *all* indictable offenses were considered, but she did establish a correlation between economic stringency and property offenses, both violent and nonviolent. W. Toytinsky, taking Thomas's property-offense indices and correlating them with the commodity index, also got high correlations. These studies seemed to corroborate nineteenth-century findings with respect to the relationship between property offenses and the financial hardships of the poor. Thomas also found, as had her predecessors, that drunkenness was correlated with prosperity.[15]

Another question that concerned researchers was whether people were more prone to commit crimes if they were out of work. A 1929 Bureau of Census study showed that of the prisoners in state and federal prisons in 1923, 70 percent were employed at the time they committed their crimes; another 25 percent had been unemployed less than six months. Furthermore, their average weekly earnings were almost exactly the same as for those who did not commit crimes. Later studies by Mary van Kleeck of Sing Sing prisoners (1931) and by Donald Clemmer of inmates at the Illinois State Prison (1931-1934) were consistent with these results.[16] They seemed to show that whatever economic causes may be involved in crime, unemployment is not one of them.

In measuring the relationship between crime and economic conditions, statisticians have used such indices of economic change as wholesale prices (Davies), composite indices (Ogburn and Thomas), industrial employment, poverty, cotton prices, real wages, and wage payments. To measure crime, they have used indices of commitments to prison, convictions in higher courts, prosecutions in higher courts, persons indicted, prosecution in lower courts, admissions to prison or probation, offenses known to the police, and delinquents brought before juvenile courts. Except for property crimes, however, the correlations have not proved to be consistent from one study to another.[17] One problem with correlating crime and economic indices has been the question of whether correlations should be synchronous, have a one-year lag, a two-year lag, or whatever. It is here, as George Vold has pointed out, that statisticians have faced a dilemma. Either they can assume that there is a relationship between crime and economic conditions, then try to find the right time lag, or they can assume the time lag, and use the coefficient of correlation to establish the relationship. The trouble has arisen from trying to do the impossible: establish both at the same time.[18] This has been a source not only of confusion but of some argument.

Although Bonger used statistics in his own work, he relied most heavily on historical examples to prove the nexus between crime and economics. The last great study of this genre was by Georg Rusche and Otto Kirchheimer, *Punishment and Social Structure* (1939), which, although it was by two German scholars, appeared first in New York. The history of this work is interesting. The International Institute of Social Research was established in Frankfurt am Main in 1923 as an affiliate of the university. It was closed by the Nazis in 1933, and it transferred its main activities to Columbia University. The first manuscript of *Punishment and Social Structure,* written by Georg Rusche, was delivered after the Institute had left Germany, and because of the unavailability of the author, it was amplified and completed in New York by Otto Kirchheimer.[d] Thus it appeared first in English translation.[19]

Bonger had shown how the class system and modes of production affect the etiology and treatment of crime. Rusche and Kirchheimer, from the same Marxist perspective, sought to show how these affect the laws that define crime and the punishment meted out to criminals. It was in every respect a classic work of

---

[d]Willem Bonger, too, was a victim of Hitler. After a distinguished lifetime in criminology, Bonger, in 1940, committed suicide rather than fall into the hands of the Nazis. He wrote to his son, "I don't see any future for myself and I cannot bow to this scum which will now overmaster us." (See article by J.M. van Bemmelen in Hermann Mannheim's *Pioneers in Criminology* (Montclair, N.J.: Patterson Smith, 1972), pp. 443-457.)

scholarship, which claimed that the changing forms of punishment—from slavery (in ancient times), to capital and corporal punishment (in the Middle Ages) to houses of correction (in the seventeenth century)—were related to labor shortages and to the modes of production. It did not concern itself with the causes of crime and is therefore not germane to the problems discussed here. Its great contribution was rather to raise the sights of penologists beyond those issues that so exclusively absorbed their attention—proportionality, incapacitation, and deterrence—and to force on them a consideration of how the economic and class interests of those who write the laws determine the means by which they are enforced. The authors' views on the matter were nicely summed up in these words of Otto Kirchheimer: "The futility of severe punishment and cruel treatment may be proven a thousand times, but so long as society is unable to solve its social problems, repression, the easy way out, will always be accepted. It provides the illusion of security by covering the symptoms of social disease with a system of legal and moral value judgments."[20]

Like Bonger's *Criminality and Economic Conditions, Punishment and Social Structure* is a classic work whose value far transcends its underlying Marxist orientation, and it is the last of its type to have appeared, at least in the noncommunist West. After World War II, economic causation faded from the scholarly literature on crime, perhaps because of the long period of prosperity, perhaps because sociologists took up the challenge of explaining crime. Drawing on the theories of such European scholars as Emile Durkheim and Gabriel Tarde, criminology was to become, by mid-twentieth century, a largely sociological and a largely American science, based on American experience and American perceptions of social reality. What the theories were and how this perception developed will be the subject of the next several chapters.

17 Familial Neglect and Criminal Association

If economic theories of criminality are based on poverty, sociogenic theories seem to find their origins in variant versions of familial neglect or criminal contagion. In their earliest formulations, either the criminal had wicked parents ("Like father, like son"), or came under the influence of an evil companion ("The rotten apple spoils the barrel"), or kept bad company ("Birds of a feather flock together"). The social contagion theory is an old and familiar one and suggests that deviant behavior, though possibly influenced by the natural perversity of human beings, is further encouraged by bad training and imitation.

In a sense, of course, we have always believed this. Otherwise, why should parents agonize over the proper way to rear their children ("As the twig is inclined, so the tree is bent"), and over the method, content, and quality of their education? Why otherwise should parents care whom their children associate with? Thus the sociogenic theory of crime, in its primitive formulations, was merely an extension of popular beliefs with regard to the importance of early training and the contagious nature of human behavior.

An early application of these ideas to criminality appeared in 1829 and 1830, when the inspectors of New York's Auburn Penitentiary wrote biographical sketches of inmates about to be discharged from prison. These biographies concentrated on the convicts' upbringing, especially their childhood. Of 173 biographies, fully two thirds, the inspectors thought, proved that childhood made the man. They used such phrases as "brought up . . . under the influence of a bad example," or, "father a very intemperate man," to explain the criminal careers on which the subjects had later embarked.[1] Not only bad example, but sheer parental neglect, was considered a factor also. In the First Annual Report of the New York Prison Association (1845), William H. Channing, a Unitarian minister, wrote this about the origins of criminal behavior: "The first and most obvious cause is an evil organization derived from evil parents. Bad germs bear bad fruit." Although this formulation sounds as though the writer is blaming poor heredity, he goes on to explain that of 156 inmates recently admitted to Pennsylvania's Eastern State Penitentiary, 14 had been orphaned by age twelve, 36 were missing one parent or another soon after, 143 had received no religious instruction, and 144 had never attended Sabbath school. "Such statistics tell at a glance that early neglect was certainly, in part, probably in great part, the cause of after crime."[2]

Thus both sins of omission (neglect, failure to send a child to Sunday school) and of commission (providing a bad home environment; setting a bad

119

example) were viewed as factors in the development of a criminal career. R.L. Dugdale's "Jukes" were as much the victims of their environment as of their heredity. Dugdale found them living in stone or log houses "similar to slave-hovels, all ages, sexes, relations and strangers 'bunking' indiscriminately." This proximity, he thought, "where not producing illicit relations, must often have evolved an atmosphere of suggestiveness fatal to habits of chastity."[3] The Jukes suffered even worse from association with each other, since they were thrown cheek-by-jowl with that extraordinary assortment of criminals, drifters, and debauchees that made up the family. But bad as they were, Dugdale thought, in a changed environment, and *if the young were caught early enough,* their will could "be so developed, organized and made steady," that it could "serve as a guide and as a restraint."[4] ("Will power" was a very popular concept in Victorian America.)

Charles Loring Brace, too, in *The Dangerous Classes of New York* (1872), devoted much of his description to the hordes of homeless and destitute children who roamed the streets and alleys by day and slept in doorways at night; he called them "the sources of domestic outbreaks and violations of law." By changing their material circumstances, he thought, and providing them with education, discipline, and religion, we could help them grow up as useful members of society. Brace believed this would be done, not only by training and example, but by the contagious influence of "the moral and fortunate classes."[5] That the upper classes, merely by association, could be a meliorating influence on the lower remained, until recently, almost an article of faith, particularly among the English, whose social climbers had long sent their sons to the "good" public schools to rub shoulders with the aristocracy. They were thus supposed to bc transformed into gentlemen by a process, one might say, of gilt by association.[a] On the other hand, the process might also work in reverse. Said the French anthropologist Léonce Manouvrier (1850-1927): "If we were to take a well-born child of a distinguished European family, and isolate him from his birth from all the influences of environment except those strictly necessary for the preservation of his life, we do not know what strange beast he would turn into."[6]

The means by which children are transformed into "beasts" or gentlemen was to be a subject of scrutiny and conjecture by psychiatrists, anthropologists,

---

[a]Just how this gilding was supposed to be accomplished—at least in the eyes of a nine-year-old English authoress—was charmingly described by Daisy Ashford in a classic work of childish imagination, *The Young Visiters, or Mr. Salteena's Plan* (published in 1919, but written some time in the latter part of the nineteenth century). Mr. Salteena, who was "not quite a gentleman," asked his friend Bernard how he might become one. Bernard sent him to the Crystal Palace in London, which, according to the young novelist, had "compartments" for people who "want to be less mere." There under the tutelage of the Earl of Clincham, Mr. Salteena was "rubbed up in socierty ways."

and sociologists. The German psychiatrist, Gustav Aschaffenburg (1866-1944),[b] thought that hereditary transmission had very little to do with the development of criminal character, even in cases where whole families, and even whole communities, were distinguished by intense criminal activity. "A child that is surrounded by criminals in its earliest youth soon learns to think like them," he said, "and never has the chance to develop other views. Crime loses its character as a reprehensible act, and punishment its disgrace; at most, the latter is regarded as an unavoidable disadvantage connected with the occupation." He cited as an example the Italian ecclesiastical state of Artena, which was for centuries a nest of rogues. In 1557 Pope Paul IV outlawed all its inhabitants and gave anyone the right to destroy the place. As late as 1887, the relative number of robberies in Artena was thirty times as great as in the rest of Italy, and the number of assaults and homicides, six or seven times as great. One of its families, the Montefortinos, maintained its reputation for crime through three centuries, said Aschaffenburg. "And yet even this high degree of criminality, that remained unchanged for centuries, does not prove the hereditary character of criminality itself. It may equally as well be attributed to the unfortunate force of example, that smothered good impulses before they could be developed."[7]

Aschaffenburg saw at work many of the same influences that Dugdale and Brace had observed. Parents worked, leaving their children "to their ungoverned impulses and the influences of the street." Living conditions were wretched "both in cities and in rural districts. The living together in close quarters, even sleeping together, of adults and children, of parents and lodgers, must arouse the sexual instincts at an early age.... A child that grows up among thieves and vagabonds, prostitutes and drunkards, forms his range of ideas after that of those about him, and scarcely requires special instruction in order to act first as assistant, then as participant, in the execution of the family's criminal plans."[8]

Gabriel Tarde (1843-1904), one of France's most eminent sociologists, suggested the mechanism by which, not only criminal behavior, but all fashions and innovations are spread. Tarde, before becoming a professor at the Collège de France, had spent many years as a provincial magistrate (*juge d'instruction*) at Sarlat, and he was dissatisfied with the biological and physical explanations for crime, which he considered preeminently a social phenomenon. The majority of murderers and thieves began as abandoned children, he claimed, and "the true seminary of crime must be sought for upon each public square or each crossroads of our towns . . . in those flocks of pillaging street urchins, who, like

[b]Aschaffenburg, with Henry Maudsley and Cesare Lombroso, was among the most distinguished pioneers of psychiatric criminology. A professor in the Cologne Academy of Practical Medicine, he was editor of the *Journal of Criminal Psychology and Criminal Law Reform (Monatsschrift für Kriminalpsychologie)*, until in 1936, when he was seventy years old, he was ousted from his editorship by the Nazis. Two years later Aschaffenburg went into exile in the United States.

bands of sparrows, associate together, at first for marauding, and then for theft, because of a lack of education and good in their homes."[9]

Tarde's great contribution to sociology is *The Laws of Imitation,* published in 1890. In the same year he applied his laws of imitation to the spread of criminal behavior in another important work, *Penal Philosophy,* so that the two books must be considered together if one is to understand his theory of crime.

His first law of imitation is that people imitate one another in direct proportion to their closeness of contact: "The honest example of an entire surrounding but distant society may be neutralized in the heart of a young vagabond by the influence of a few companions."[10] His second law says that although superiors sometimes imitate their inferiors, most customs spread from above down: from the upper to the lower classes, from the great cities to the country. "When two men are together for a long time, whatever may be their difference in station, they end by imitating each other," and what is imitated is "the most superior one *of those that are nearest."* The influence of the model's example is efficacious in inverse proportion to its *distance,* as well as in direct proportion to its superiority.[11]

The result of immigration to the cities has been an unusual rush of inventions. What Tarde calls "imitation-fashion" (copying the new) makes greater gaps in the old ways, "imitation-custom," and it provides many prosperous days for crime until custom absorbs and assimilates those currents of example that have in turn become traditional. The vices and crimes of the lower orders are descended from above: drunkenness, poaching (which is really an attempt to imitate the hunter-aristocrat), poisoning (cf. the Borgias), arson and brigandage (a major occupation of the feudal upper classes). "If heredity were the principal 'factor' as far as morality is concerned, could this be as it is?" he asks. Crime once spread from the nobility to the people; now it spreads from city to country. Indecent assaults on children are an urban crime; so are throwing vitriol (a Paris fashion) and mutilating women (which started in London with Jack the Ripper). And he quotes Armand Corre, *Crime et Suicide:* "Infectious epidemics spread with the air or the wind; epidemics of crime follow the line of the telegraph."[12]

Tarde's third law of imitation is the law of insertion. There is an intermittent insertion of new buds or grafts of imitation-fashions, he said, and these may either replenish, nourish, or even displace the previous imitation-customs. Thus guns replace knives (new fashion replaces older custom). Sometimes, however, when two fashions compete, they may both increase; for example, labor and stealing both have the same purpose, making money, but the spread of industrialism, by increasing wants, may cause both labor *and* crime to multiply.[13]

In republican times, says Tarde, Roman morality held its own. But from the end of the Punic Wars, there was great confusion and a continuous growth in crime and immorality. "If the morals of this great city of olden times never improved, is it not because the continuous arrival of exotic religions, of heterogeneous civilizations, did not leave her any time to put a little order into this chaos?"[14] Or, to put it in his own theoretical terms, the insertions of imitation-fashion were so rapid and continuous as to keep Roman society in turmoil.

To summarize his views, Tarde believed that crime is spread by imitation, that people imitate each other in direct proportion to propinquity, that like all fashion, crime spreads from superior to inferior, and that new criminal fashions, grafted onto the old, either increase the total amount of crime or replace an older method with a newer and more innovative one.

An interesting variant on Tarde's laws of imitation is the differential association theory of the American sociologist, Edwin H. Sutherland (1883-1950). Sutherland was a professor at the University of Minnesota, the University of Chicago, and Indiana University. His ideas in many respects parallel those of Tarde, while providing new dimensions to a theory of criminal contagion. According to Sutherland, criminal behavior is not inherited and not invented, it is learned from other persons, both by verbal communication and gestures. Most of this learning is not from movies or newspapers but occurs in intimate personal groups (cf. Tarde's first law of imitation); it includes both the techniques of crime and "the specific direction of motives, drives, rationalizations and attitudes." These last are learned from definitions of the legal codes as favorable or unfavorable. In some societies an individual is surrounded by those who believe the laws are to be observed; in others, he is surrounded by those who do not. In American society, said Sutherland, these definitions are almost always mixed, so that Americans have a culture conflict in relation to the legal codes.

The principle of differential association says that a person becomes delinquent because of an *excess* of definitions favorable to lawlessness over definitions unfavorable to such violations. Differential associations may vary in frequency, duration, priority, and intensity. Priority is important because both lawful and delinquent behavior, developed in early childhood, may persist throughout life. "Intensity" refers to the prestige of the source of the behavior pattern, whether criminal or anticriminal (cf. Tarde's second law of imitation). The learning of crime involves the same processes as any other learning. Although criminal behavior is an expression of general needs and values, it is not explained by them since noncriminal behavior is an expression of the same needs and values: thieves, for example, steal to get money, while honest laborers work.[15]

Sutherland's was a more complex theory than the earlier ones that dealt with crime by imitation. It provided an explanation for the observable fact, so often commented on, that of two boys raised in the same home in the same slum, one becomes a criminal while the other does not. Where the delinquency rate is high, said Sutherland, a boy who is athletic and gregarious is likely to come in contact with other neighborhood boys and learn delinquent behavior from them, while the shy introvert, even a psychopath, may stay at home, not learn such behavior, and consequently not become delinquent. Differential association has been criticized for not explaining why not everyone in contact with criminality becomes a criminal. But this, say his defenders, is to overlook the words "differential" and "excess." The association does not have to be with *criminals* but only with definitions of the legal codes as favorable or unfavorable, or with criminal and anticriminal patterns. One can learn criminal behavior patterns even from those who are not themselves criminals.[16]

It may be noted that on two important points Sutherland agreed with Tarde. First, he believed that learning comes from close personal contacts. Second, he agreed that the prestige of the source is important in criminal learning. Sutherland called this "intensity," and it corresponded to Tarde's second law of imitation, that fashions spread from superior to inferior—from the more prestigious person to the less prestigious—even if the admired model is a criminal. But in Sutherland's theory of differential association there was a very curious omission: He provided for imitation, but he *did not provide for innovation.* One would think, from reading Sutherland, that innovations in criminal behavior are nonexistent—that criminal conduct, somehow, in all its manifestations, goes back to the time when the mind of man runneth not to the contrary. "God hath made man upright," says Ecclesiastes "but they have sought out many inventions." Sutherland would amend this to read: "God hath made man upright, but they have sought out wicked models."

Sutherland has been criticized for a number of shortcomings. Some critics say his view of "excess of definitions" favorable to unlawful behavior is too mechanistic, if not really meaningless. Others argue that in fact many delinquents recognize that what they have done is wrong and that their moral and value judgments do not differ widely from those of the "straight" society. Still others say that differential association explains some crime, but it certainly does not explain all. And finally, of course, there is the undeniable problem of empirical verification: How do you prove—or disprove—such a theory? Nevertheless, for a period of some twenty years Edwin H. Sutherland was considered America's premier criminologist. As late as 1954, Donald R. Cressey wrote that differential association was "considered by most sociologists as the best formulation to date of a general theory of criminality,"[17] and few then would have quarreled with that statement.

However, even at the height of its influence, differential association was by no means the only sociogenic theory of crime. There were a number of others—some American in their origin and development, some with their roots in earlier European thinking. Among the former, one of the most influential on Sutherland himself was the theory of social disorganization, which arose from the immigrant experience in the United States.

18 Social Disorganization

In the early years of the twentieth century, American immigration was at flood tide. For three quarters of a century there had been successive waves of Irish, Germans, Swedes, Norwegians, Italians, Serbs, Croats, Bohemians, Poles, Russians, Armenians, Greeks, Turks, Syrians—their nationalities and numbers were legion. It was a period of unprecedented world migration. In the period 1840-1924, over forty-five million people left the Old World for North and South America, Australia, and New Zealand; and of this number, the United States received about two thirds. In the nineteenth-century United States, the average rate of population growth per decade was 29 percent.[1] By the twentieth century there was a visibly decreased enthusiasm for the newcomers, disproportionate numbers of whom were crowding American prisons. The prevailing theory was that "bad blood" was involved—that these Johnnies-come-lately were of inferior strains that would soon overwhelm the superior genetic inheritance from England. In this view, Protestant immigrants from Northern Europe were acceptable—law-abiding people, high on the evolutionary scale, who blended in well with the old American stock.[a] But the Southern and Eastern Europeans were not only racially inferior, they were a major cause of crime and delinquency. So went the popular feeling, which eventually found its outlet in the Immigration Acts of 1921 and 1924. America no longer lifted its lamp to the "huddled masses, yearning to breathe free."

It was in the midst of a spirited public debate over immigration that W.I. Thomas and Florian Znaniecki published a massive study of *The Polish Peasant in Europe and America* (1918-1920).[b] Thomas and Znaniecki looked first at the villages from which these peasants had emigrated; read the correspondence between the Old World and the New; saw how the immigrants assimilated and adjusted (or did not assimilate and adjust), and came up with what they called the concept of social disorganization. They were not talking primarily about *individual* disorganization—that is, a person's inability to organize his own life productively. What they meant by social disorganization was a decrease in the influence of existing social rules of behavior over members of a group. They had

---

[a]Needless to say, by "old American stock," Americans did not mean the native Indians, whom they had done their best to exterminate. They meant rather any white European—Scotch, Dutch, English, or Scotch-Irish—who had arrived before the Irish potato famine.

[b]William Isaac Thomas (1863-1947) was a professor at the University of Chicago. Znaniecki (1882-1958), who was a Pole, met Thomas in Europe, spent several years as a teacher at Chicago, then returned to Poznan as a professor of sociology.

seen this, of course, in the Polish peasants who had come to the United States from small farming communities. In these villages, there had been little crime. Social ties were strong, customs and standards well understood and accepted. But suddenly these Polish peasants were thrust into a different world. It was one that neither understood nor supported their customs, language, or ways of behavior.

The older immigrants were relatively resistant to social disorganization; they had never ceased to be small-town peasants, even in the slums of America. But their children were in a different situation. They were not Polish peasants, they were urban Americans, and in the strain of their rebellion and adjustment, the Polish-American communities experienced what Thomas and Znaniecki called "social disorganization." These Polish-Americans were not necessarily *personally* disorganized, the authors said; what became increasingly disorganized, rather, were the transplanted social groups that had set and enforced standards of behavior in the Old World.

Social disorganization is not an exceptional phenomenon limited to certain periods or certain societies; some of it is found always and everywhere, since always and everywhere there are individual cases of breaking social rules, cases which exercise some disorganizing influence on group institutions and, if not counteracted, are apt to multiply and to lead to a complete decay of the latter. But during periods of social stability this continuous incipient disorganization is continuously neutralized by such activities of the group as reinforce with the help of social sanctions the power of existing rules. The stability of group institutions is thus simply a dynamic equilibrium of processes of disorganization and *reorganization*. This equilibrium is disturbed when processes of disorganization can no longer be checked by any attempts to reinforce the existing rules. A period of prevalent disorganization follows, which may lead to a complete dissolution of the group.[2]

To explain any given case of social disorganization, said Thomas and Znaniecki, it is necessary to seek out the particular attitudes whose appearance manifests itself in the loss of influence of the social rules and determine the cause of these attitudes. The decay of the rules or institutions is symptomatic only—a superficial manifestation that the new attitudes are there.[3]

The theory of social disorganization was especially well suited to the American experience. The United States comprised the most diverse nationalities, religions, languages, and cultures. The English playwright Israel Zangwill called it "God's crucible, the great Melting Pot," and it was certainly that; there was a conscious national effort to break down Old World attitudes and loyalties by disparagement and ridicule. The American crucible proved to be a very hot experience indeed for those immigrant communities that had settled in the major urban centers, seeking to maintain their native culture even as they underwent Americanization. To the young, however, growing up in these ethnic enclaves, the traditional rules and customs seemed increasingly irrelevant. At the same time, the new rules had little hold on them because they were too foreign and unfamiliar. The result was a very weak sense of any kind of behavior standards, and for the immigrant communities, an increasing problem of delinquency and crime. This process, in the individual case, Thomas called "individualization," and in the case of the community, "social disorganization." It was not unlike the problem described by Tarde of Rome after the Punic wars when under the flood of immigration, exotic fashions overwhelmed the traditional customs that had held society together. The metaphors of Tarde were different from those of Thomas, but the problems described were the same.

W.I. Thomas was a member of the Chicago School of sociology, which related problems of all kinds—mental illness, delinquency, suicide—to the urban setting of twentieth-century America. But, as we have seen, it had long been noted by criminologists that there are regional and rural-urban differences in crime rates. Lombroso, in his *Crime, Its Causes and Remedies,* had pointed out that in every part of Italy there existed some village renowned for having furnished an unbroken series of criminals, specializing in a particular crime. Aschaffenburg had noted the same thing; so, in his work with French statistics, had André-Michel Guerry, who as early as 1833 had used shaded ecological maps to relate crime rates in the eighty-six departments of France to geographical and educational factors.[c] There had been similar studies in England, Wales, and Germany that showed regional differences from one part of the country to another. And, of course, all commentators on crime had long noted the greater criminality in urban areas, which from Biblical times had been considered centers of turpitude and vice.

Urban crime became the great theme of the Chicago School, and that midwestern metropolis was to prove the sociological laboratory for a generation of studies. In 1912 Sophonisba P. Breckinridge and Edith Abbott had pointed out that various parts of Chicago had widely differing rates of delinquency; most delinquents, they said, came from the west side of Chicago, particularly from the wards lying along the river and canals, the Italian quarter, the Black Belt, and the area around the steel mills and stockyards. In 1925 Ernest W. Burgess published a study claiming that in industrial societies, the characteristic urban spatial pattern is a series of concentric circles, with the business and industrial areas in the center, a blighted area farther out, then zones of two-family dwellings, single-family dwellings, and suburbs, in that order.[d] Then in 1929 Clifford R.

[c]Guerry found that the number of people accused of crime against the person had varied from one out of 2,199 inhabitants in Corsica to one out of 37,014 in Creuse. The number accused of crime against property varied from one out of 1,368 inhabitants in the Department of the Seine, to one out of 20,235 in Creuse. [André-Michel Guerry, *Essai sur la statistique morale de la France* (Paris, 1833); quoted in Clifford R. Shaw and Henry D. McKay, *Juvenile Delinquency and Urban Areas* (Chicago: University of Chicago Press, 1969), p. 5.]

[d]This spatial pattern, while characteristic of some American cities, does not apply to Europe or Latin America, where working-class districts have been typically suburban.

Shaw reported that in Chicago, rates of crime, truancy, and juvenile delinquency varied inversely with distance from the center of the city. In a study by Shaw and Henry D. McKay for the National Commission on Law Observance and Enforcement (1931), this finding was reported for a number of other cities also.[4]

In 1942 Shaw and McKay published the classic work *Juvenile Delinquency and Urban Areas.* What Shaw and McKay did was to study males brought into the Cook County Juvenile Court on delinquency charges in 1900-1906, 1917-1923, and 1927-1933. They discovered that over this thirty-three year period, a preponderance of the delinquent boys lived either in an area adjacent to the central business and industrial areas or along two forks of the Chicago River (Back of the Yards, or South Chicago). Then applying Burgess's model, they constructed a series of concentric circles, like the circles on a target, with the bullseye in the central city, and measured delinquency rates by zone and by areas within the zones. In all three periods, the highest delinquency was in Zone I (the central city), the next highest in Zone II (next to the central city), and so on, in progressive steps outward to the lowest in Zone V. Although the delinquency rates changed from one period to the next, they said, the *relationship* among the different zones remained constant: the farther out one moved from the center of Chicago, the lower the rate of juvenile delinquency. Of the twelve most delinquent areas in the city in 1900-1906, nine were among the twelve highest in 1927-1933, and all twelve were still among the high-delinquency areas of the latest period, *even though the ethnic composition of the population had, in some neighborhoods, changed completely.* During the first decade, a large proportion of delinquents were German or Irish; thirty years later they were Polish and Italian.[5]

If the nationality of these high-delinquency areas was not the constant, what was? The answer appears to be economic status.

The number of recorded delinquents corresponded with variations in family income: the poorer the neighborhood, the higher the delinquency, or as Shaw and McKay put it, "The communities with the highest rates of delinquents are occupied by those segments of the population whose position is most disadvantageous in relation to the distribution of economic, social, and cultural values."[6] This conclusion, of course, would not have surprised Bonger or any of the Marxists. Nor would Sutherland have been surprised at the further conclusion that in the better neighborhoods, children were indoctrinated with conventional values, whereas in the poorer neighborhoods, they were exposed more frequently to deviant ones. And Tarde and Sutherland would both have approved of the authors' observation that in neighborhoods with high concentrations of delinquents, criminal skills were transmitted from the older to the younger boys: "Jack-rolling, shoplifting, stealing from junkmen, and stealing automobiles are examples of offenses with well-developed techniques, passed on by one generation to the next," they reported. By tracing the names of boys who had appeared together in court (most boys committed their offenses in groups), Shaw and McKay found that some members of each delinquent group had previously taken part in crimes with older boys, providing an unbroken continuity of training from one generation to the next, much as baseball players are trained "in backyards, playgrounds and sandlots."[7]

The authors even gave support to Garofalo's Cup of Tantalus theory, reasoning that children in poor neighborhoods are exposed to the same luxury values and success patterns as those from the more affluent classes. What is different for them is that they have no legitimate means of achieving them. "Crime, in this situation, may be regarded as one of the means employed by people to acquire, or to attempt to acquire, the economic and social values generally idealized in our culture, which persons in other circumstances acquire by conventional means." And finally, Shaw and McKay saw the youths in high-delinquency areas exposed to conflicting standards and forms of behavior. On the one hand, there are the legal and social norms of the broader society—on the other, the values of a neighborhood (or peer group) whose folk-heroes are often pimps, hustlers, and racketeers.[8]

It would be difficult to call the authors' conclusions original: They echo nearly a century of sociological thinking, both European and American. Their ecological approach, however, was graphically presented. The bullseye in the central city, with its rings of concentric circles like those on a target, captured the sociological imagination. Furthermore, by laying out the high-crime areas and looking at them over a period of three decades[e] Shaw and McKay were able to make an excellent case that, not ethnic degeneracy, but social contagion was responsible for the persistence of deviant and criminal behavior in immigrant neighborhoods. They showed that although the people had changed and their ethnic backgrounds (and hence their cultures) were different at different periods, criminal and deviant behavior had somehow been transmitted intact to the newcomers as they moved in. Clearly, the finger did not point to biogenic transmission: The peasants who settled in the slums of Chicago were not criminals in the old country; if they became so in the new, it must be by some process of social learning.

Tarde would have been pleased with Shaw and McKay, who had so brilliantly documented his theory of imitation. In their work, too, Sutherland

---

[e]In 1969 a revised edition of *Juvenile Delinquency and Urban Areas* was published, including three new series of male commitments to juvenile court: 1945-1951, 1958-1962, and 1963-1966. In the new work the zones were abandoned in favor of area maps. The authors' conclusion, covering now sixty-five years of Chicago history (more than half the life of the city), was that "the most persistent finding . . . has been the absence of significant changes in the production of delinquents in most city areas relative to other city areas," but that in a few areas, rates have been increasing rapidly, while in some others, decreases have been similarly rapid. This they attributed to the assimilation of some immigrants in stable neighborhoods and the arrival of new groups in neighborhoods further removed from inner-city areas. See Clifford R. Shaw and Henry D. McKay, *Juvenile Delinquency and Urban Areas* (Chicago: University of Chicago Press, 1969), pp. 329-375.

found support for his theory of differential association. The Marxists could take comfort; the one persistent factor Shaw and McKay demonstrated through the years was the economic one: High-crime neighborhoods were poor neighborhoods. In fact, it may simply be said that almost any sociogenic theory of criminal behavior would be buttressed by a work like this, even though the authors themselves felt their study was primarily significant for offenses against property.

19 Cultures, Subcultures, and Anomie

In the United States the period of 1920 to 1970 was one of extraordinary ferment in the sociology of deviant behavior. Just as the European criminologists of the last century knew and were strongly influenced by each other, so the American criminologists of this century were in continuous contact and debate. Theirs was a more decorous discussion, certainly: To American scholars, the lively cut-and-thrust of European polemics, so often witty as well as wounding, would seem the ultimate in academic bad manners. The Europeans wrote better, argued better, and were more entertaining than their American successors; they were probably more original. But nowhere have scholars marshalled such an array of facts, pursued them as doggedly, or subjected them to such prodigies of statistical analysis as in the United States. The result is that anyone hoping to give a brief synopsis of these sociogenic theories is faced with a very difficult task.

There are almost as many American theories of what causes crime as there are American automobiles. They overlap and complement (and sometimes disagree with) each other, but they have one thing in common: They do not, like the positivists, find the causes of danger in the offender himself, in some supposed biological anomaly, but rather in the environment that shaped him. In short, what they are concerned with is not so much the dangerous offender as *the dangerous society.* This is not to say that the sociological school of criminology denies the influence of biological and personality differences; it does say that looking at the criminal problem as a whole, these criminologists find the major causes of dangerous behavior—and the only ones we can do much about—in society itself.

But what do we mean when we talk of the "causes" of crime? The Swedish-American criminologist Thorsten Sellin[a] in his *Culture Conflict and Crime* (1938) said that "cause" has been applied to widely different concepts. He quotes the Scottish philosopher Dugald Stewart (1792) as saying; "When we speak of one thing being the cause of another, all that we mean is that the two are constantly conjoined, so that when we see the one we may expect the other. These conjunctions we learn from experience alone."[1] Applying this concept to crime, Sellin said that when we speak of "causes" we mean merely "the

[a]Johan Thorsten Sellin (b. 1896) received his primary and secondary education in Sweden. He came to the United States in 1913, graduated from Augustana College, and completed his graduate education at the University of Pennsylvania, where he spent his life as a professor. Sellin is considered the dean of the Philadelphia school of criminology.

131

necessary antecedents and the establishment of constants in their relations to criminal conduct."[2]

The fact that crime and criminals are defined by statute, he continued, is *the* crucial problem in criminology, because science does not recognize such arbitrary boundaries. The social values protected by criminal law are inevitably those of the dominant interest group. There may, therefore, be a clash between the law and the majority local customs of the "submissive" group. For example, the laws of Mexico copy European models, but Indian peasant culture may be in conflict with them. Also, what is criminal today may be legal tomorrow, and vice versa. The only safe generalization one may draw from history is that everything a state prohibits today will not be prohibited tomorrow, unless there is complete social stagnation, an experience thus far unknown to the social historian.

The variability in defining crime, said Sellin, should raise questions in the mind of the social scientist. An unqualified acceptance of *legal* definitions violates a fundamental criterion of science, which should be based on the intrinsic character of the material and on the properties in that material that are assumed to be universal. Therefore, data must be selected and classified independent of their *legal* form. In other words, the social scientist must throw off the shackles of the criminal law. Had psychiatry been thus confined only to the study of those declared incompetent by courts of law, it would have learned very little.[3]

Man, born into a particular culture, Sellin said, is biologically equipped to receive and adapt knowledge, ideas, instructions, and precepts. Thus cultural elements, embodied in the mind, become personality elements, and the sum total of all such elements may be called "personality." There is no doubt that personality rests on a biological foundation which fixes the limit of personality development and thus influences the expression of the latter in social behavior. "If all individuals were biologically alike and subjected to identical cultural influences," he said, "all personalities would be identical. If all individuals were biologically alike, but each subjected to different cultural influences, each would present unique personality configurations." The behavioral scientist is faced with the problem of offering scientific descriptions of growth and manifestations of unique personalities in unique biological individuals. But the scientific method cannot be applied to unique phenomena: It can only deal with classes and types.[4]

People faced with decisions are influenced by the norms that mark their culture. Conduct, in short, has been *socially conditioned*. But the more complex a culture becomes, the more normative groups there are within that culture and the greater the chance their norms will fail to agree. They may overlap; they may also conflict. Conduct norms are universal. They are not the creation of any one group; they are not confined with political boundaries; they are not necessarily embodied in law.

From one point of view, abnormal conduct is merely a violation of a group norm; from another, it is the expression of a personality which in its growth and development has incorporated the cultural elements leading to such conduct. It is the task of etiological research, therefore, to formulate generalizations that permit us to distinguish the violator from the conformist in terms of personality structure or growth process. "The goal of the scientist should be the arrival at generalizations which would state that if a person of type A is placed in a life situation of type B, he will violate the norm governing that life situation."[5]

All culture conflicts are conflicts of meanings: social values, interests, norms. There can be no clashes between the material objects of a culture. Our industrial and mercantile society shows a multitude of competitive interests and groups. Interpersonal relations are poorly defined. Social anonymity, a confusion of rules and standards, and the vast extension of control agencies characterize a society that tries to enforce rules of behavior that could be enforced only if they really grew out of emotionally felt community need. To a large number of people, certain life situations are such that no matter what response they make, they will violate the norms of *some* social group. People are expected to limit their greed yet compete vigorously for the goods of this world; they must acquire property and wealth but be altruistic and generous; or, as Alfred North Whitehead once put it, "*Thou shalt not murder; but tradition approves all forms of competition.*" Society also expects people to respect the truth, but to tell white lies, and to have strong normal sex drives, yet inhibit them. And, of course, for immigrants, conflicting cultural norms may pose special dilemmas. The Sicilian father in New York kills the seducer of his daughter because this is what Sicilian family honor demands. He has not assimilated the new cultural norms, and mentally he cannot accept them.[6]

Thorsten Sellin's theory of culture conflict was not original with him. It was in part at least a development from the social disorganization studies of the Chicago school and may also have owed something to the Freudian theories of culture conflict as a struggle between deeply rooted biological urges that demand expression and culturally created rules that thwart this expression.[7] In any case, *Culture Conflict and Crime* was the classic exposition of this theory, which is always associated with Sellin's name. It provided one of the three sociological explanations for the observed differences in crime rates among various nativity groups in the United States. The other two were that differential crime rates are caused by the migration of people from rural to urban environments and/or by moving from well-organized, homogeneous societies to disorganized and heterogeneous ones.[8] These three explanations may be viewed as either complementary, overlapping, or alternative, depending on one's point of view.

A related sociogenic theory ascribes the growth of crime in modern society to what Emile Durkheim called "anomie." Webster defines anomie as "a state of society in which normative standards of conduct and belief are weak or lacking; also, a similar condition in an individual commonly characterized by disorientation, anxiety and isolation."[9] In his classic work *Suicide* (1897), Durkheim had contrasted a hierarchical, traditional society where everyone knew his place and was content with it, with a society in rapid transition. When there are sudden economic disasters or when "beneficent but abrupt transitions" provide growing wealth, the relative scale of values between classes and people is upset: "The limits are unknown between the possible and the impossible, what is just and what is unjust, legitimate claims and hopes and those which are immoderate." Appetites become disoriented, desires increase. This occurs at the very moment traditional rules and standards have lost their authority. Passions become undisciplined precisely when they need more disciplining. Prosperity may grow, but ambition always exceeds it. Where poverty requires self-discipline, wealth, by "exalting the individual, may arouse the spirit of rebellion which is the very source of immorality."[10]

In his work Durkheim was explaining the high suicide rate in developed societies as compared to backward ones. Robert K. Merton, in *Social Theory and Social Structure* (1949), applied Durkheim's concept of anomie to "aberrant behavior." To Merton, "aberrant behavior" was not limited to crime but included a whole series of responses to anomie from vagrancy to conformism; he termed it "a symptom of dissociation between culturally prescribed aspirations and socially structured avenues for realizing these aspirations." No society, he said, lacks some kind of norms to govern conduct; but societies do differ in the extent to which "the folkways, mores and institutional controls are effectively integrated with the goals which stand high in the hierarchy of cultural values." When ends are emphasized, so that all successful means are accepted, there develops the normlessness that Durkheim called "anomie." Thus when the emphasis in sports is on winning, not on rules, cheating and violence become rampant. The United States, said Merton, is an example of a society where there is an emphasis on success without an equivalent emphasis on the institutional means for achieving it. Money has been consecrated as a value in itself. However acquired, fraudulently or institutionally, it can be used to purchase the same goods and services.[11] Dollars, in other words, carry no odor.

Merton's anomie, Garofalo's Cup of Tantalus, and Sutherland's differential association theories come together in the works of Albert Cohen, Richard Cloward, and Lloyd Ohlin on the delinquency of young lower-class males whose opportunities for advancement through legitimate channels are blocked. According to Cohen (*Delinquent Boys*, 1955), the delinquent subculture provides a group solution for "status frustration." This subculture is found in the institution of the gang, and it explains crime that is nonutilitarian, malicious, and negativistic—in other words, crime "for the hell of it." We usually assume, says Cohen, that stealing is a means to an end. Unquestionably, some is. But in many delinquent acts there is a kind of *malice* involved. "The delinquent subculture is not only a set of rules, a design for living which is different from or indifferent to or even in conflict with the norms of the 'respectable' adult society. It . . . is defined by its 'negative polarity' to those norms. That is, the delinquent subculture takes its norms from the larger culture but turns them upside down."[12] On the other hand, Ohlin and Cloward (*Delinquency and Opportunity*, 1961) see gang criminality as a means to wealth or power for those excluded from the "opportunity structure." In fact, "certain forms of delinquency are essential requirements for the performance of the dominant roles supported by the subculture."[13]

Another related view is that there are certain subcultures in our society characterized by religious peculiarity, poverty, crime, ethnic origin, or whatever. Said Marvin E. Wolfgang and Franco Ferracuti in *The Subculture of Violence* (1967): "Just as man is born into a culture, so he may be born into a subculture." Examples of subcultures include the Amish, the Mormons, delinquents, prisoners, ethnic groups, and social classes. A subculture is only partly different from its parent culture. In a heterogeneous society the individual may participate in a number of subcultures as long as they do not conflict or as long as he can stand the conflict. Among the many subcultures that might be defined, say the authors, is a *subculture of violence*. It may be found in such countries as Colombia, such regions as Sardinia, or in the lower-class social structure of many countries, where physical aggression is seen as a manifestation of masculinity and toughness. The existence of a subculture of violence may be demonstrated by examining those groups and individuals who experience the highest rates of violence. People are integrated into this subculture by the "differential association" described by Sutherland.[14]

To this thesis of a subculture of violence, Wolfgang and Ferracuti appended the following corollary propositions: (1) No subculture can be totally different from, or in conflict with, the parent culture. (2) The actors in such a subculture do not express violence in all situations. (3) Their willingness to resort to violence in a variety of situations emphasizes "the penetrating and diffusive character of this culture theme." (4) The ethos of violence is most prominent from late adolescence to middle age. (5) The member who fails to live up to the gang's conflict requirement is pushed out. (6) The development of violent attitudes involves learned behavior and a process of differential learning, association, or identification. (7) The use of violence in a subculture is not necessarily viewed as illicit; members do not feel guilty about their aggression.[15]

The social criminologists we have been discussing in these last three chapters share a perspective that is especially, although not uniquely, American. However much they owed to the great European sociologists, they owed even more to the American experience of urbanization and acculturation. Only Israel has provided as remarkable a laboratory for the social scientist as the United States. What happens when pockets of rural peasant cultures seek assimilation into an urban society that is alien to them in language, technology, customs, and religion? The subject has fascinated two generations of American sociologists, and their studies are so many that even those dealing with crime are impossible to summarize, let alone do justice to. One writer may differ in emphasis from another. But whether one calls the problem "social disorganization" or "anomie" and the groups "cultures" or "subcultures," and whether one calls the learning process "imitation," "social learning," or "differential association," there is a core of thinking common to these theories. They all see some conflict between the culture of the group and the standards and norms of the greater society in which it has its being. They see the process of rapid secular change as creating disorientation. They see poverty not as an economic issue but as a social problem that affects the lives, thinking, and opportunities of its victims. And, finally, they see crime and delinquency as one of the natural responses to these life conditions.

For American criminologists of this school, most criminals are normal people who have been conditioned by abnormal life situations. They would not deny that *some* criminals are biologically abnormal; they simply do not concern themselves with them because they are sociologists, not physicians. Their concept of a "dangerous offender" is that of a normal human being who has been so conditioned by his life and environment that he has become dangerous to others. As for Lombroso's "born criminal," he has no more objective validity for them than has the Abominable Snow Man; those who follow his tracks through the wilderness they view as romancers and not serious scientists.

20 Societal Reactions and Self-concept

Among the many sociogenic theories of criminality that have been popular in the United States are a number revolving around societal reactions. According to these theories, the way those around us react to our behavior determines whether we shall be seen as deviants and ultimately forced into playing that role. Or, as Shakespeare might have said, no one is either good or bad but thinking makes him so.

In its most popular version, the process works like this. A small child gets into trouble; eventually he comes to be known as a "juvenile delinquent," at first by the neighbors, then by police and juvenile authorities, until finally he accepts this view of himself and becomes what others believe him to be. This theory has been widely accepted, not only by American sociologists, but by psychologists and social workers as well. Its great strength is that it conforms so well with popular observations. Its weakness, of course, is that it leads to a chicken-and-the-egg argument: Are people labeled as "delinquents" because they behave badly, or do they behave badly because they are labeled as "delinquents"?

The consequence of this labeling process Edwin H. Lemert called "secondary deviation." According to Lemert, delinquency has no substantive meaning independent of the judgment (and reaction) of others. Primary deviation represents a series of deviant acts—heavy drinking, fighting, shoplifting, or whatever—that do not affect an individual's concept of his own real self. But if he meets with penalties, rejection, and hostility, he may ultimately accept for himself the role of deviant. "Secondary deviation is deviant behavior, or social roles based upon it, which becomes a means of defense, attack, or adaptation to the overt and covert problems created by the societal reaction to primary deviation. In effect, the original 'causes' of the deviation recede and give way to the central importance of the disapproving, degradational, and isolating reactions of society."[1]

Stigmatization, he said, has long been practiced by society in such rituals as drumming the coward out of the regiment or administering the pauper's oath, but its success is to be found less in the drama of enactment than in its consequences. To be successful, stigmatization must be disseminated. Lemert, quoting William Lecky, points out that in the nineteenth century an unchaste woman, *once labeled unchaste*, was forced by the resulting stigma into a life of prostitution.[a,2] Accord-

---

[a]The relentless nature of this stigmatization has long been the subject of literature and drama. In Edith Wharton's *The House of Mirth*, Lily Bart, the heroine, is seen coming out of a man's apartment where she has innocently been taking tea. As a result, she is stigmatized as unchaste and unmarriageable by her social set. The irony of her destruction is driven home by the fact that among its chief agents are the "fast" women of upper-class society who have avoided having their indiscretions noticed.

137

ing to Lemert, "The general principle at work is a simple one: when others decide that a person is *non grata*, dangerous, untrustworthy, or morally repugnant, they do something to him, often unpleasant, which is not done to other people." In modern societies these controls are exercised through "welfare, punitive, or ameliorative agencies."[3]

A similar view has been expressed by Howard Becker, namely, that "deviance" is not a quality of the act a person commits but a consequence of what is done to him: "The deviant is one to whom that label has successfully been applied; deviant behavior is behavior that people so label."[4] This is a view that became popular in the 1960s. Some sociologists carried it further than others, asserting that *all* criminality is a matter of labeling. Said the Israeli criminologist, Shlomo Shoham:

By the process of elimination we have concluded that divinity and sin, justice and injustice, morality and immorality cannot be fruitfully related to crime, delinquency and deviation. This may uphold our hypothesis that the main difference between crime and honesty, deviation and conformity, is a formal, external one. *A criminal or an antisocial person is one who is branded as such by a group (or an individual who has power to do so) and treated accordingly.* [Emphasis added.]

The stigma of conviction, said Shoham, limits the individual's opportunities; his role and status are thereby affected. He may then seek the company of other outcasts where his stigma becomes a status symbol. "The Mark of Cain is, therefore, primarily an exercise of power by the branders in putting tags on individuals or groups who 'don't fit in.' " These square pegs are "pushed and run over hard and fast by the branding wheels."[5]

A related idea is that of social identity transformations. Theodore Sarbin has said that assaultive or violent behavior that leads us to label a man "dangerous" is the predictable outcome of the degradation that transforms a man's social identity in prison. Identity transformation puts him in a condition of strain where he must either accept the identity of a nonperson, a brute, or engage in behavior that radically alters the social system and reverses the *dominium*, or power relationship, thus giving himself a more acceptable social identity. Such a solution is perceived as dangerous by those whose grant of power is thus repudiated.

The transformations of social identity that occur in prison, if extreme enough, said Sarbin, may set the stage for extreme and dangerous behavior. When a person is cast in the role of a nonperson, he is denied a social identity. The ultimate derogation, to be labeled and treated as a nonperson, arises out of the valuational practices of significant persons in one's society who have the legitimate power to declare such valuations. Attitudes, conventions, customs of the police, jailers, court employees, and prison personnel contribute to shaping the social identity of prisoners. Instances of dangerous conduct follow from practices that transform a man's social identity downward and leave no room for substitute identities. Thus the dangerous offender is an outcome of the institutions we have created to manage him.[6]

A theory related to labeling is that of the self-fulfilling prophecy. W.I. Thomas once set forth the theorem that if men define situations as real, they are real in their consequences. According to Robert K. Merton, prophecies and predictions tend to become an integral part of a situation and affect its development; predictions of a bank collapse may cause a run on a bank and bring about its insolvency; predictions of war often lead to war. The self-fulfilling prophecy is, at first, a false definition of the situation. But by evoking new behavior, it may bring the prediction to pass; social beliefs father social reality. The fact that the initial idea may be false does not mean that the truth may dispel it, any more than paranoiac delusions will vanish when the patient is informed that they are groundless. "If psychic ills could be cured merely by the dissemination of truth, the psychiatrists of this country would be suffering from technological unemployment rather than from overwork."[7]

The self-fulfilling prophecy states that if a teacher believes a student will do well, he will do well. If the teacher believes that the student will fail, he will fail. If others predict that a boy will turn out bad, become delinquent, end in prison, he will do that—not because his destiny was written in the stars, but because the expectations communicated to him, the treatment he is accorded because of those expectations, make the prophecy come true.

Simon Dinitz, Frank Scarpitti, and Walter Reckless thought that the basic mechanism involved in delinquency is the person's concept of himself. In a study of lower-class white boys in a high-delinquency area of Columbus, Ohio, the authors sought to answer the question, Why do some children in such neighborhoods, with all the disadvantages of association and environment, nevertheless turn out well, while their classmates become dropouts, delinquents, and criminals? By carefully testing the children for self-concept, then observing them over a period of four years, they concluded that a good self-concept, "undoubtedly a product of favorable socialization, veers slum boys away from delinquency, while a poor self-concept gives the slum boy no resistance to deviancy. . . ." In their view, a good concept of self acts as an inner buffer or containment against negative influences in the environment, steering the individual "toward middle-class values, and to awareness of possibility of upward movement in the opportunity structure."[8]

These observations are consonant with both the labeling theory and the theory of the self-fulfilling prophecy. It is conceivable—and perhaps, given the nature of social interaction, inevitable—that a child who is seen by others as "deviant" and who is so treated would respond by developing a poor concept of himself. In such a case, society becomes the mirror that reflects back the image others hold of him. It is this image that he sees and incorporates into his own self-concept.

140

All the theories discussed in this chapter deal with a process by which sporadic and occasional behavior that others consider "deviant" is transmuted into the full-blown delinquent or criminal persona—from the action to the *thing*, so to speak. As seen by these sociologists, the process is both social and psychological. It applies as well to the successes of this world as to its failures, to the good students as to the dunderheads; not only the role of *homo delinquens*, but of doctor, artist, scholar, even saint, is created by the social process, and the interplay between what you think I am, and how I come to see myself.

We know what it is to be a doctor, an artist, a scholar; but what is it to be "deviant"? Deviant by what standards, and from whose norms? Dinitz, Scarpitti, and Reckless answered explicitly the question most sociologists do not bother to ask: deviant from *middle-class values.* "Good" self-concepts are those that set a person on the ladder of upward mobility in the "legitimate opportunity system"—bad ones are those that do not.[9]

It is precisely this tacit standard of values, which underlies so many sociogenic theories, that has been challenged by the "new criminology," as its adherents call it.[b] The new criminology, otherwise known as conflict theory, is not all that new; but in the past few years it has mounted a powerful attack against establishment sociologists, including the leadership of the American Sociological Association, asking the same questions we heard from Engels and Bonger, Rusche, and Kirchheimer: Is what we call "crime" merely an aspect of class war? Do those who control the state apparatus define delinquency to suit their own interests? Why is violence by the police more acceptable than violence by the poor? What is the legitimacy of law? Old questions, but in the revolving door of criminologic fashion, they are once more the subject of hot debate. The conflict theorists, many of whom are Marxists (and some of whom are not), do not always agree among themselves. They do, however, share a common point of view, and it will be considered in the next chapter.

---

[b]Cf., Lombroso's *Scuola Nuova*, or New School, of criminology. The trouble with new schools is that it is impossible to be "new" very long (although it is exhilarating while it lasts).

21 Crime, Power, and Conflict

In America the rules for academic discourse prescribe a kind of bloodless disputation, unemphatic in tone, scientific in appearance (if not always in nature), and limited to the scholarly journals, which is to say, to an audience of one's peers. If these are the norms, then the late C. Wright Mills, professor of sociology at Columbia, was one of the most striking "deviants" of his generation. Dennis H. Wrong of New York University called his work "an uneven blend of journalism, sociology, and moral indignation."[1] Philip Rieff of the University of Pennsylvania said Mills was one of the "caretakers of the socialist polemical tradition . . . the angry man of American social letters" and a "virtuoso heretic striking blindly at where dogma used to be."[2] On the other hand, his Columbia colleague Robert S. Lynd called him "bold and candid,"[3] and economist Paul Sweezy thought that C. Wright Mills "stands out as a man of courage and imagination, an iconoclast who cares little for the sacred cows of university administrators and foundation trustees." He was, said Sweezy, "an innovator who wants to get along with the important business of understanding the United States of America in the middle of the twentieth century."[4]

Who was C. Wright Mills, and why did he attract such lightning from the academic community? Mills could fairly be described as a polemical sociologist. He not only challenged the orthodoxies of his discipline, he did so with so much verve and color that his most famous works—*White Collar* (1951) and *The Power Elite* (1956)—became best sellers. It is hard to say whether he was resented more for his attacks on accepted dogma or for the popularity of his writings. To the academic community, Mills was a maverick in a time of high conformity, and if they attacked *him*, it was only because he attacked them first.

In 1943, with the ink scarcely dry on his doctoral diploma, Mills published an article in the American Journal of Sociology that he titled "The Professional Ideology of Social Pathologists." In it he took aim at American sociologists who defined social problems as deviations from some unexamined "norms." By defining norms as the standards of "society," he said, social pathologists assumed these norms, and in fact, tacitly sanctioned them. " 'Socialization' is either undefined, used as a moral epithet, or implies norms which are themselves without definition." The works of such writers was of such a low level of abstraction, he said scornfully, that it did not permit an examination of the norms themselves, or ask why they are transgressed.[5]

Mills thought that most social pathologists were unable to see class structures because they came from small towns or farms, where class is not a

141

determinant of conduct, rather than from cities, where it is. Unable to perceive anything but a scatter of situations, they thus viewed the problems of immigrants as those of assimilation, instead of class ceilings. Because of their organic view of society and their emphasis on social process, Mills said, they either missed dislocations altogether or saw them as signs of "pathology." Social pathologists typically used terms like "society," "the social order," "mores," and the like, not only descriptively but *normatively*. "Social," to them, was a good term, in contrast with such pejorative expressions as "individualism," "selfishness," "lack of altruism," and "antisocial sentiments." They failed to understand pathological behavior in either a structural or a statistical sense; otherwise, how could one explain the claim that pathological conditions "abound" in the city? If conditions "abound," how can they be abnormal?[6]

For the concept of "maladjustment," so dear to his fellow sociologists, he had only contempt. Nowhere, he said, did they define the social type within which one is maladjusted. The whole concept of "adaptation" is quasibiological, drawing prestige from the vogue of evolutionism. Writers using these terms assume the desirability of certain goals, then suggest techniques or means to attain them. They never ask themselves whether the economically underprivileged can possibly reach these goals "without drastic shifts in the basic institutions which channel and promote them."[7]

C. Wright Mills was not a criminologist, but his concepts were to influence sociological criminology through the development of "conflict theory." To him, America was run by a self-perpetuating power elite of the corporate rich, the military, and the political directorate. Below them was a middle level of power, composed of special-interest groups struggling among themselves for wealth and position. Finally, below both of these levels came the "mass society," the people who don't count, a class without traditions, unity, or power. This is not a Marxist view, because it deals not with the ownership of the means of production, but with the ownership of *power*. But it has similar implications for the criminal law. It calls into question the legitimacy of a legal system enacted and administered by a power elite and imposed from above. It asks of law the question *for* whom—*to* whom? Is law the reflection of special interests, a kind of sanctioned force against the poor and helpless?

Mills was not a Marxist; he was a maverick who fell chronologically between such Marxists of the 1930s as Rusche and Kirchheimer and the conflict school (both Marxist and non-Marxist) of the fifties and sixties. With his iconoclastic views, his scorn for such concepts as "the social order," and his refusal to accept a term like "deviation" without specifying norms, he swam very much against the mainstream of American sociology. But American scholars were coming under fire for other reasons, especially their excessive addiction to the meaningless accumulation and refinement of data. T.H. Marshall,[a] in a 1949 inaugural

---

[a]T.H. Marshall, a distinguished sociologist and economic historian, taught at Trinity College, Cambridge, the University of London, and the London School of Economics. He was at one time president of the International Sociological Association.

lecture at the London School of Economics which he called "Sociology at the Crossroads," said that there are two paths in sociology—the "way into the stars" (by which he meant the elaboration of broad theoretical concepts as a substitute for research) and the "way into the sands," the expenditure of great energy on the indiscriminate collection of facts with "an inadequate sense of the purpose for which they are being collected." The Americans, he said, had chosen the way into the sands because of the vast number of sociologists "looking for something to do." He cited statistics to show that in 1940-1941 there were in the United States 441 "institutes" with departments of sociology, and that these offered a total of 5,260 courses in the subject. It is one thing to say that measurement should be used when there are relevant data to measure; it is quite another to hold that everything measurable is worth measuring. The theoretical sociologist, he warned, may become a slave to his concepts—the empirical sociologist to his methods. It is one thing to say "Give us the tools and we will finish the job"; but it is hard to respond eagerly to the scholar who says, "Give me a job, and I will spend the rest of my life polishing the tools."[8]

Thus mainstream American sociology (and with it, sociological criminology) came under fire for being too hypnotized by facts, too concerned with the refinements of statistical methods, too blind to the realities of class, power, and poverty, and too uncritically accepting of norms and values that were essentially those of small-town, middle-class America. This dissatisfaction was, at first, very much a minority view. American criminology was clearly the busiest and most productive in the world. It was widely viewed as a branch of sociology rather than as a branch of law. It did indeed spend a great deal of time polishing its statistical tools and using them to measure, count, study, and amass data. Although on the continent of Europe, most professors of criminology remained, as they always had been, lawyers or forensic psychiatrists, the younger European sociologists, too, were beginning to follow the "way into the sands." For them, the theories of such figures as Durkheim and Max Weber were by the early 1950s considered stale and fusty.[9]

It was at this juncture that conflict theory attracted adherents among the Young Turks of sociology. One of the seminal works in conflict theory was Ralf Dahrendorf's *Class and Class Conflict in Industrial Society*, first published in Germany in 1957.[b] According to Dahrendorf, there have been throughout history two views of how societies cohere. One is the view of the *consensus omnium*—Rousseau's *volonté générale*, or "general will." The other is the view that coherence and order are founded on force and constraint, the domination-subjection school. The integration theory Dahrendorf called "Utopian": the coercion theory he called "rationalist." Marx was a rationalist. His dictum was,

---

[b]The work had its origin in a small informal group of young sociologists from divers countries who met in the Thursday Evening Seminar at the London School of Economics in 1952-1954. It was published as *Soziale Klassen und Klassenkonflikt in der Industriellen Gesellschaft* and was translated and expanded by Dahrendorf for the American edition of 1959.

"Without conflict, no progress; that is the law which civilization has followed to the present day."[10]

According to Dahrendorf, the integration theory had predominated in recent years. But, in fact, society is Janus-headed: There are problems for which each view is adequate, others for which only one is. The integrationists believe that every society is relatively persistent, stable, and well integrated. Coercion theory holds, however, that every society is at every point subject to processes of change, and that it displays at every point dissensus and conflict. In this view society is based on the coercion of some by others. This means that authority relations are always those of superordination and subordination. Authority relations are supported by legal systems, but they also generate conflict groups.[11]

What conflict theory meant for criminology was a view of the criminal law as a weapon in the age-old struggle among groups holding, or seeking to attain, power. In his description of conflict theory (1958), George B. Vold said that "the whole political process of law making, law breaking and law enforcement becomes a direct reflection of deep-seated and fundamental conflicts between interest groups and their more general struggles for the control of the police power of the state."[c] In this view a juvenile gang is merely a minority group that is out of sympathy with the dominant majority. Criminal acts are behavior on the "front-line fringes" of groups struggling for power, just as are revolutions, racial violence, and jurisdictional conflicts between unions. To conflict theorists, criminological theories based on individual responsibility are no more germane in such situations than holding an individual soldier responsible for violence done in battle.[12]

Where adherents of this theory differ from the orthodox Marxian criminologists is in their emphasis on power and status relationships rather than economics. But they agree with Marx in seeing society as based, not on the general will, but on force, constraint, and domination. On the other hand, while most American sociologists (and sociological criminologists) view culture conflict as a fact, they nevertheless see society as an integrated social structure, based on consensus, and seeking, if not always achieving, stability. These two views result in strikingly different conclusions.

Traditionally, law has been seen as a means of settling disputes and promoting justice. But if law is no more than a weapon for the maintenance of a power relationship, then its moral foundations are called into question. In his "Law as a Weapon in Social Conflict" (1976), Austin T. Turk, himself a conflict theorist, said that the "empirical reality of law" seems to be "that it is a set of resources for which people contend and with which they are better able to promote their own ideas and interests against others. . . ." This conception of law as power, he said, is methodologically superior to the conception of law as a

---

[c]It should be noted that Vold is here merely describing, and not necessarily subscribing to, conflict theory.

conflict regulator. "Instead of asking *how* law regulates conflict, the investigator is encouraged to ask *whether* law regulates or generates conflict. . . ."[13]

Another conflict theorist, Richard Quinney, in *The Social Reality of Crime* (1970), proposed the following analysis of what we call "crime." (1) "Crime is a definition of human conduct that is created by authorized agents in a politically organized society." The definition is conferred by some persons on the acts of others: thus *crime is created.* The greater the number of definitions, the greater the amount of crime. (2) What is defined as crime is what conflicts with the interests of those in power. (3) Crime is defined by those with power to shape the law. The more the behavior of the powerless conflicts with their interests, the greater the probability that criminal definitions will be applied. (4) Crime is relative to the behavior patterns of the group that formulates criminal definitions; thus lower-class behavior is more likely to be defined as criminal than upper class. (5) Concepts of criminality depend on the portrayal of crime in personal and mass communications. (6) In summary, "The social reality of crime is constructed by the formulation and application of criminal definitions, the development of behavior patterns related to criminal definitions, and the construction of criminal conceptions."[14]

In *Crime and Privilege* (1975), Barry Krisberg put the matter even more baldly. Crime, he said, is related to the maintenance of privilege. The whole concept of crime deflects attention from "the violence and social damage that those with power inflict upon the mass of the people in order to keep them subordinate and oppressed." Citing Balzac's dictum that "behind every great fortune there is a crime," Krisberg claimed that the history of wealth in America is the story of "relentless fraud, violence, and theft." The great fortunes of the nineteenth century were produced by the "sordid and brutal exploitation of labor." To Krisberg culture is a system of guidelines for behavior that rewards those who conform and censures those who break the rules. "Cultural domination may be anchored in appeals to tradition, in claims of the superiority of the ruling clique, or . . . in appeals to abstract legal systems. . . ." The elite use their power to enforce their belief system, but to ensure its success and long life, they first try to convince the population of its correctness.[15]

With conflict theory we have, in a sense, come full circle back to nineteenth-century Marxism. By defining criminal law as a tool to control the powerless, this theory strips it of any pretense to moral authority. Conflict theory was quite popular during the turbulent sixties when masses of young whites and blacks were involved in a wholesale, violent challenge to existing laws and institutions. It received support in newspapers, magazine articles, and such quasipopular books as *Struggle for Justice,*[16] which stressed the anomaly that while all classes commit crimes, only the poor, seemingly, are ever punished. Or as a black inmate in The Tombs once demanded of a *New York Times* reporter, "How come you're always reading about the Mafia, but all you see in prison is black faces?"[17]

It is this kind of question that today haunts the criminal justice system of the United States and all democracies. Why are our prisons stuffed to overflowing with the losers of society? By offering us an ideological answer, conflict theory elects the way, not into the sands, but into the stars. That answer may be correct, or it may be partial, misguided, even perverse. Nevertheless, like their nineteenth-century predecessors, conflict theorists pose a tough challenge to the justice of a social order that all too often selects the powerless and the deprived to be a full, perfect, and sufficient sacrifice for the sins of the whole world.

22 Some Reflections on the Social Science of Criminology

Those who have followed the narrative thus far must be aware how numerous and diverse are the etiological theories of crime and how difficult to summarize—none more so than those of societal causation, which would require a large volume to do justice to their variety. We have seen the criminal celebrated as a soldier in the class struggle (Engels and Turati), and as the victim of familial neglect (Channing), bad example (Tarde and Aschaffenburg), differential association (Sutherland), social disorganization (Thomas and Znaniecki), anomie (Merton), culture conflict (Sellin), delinquent subcultures (Cohen et al.), class oppression (Loria and Bonger), or powerlessness and lack of status (the conflict theorists). Because of the theoretical nature of the present work, it has not been possible even to summarize the many empirical studies by scholars in this field. There was as much truth as humor in T.H. Marshall's lament about the number of sociologists engaged in the pursuit of data.

If causation is really no more than an observed relationship between two sets of facts—or as Dugald Stewart put it, if all we mean when we speak of one thing causing another is that the two are constantly conjoined, so that when we see the one, we may expect the other—then it becomes clear that serious difficulties attend sociogenic theories of crime. Those who study society are never dealing with two simple sets of facts. They are concerned, rather, on the one hand with the human personality, in all its diversity and unpredictability, and on the other with milieus so tangled and complex that causation loses meaning.

Sociogenic theories of crime have been attacked from many points of view. The criminal justice system of all countries follows the classical tradition, which assumes that men are free agents and that when they transgress the law, they deserve to be punished. There is nothing that makes the average law-enforcement officer more impatient than claims that the criminal is the "victim" of society. If police, prosecutors, and judges accept any determinism at all, it is the biological determinism that claims some people are by nature too dangerous to be at large.

The positivists did not necessarily ignore the social component in criminality, but they felt that it was insufficient to explain what Ferri dubbed "the born criminal." Both classical and positivist criminology accepted punishment—the former because the criminal deserved it, the latter because he needed to be somehow removed from society. But as we have seen, classical theory thinks punishment should fit the crime, and positivism, that punishment should fit the criminal. Societal causation theories, on the other hand, raise the gravest

147

questions about punishment. If society is the criminal, why should the individual malefactor be punished? It is the very nature of this question that has caused sociologists to be so vehemently attacked. Their views seem contrary to common sense; they are widely dismissed as "bleeding hearts."

But sociological criminology has been criticized on other grounds as well. In *Art and Prudence* (1937), Mortimer J. Adler, the philosopher and neo-Thomist, was critical of both its methodology and its unexamined ethical and philosophical assumptions. The first mistake the social scientists make, he thought, is trying to create a science of human behavior in the sense in which the natural sciences exist. Echoing both Christian theology and the classical criminologists, Adler claimed that man has free will, and *reason* is the first cause of human behavior, which is therefore essentially contingent and relatively unpredictable. Human behavior ultimately lies in the field of opinion, even though one can say what, under certain circumstances, and in the light of their characters, men will *probably* do.[1]

Consider by contrast, he said, the case of the natural sciences. Our knowledge of natural phenomena is based on the fact that natural changes are *involuntary*. Because human behavior is voluntary change, its phenomena are indeterminate, and scientific knowledge about them impossible. Human behavior can be investigated and generalizations drawn; in that sense, one can speak of a "science" of human behavior. "But this science is much more like opinion than natural science," said Adler: "its conclusions can never be better than probable." It is not enough for social scientists to be speciously technical about what is already widely assumed—to document the obvious. "Thus, little of what has been accomplished by research in the field of criminology has improved upon the state of common and expert opinion—the 'unscientific' opinion of men experienced in dealing with criminals. At best, research has been confirmatory of our doubt about any factor or set of factors as causative of crime."[2]

Adler accused social scientists of "methodological incompetence," saying that their work was not only inferior to the natural sciences with regard to the status of their conclusions but that "in their short career they have again and again transgressed or ignored the simplest canons of scientific procedure." Their greatest offense, he thought, was that in the investigative study of human behavior, they had suppressed "its intimate affiliation with such normative disciplines as ethics and politics," seeking by this means to avoid all questions of value and all criteria of moral judgment. Yet by making normative judgments, the social scientist does appeal to principles beyond the domain of pure science, concealing "this duplicity from himself as well as from his audience." Social scientists "moralize surreptitiously" while denying the principles of morality. "Empirical psychology and social science, insofar as they attempt to investigate human behavior, would better achieve the status of science if they recognized their limitations in the speculative order, and their subordination to ethics and politics, in the practical order."[3]

Adler's criticism is not relevant to Marxism, which has always been political, or to conflict theory, which leveled much the same charge of unexamined normative assumptions against mainstream sociology. That charge may be well founded. It is difficult to divorce a science of human behavior from what one might call a "philosophy of oughtness"—a belief, however tacit and unexamined, about what people and society *ought to be*. What is "social pathology" if it is not a violation of some standard of how humans and society should behave? Can we measure it if we have no yardstick?

The physicist observes the atom; he does not say how its particles should act. If he sees unexplained irregularities, he does not attribute them to "atomic pathology," any more than the astronomer attributes the irregular movement of comets or the bursting of stars to some heavenly pathology. It is only when we speak of living things that we begin to call this state or that "pathological." To diagnose sickness, the physician must have a clear idea of what is health—to diagnose a sick society, the sociologists must know a healthy one. Where societies are concerned, the question is not medical; it is ethical, political, and philosophical and until it is recognized as such, is unlikely to be resolved.

It must have occurred to the reader how far we have come in this section from a concept of "the dangerous offender" to a concept, however unformulated, of "the dangerous society." *Homo delinquens* is seen as a lone, lost entity, buffeted by forces he cannot understand, in a world he never made. He is subjected to conflicting loyalties and standards of behavior, exposed to evil companions, denied status, ground down by ignorance and poverty, and victimized by a normless, disorganized society. Not only is man today acting out his life on a different stage, it is a different man who acts. Was life less hard or society less brutal in Shakespeare's time, when Hamlet could exclaim: "What a piece of work is a man! how noble in reason! how infinite in faculty! in form and moving how express and admirable! in action how like an angel! in apprehension how like a God!" For such a being, in such a world, good and evil are freely chosen. Man is not the victim; even when he loses, he is the protagonist. The criminal, too, has his own dignity because, like Lucifer, he has freely chosen to rebel.

Criminology, however scientific, can never divorce itself from the mythos that underlies it. If we see *homo delinquens* as the protagonist of his own story, then justice has one kind of meaning; if we see him as victim, it has another. Ever since the rise of biological determinism in the late nineteenth century, law and criminology have diverged because their assumptions are different. Where the law posits free will, criminology, both biogenic and sociogenic, posits determinism. Where the law sees a criminal who acts rationally, criminology sees someone who does not—who is, in fact, driven by forces beyond his control or understanding. It is not that the law is less "scientific" than the biological and behavioral sciences, rather that it operates in the classic Christian tradition, under different assumptions about human nature. The law appeals to precedent and common sense, criminology to its data; but at bottom, the real, if unrecognized, difference between them is philosophical. The reason we argue fruitlessly over what should be done about criminals is that we cannot agree on who—and what—is man.

**Part IV
The Mind of the Dangerous
Offender**

23 Psychoanalysis: The Search for Motive

The three figures from the nineteenth century who most profoundly influenced the ideas of the twentieth were Charles Darwin, Karl Marx, and Sigmund Freud. Each proposed a world view, each provided a perspective different from the others; and their works gave rise to deterministic theories in fields as diverse as psychiatry, politics, the social sciences, and biology. In fact, these three men left almost no aspect of intellectual life untouched. We have already seen how Marx and Darwin affected the fledgling science of criminology. It is now time to consider the influence of Sigmund Freud (1856-1939), who was the founder of psychoanalysis, and for thirty-six years (until forced to flee by the Nazis), held the chair of neuropathology at the University of Vienna.

When Freud received his degree, the medical profession explained mental symptoms physiologically; if nothing physical was found, the disturbance was attributed to some organic (if unknown) problem in the brain. At the Vienna General Hospital (*Allgemeine Krankenhaus*), Freud became an expert on the anatomy of the brain, and he wrote a number of works on diseases of the nervous system that were highly regarded by his contemporaries. Then in 1885 he went to the Salpêtrière in Paris to study with the great French neurologist Jean-Martin Charcot (1825-1893), whose studies of hysteria had led him to the use of hypnotism in curing hysterical blindness and paralysis. Freud was profoundly impressed by what he saw; not only could hypnotism alleviate such symptoms, but it could also induce states of cataleptic rigidity in people who were normal. At that time hypnotism was widely considered no more than sideshow quackery; this was certainly the view among the medical fraternity. Freud, however, returned to Vienna and to private practice and began to treat his hysterical patients with hypnosis.[a,1]

At this time Dr. Josef Breuer, a friend of Freud's, was also treating hysterical patients by hypnotizing them and asking them while they were under hypnosis to give verbal expression to the problems that oppressed them. Through a catharsis of the emotions, giving expression to long-repressed feelings, these patients were able to cure their symptoms. Freud was much struck by Breuer's cathartic method, which he adopted himself, and he and Breuer in 1893 jointly issued a preliminary communication they called *On the Psychic Mechanisms of Hysterical Phenomena*, in which they concluded that hysterical

---

[a]Later Freud adopted his method by which the patient's problems were explored through the free association of ideas ("talk therapy") and by the interpretation of dreams. Hypnosis was abandoned because its effects proved temporary.

syymptoms were the result of some disagreeable and forgotten episode from the past. When the patient was unable to express affect (i.e., feeling or emotion), but rather repressed it from consciousness, the psychic energy thus dammed up took a wrong path to bodily innervation, thereby producing the hysterical symptom.[2] This has been called the "hydraulic model" of personality. It is based on the analogy of liquid held under pressure: When the pressure gets too high and there are no channels for drainage, the walls begin to leak.[3] This is the physical principle of the conservation of energy, which Freud, for the first time, applied to psychic processes.

Freud eventually abandoned hypnotism, and Breuer abandoned Freud, who was rapidly becoming a controversial figure in medical circles. Nevertheless, both in theory and treatment, psychoanalysis was, in Freud's own words, "the administrator of the estate left by hypnotism."[4] For the first time it directed attention to the dynamic processes and *unconscious* motivation of human behavior. Not only hysteria, but the other neuroses, and what Freud called the "psychopathology of everyday life"—slips of the tongue, forgetting names and words—were explained by this new science, for which Freud and his disciples constructed an elaborate theoretical framework. The term "psychoanalysis" came to have two meanings: first, a particular method for treating nervous disorders, and second, the science of unconscious mental processes.

In Freud's original topography of the mind, there were three levels: the conscious, the preconscious (which could, with effort, be summoned into consciousness), and the unconscious, which is beyond deliberate recall. Later he developed a structural theory of the mind. One part of the mind he called the "id," a primitive, unorganized reservoir of the instincts, which seeks immediate gratification. A second part he called the "ego," which he described as "that part of the id which has been modified by the direct influence of the external world." And finally, there is the "superego," formed by the ego out of the id. The superego dominates the ego and represents the inhibitions of instinct that are characteristic of men. The superego, Freud said, "is the representative of our relation to our parents. When we were little children we knew these higher natures, we admired them and feared them; and later we took them into ourselves." The superego "represents the whole demands of morality, and we see all at once that our moral sense of guilt is the expression of the tension between the ego and the super-ego." The activities of the superego are "self-observation, conscience and the holding up of ideals." Because the superego is repressive and often tyrannical, in its struggle for control it creates conflict and a sense of guilt. The ego, superego, and id are not sharply divided, but are like "areas of colour shading off into one another. . . ."[b,5]

---

[b]Two points should be noted about Freudian doctrine. First, Freud's patients were of the Viennese (and later, European and American) middle and upper classes. Second, his doctrines were developed in the nineteenth and very early twentieth centuries, which were marked by a strong Puritanism, and in the case of women, by excessive demands for the repression of the sexual instincts. Because of the character of the times, his patients were

S.H. Foulkes has compared these three layers of the personality to the criminal (id), society (ego), and judge (superego), with the ordinary citizen standing in the middle.[6] In this metaphoric topography—Freud was not relating these layers to any *physical* locus within the brain—the ego is attacked from above and below. On the one hand are the instinctual urges of the id for immediate gratification, and on the other, the censorship and repression exercised by the superego. One way to mediate is *sublimation*, or turning one's baser instincts into socially acceptable channels. Where this doesn't work, repression takes place, and these instincts are thrust back into the unconscious where they give rise to obsessions, phobias, compulsions, hysterical symptoms, and even criminal acts.

If one views the id as the criminal within man, then man—*every man*—is a "born criminal." The newborn baby has neither ego nor superego; he is a bundle of instincts seeking immediate gratification. Lombroso's idea that only evolutionary throwbacks are "born criminals" is scornfully dismissed by psychoanalysis. In *The Criminal, the Judge and the Public* (1931), Franz Alexander and Hugo Staub wrote, "The attempt of Lombroso and his school to draw a sharp line between the normal and the criminal comes from the narcissistic wish of the scientist to separate himself and his normal fellow men from the criminal, as if the latter belonged to a different race of beings. . . ."[c,7]

All of us, said Alexander and Staub, enter the world as criminals, not socially adjusted, and we preserve that criminality until the Oedipus complex is overcome, during the so-called latency period.[d] At this point the normal individual represses his criminal drives, but *the future criminal fails to do so*. The criminal behaves as the child would if he could. Criminality is therefore not a congenital defect, as Lombroso would have it, but a defect in upbringing. If all children between two and six could acquire adult size and act out their fantasies, dominating adults who had in turn shrunk to the size of children, this would represent 100 percent criminality in action.[8]

---

often marked by a severe sense of guilt. Thus much of the early efforts of psychoanalysis were directed toward moderating the demands of the superego. However, times and problems change. Recent psychotherapists have commented on the apparent disappearance of both the ego and the superego in late twentieth century patients, who seem to be lacking either a conscience *or* a sense of identity. Thus, apparently, does culture alter the topography of the mind! (Cf. Mary Harrington Hall, "A Conversation with Bruno Bettelheim," *Psychology Today*, May 1969, p. 22.)

[c]Franz Alexander was born in Budapest and taught at the Berlin Psychoanalitical Institute before coming to the United States in the late twenties. He and Hugo Staub, a Berlin attorney, conducted a seminar at the institute for members of the legal profession. Their book was published in Vienna (1929) under the title *Der Verbrecher und seine Richter*.

[d]Freud believed that the most important conflict with which the child has to grapple is the desire, manifested at about the age of three, to have sexual relations with the parent of the opposite sex. This he called the Oedipus complex after the hero of Sophocles' tragedy who unknowingly killed his father and married his mother. The Oedipus complex, according to Freud, causes a feeling of hatred and rebellion toward the parent of the same sex that must be surmounted during the period of sexual latency (roughly from age five until the onset of puberty). If it is not, serious neurotic conflicts ensue.

Alexander and Staub applied psychoanalytic theory, not only to the individual criminal, but to the whole concept we call "justice." The psychoanalytic theory of ego development says that we restrain our impulses through fear of pain and expectation of pleasure. This restriction expresses the adjustment that our subjective instinctual drives make to the demands of reality. We hold back present impulses in expectation of future reward: Freud called this the evolution from the "pleasure principle" to the "reality principle." Thus the reality principle is the pleasure principle adjusted to the demands of reality. Fear of punishment and of not being loved (which is also a kind of punishment) are the two factors of education which, throughout life, remain the chief regulators of human instinctual behavior.[9]

In restricting our instincts, they said, we deal with an outer world whose power to restrict is stronger than our demands, whether we think of nature, an educator, a public leader, or a more powerful social class. Our psychic apparatus renounces just the minimal amount necessary to achieve the maximum security in gratifying the remainder of our instinctual demands. This equilibrium we call social order; it is a contract between the restricting powers and our instinctual demands. The *sense of justice* is the sensitive emotional regulator of this balance. Purely instinctive, it is something comparable to anxiety or even pain. Miscarriages of justice shake the stability of this balance and threaten a breakdown in the restrictions, either voluntary or forced, that men impose on their instinctual impulses. When the common sense of justice is seriously offended, the following two consequences ensue: First, acts of injustice become increasingly a center of interest, and the individual identifies with the victim of injustice, as if to say: "This might happen to any one of us." Second, the equilibrium between social restrictions and one's antisocial impulses is disturbed. Regression then takes place from instinctual restriction to a breakthrough of instinctual drives. Before every great social revolution, people observe—or think they observe—an increasing number of miscarriages of justice. Revolutions themselves represent the breaking through of those instinctual impulses that were previously held in check by accepted social restrictions.[10]

According to these authors, whenever the expected gratification is threatened that is to reward restriction, man reacts with a strong notice that the contract has been violated; then a regression takes place from instinctual *inhibition* to instinctual *expression*. Thus, they claim, the sense of justice is but a form of the pleasure principle wearing the mask of defender of the right; by means of it, man "keeps a constant and desperate watch over the remnants of his personal liberty, which is so badly curtailed."[11]

Alexander and Staub thought there are three types of criminals: the neurotic, whose behavior is the result of internal conflict between the social and antisocial components of his personality; the normal criminal, whose psychic organization resembles that of the normal individual, but who has identified himself with criminal prototypes; and the criminal whose delinquency has a biological cause. In addition to these three permanent types, there is the "acute criminal" who commits an act under the stress of circumstances. All persons may be found somewhere along a continuum from the pure criminal who has not formed a superego to the perfectly adjusted social individual whose superego and ego are so fused that he always considers the interests of society before his own. This last type, unfortunately, remains hypothetical; in the real world, he does not yet exist.[12]

In the Freudian view of human behavior, crime and punishment are not a drama that occurs only "out there," in society, but in fact they underlie all neurosis. In our unconscious psychic life we all punish ourselves for transgressions, real and imagined, against the parental demands of the superego. That punishment may take the form of conversion symptoms like paralysis and even blindness; or it may appear as phobias, compulsions, anxieties, and depressive states. Neurotics have a deep need to punish themselves. "That spirit of the criminal code which claims that punishment expiates a crime is thus made eternally active in the psychology of the neurosis. . . ." It is also seen as a license to indulge in the gratification of forbidden wishes ("I have paid for my crime; now I can do as I please"). In the case of many neurotic criminals, punishment serves to lift the moral inhibitions and is the necessary condition for the repetition of their crimes.[13]

Freud described a type he called "the criminal out of a sense of guilt." This sense of guilt is of unknown origin and long standing and involves unconscious forbidden wishes that the criminal's superego condemns more severely than it condemns his real transgressions. By being punished for the crimes he actually commits, he pays for that which is only an unconscious wish; in this way he is able, albeit temporarily, to rid himself of a sense of guilt. And what is this unconscious, forbidden wish? Often, said Freud, it is rooted in the Oedipus complex—the wish to kill the father and possess the mother. But in the case of the neurotic criminal, unlike the ordinary neurotic, he does not fantasize his crimes, he acts. It does no good to punish the neurotic criminal, because *punishment is what he is seeking.* Only through punishment, endlessly repeated, can he assuage his sense of guilt.[14]

William Healy, who in the early years of this century was director of the Psychopathic Institute of Chicago's Juvenile Court, reported that in his experience this kind of mental conflict underlies delinquency in about 7 percent of all cases. Because of the recurrent impulse to misbehavior, however, these include some of the most important cases. It is less important to know what an individual is structurally than to understand the dynamics of his mental powers, Healy claimed. Conduct cannot be understood by looking at the superficial facts and the obvious workings of the mind. What is important is not only that there are driving inner forces making for misconduct, but "that these forces prove to be so powerful and are so persistently recurrent."[15]

Repression is a form of mental dissociation. The conscious mind "forgets":

the unconscious *never forgets.* No psychic energy is ever lost: "Conservation of energy takes place here," said Healy, "as in the world of matter." Thus if an experience is thrust back into the unconscious with a strong emotional tone attached to it, it retains the capacity for releasing energy and causing a disturbance.[16] The disturbance may take many forms: hysterical paralysis, "forgetting," compulsive gambling, obscure phobias, even crime. The neurotic, the neurotic criminal—indeed, all of us—are alike prisoners of the past. Our past not only grows without ceasing but, in the words of the French philosopher Henri Bergson (1907),

it follows us every instant; all that we have felt, thought, and willed from our earliest infancy is there, leaning over the present which is about to join it, pressing against the portals of consciousness that would fain leave it outside. The cerebral mechanism is arranged just so as to drive back into the unconscious almost the whole of this past, and to admit beyond the threshold only that which can cast light on the present situation or further the action now being prepared.... Doubtless we think with only a small part of our past, but it is with our entire past, including the original bent of our soul, that we desire, will and act.[17]

And what of that faculty, so dear to our grandfathers, which we call "willpower," and which, aided by common sense and guided by conscience, was supposed to be trainable through parental discipline, providing us with a kind of automatic pilot to keep us morally upright? The discoveries of Freud changed this view. Ego (willpower) can indeed "suppress, divert, sublimate, or otherwise handle the dangerous impulses," said Karl Menninger in *The Crime of Punishment* (1968); but there is also an unconscious part of the conscience that is often rigid, prejudiced, corruptible, and cruel.[18] It is in response to this terrible judge, which Freud called the superego, that some people commit suicide, some people commit crimes, and some people go mad. In *Whatever Became of Sin?* (1973), Menninger saw each of us existing in a complicated balance of relationships with other persons and things and with the intricate parts of ourselves that lie within. Sometimes we make serious sacrifices to compensate for overstress. "*What we call illness and what we call crime are often just these sacrifices....* Many a crime is committed to avoid committing suicide; many a theft is a substitute for mayhem."[19]

In this view crimes are seldom what they seem. Sometimes they are motivated by a desperate need to act, to do something to break out of a state of passivity and frustration and redress grievances too long endured. These are the crimes of quiet desperation, committed by people who have always seemed to their neighbors or fellow students to be gentle and well behaved. Some suicides, said Menninger, are committed to forestall murder, some rapes committed to forestall impotence; and many murderers do not realize that they are killing the wrong person. The crime of bravado is usually the work of a man who mistrusts his own strength and manhood. Crime gives the criminal a sense of power, of magic, of controlling his own destiny. Often it is an alternative to mental illness. "In other words," he said, "many individuals perform criminal acts in order not to 'go crazy,' or not to become neurotically inhibited or highly disorganized."[20]

Although psychoanalysis has always claimed to be a "science," it can perhaps better be understood as poetry with certain elements of religion. Like Original Sin, the id is a metaphor for all that is messy, primitive and instinctual within the human personality. As for psychoanalytic criminology, it is almost Calvinistic in its determinism. If our unconscious is hidden from all but the most prolonged analytic probing, if it is the determinant of behavior for good or evil, the motive force that drives us blindly to our fate, then salvation or damnation lies, not in our selves, but in our analyst. The elect are the same elect of our social, economic, and criminal justice systems—the wealthy—because only they can afford this Rolls-Royce of therapies.[e]

This is not to say that psychoanalysis is untrue, any more than Goethe or Shakespeare are untrue, only that as a science it presents great difficulties: How can one prove or disprove such a theory? As George Vold put it in his *Theoretical Criminology* (1958), "A methodology... under which only the patient knows the 'facts' of the case, and only the analyst understands the meaning of those 'facts' as revealed to him by the patient, does not lend itself to external third person, impersonal verification...."[21] Nevertheless, for several decades psychotherapy as practiced in American prisons was strongly influenced by psychoanalytic concepts. So were the so-called psychological reports sent by prison social workers and psychologists to parole boards. So, sometimes, were the prisoners themselves, who often follow popular fashion in explaining their misdoings. In 1972 Associate Warden James W.L. Park of San Quentin observed that:

when the theologians determined that crime was the result of Satanic forces, the offender was quick to admit, "The devil made me do it." When physiognomy was an accepted means of diagnosis, the prisoner could resign himself to the fate ordained by his cranium.

During the fifty years of the psychoanalytic fad, prisoners became quite skilled in tracing their aberrations to unhappy early experiences and were able to diagnose their psychic flaws in credible detail. They also diagnosed each other and even today some can be heard on the prison yard calling out to a colleague: "Hey, you mother—," itself a perfectly sound Freudian concept.[22]

---

[e]A typical course of psychoanalysis consumes several hours a week for six or seven years. It is thus the most expensive of all kinds of psychotherapy, a problem that has contributed to the recent decline in its popularity.

24 Mad or Bad? The Issue of the "Guilty Mind"

From Lombroso to the modern prison psychiatrist, mental health professionals have probed the minds of offenders, seeking to understand how they think and why they behave as they do. The Freudians in particular have directed attention to the question of *motivation*. What dark impulses lie behind the apparently senseless crimes that fill our newspapers—the assassinations, mass murders, mutilation killings, and acts of terror that fill us with wonder and revulsion? What should be done with the perpetrators of such crimes? Psychiatry, which is still an infant science, has concerned itself with these questions for no more than a century, and then, for the most part, from the medical and therapeutic points of view. The *law*, on the other hand, has had to deal with them since the first codes were set down on clay tablets, but from an altogether different perspective. In jurisprudence the issue of motivation is most often posed narrowly, in terms of *mens rea*—the guilty mind, or criminal intent, of the offender.

What is the legal responsibility of, and what should be done with, a person who commits an offense when he is mentally ill or driven by some strange compulsion that he does not understand and over which he seems to have no control? Every day, in some courtroom, this question is asked, as it has been for centuries—and it is answered, as it has been for centuries, with perplexity, and a pained awareness that we have not yet found the *right* answer. In dealing with the insane criminal, the law must satisfy two often antithetical objectives: on the one hand, to do justice, and on the other, to protect society.

This chapter will look at the criminally insane as they have been understood and treated in Anglo-American law: The following chapter will consider the way our institutions have tried to cope with the offender who has been found mentally ill, either at arraignment, during trial, or after confinement. As the reader will discover, though the issue of criminal responsibility may seem to be a narrow one, in practice it involves questions of enormous ambit—not merely legal, but medical, behavioral, philosophical, and religious. There is no more controversial area in the criminal law, and certainly none more difficult.

Both the Greeks and the Romans accepted the notion that for an individual to be held morally and legally responsible for his actions, he must have the capacity for free choice. The Greeks distinguished between intentional and unintentional crimes; Aristotle stated that moral blameworthiness requires that an individual be capable of free choice and said that such capacity is lacking in the insane, in animals, and in children. Roman law divided the insane into two classes, those whose understanding is weak (*mente capti*) and those who are mad (*furiosi*), and required a guilty mind before a person is held responsible for criminal behavior.[1]

In Anglo-American law, too, criminal *intent* must be proved, a doctrine that was used to exculpate the insane by the time of Ethelred the Unready (978-1016). The laws of Henry I (1100-1135) made special provision for "insane persons and evildoers of a like sort," who were to be "guarded and treated leniently by their parents." The custom in the Middle Ages seems to have been to lock up such people until they seemed no longer dangerous, at which point application would be made to the king for pardon. In 1270, for example, Richard of Cheddestan, who killed his wife and two children while "suffering from a frenzied seizure," was locked by the sheriff of Norfolk into the prison at Norwich. After six years King Edward I made inquiry whether Richard were restored to his former soundness of mind or whether it would be dangerous to release him. Accordingly, a jury was convened. They reported back to the king that Richard was "well enough," but "it cannot safely be said that he is so restored to soundness of mind that there would not be danger in setting him free, especially when the heat of summer is increasing, lest worse befall."[2] ("If this ruling sounds strangely similar to the decision of a modern American parole board," comments Alan Dershowitz, "it simply demonstrates that human nature, fears, and attitudes have not changed radically over the centuries.")[3] Nor, it should be added, have our predictive powers.

By the sixteenth century it was no longer necessary for the king to pardon the criminally insane; they could be acquitted by the judge or jury, after which they would probably be put in the local jail for safekeeping. Private asylums were few, and such as there were were for the well-to-do. By the eighteenth century most of the modern elements of the insanity defense were in place. This may be illustrated by the charge to the jury in *Rex* v. *Arnold* (1724). One Edward ("Mad Ned") Arnold, a delusional eccentric well known in the neighborhood for his strange behavior, was accused of maliciously and wilfully wounding Lord Onslow. (Arnold believed that Onslow had sent imps and devils to disturb his sleep, and that he plagued and bewitched him by getting into his belly or bosom, so that Arnold could neither eat, drink, nor sleep.)[4]

The facts were not in dispute: "Mad Ned" had planned the crime and announced it in advance. He had bought the powder and shot the same day, asking for the biggest shot in stock, then inquired whether Lord Onslow were out hunting, saying, "God damn him, if I see him I will shoot my Lord Onslow." The question was, said Mr. Justice Tracy in his charge to the jury,

whether this man hath the use of his reason and senses. If he was under the visitation of God, and could not distinguish between good and evil, and did not know what he did, though he committed the greatest offence yet could not be guilty of any offence against any law whatsoever: for guilt arises from the mind, and the wicked will and intention of the man. If a man be deprived of his reason, and consequently of his intention, he cannot be guilty: and if that be the case, though he had actually killed Lord Onslow, he is exempted from punishment: punishment is intended for example, and to deter other persons from wicked designs; but the punishment of a madman, a person that hath no design, can have no example.

On the other hand, warned the judge, "not every frantic and idle humour of a man" will exempt him from justice: "It must be a man that is totally deprived of his understanding and memory, and doth not know what he is doing, no more than an infant, than a brute or wild beast...."[a] The jury, following the instructions of the judge, decided that "Mad Ned" was not quite mad enough to meet the "wild-beast" test: he was found guilty and sentenced to death.[b] However, his intended victim, Lord Onslow, interceded to secure a reprieve for him, and Arnold spent the remaining thirty years of his life in the jail at Southwark.[5]

Then, as now, there was a great reluctance to let criminals escape their "just deserts" on an insanity plea. Sir Matthew Hale, whose *Pleas of the Crown* (1678) was the Bible in such cases, had clearly distinguished between *partial* and *total* insanity. Many people, he thought, are insane on one subject or another, but this sort of dementia is not enough to excuse criminal behavior. "It is very difficult to define the invisible line that divides perfect and partial insanity; but it must rest upon circumstances duly to be weighed and considered both by judges and jury, lest on the one side there be a kind of inhumanity towards the defects of human nature;—or, on the other side, too great an indulgence given to great crimes."[6] Mr. Justice Tracy, in the Arnold case, was following Hale's injunction in his charge to the jury, as he distinguished between what he called the "frantic and idle humour of a man," on the one hand, and total deprivation of understanding and memory, on the other. But in *Rex* v. *Hadfield* (1800), the defendant for the first time won acquittal on a claim of partial insanity, rather than on the "wild-beast" standard that then ruled.

---

[a]The "wild-beast" test was derived from the thirteenth-century English jurist, Henry de Bracton, who wrote *On the Laws and Customs of England*, and who said that madmen "are not very different from animals." *Brutus*, meaning animal, as distinct from human, had, through the intervening centuries, been transmuted into brute, or wild beast, a meaning that went far beyond Bracton. See Nigel Walker, *Crime and Insanity in England*, vol. 1 (Edinburgh: Edinburgh University Press, 1968), pp. 27-28, 56-57, and Laurence R. Tancredi, Julian Lieb, and Andrew E. Slaby, *Legal Issues in Psychiatric Care* (Hagerstown, Md.: Harper & Row, 1975), p. 2.

[b]The outcome may have been somewhat affected by the fact that at this time English law did not permit the defendant in a felony case (other than treason) either to testify in his own defense or to be represented by counsel. Counsel might be present, but only to speak to legal questions that might arise during the course of the trial. For an untutored defendant to conduct his own defense must have been difficult enough—for a madman to do so rather boggles the mind. It was not until the end of the eighteenth century that defense counsel were allowed to examine witnesses (they still could not make speeches on the defendant's behalf); and it was not until 1836 that English law permitted a defendant not only to be advised by counsel, but also to have him speak in his defense at the end of the prosecution's case. See Walker, pp. 53, 58, 60, 64-5, 68-70, 231.

James Hadfield had attempted nothing less than the assassination of King George III. The case was therefore one of high treason, presided over by Lord Kenyon, the Lord Chief Justice. From the defendant's point of view, the treason charge was fortunate, because it permitted Hadfield's counsel to argue his case. He was defended by the most brilliant advocate of the day, Thomas Erskine, who had won acquittals for such famous but unpopular clients as Admiral Lord Keppel, Lord George Gordon, and Thomas Paine.[c] Erskine marshalled an army of witnesses to testify to the fact that the defendant, though rational on some subjects, was clearly delusional in others and that he was given to fits of terrifying madness. The attorney-general had told the court that to protect a person from criminal responsibility, there must be a *total* deprivation of memory and understanding. To this, Erskine replied that "no such madness ever existed in the world." On the contrary, "in all the cases that have filled Westminster Hall, with the most complicated considerations, the lunatics and other insane persons, who have been the subjects of them, have not only had memory, *in my sense of the expression*—they have not only had the most perfect knowledge and recollection of all the relations they stood in towards others, and of the acts and circumstances of their lives, but have, in general, been remarkable for subtlety and acuteness. Defects in their reasonings have seldom been traceable—the disease consisting in the delusive sources of thought:—all their deductions, within the scope of their malady, being founded on the *immovable* assumptions of matters as *realities*, either without any foundation whatever, or so distorted and disfigured by fancy, as to be nearly the same thing as their creation." Instead, Erskine proposed *delusion* to the court as a test of insanity.[7]

So masterly was Erskine's defense, so strong the evidence, and so persuasive his arguments that even before the case was sent to the jury the judges began to discuss publicly what ought to be done with Hadfield. Said Lord Kenyon:

... The prisoner, for his own sake, and for the sake of society at large, must not be discharged; for this is a case which concerns every man of every station, from the king upon the throne to the beggar at the gate; people of both sexes and of all ages may, in an unfortunate frantic hour, fall a sacrifice to this man, who is not under the guidance of sound reason; and therefore it is absolutely necessary for the safety of society that he should be properly disposed of, all mercy and humanity being shown to this most unfortunate creature. . . .

It was suggested to the jury that they should acquit Hadfield but give their reason for doing so. They found that "the prisoner is not guilty of the treason whereof he is indicted, being under the influence of insanity at the time," but,

[c]Thomas, first Baron Erskine of Restormel, had been attorney-general to the Prince of Wales (1783), and was to become Lord Chancellor in 1806. He advocated black emancipation, worked for Greek independence, and was an early sympathizer with the French Revolution. His advocacy of radical causes and unpopular clients seems not to have injured his career, possibly because of his impeccable establishment credentials (his father was the tenth Earl of Buchan, and his brother Henry, the Lord Advocate of Scotland).

because he was dangerous, remanded him to "the custody of the keeper of his Majesty's gaol at Newgate."[8]

Startled by the case and fearful that dangerous madmen might be acquitted and turned loose, Parliament passed the Act of 1800 "for the safe custody of insane persons charged with offenses." It stipulated that in cases of treason, murder, or felony, the only permissible verdict where the jury found the defendant insane was the special verdict, "not guilty by reason of insanity." The court must then order the accused "to be kept in strict custody, in such a place and in such manner as to the court shall seem fit, until His Majesty's pleasure be known," after which the King would provide for his custody. This phrase was made to apply retroactively—i.e., to Hadfield. A similar arrangement provided for those found mentally unfit for trial at the time of their arraignment. The Act of 1800 formalized and made mandatory what amounted to two levels of acquittal, with two very different consequences. As Nigel Walker has commented, the insanity verdict was an *acquittal in name only*. By finding the accused insane at the time of the act, it permitted a judge to return the offender to custody. However morally innocent the offender might be, he could not be *treated* as innocent: He was simply too dangerous to be at large. "The solution," said Walker, in his *Crime and Insanity in England* (1968), "was to pay lip-service to his innocence but use the law to make sure he remained in custody."[9]

Here, now, are the two issues that may be observed in the tangled relations of law with psychiatry: on the one hand, the responsibility for dangerous behavior, which includes the test of *mens rea*, or guilty mind; on the other hand, the control of those who, because of impaired mental function, are incapable of reasoned criminal intent but might be dangerous to themselves or others. Even though the verdict "not guilty by reason of insanity" may in fact condemn the acquitted to longer incarceration than a simple guilty verdict, the indeterminate nature of the confinement, and the fear that a madman might be turned loose prematurely, have often inhibited judges and juries in rendering such verdicts. Their dilemma has been made no easier by changing legal definitions of insanity, by disagreements among professionals, and by the obvious clash between considerations of justice (not punishing the innocent) and social defense (protecting the public).

Although the *Hadfield* case startled the British Parliament into legislation for legal control over those found insane, it remained an aberration because the ordinary defendant did not have counsel to plead his case. Thus judges, using ancient precedent, continued to follow the traditional test of insanity. In France, by contrast, the *Code Napoléon* (1810) was generous in exculpating the mentally ill offender. "There is neither crime nor offense," said the French criminal code, "when the accused was in a state of insanity at the time of the action. . . ." This law required no investigation into the relationship between the "state of insanity" and the act,[10] and in practice French juries, who were allowed great liberty in phrasing their verdicts, construed it in their own way. In one celebrated case a French jury stated in their verdict that the accused acted voluntarily *and* with premeditation, and that furthermore, he was *insane at the time.* This verdict, which appeared contradictory (but would certainly have fitted the facts in *Arnold*), was understood by the court to mean that the accused possessed the will of a madman, a merely animal will, excluding legal culpability, and that he was therefore not guilty.[11]

In 1838, Isaac Ray, a thirty-one-year-old general practitioner in the small fishing village of Eastport, Maine (population 2,840), published *A Treatise on the Medical Jurisprudence of Insanity*, a book that went into five editions and was for a century to remain the outstanding contribution in English to the literature of forensic psychiatry.[d] Its influence is to be traced through two lines of judicial decision, to the so-called New Hampshire, or *Durham*, test for insanity and to the "irresistible-impulse" defense, both of which will be discussed later. Ray reviewed English writings and precedents that, *faute de mieux*, were also followed in the United States, and he dismissed them as psychiatric and legal nonsense.

One reason why the criminal law of insanity has undergone so little improvement in England is probably that the accused, not being allowed counsel to speak in their defense except in trials for high treason, the officers of government have always been at liberty to put their own construction on the law, and urge it on the jury as the only correct one, without fear of being contradicted or gainsayed. Thus the old maxims have been repeated year after year, and, not being questioned, their correctness has remained undoubted, both in and out of the legal profession.

Could anyone doubt, he said, that had any of the insane criminals of the last half-century been defended by Erskine, "many of them would have been acquitted, and a great advance made in the law of insanity that would have prevented some of those exhibitions of presumptuous ignorance which will one day be universally regarded with feelings of disgust and pity?"[12]

Ray analyzed the doctrine, enunciated in *Arnold*, that if the accused knew right from wrong at the time he committed a criminal act, he was guilty. "That the insane mind is not entirely deprived of this power of moral discernment, but on many subjects is perfectly rational and displays the exercise of a sound and well balanced mind is one of those facts now so well established that to question it would only betray the height of ignorance and presumption." Under this test no one could successfully plead insanity, said Ray. It is not the partial possession of reasoning power—i.e., partial *sanity*—that matters, but "the undiminished

---

[d]After publication of his work, Ray was made superintendent of the Maine Insane Hospital, where he remained until 1845. During this period he joined with twelve other psychiatrists in founding what is now known as the American Psychiatric Association, the oldest national medical organization in the United States. In 1845 he was chosen to build and head the Butler Hospital, a private psychiatric institution in Providence, Rhode Island. He is annually honored by the APA in the granting of the Isaac Ray Award to a lawyer or psychiatrist who has promoted closer relations between law and medicine.

power of the mind to contemplate some objects or ideas in their customary relations, among which are those pertaining to their right or wrong, their good or evil tendency; and it must comprise the whole of these relations, else the individual is not sane on these points."[e][1][3]

Why, asked Ray, is this power to distinguish right from wrong only agitated in criminal cases? Why, on very slight evidence of eccentricity, can an individual be denied his civil power of concluding contracts or making a will, when on overwhelming evidence of madness he is denied the right to an insanity plea? "If it is proper to make those who possess this power [of distinguishing right from wrong] responsible for their criminal acts, how unjust and absurd is it to deprive them of their liberty and seclude them from their customary scenes and enjoyments before they have violated a single human law." No doubt this would prevent them from injuring themselves or others, but on such grounds, why not lock up "every other unprincipled and reckless individual who bids fair to be a pest to society"? It is said that the latter is morally and personally free until he commits some unlawful act. But if moral freedom consists in the power of distinguishing right from wrong, why should not the civilly insane claim the same immunity from personal constraint?

This preposterous distinction between civil and criminal cases gives rise in practice to one of the most curious and startling inconsistencies that human legislation ever presented. While the mental impairment is yet slight, comparatively, and the patient is quiet and peaceable, the law considers him incapable of managing himself or his worldly affairs and provides him with a guardian and a place in the wards of a hospital; but when the disorder has proceeded to such a height as to deprive the maniac of all moral restraint and precipitate him on some deed of violence, he is to be considered as most capable of perceiving moral distinctions and consequently most responsible for his actions![1][4]

Ray dismissed as irrelevant the question of whether the crime was planned. In the *Arnold* case, much was made at his trial of the fact that "Mad Ned" had purchased shot of a larger than usual size. The power of design, said Ray, is *not* incompatible with the existence of insanity. "What must be thought of the attainments of those learned authorities, in the study of madness, who see in the power of systematic design a disproof of the existence of insanity, when from the humblest menial in the service of a lunatic asylum they might have heard of the ingenuity of contrivance and adroitness of execution that preeminently characterize the plans of the insane?"[1][5]

In his defense of Hadfield, Erskine had proposed the test of *delusion.* This is not broad enough, said Ray. It is not only the *intellectual* powers that are subject to derangement, but the *moral* faculties—"the various sentiments,

[e]Ray gives as an example the case of a parent who loves his child very much, but he believes heaven has commanded him to sacrifice the child to secure its eternal happiness. "Before, therefore, an individual can be accounted sane on a particular subject it must appear that he regards it correctly in all its relations to right and wrong." (Query: Would Ray have regarded Abraham as insane?)

propensities, and affections, which, like the intellect being connected with the brain, are necessarily affected by pathological actions in that organism." Such illness may turn a peaceable and retiring individual into a "demon of fury," an upright man into a debauchee, "while the intellectual perceptions seem to have lost none of their ordinary soundness and vigor." Insanity is a disease whose existence is never established by a single diagnostic symptom but rather a whole body of symptoms, intellectual and emotional.[16]

In the fifth edition of his *Treatise* (1871), Isaac Ray considered the various national codes on insanity—those of France, Prussia, Wurtemburg, Switzerland, Hesse, and the Duchy of Baden, most of which he found too broad because they did not relate the offense to the illness, e.g., the French statute that "there is neither crime nor offense when the accused was in a state of insanity at the time of the action." That makes no sense, he said, unless the insanity was related to the crime. He then considered the Revised Statutes of the State of New York (II, 697): "No act done by a person in a state of insanity can be punished as an offense," and proposed the following revision of that statute:

No act done by a person in a state of insanity or any other condition of mind in which the person is involuntarily deprived of the consciousness of the true nature of his acts can be punished as an offense unless it can be proved that the act was not the offspring of such condition.[17]

Isaac Ray believed, and argued throughout his book, that insanity is a question of fact, to be determined by the jury, and not a question of law to be laid down in "rules of insanity," a view that was adopted from him by the supreme court of New Hampshire in 1869. Long before Freud, he taught that affect, the emotional content of behavior, is as important as intellect, and he stressed the emotional role in mental disorders. He followed Prichard and Pinel in pointing out that a person could be free of overt cognitive delusions and still, because of "moral mania," be unable to control his behavior.[f] This was the doctrine of "irresistible impulse," and it was to be argued throughout the nineteenth century and into the twentieth. Can a person, not from any impairment of reason, but purely because of an affective disorder, be driven into the commission of a crime? Isaac Ray thought he could. So did Sigmund Freud.

The criminal law of England and the United States, however, was not ready for psychiatric counsel on this or any other subject. In 1843, five years after the publication in America of Ray's *Treatise on the Medical Jurisprudence of Insanity* (and four years after that work was published in England), the *M'Naghten* case was to lead to a reaffirmation of the old rules on insanity.

[f]Like many nineteenth-century physicians, Ray seems to confuse manic behavior with what was later dubbed "psychopathic moral inferiority," or as we should now say, "psychopathy" (or "sociopathy"). Other problems that were dumped by nineteenth-century psychiatrists into the same nosological wastebasket included homicidal mania, pyromania, and kleptomania.

Daniel M'Naghten was a Scottish woodturner who would nowadays be described as a paranoid schizophrenic. Although he was described as mild mannered, inoffensive, and "humane," M'Naghten was profoundly convinced that the police, the Tories, and the Catholic Church were all persecuting him. Eventually his animosities settled on the British Prime Minister, Sir Robert Peel, who was not only a Tory, but also the founder of the metropolitan police force. Mistaking Edward Drummond, the Prime Minister's secretary, for Peel himself, M'Naghten, in January 1843, shot and killed him. When examined at the Bow Street police station, M'Naghten made a statement in which he said that the Tories of Glasgow "have compelled me to do this. They follow and persecute me wherever I go, and have entirely destroyed my peace of mind. They followed me to France, into Scotland and all over England. . . . They have accused me of crimes of which I am not guilty; in fact they wish to murder me."[18]

On March 3, M'Naghten went on trial with the lord chief justice, Sir Nicholas Tindal, presiding, along with two other judges. The accused was represented by Alexander Cockburn, Q.C., who was later to become attorney-general, and, still later, lord chief justice. The prosecutor was the solicitor-general Sir William Webb-Follett. In attacking the defense claim of insanity, the solicitor-general quoted Sir Matthew Hale and other distinguished authorities on the subject, while Cockburn argued, in effect, not only Erskine's pleadings in the *Hadfield* case, but also Ray's doctrine of irresistible impulse. Cockburn claimed that the prisoner's insanity took away from him all power of self-control, that "the disease of partial insanity can exist—that it can lead to a partial or total aberration of the moral senses and affections, which may render the wretched patient incapable of resisting the delusion, and lead him to commit crimes for which morally he cannot be held responsible. . . ." Cockburn relied also on Isaac Ray's arguments against Hale, whose views on partial insanity, Ray had said, derived from the fact that insanity was a much less frequent disease in the seventeenth century: "Could Lord Hale have contemplated the scenes presented by the lunatic asylums of our own times, we should undoubtedly have received from him a very different doctrine for the regulation of the decisions of after generations."

In summing up, the lord chief justice told the jury that the question for them to decide was whether at the time of the shooting the accused had been "sensible that it was a violation of the law of God or of man." If they thought he had been "capable of distinguishing between right and wrong, then he was a responsible agent and liable to all the penalties the law imposes." Impressed by Cockburn's arguments, the jury brought in the special verdict, that is, "Not guilty by reason of insanity": no doubt the quality of defense counsel, as in *Hadfield*, had much to do with the outcome. M'Naghten, instead of being executed, was removed to Bethlem Hospital, and a public uproar ensued, during which there were demands in Parliament for a revision of the Act of 1800 that regulated the insanity verdict.[19]

After much debate, the House of Lords decided to put five questions to the fifteen judges sitting in that house. Briefly summarized, these were: (1) What is the law with respect to persons inflicted with insane delusions on particular subjects who know they are acting contrary to law but who act under the influence of such a delusion? (2) What are the proper questions to be submitted to the jury in such a case, if insanity is set up as a defense? (3) In what terms ought the question to be left to the jury, as to the prisoner's state of mind when the act was committed? (4) If a person is delusional as to the facts, and in consequence commits an offense, is he thereby excused? And (5) can a medical man who never saw the prisoner prior to trial, but who was present during the trial and examination of witnesses, be asked his opinion as to the state of the prisoner's mind when the alleged crime was committed? (This was a reference to what had happened at M'Naghten's trial.)

Lord Chief Justice Tindal replied for the judges. With respect to the first question, he said that if the offender was laboring under partial delusions only and acted under such delusion, "he is nevertheless punishable according to the nature of the crime committed, if he knew at the time . . . that he was acting contrary to law. . . ." With respect to the fourth question, also dealing with delusion, he said that, again, if the delusion was partial, "we think he must be considered in the same situation as to responsibility as if the facts with respect to which the delusions exist were real." For example, if in his delusional state, he kills a man in what he believes to be self-defense, he would be exempt from punishment; if he kills in revenge, he would not. Tindal answered the second and third questions together, "that the jurors ought to be told in all cases that every man is to be presumed to be sane, and to possess a sufficient degree of reason to be responsible for his crimes, until the contrary be proved to their satisfaction; and that *to establish a defence on the ground of insanity, it must be clearly proved that, at the time of the committing of the act, the party accused was labouring under such a defect of reason, from disease of the mind, as not to know the nature and quality of the act he was doing; or, if he did know it, he did not know he was doing what was wrong.*" [Emphasis added.] Finally, with respect to the testimony of a doctor who had not examined the patient before the trial, the judges said that, strictly speaking, he could not "be asked his opinion in the terms above stated" because it is the jury's responsibility to determine the truth of the facts deposed to. However, where the facts are not in dispute, the question becomes substantially one of science only, and it may be allowed by the judge, "though the same cannot be insisted upon as a matter of right."[20]

The M'Naghten rules were, and remain, an anomaly in the history of Anglo-Saxon jurisprudence. The case put to the law lords, although prompted by *M'Naghten*, was in fact hypothetical. Normally judges give judgment after hearing the arguments in an actual case. Thus technically, the M'Naghten rules do not constitute a judicial precedent; in fact, however, their authority has been very great. Not only did they affect England but they were also adopted virtually verbatim in the United States. For example, New York changed its penal law to read, "A person is not excused from criminal liability as an idiot, imbecile, lunatic or insane person except upon proof that, at the time of committing the alleged criminal act, he was laboring under such a defect of reason as not to know the nature and quality of the act he was doing, or not to know that the act was wrong" (sect. 1.120). A comparison with the previous statute makes clear the effect the M'Naghten rules had on New York, and, indeed, on the criminal law of most American states. Implicit in the M'Naghten definition of insanity is the subsidiary principle, enunciated in Tindal's answer to the fourth question and propounded in many American courts, that a person suffering from insane delusions must be judged as to his knowledge of the nature and quality of his act by the supposed facts presented in the delusion. Or to take the example the law lords gave, if, in his delusional state, the accused thought he was acting in self-defense, he is innocent; but if, when he committed the act, he thought he was acting to redress or avenge some wrong, then he is guilty.[21]

Isaac Ray was extremely displeased by the M'Naghten rules. In his 1871 edition, he wrote that "it is a truth which no assumption of superior wisdom, no blind conservatism can destroy, that with hardly a single exception these 'rules of law' on the subject of insanity are in conflict with the well-settled facts of mental disease." In every hospital for the insane, he said, there "are patients capable of distinguishing between right and wrong, knowing well enough how to appreciate the nature and legal consequences of their acts, acknowledging the sanctions of religion, and never acting from irresistible impulses, but deliberately and shrewdly. Is all this to be utterly ignored in courts of justice?"[22]

Not quite utterly, but almost. In 1869 the supreme court of New Hampshire adopted Isaac Ray's views, and in *State* v. *Pike* (49 N.H. 399, 1870)[g] Chief Justice Perley instructed the jury "that, if the killing was the offspring or product of mental disease in the defendant, the verdict should be, 'not guilty by reason of insanity'; that neither delusion nor knowledge of right and wrong, nor design or cunning in planning and executing the killing and escaping or avoiding detection, nor ability to recognize acquaintances, or to labor, or transact business, or manage affairs is, as a matter of law, a test of disease; but that all symptoms and all tests of mental disease are purely matters of fact to be determined by the jury."[23]

It took eighty-five years for the mental-disease test to be adopted by another jurisdiction. Then in 1954 a landmark case reached the Court of Appeals for the District of Columbia. The appellant, Monte Durham, had been convicted of housebreaking. His history included both prisons and mental hospitals.

[g]This case was decided in June 1869, but through an error did not appear in the New Hampshire *Reports* until volume 49 (1870). It was heard by Chief Justice Perley and Justice Doe, a friend of Ray's, but was evidently decided by a jury, acting on instructions from the court.

Psychiatrists testified that he was a psychotic with a psychopathic personality; he suffered from hallucinations, heard nonexistent voices, and thought his fellow employees in the store where he worked watched him and talked about him. But, said the psychiatrist, "if the question of the right and wrong were propounded to him, he could give you the right answer." Clearly, Monte Durham, delusional though he might be, had failed the M'Naghten test, and he was convicted in the lower court. The court of appeals, however, reversed his conviction, and borrowing directly from *Pike*, stated that:

The fundamental objection to the right-wrong test . . . is not that criminal irresponsibility is made to rest upon an inadequate, invalid or indeterminable symptom or manifestation, but that it is made to rest upon *any* particular symptom. In attempting to define insanity in terms of a symptom, the courts have assumed an impossible role. . . . The rule we now hold . . . is simply that an accused is not criminally responsible if his unlawful act was the product of mental disease or mental defect. We use "disease" in the sense of a condition which is considered capable of either improving or deteriorating. We use "defect" in the sense of a condition which is not considered capable of either improving or deteriorating and which may be either congenital, or the result of injury, or the residual effect of a physical or mental disease. [*Durham* v. *United States*, 214 F.2d 862, 872-875 (D.C. Circuit, 1954).]

The *Durham* decision was one of the most controversial ever handed down in the United States, notwithstanding the fact that its legal reasoning was eighty-five years old. Innumerable books and law articles were written about it. On the whole, psychiatrists hailed it; but with their customary caution and adherence to precedent, almost every state court that was asked to adopt the mental-disease-or-defect test refused to do so. As the debate continued, and the District of Columbia acquired more experience with the *Durham* decision, the questions it raised became clear.

First, more defendants would be exculpated under *Durham* than under the M'Naghten rules. This was worrisome, both to the hardliners, who thought insane defendants were probably better off in prison, and to the liberals, who thought mental hospitals were, in some respects, worse than prisons, and that, in any case, commitments for insanity were much longer than commitments under the penal code. According to Judge David L. Bazelon, who wrote the *Durham* decision, from July 1, 1954 (when the decision went into effect) until November 1960, 229 persons in the District were found not guilty by reason of insanity and committed to St. Elizabeth's Hospital—100 in the last year alone. Though this represented an increase over earlier years, the increased acquittals were largely offset by a decrease in the number of defendants found incompetent to stand trial, so that the total number hospitalized did not change much.[24] This suggests that with the liberalized rules, judges were more willing to let a defendant go to trial whose mental condition was questionable.

Second, both *Durham* and the M'Naghten rules require that the psychiatric evidence be introduced at the trial in the usual adversary procedure. In the post-*Durham* insanity cases within the District of Columbia, a striking feature of the testimony was the failure by nearly all the psychiatric experts to utilize the new rule.[25] In fact, it has been observed that the battle of the experts is no different under *Durham* than under M'Naghten. According to Jerome Hall:

Although the M'Naghten Rules are phrased in terms of cognition, they are generally interpreted broadly by the courts, with the result that all psychiatric evidence relevant to the defendant's mental condition is admitted. And not a few of the most experienced forensic psychiatrists believe the M'Naghten Rules function very well in practice, without miscarriages of justice attributable to the use of the Rules, and that no better substitute has been proposed.[26]

Judge Bazelon, six years after *Durham*, expressed disappointment with the testimony of psychiatrists under the new rule: ". . . An open rule like Durham asks [the psychiatrist] for something the law has never consistently received, welcomed or appreciated—namely, profound insight into the nature and motivations of the defendant. Well, what happens? By and large the answer is—nothing much. And that is true whether the psychiatrist is forced to testify within M'Naghten, or simply reluctant to expand within the framework of Durham. . . . In general, the *practice* under Durham is not yet decisively—or anything like satisfactorily—different."[27]

A third problem, say the critics, is that psychiatric testimony, always so confusing and contradictory, becomes even more complex and speculative under *Durham*, where the question is no longer, "Did the defendant know his act was wrong?," but "Was his act the product of a mental disease or mental defect?" What is a "product"? Even more to the point, what is a "mental disease"? According to C.R. Jeffery (*Criminal Responsibility and Mental Disease*, 1967), an acceptable definition of mental disease has not been put forth by psychiatrists and psychologists, and neither has acceptable treatment, whether the problem be labeled "crime" or "mental disease," or both. The *Durham* rule assumes that such knowledge exists, when in fact it does not. Also, said Jeffery, it raises serious constitutional questions by first finding a defendant *not* guilty and then incarcerating him in an institution, perhaps indefinitely.[28] (In this, of course, it is no different from any other insanity verdict.)

Unlike Isaac Ray, who thought juries should decide insanity as a question of fact, Jeffery was troubled by the dilemma posed, no matter who makes the decision. "If behavioral experts are allowed to make these decisions," he said, "then one must recognize the fact that much of what passes for science in psychiatry, psychology, and sociology is not science but unverified opinion. If, on the other hand, judges, lawyers, and jurors are allowed to make these decisions, then we are not utilizing to the best of our ability the knowledge we now possess concerning human behavior."[29]

He criticized the *Durham* decision for failing to resolve "the philosophical notion of free will versus the scientific notion of determinism," thereby perpetuating "this dualistic and conflicting system." Jeffery concluded by arguing that the insanity defense, under the *Durham* rule, defines crime as a *medical* problem, when it is in fact a *social* problem.[h] Experts on criminal behavior from the fields of sociology and experimental psychology, said Jeffery, are not called on to testify in criminal trials. For this reason evidence introduced in trials is often out of date, and there is a lag between scientific knowledge and courtroom testimony "which makes it almost impossible at times for the behavioral expert to communicate with the legal expert. This gap in communication must be overcome before any legal definition of criminal responsibility can be created which will make sense to both the scientific community and legal community."[30]

Though the M'Naghten rules have never been entirely abrogated, they have gradually been eroded, not only through the common sense of juries, but through statutory enactment. In 1964 England adopted from Scottish law the concept of "diminished responsibility" as an alternative in murder cases to the insanity plea—that is, the defendant could claim to be insane, under the M'Naghten test, or alternatively plead that "he was suffering from such abnormality of mind (whether arising from a condition of arrested or retarded development of mind or any inherent causes or induced by disease or injury) as substantially impaired his mental responsibility. . . ." If this latter defense were successful, the accused became liable to a conviction for manslaughter (in Scotland he would be convicted of "culpable homicide"). This freed the judge from the necessity of pronouncing the death sentence and allowed him a choice between life imprisonment, imprisonment for a specified term, a fine, probation, or an absolute or conditional discharge.[31] "Diminished responsibility" became a popular defense because it is easier to sustain than the old insanity plea. It also provides for those mental disabilities that fall between absolute rationality at one end of the spectrum, and the raving madness of a "wild beast" at the other.

In the United States, "irresistible impulse" has also made its inroads as an exculpatory defense, usually as an addition to the M'Naghten rules. It provides that the defendant will be relieved of the consequences of his criminal act if he suffered from such a "diseased mental condition" as to create in his mind an uncontrollable impulse to commit the offense charged. "Irresistible impulse" is recognized in federal courts, and in many states, as a gloss on M'Naghten but it, too, has been criticized by those who say the rule does not clearly distinguish between the kind of rage which it is the purpose of the criminal law to deter and that which is, in effect, undeterrable. This formula, they say, because of its ambiguities, is an invitation to the jury to avoid applying the criminal law and thereby tolerate the defendant's taking the law into his own hands.

Thus the debate rages while the insane defendant remains poised precari-

---

[h]Then, of course, there are sociologists who claim it is a *legal* one, since it is always a matter of definition (cf. Sellin).

ously between two stools, one labeled "law" (and "free will") and the other "psychiatry" (and "determinism"). Sometimes he comes down on the one, sometimes on the other; but more often he falls helplessly in between. In the next chapter we shall consider what happens to those we call the "criminally insane"—those too innocent to imprison, too sick to hang, too criminal to be put in a mental hospital, and too dangerous to be at large.

25 The Insane Dilemma of the United States

No area of American criminal justice is murkier or more controversial than that legal and conceptual no-man's-land that lies in the penumbra between corrections and mental health. There, in a tangle of confused legislation, inconsistent treatment, and anomalous, hybrid institutions are to be found malefactors by the hundred thousands. They include persons found incompetent to stand trial, those not guilty by reason of insanity, those we call the "criminally insane," and the myriad psychotics who crowd our prisons, undiagnosed and untreated. Why are some deviants sent to mental hospitals, some imprisoned, and some turned loose? Is there something uniquely dangerous about the mentally ill offender as opposed to the calculating criminal?

Sir William Blackstone, whose *Commentaries on the Laws of England* (1765-1769) was once the Bible of American jurisprudence, said that "if a man in his sound mind commits an offense, and before arraignment for it he becomes mad, he ought not to be 'called on to plead to it, because he is unable to do so' with that advice and caution that he ought. And if, after he has pleaded, the prisoner becomes mad, he shall not be tried; for how can he make his defence? If, after he be tried and found guilty, he loses his sense before judgment, judgment shall not be pronounced; and if, after judgment, he becomes of nonsane memory, execution shall be stayed. . . ."[1] Practice in the United States has reflected these rules of common law, so that a mentally ill offender may effect an escape from the judicial system (at arraignment or during trial), from the correctional system (after conviction), and even from death row itself; it is, unfortunately, all too often the escape of a man who runs away from a tiger, only to be consumed by a bog.

Until the middle of the nineteenth century, no special provision was made for the mentally disordered offender. As had been the custom since the Middle Ages, the psychotic criminal was usually cared for in jails or prisons—in fact, many noncriminal psychotics were thrown into common jails where they kept company with felons and were often barbarously treated. It was a visit to the East Cambridge, Massachusetts, jail in 1841 which launched Dorothea Dix on her lifelong career as a mental health reformer. Horrified by the treatment of the insane in this jail, she petitioned the court for a correction of conditions; then, notebook in hand, she visited every jail and almshouse from the Berkshires to Cape Cod. There, she told the state legislature, she found insane persons confined in "*cages, closets, cellars, stalls, pens; chained naked, beaten with rods, and lashed into obedience!*"[2] Having shocked the Massachusetts legislature into

177

building additional beds at the Worcester State Hospital, "this terrible reformer, yet gentle lady"[3] made the sweep of North America, from Mississippi to Canada, stirring legislators into action. She even carried her investigations into the British Isles, where in 1855 she persuaded the home secretary, Sir George Grey, to appoint a royal commission to look into the treatment of the insane in England.[a]

Nevertheless, the removal of patients from jails to mental hospitals did not resolve the problem of what to do with the criminally insane. These were unwelcome in the institutions for the mentally ill because of the supposed danger they posed to the morals and safety of inmates and staff; they were unwelcome in prisons because of the special problems they posed to custody. Nevertheless, insane murderers were confined, untreated, for life in ordinary prisons, which also housed psychotics and mentally retarded offenders of all kinds. (One eminent alienist even declared that he preferred sending an insane criminal to prison rather than to a hospital because he believed the discipline and severity of prison life more serviceable than the lax discipline of hospital treatment.)[4]

In New York a law passed around 1850 provided for the transfer of insane criminals from the jails and prisons to the Utica State Hospital. So great, however, was the number of transfers that they threatened to crowd out the civilly committed. As a result, the first mental hospital for criminals, the State Lunatic Asylum for Insane Convicts, was opened at Auburn, New York, in 1855 as an appendage of the state prison. In 1892 the inmates were moved to a second, larger institution at Matteawan, and in 1900 a third hospital was opened at Dannemora.[5] In 1863 England, also, opened its first special criminal lunatic asylum at Broadmoor. There, from Bethlem Hospital, the unfortunate Daniel M'Naghten was transferred, and there he was eventually to die of tuberculosis.[6] In the years since 1855, institutions of this type have become common in both Britain and the United States.

Sometimes these hospitals make provisions for patients who have not been accused of crime but who prove unmanageably violent, so that they need greater security than what may be afforded at the ordinary mental hospital. Their chief function, however, is within the criminal justice system, where they typically serve multiple purposes: a defendant may be sent there to see whether he is competent to stand trial; he may be sent after trial, if he is found not guilty

---

[a]Dorothea Lynde Dix (1802-1887) was one of the most remarkable reformers of a reforming generation, in spite of lifelong ill health. Like that other quasi-invalid, Florence Nightingale, she had an uncanny knack for enlisting the leaders of public opinion in her crusades. Her power over legislators and governments, foreign and domestic, was awesome. Probably no one has ever visited more prisons, jails, almshouses and mental hospitals, or achieved more of her objectives with less argument from the political establishment. Her strength seems to have derived from the firm conviction that Providence willed her success—as perhaps He did.

by reason of insanity;[b] and he may be transferred from prison to such a hospital if he is found mentally ill or especially troublesome while in confinement. Some states, such as California, have different institutions for those found incompetent to stand trial or found not guilty by reason of insanity, and for those who become ill while incarcerated. Practice differs from state to state, as does the quality of the institutions. A few provide intensive treatment, but it is fair to say that in the United States, hospitals for the criminally insane are little more than wastebaskets for people who are deemed particularly dangerous and troublesome and who have been rejected by both the correctional and mental health systems.

Because of the constitutional issues involved, the treatment of the mentally disordered dangerous offender poses special problems for American jurisprudence. From competence to stand trial to eventual discharge from a hospital or prison, the questions of due process and equal protection are justiciable.[c] Furthermore, over the past fifteen years, both the due-process issue and the problem of cruel and unusual punishment have been extensively litigated, and a large body of case law accumulated in the fields of mental health and corrections. The mentally disordered offender falls somewhere between the two systems and often receives the worst of both.

The first question that may arise at arraignment is whether the defendant is competent to stand trial. In the majority of jurisdictions, this is a different question from that of "insanity," however defined. It asks only whether he is able to understand the proceedings against him and assist counsel in the conduct of his defense.[d] It is not impossible for a defendant to be both competent *and* "insane" (in the M'Naghten or *Durham* sense). But if the accused should be found incompetent to stand trial, the question of whether he in fact committed the act charged may *never be decided.* Under these circumstances, many an unfortunate has spent the rest of his life in what is technically a mental hospital, but what is, in reality, a prison. According to Alan A. Stone (1975), far more persons in the United States are confined on a finding of incompetence than of insanity.[7] A 1961 Michigan study by John H. Hess, Jr., and Herbert E. Thomas showed that of 1,484 defendants committed for incompetency to stand trial, six years later only 105 had been returned to the committing courts. Their findings

---

[b]In the United States the verdict is "not guilty by reason of insanity." In England from 1800 to 1883 the verdict was "not guilty by reason of insanity"; from 1883 to 1964 it was "guilty but insane"; and now it is once again "not guilty by reason of insanity." See Nigel Walker, *Crime and Insanity in England*, vol. 1 (Edinburgh: Edingburgh University Press, 1968), p. 244.

[c]The Fourteenth Amendment provides that "no State shall make or enforce any law which shall abridge the privileges or immunities of citizens of the United States; nor shall any State deprive any person of life, liberty or property without due process of law; nor deny to any person within its jurisdiction the equal protection of the laws." (The due-process clause originated in the Fifth Amendment, where it applied only to Congress. By the Fourteenth, it was extended to the states.)

[d]In fourteen states, however, incompetence is defined as "insanity." In seven, the term is undefined.

indicated, said the authors, that well over one half of the individuals committed as incompetent will spend the rest of their lives confined to a hospital. Yet the issue of incompetency was "most frequently raised not on the basis of defendant's mental status, but rather was employed as a means of handling situations and solving problems for which there seemed to be no other recourse under the law."[8]

In 1971 the United States Supreme Court, in *Jackson* v. *Indiana*, considered the situation of a mentally retarded deaf-mute who, being unable to understand the charges against him or communicate with his counsel, was committed to the Indiana Department of Mental Health until certified "sane." Psychiatrists had said that, in their judgment, he would never be able to understand the charges against him. His counsel argued that under the circumstances Jackson's commitment amounted to a life sentence and that he should have been committed under the regular process for civil commitment, which would make him eligible for release under more lenient standards. The court ruled that it was a denial of equal protection under the Fourteenth Amendment to institutionalize Jackson under a standard that made it easier to commit him and more difficult for him to obtain release:

We hold, consequently, that a person charged by a state with a criminal offense who is committed solely on account of his incapacity to proceed to trial cannot be held more than the reasonable period of time necessary to determine whether there is a substantial probability that he will attain that capacity in the foreseeable future. If it is determined that this is not the case, then the State must either institute the customary civil commitment proceeding that would be required to commit indefinitely any other citizen, or release the defendant. Furthermore, even if it is determined that the defendant probably soon will be able to stand trial, his continued commitment must be justified by *progress toward that goal.* [Emphasis added] (406 U.S. 715 at 738)

At the present time no more than half a dozen states have statutes that meet the standards in *Jackson*.

The whole area of incompetence is a judicial quagmire. A defendant who is examined at a state hospital for the criminally insane and found competent to stand trial may then be found not guilty by reason of insanity and remanded once again to the same hospital for an indefinite stay. If this seems anomalous, it is only because of the different definitions of "incompetence" and "insanity." One may be both competent *and* insane; furthermore, one may be insane at the time of trial, but sane during the commission of the crime, or vice versa.

The prisoner who, on examination, is found incompetent to stand trial may be treated or simply warehoused. Although warehousing would now seem to fall afoul of the *Jackson* decision, "treatment" raises questions no less interesting. In 1971 catatonics at California's Atascadero State Hospital were being made "competent" by the most heroic measures. One patient who faced murder charges in San Francisco if he could only be brought out of his rigid state was given electric shocks (aversive therapy) to force him to clean and feed himself. Under this treatment, the patient recovered sufficiently to be shipped back to court, but before he could be tried for murder, he became mysteriously catatonic once again and had to be returned to the hospital. There seems to have been as much method as madness in the behavior of the patient—there certainly was as much madness as method in what was being done to him. The program coordinator who now supervised his second course of aversive therapy (including more electric shocks) considered the patient hopelessly schizophrenic— "incurable," he said—but he was performing his duty of making him competent to stand trial.[9]

Once returned to competency, a defendant will be tried. He may now plead not guilty by reason of insanity. Should his claim prevail, he will be sent to a state hospital for the criminally insane to be kept there until cured, or considered no longer dangerous, or, in a few states, for the term provided by law. Most defendants who are "acquitted" on grounds of insanity will spend more time under lock and key than if they had been convicted. The chance is excellent that they will receive no better treatment than they would have in prison, and in many cases, they will receive worse.

On the other hand, should the defendant be found guilty and sent to prison, and should he, in fact, be mentally ill, he may spend part or all of his sentence in a prison, or part or all of his sentence in the same kind of institution for the criminally insane. Whether he will wander the prison yard undiagnosed or be shipped out to a hospital depends on how much of a problem he poses to custody. So long as an inmate does not attract unwelcome attention, his mental problems, however serious, are likely to be ignored. On the other hand, let his behavior be troublesome enough, and he stands an excellent chance of being transferred to a mental institution, *whether he is insane or not.*[e] The standards for transfer to and from such institutions have traditionally been so vague as to raise serious constitutional questions. The custom at the Ohio Penitentiary as late as the 1960s was for the warden to call the superintendent of the Lima State Hospital and simply announce the transfer. Sometimes the warden would say candidly that the prisoner "is causing us some trouble down here. Will you keep him for a while?" Agitators and other troublemakers who could not be discouraged by solitary confinement were frequently handled this way.[10]

The concept of due process in hospital transfers began to be seriously litigated in the 1960s. One reason for the litigation was the indeterminate nature of hospital confinement. A prisoner in a correctional institution may obtain early release on parole and must receive unconditional release when his sentence is up. In most jurisdictions a prisoner is not permitted parole from a state

---

[e]Among the kinds of troublesome behavior with which most wardens cannot cope are suicide attempts (real or pretended), long hunger strikes, setting fires, throwing food or feces at the staff, and so forth. This behavior may signal mental disturbance, or it may represent a protest against prison treatment or conditions, or both.

182

hospital, and in fact, may spend the rest of his life there.[f] No less important than the problem of release for most prisoners is the onerous nature of the confinement in a security mental hospital, which often combines the worst features of a prison and an insane asylum. Some of these institutions are as barbarous as anything from the nineteenth century. At the Lima State Hospital, until 1970, new admissions were routinely put into strip cells with a chamber pot but no running water or toilet; there they lay for weeks on a bare mattress thrown onto the floor, observed through a slot in the door, not by psychiatrists—they might not see a psychiatrist for six months—but by ward attendants.[11] In 1971 the same admissions routine prevailed for violent cases in S-Wing of the California Medical Facility at Vacaville, one of the most modern in the world. There new arrivals were placed on mattresses in soundproof cells and observed through a window in the back of the cell by attendants on a catwalk. Although there were twenty-five psychiatrists on the Vacaville staff, ten of them full-time, the patients received no treatment except tranquilizers and other medication. Food was passed to them three times a day through a slot in the door. After a month, if they showed "improvement"—presumably by not butting their head against the wall or tearing the mattress—they were promoted through various wards of S-Wing to the Intensive Treatment Unit, described by the physician in charge as "the most richly staffed psychiatric unit in the world." There they participated in a ward self-government program and a course of group therapy. Even the ITU, however, had six "quiet cells," soundproof rooms where recalcitrant inmates were fed through slots, and if they screamed, nobody could hear them.[12]

Like Atascadero, Vacaville is proud of its innovative treatment programs. At these two California hospitals[g] during the late 1960s there took place one of the most controversial treatment programs ever undertaken. Over a three-year period, 157 patients were subjected to experiments in which they were injected with Anectine (succinylcholine chloride), a derivative of the South American arrow-tip poison, curare, which causes instant paralysis of all muscles including those needed to breathe. According to Dr. Arthur G. Nugent, who was in charge of the program at Vacaville, "The sensation is one of suffocation and drowning. . . . The patient feels as if he is on the brink of death." At this juncture, a

[f]In 1971 I interviewed a prisoner at the Chillicothe Correctional Institute in Ohio who had been denied parole because he had, within the last six months, returned from the Lima State Hospital. He was ordered by the parole board to go back for a psychiatric evaluation before the board would consider him safe to release—and was again, at his next hearing, denied parole on the grounds he had been at Lima (for his psychiatric evaluation) within the past six months. "How do I get out?" he asked plaintively. How, indeed?

[g]The Atascadero State Hospital, which is under the Department of Mental Hygiene, is for patients who during arraignment show signs of incompetency to stand trial or who are found not guilty by reason of insanity. The California Medical Facility at Vacaville, under the Department of Corrections, is for patients who become ill while incarcerated. Transfers between the two can be (and are) arranged on criteria which John Conrad, a former California official, describes as "metaphysically slippery."

medical technical assistant would scold him for his wickedness. The experimenters believed that the patient would connect the behavior he was being scolded for with the feeling of dying, and therefore refrain from this behavior.[13] Candidates for this program were selected because of frequent fights, verbal threatening, deviant sexual behavior, stealing, or unresponsiveness to group therapy in the hospital. When the resulting public uproar forced suppression of the program, Dr. Nugent told the San Francisco *Chronicle*, "I'm at a loss as to why everybody's upset over this."[14]

In recent years the courts have wrestled with a number of questions with respect to institutions for the criminally insane. One would suppose that there would be some objective standard for keeping a prisoner confined in one. Yet in *Schuster* v. *Herold* (1969), the federal court confronted the case of a prisoner who had spent twenty-nine years in the Dannemora State Hospital for asserting that officials at Clinton State Prison were corrupt. A prison physician had in 1941 found Roy Schuster to be "paranoid and suspicious"—the evidence being that he criticized the way the Regent's examination was conducted there. At a habeas corpus hearing in 1963,[h] a psychiatrist testified that his claim of corruption was his only symptom of mental illness. Although the court ordered a sanity hearing for him within sixty days, Schuster was still confined in 1975, thanks to a series of delays and objections by the State of New York. Saying that "we can no longer sit by and permit the State to continue toying with Roy Schuster's freedom," the court, on September 23, 1975, ordered the unfortunate Schuster to be unconditionally released.[15]

The question of administrative transfers from prisons to mental hospitals has been litigated in various jurisdictions. In *Matthews* v. *Hardy* (1969) a District of Columbia court considered the case of a Lorton Reformatory inmate who had been transferred to St. Elizabeths Hospital and found that such transfers require protective procedures similar to those in civil commitments because, "although regrettable, it is a fact that there is a stigma attached to the mentally ill which is different from that attached to the criminal class in general. Thus a prisoner transferred to St. Elizabeths might well be described as 'twice cursed.'" Furthermore, said the court, the restrictions and routines of a mental hospital differ significantly from those in prison, and an inmate in such a hospital may be incarcerated longer than someone at Lorton. Finally, a person mistakenly placed in a mental hospital might suffer severe emotional and psychic harm. If he is confined with the insane, told he is insane, and treated as insane, he may in the end become insane.[16]

The American federal system, however, in the absence of a definitive decision by the Supreme Court, does not provide a national standard for

[h]Schuster had filed habeas corpus petitions in either state or federal Courts in 1950, 1960, 1962, 1963, and 1967; they were all dismissed. The present case was a federal appeal of the last dismissal. Had Schuster remained at Clinton he would have been eligible for parole in 1948.

commitment of offenders to a mental hospital, and therein lies the peculiarity of America's insane dilemma. In a country which, unlike the United States, has but a single jurisdiction, with no constitutional bars to any kind of treatment, an individual may be confined, treated in any fashion, and kept—or released—at will. There may be some therapeutic advantage in this: Many psychiatrists believe there is. Nothing in the American experience, however, suggests that this is so. As Herbert Fingarette has observed in *The Meaning of Criminal Insanity* (1972), "Medical efficiency cannot be purchased at the price of injustice; protection of society cannot be purchased at the price of stripping a person of his human rights. . . ."[17] In its everyday application, this kind of power can result in the warehousing of thousands of men and women whose major offense is that they are troublesome to their custodians, or that nobody can guarantee that they may not in some distant, but unknown future, prove dangerous to others. At its worst, it entails abuses that are an affront to the human spirit: in the Soviet Union, political dissidents are committed to mental hospitals.[i]

Nevertheless, the dilemma of the mentally ill offender remains a real one. Every prison system contains individuals who, but for chance, might have ended up in a mental hospital, just as every mental hospital contains individuals who, but for chance, might have gone to prison. A study by David Levine of patients in a large state mental hospital showed that 71 percent of them had been committed after behavior that was against the law—their actions involved either felonies or misdemeanors, and they could as easily have been jailed as hospitalized. He concluded that the mentally ill whose symptoms threaten the community are more likely to be admitted to mental hospitals than those whose symptoms do not threaten the community; that a sizeable proportion of patients diagnosed as mentally ill will have broken the laws; and that there will be a positive correlation between the threat to the community and their stay in the hospital.[18] A similar study of prison inmates would show the reverse face of this coin: that many inmates are mentally ill or retarded and could as justifiably have been hospitalized as imprisoned. In every jail and prison, officials must deal with inmates who are psychologically impaired, sometimes to a very serious degree. They cannot conform themselves to the demands of custody; they invite the most brutal kind of retaliation by their frequently intractable behavior; and they are likely to spend a great deal of time in maximum-security units, in solitary confinement. Needless to say, much treatment does little to improve their mental health.

Efforts to formulate a practical, rational, or theoretical relationship between crime and mental illness, says Levine, have largely failed. From the legal point of

---

[i]The Soviet rationale for giving psychiatric treatment to their political troublemakers is that since communism is the best of all possible systems, anyone who denies its validity must be *non compos mentis*. This is not unlike the reasoning of the New York authorities in sending Schuster to Dannemora: Anyone who denies the uprightness of prison authorities must be hallucinating.

view, the criminal act is inextricably entangled with the concept of responsibility. The concept of mental illness, on the other hand, stemming as it does from a deterministic philosophical and scientific framework, has largely ignored considerations of responsibility. In *The Mentally Abnormal Offender and the Law* (1969), the British psychiatrist Henry R. Rollin asked, "Should [the mentally abnormal offender] be treated for his mental illness or should he be punished for his offence?" Levine commented that asking the question in this way assumes there is a difference between "treatment" and "punishment."[19]

In his study of English practice, Rollin found no more satisfaction than do critics of the American scene. "The same mentally abnormal offender may be lobbed over the judicial net and land in the court cared for by the psychiatrist on one occasion and, on another by the prison officer," a game of Ping-Pong that might go on indefinitely. "There must be far more communication between jurists and psychiatrists," he wrote, "so that the strong arm of the law knows what the weak hand of psychiatry is doing, and even more important, perhaps, capable of doing.... Unless and until something of this sort is brought about, the Gilbertian situation which now obtains will continue, and psychiatrists and jurists, instead of being . . . brothers-in-law, will become increasingly partners-in-crime."[20]

Thomas S. Szasz, in *Law, Liberty and Psychiatry* (1963) argued that lawbreakers, irrespective of their sanity, ought to be treated as *offenders*. This would, he thought, provide some possibilities for "therapy" in a context where personal liberties are protected.[j] In his view, society's ambivalence toward the mentally ill had found new expression in the *Durham* and post-*Durham* rulings, placing mental patients and criminals once more in the same category. In the past we did this by asserting that mental patients are criminals; now we achieve the same end by claiming that criminals are mental patients. Thus, he said, the psychiatrist attempts simultaneously to protect the patient from society, and society from the patient, forgetting "the most important lesson which the history of democratic institutions and popular revolutions has taught us; namely, that the misbehavior of those who govern is no less a danger to society than the misbehavior of those who are governed. In other words, so-called mental patients are not the only persons in society who may be dangerous. Jurists, legislators, and psychiatrists may also be."[21]

Power relationships often have as much to do with the decision on who is crazy as the decision on who is criminal. David Levine has observed that people or groups with substantial power in the community are rarely seen as "dangerous."[22] Similarly, Thomas Szasz has pointed out that teachers and public school administrators may view their pupils as psychiatric problems: Students are not

---

[j]It is not clear why Szasz supposes that personal liberties are "protected" in prison. On the other hand, it is arguable that they are more protected in this frankly malevolent institution than in the supposedly more benevolent setting of a hospital for the criminally insane — which is saying little enough.

permitted such conclusions with respect to their teachers. Similarly, in psycho-analytic education, the training analyst may decide his student needs further analysis—but woe to the student who questions his analyst's mental health! And, says Szasz, "In courts of law, the same rule prevails: only the sanity of the defendant can be questioned, not that of the prosecutor or the judge."[23]

Does this mean that "mental disease" is no more than a convenient label for those who are both powerless and, at the same time, eccentric in their behavior? According to Herbert Fingarette, a review of the psychiatric and psychological literature shows no definition whatever of "mental disease," a phrase "notable by its absence in most of the theoretical, textbook, clinical, and dictionary literature." When it comes to defining the term in court, he says, psychiatrists and hospitals take many different positions: (1) There is no such thing as mental disease, or (2) mental disease is a psychosis but it is not neurosis, or (3) mental disease is any significant mental disturbance, or (4) mental disease is social maladaptation or incompetence (as judged by legal criteria), or, finally, (5) mental disease is a "failure to realize one's nature, capacities, or true self."[24]

But as we have seen, the law's attempts to define such terms as "insanity" or "mental disease" are hardly more satisfactory. Where there is so much semantic confusion, it is fair to suspect that more than semantics is involved. What is really involved, perhaps, is ignorance: we can give names to erratic behavior and describe symptoms, but much of the field of psychiatry is, like those nineteenth-century maps of Africa, to be marked Terra Incognita. Until we know a great deal more than we do about mental illness, it is unlikely that medicine can salvage the courtroom from its insane dilemma.

It would be nice to believe, with Henry Rollin, that simple communication between the disciplines of law and psychiatry would solve a problem that has vexed the common law for centuries. His suggestion that the two disciplines talk more to each other reminds one of the remark by Thoreau on the proposal to link Maine and Texas by "magnetic telegraph"—it may be, he said, that Maine and Texas "have nothing important to communicate." What should the law propose to psychiatry, or psychiatry to the law, that will not further compound their confusion? These two disciplines are like the man in Thoreau's story who worked hard at being introduced to a distinguished deaf lady, only to find, after she extended him her ear trumpet, that he could think of nothing to say.[25] It is hard to enlighten others when one is in the dark oneself.

Thus we stumble along, for lack of anything better, sending madmen to prison, and lawbreakers to mental hospitals. In the present state of our ignorance, the best we can hope for is that both types of institution be made somewhat more worthy of a civilized society.

26 The Psychiatric Diagnosis of Dangerousness

In the popular mind there is something uniquely threatening about the mentally disordered offender. He is indeed "twice cursed"—once for the evil he has done or may do, and once because the evil seems unmotivated. Society can be comfortable with crimes committed out of greed, jealousy, or anger because we all share these passions. We still believe it possible to deter the criminal who acts out of simple self-interest. And we can forgive someone who acts out of passion. The ones who worry us are, in Lady Caroline Lamb's wonderful phrase, the "mad, bad and dangerous to know":[a] those who commit the sudden violent, irrational crimes that bloody the front pages of our newspapers. In *Violent Men* (1969), Hans Toch described them thus:

In the ranks of these ogres are assassins and those who lynch them; stranglers of women and torturers of children; practitioners of patricide and killers of offspring; and among them we find the quiet veteran who converts his home town into a target range. Such men strike terror for several reasons: for one, they cast doubt on the sanctity of life, because they assault victims who have done them no harm and who are frequently unknown to them; they raise questions about the meaningfulness and predictability of human motives, because their lives typically do not foreshadow their tragic fate. Frequently these are the mildest, gentlest souls, immune to anger and unconcerned with their surroundings. Frequently they are shy, brooding, and shadowy, unnoticed until the moment when they explode into horrible prominence.[1]

Laws do not deter them, because they are not calculating. Their crimes cannot be prevented, because they give no warning. They are like sleeping adders, and when they strike, it is often to awesome effect. The law has never known what to do with them, and it has consequently turned to the psychiatrists for guidance. Unfortunately, said Frederic Wertham in *A Sign for Cain* (1966), "In no other area of the administration of justice is there so much injustice, so much confusion, and so much flouting of scientific and moral principles on a large scale." Although there is a substantial body of psychiatric knowledge on which all competent psychiatrists agree, he said, it "is surrounded by a wider field where differences of opinion are all too frequent."[2]

Wertham pointed out that the current *Diagnostic and Statistical Manual: Mental Disorders,* which was binding for all clinical and hospital psychiatrists, required them to distinguish between such terms as "sociopathic," "antisocial,"

---

[a]She was, however, referring not to a convicted criminal but to Lord Byron (who nevertheless well fitted the description).

187

"dyssocial," "pseudosocial," and "asocial." Another much-used term, "passive-aggressive personality," had three subdivisions in the *Diagnostic Manual*, and the third again had two subdivisions. Said Wertham: "This is clearly a terminology of confusion." Vagueness is not inherent in psychiatry, he thought, "though it sometimes is in psychiatrists." He described the judge who was seeking to have a psychiatric witness explain the term "antisocial": "Now in simple terms," said the judge, " 'antisocial personality'—doesn't that mean he is a crook?"[3]

Thomas Szasz was also critical of what he termed "our chaotic nosology" and blamed it on psychiatric eclecticism. He noted that in the standard nomenclature there is a tendency to combine physiochemical phenomena such as general paresis with behavioral events like hysteria and reactive depression. We now recognize, he said, that in physics the term "ether," and in biology, the term "protoplasm," obscured important problems; why, then do we fail to recognize that words like "schizophrenia" or "psychosis" may similarly obscure important problems in psychiatry? A label may have important consequences. Drunken drivers injure and kill more people than persons with paranoid delusions; but people labeled "paranoid" are committable—drunken drivers are not. Thus, he thought, it is not so much *dangerousness* that is involved here as "the manner or style in which one is dangerous."[4]

In a 1975 article "On Involuntary Psychology," Szasz argued against the involuntary commitment of psychiatric patients who are supposed to be dangerous. In American law, he said, dangerousness is not some abstract psychological condition but an inference drawn from the fact someone has committed an illegal violent act and has been found guilty—in which case he should be punished, not treated. The kind of "dangerousness" which is identified by psychiatrists but cannot legally be proven, he dismissed as "secular heresy." It cannot, under American law, he said, be the grounds for depriving anyone of his civil liberties.[5]

Thomas Szasz, it must be explained, is considered somewhat of a maverick by his fellow psychiatrists; actually, "heretic" may be a better term. For good or ill, psychiatry has increasingly been given the responsibility for identifying and treating those persons who pose a special threat to society, and with or without excessive eclecticism and a "chaotic nosology," its practitioners have struggled as best they can to satisfy the courts and the public. Rightly or wrongly, society believes that some people are indeed very dangerous. They commit dark and bloody crimes, often with little or no warning to those about them. Can such individuals be identified beforehand? Can their deeds be prevented? The American Psychiatric Association appointed a task force on the clinical aspects of the violent individual which in 1974 attempted to answer these questions.

First, it identified those groups of patients who are "suitable candidates for clinical concern to psychiatrists." These included: (1) Those who seek help because of repetitive problems with aggression and impulsivity and who often express fears of running berserk. (2) Those incarcerated for violent acts, who need diagnostic, presentence, or preparole evaluation. Among these are some people whose previous behavior may not have come to legal attention but who have a history of "sudden, senseless or bizarre acts, with or without psychotic behavior": e.g., an absence of apparent motive, no attempt to conceal the crime, impulsive action, murders of close family members, particularly brutal murder, complete emotional indifference, and a past history of mental disorders.

Other groups of concern to psychiatrists, they said, include (3) persons with a history of child abuse; (4) those with childhood behavior disorders accompanied by psychomotor agitation, aggressiveness, and belligerence; (5) persons suffering from such toxic or organic states as amphetamine psychosis or viral encephalopathy, and finally, (6) individuals with a history of dangerous driving.

Patients who are of clinical concern to psychiatrists may be distinguished from other violent persons on the basis of some or all of the following characteristics: they perceive their violent acts or urges as unwanted, as ego-alien or ego-dystonic; they exhibit a diagnosable mental disorder; their violence is associated with an underlying psychological abnormality, e.g., an organic state or an intoxication; their individual management is within the competence and scope of the psychiatric clinician.[6]

The task force said that "violent patients are seldom randomly or irrationally violent, but respond with violence" to stress situations. Their social history reveals that they have frequently come from homes where there was violence or parental deprivation. Alcoholism and parental brutality are commonly noted in their histories. However, situational factors do not necessarily exclude organic ones. While no positive association has been demonstrated between the actual clinical diagnosis—for example, schizophrenia—and crimes of violence, the clinician should take seriously the delusional patient with violent fantasies, the suicidal, and those who fear losing self-control. They should also be wary of schizoid or obsessive patients who report violent urges in a clinically detached way, and, pace Fredric Wertham, those with certain personality disorders, such as explosive, antisocial, or passive-aggressive types.[7]

Certain factors, said the task force, predispose and contribute to violence. One such is alcohol, which may lead to a state of "pathological intoxication," a transient psychotic-like state that is often accompanied by violent behavior. Other drugs contribute also, among them, the amphetamines, LSD, and barbiturates. Victims may contribute as well. Certainly the availability of weapons is a factor. Then there are certain organic conditions: in women, premenstrual tension; in men, perhaps, testosterone levels, although the evidence on this point is mixed. Other conditions include tumors of the limbic system, normal pressure hydrocephalus with dementia, encephalitic disorders, and metabolic conditions such as hypoglycemia. Nevertheless, to the questions, "What is the potential for future violence?" and "Is this man dangerous?" the task force saw no satisfactory or reliable answers. Such judgments, they said, "are fundamentally of very low reliability, much as would be the prediction of 'altruism' or other human behaviors." Clinical labels have long-term implications that warrant the utmost caution.[8]

Predictions of dangerousness, they said, like those of suicide, are predictions of rare events. A clinician might fairly expect a parent who has repeatedly abused his own children to do so again, just as he might safely predict arson from someone who can find sexual release only in setting fires, and who has repeatedly done so in the past. The reliability of t... ...dictions is a function of knowing that the base rates of such behavior are high. Not so, however, with threats of (unspecified) violence. In one reported study of one hundred persons, who, after threatening violence, were followed for five to six years, it was shown that three persons actually did commit murder, while four committed suicide. "The future dangerousness of persons who threaten violence would appear to be as much to self as to others." Unfortunately, to be safe, psychiatrists over-predict, especially in the case of the mentally ill offender, who may then be simply lost in a hospital somewhere, the victim of administrative oversight and excessively conservative release policies.[9]

The task force pointed out that dangerousness is an attribute, not only of individuals, but of environmental situations. The immediacy of some expected harm and its likelihood are clearly "a function of the potentially violent person's *future* or *expected environment* and not merely a function of any existing psychopathology." They concluded: "Violent behavior results from complex interactions, psychological, social, cultural, environmental-situation and biological factors. Despite various attempts at classification, there exists no adequate typology of violent persons."[10]

On the other hand, John R. Lion and Russell R. Monroe, writing in the *Journal of Nervous and Mental Disease* (1975), argued that while humility and social consciousness are all very well for a psychiatrist, "it would be clinically irresponsible to overlook the fact that individuals do exist who are troubled by violent urges and behavior and who would seek help to control these urges if appropriate treatment were available."[11] John R. Lion and Manoel Penna, in "The Study of Human Aggression" (1974), thought that the most common form of deviant human aggression occurs in the class of personality disorders labeled variously "explosive," "passive-aggressive," or "antisocial." Most prisoners, they said, fit one or the other of these labels. Such individuals demonstrate recurring and labile hostile episodes, rage attacks, temper outbursts; many have trouble with impulse control. Others, though able to plan and premeditate criminal activity, are nevertheless bothered by paroxysmal aggressive and impulsive acts that hamper their lives and actions. Prisoners say they "blow up easily" or "get mean streaks." Their outbursts, thought Lion and Penna, may reflect brain dysfunction.

A second type of deviant aggression may stem from a thought disorder such as schizophrenia, they said. While not impulsive, persons of this sort are often belligerent because of their delusional beliefs, hallucinations, and paranoid ideation; they are often suicidal as well as homicidal. Lion and Penna also listed other groups of aggressive persons: those who exhibit hyperkinetic behavior as a result of minimal brain dysfunction; those with hypersexual disorders; those with organic brain syndromes; and those with toxic paranoid psychoses induced by alcohol or other drugs. *Any* alteration in brain function, they said, can lead to violence. But prediction is very difficult; no test or set of qualities has been shown to be predictive in follow-up studies. It is as difficult to predict violence, they thought, as it is to predict any other human trait, such as altruism, fortitude, or courage.[12]

Much the same conclusion was reached in 1975 by the British Committee on Mentally Abnormal Offenders in a report to Parliament by the secretary of state for the Home Department:

The practice of referring to some individuals as "dangerous" without qualification creates the impression that the word refers to a more or less constantly exhibited disposition, like lefthandedness or restlessness. It is true that there are people in whom anger, jealousy, fear or sexual desire is more easily aroused and whose reactions are more extreme than in most people, prompting them to do extremely harmful things. But these emotions are aroused and lead to harmful behavior only in certain situations. A persistent housebreaker may go right through his criminal career without physically harming anyone; but if one day he is surprised, or cornered, he may have it in him to commit an offence of violence.

In releasing such patients, said the report, doctors "have to take into account the prospect of their being exposed to situations likely to have a 'trigger' effect."[13]

Does this mean that the search for some diagnostic and predictive test is chimerical—that we are no more likely to find it than the medieval alchemist was to find the philosopher's stone? There are many who think so. On the other hand, Dr. Harry L. Kozol, Richard Boucher, and Ralph F. Garofalo, reporting ten years of data from the Bridgewater (Massachusetts) Center for the Diagnosis and Treatment of Dangerous Persons, claimed in a 1972 study that dangerousness *could* be reliably diagnosed and treated, citing as proof their own experience at the center. Among those patients initially diagnosed, found not dangerous by staff, and released at the end of their sentences, they said, only 8.6 percent subsequently committed serious assaultive crimes. Among those released on recommendations by the staff after treatment, only 6.1 percent subsequently committed serious assaultive crimes. But of those patients released by court order *against* the advice of the clinical staff, 34.7 percent subsequently committed serious assaultive crimes, including two murders. From this experience, covering a total of 592 male offenders, the authors concluded that a reliable diagnosis of dangerousness was possible, at least where there was a history of violent assaultive behavior by the patients, as in these cases there was.[14] This conclusion was strongly questioned by John Monahan in a subsequent critique of their report (1973). Pointing out that these prognoses had a false positive rate of 65 percent—i.e., 65 percent of those they predicted as dangerous turned out not to be—Monahan added: "When an extraordinarily thorough clinical examination by at least five mental health professionals combined with an extensive social history and psychological test battery is inaccurate in two out of three predictions of dangerousness one cannot conclude that 'reliable diagnosis' of dangerousness has been achieved."[15]

Whether or not dangerousness can be reliably diagnosed, the fact is that thousands of those who are mentally disturbed and presumed dangerous are being scooped annually into the seines of our psychiatric or criminal justice systems. There they are either treated or not treated, released or kept in institutions, "cured" or forgotten. George B. Vold has estimated that approximately 30 percent of those in prison come under the heading of the "psychologically disturbed."[b,16] (By this he presumably does not mean those psychologically disturbed *by* prison, but those whose crimes are related to their mental problems.) It is, of course, impossible to set a figure for the psychiatric casualties in American prisons; most of them remain undiagnosed and untreated. The figure would certainly vary from one prison population to another.

In 1971 Dr. William E. Gordon, chief psychiatrist at the California Men's Colony-East, called this prison near San Luis Obispo "a huge warehouse for hundreds of men who are very sick mentally and not receiving treatment." Asked why something was not being done about the problem, he replied, "Well, sometimes I have the feeling that people don't really want to admit the problem exists. They just want to keep hiding their heads in the sand. If they looked, they would see that we are drowning in crazy people here and can't do anything to help them." At the time of this interview, half the population of CMC-East, some 1,200 prisoners, were so-called psychotics in remission; yet a prisoner who had been denied parole because he needed therapy, after waiting thirteen months for admission to a group, was told by Dr. Gordon, "I have been instructed [by the superintendent] to start no more groups at this time as group therapy was interfering with industries."[17]

Not all the psychiatrically disordered offenders, however, remain untreated. Many critics are even more alarmed by what is done in the name of treatment than by what is not done at all. As California criminologist James Robison put it in 1971, "Vengeance I can understand. We can then think about limits we put on our hostilities. But it's *rehabilitation* that really scares me."[18] What this rehabilitation consists of, and the debate that has grown up around the various treatment modalities, will be the subject of the next two chapters.

---

bThe other categories listed by Vold are: the unskilled, uneducated, and those of low ability, 40 percent; the ideational, high-grade, white-collar, political, or philosophical offender, 10 percent; the professional, crime-as-business type, 20 percent.

27 Treating the Intractable: The Experimental Sixties and Seventies

Lombroso was the first psychiatrist to practice criminology, and the first criminologist to formulate a psychiatric concept of criminality. To him, the "born criminal" was different from other people in his mental, physical, and moral constitution. The reason for this was evolutionary, said Lombroso, but the effect was decisive and final: A person so constituted could not be cured, no matter what was done to him. The positivist answer to this kind of innate infirmity was simply to remove such dangerous people from society forever. Garofalo recommended "transportation with abandonment"; taking the offender to some distant part of the globe and stranding him there.

But in the century since the publication of *Criminal Man,* the world has grown very small. Penal colonies have become emerging nations; no place in the world is more than a few hours away from any other; and unless we wish to colonize the moon with our dangerous offenders, society has been forced to contemplate seriously the question, what shall be done with people who are predatory, dangerous, and apparently intractable? Lock them up for the rest of their lives? Treat them in some way, in hopes that a cure will be found for their mental—or is it moral—infirmities? Americans, a perennially optimistic people, have inclined to the view that sooner or later, all problems, including the insoluble, can be solved. (During World War II, the motto tacked up in many army headquarters was, "The difficult we do at once: The impossible may take a little longer.") As earnest of their faith, they filled their landscape with penitentiaries and insane asylums to cure the morally and mentally infirm; and when they were faced with individuals who were both bad *and* mad, they created hospitals for the "criminally insane."

As we have seen, however, this did not dispose of the problem of the mentally ill offender. People with severe character and mental disorders were as likely to be found in prison as in a mental hospital. In the full flush of reformist penology, after the Second World War, it was decided to bring psychotherapy to these unfortunates, in hopes of curing them (if possible), but at least of making them less of a problem to custody. The more advanced penal systems hired psychiatrists, psychiatric social workers, and psychologists to see what they could do about the mental and emotional ills of their charges. It would be nice, of course, if they could "cure" them. But if not, could they make them a bit less troublesome?

The new professionals confronted a difficult dilemma. In most settings the therapist is called on to minister only to the needs of the patient. Here they were called on to fulfill a dual function—not only to treat the patient but to protect society. The prison psychologist or psychiatrist was not hired by the patient, but by the state. The usual considerations did not apply: There was no confidentiality between patient and doctor; there was no free choice of therapists or treatment modalities, either for the patient, or for the physician, who had always to subordinate clinical judgment to the demands of custody. In short, the prison psychotherapists found themselves not so much agents of therapy as of social control.

From the beginning their therapeutic treatments had a dual purpose: to cure the offender of his disorder, if that was possible, but in any case to keep him relatively quiescent in the prison setting. The first efforts in this direction were benign. During the ascendancy of psychoanalysis in the United States, particularly in the 1950s, California pioneered in the use of individual counseling and group therapy. John Irwin, author of *The Felon* and a professor at California State University, San Francisco, was himself a convicted robber during the heyday of this therapeutic experiment. "When I was in," he said, "the guys thought that they were sick and that the administration would cure them. . . . This was the era when all of the cons carried Freud or the Bible under one arm."[1] Therapy groups, however, tended to fall into disrepute when it could not be proven they did anything to reduce recidivism,[a] and although they were not entirely abandoned, other methods of treating psychiatric and emotional disorders became much more common, especially since the number of therapists in correctional institutions has always been limited.

The decline of psychotherapy as a treatment modality was paralleled by the rising popularity of various psychoactive agents that could be administered by mouth or injection. Since the primary concern of prison administrations was not the cure but the control of criminals, tranquilizers became the most widely used (and abused) of these agents. Known medically as ataraxics (from the Greek, *ataraxia*, calmness) these included such popular pharmaceuticals as Miltown and Equanil (meprobamate), Valium (diazepam), Librium (chlordiazepoxide hydrochloride), Serpasil (reserpine), and the phenothiazine derivatives, Stelazine, Thorazine, and Prolixin. In small doses, tranquilizers were used to relieve anxiety and tension states and agitated, hyperactive behavior. In large doses, such drugs as Stelazine, Thorazine, and Prolixin were prescribed for acute and chronic schizophrenias and manic-depressive psychoses. Unfortunately, these ataraxics came to be very badly abused in the prison setting, not only by physicians, who in some cases prescribed them with prodigal abandon, but by inmates, who traded and sold them on the prison black market.[b]

aCalifornia prison administrators to whom I talked in 1971 mourned the passing of group therapy. Said one official, "The men were much easier to handle when they were in therapy."

bIn the wake of 1973 disturbances at the Southern Ohio Correctional Facility at Lucasville, the Ohio Governor's Task Force on Corrections discovered that more than half the prison

Ataraxics were not to be taken lightly. Their side effects (differing, of course, from one drug to another) included fever, chills, angioneurotic edema, severe depression, hypotensive crises, aplastic anemia, parkinsonism, liver damage, and in massive overdoses, shock, coma, and vasomotor and respiratory collapse.[2] In prisons, unfortunately, despite efforts by staff to control their distribution, tranquilizers were often hoarded by inmates and taken in large overdoses (or mixed with other potent chemicals) to produce intoxication. Thus the very medications that, properly prescribed and taken, could relieve such psychotic symptoms as agitation, delusion, and hallucination in the mentally disordered offender could also, once they circulated on the prison black market, create general havoc.

On rare occasions inmates themselves protested the widespread prescription of tranquilizers in penal institutions. In her book *Kind and Usual Punishment* (1973), Jessica Mitford reported a petition against Prolixin by a group of Chicano prisoners in the California Men's Colony, who told the California Senate Committee on Penal Institutions that "a number of prisoners are walking the yard in this institution like somnambulists, robots and vegetables as a result of this drug. ... No prisoner feels safe because he never knows when he will become a candidate for it."[3]

More popular than tranquilizers with prisoners were the various stimulants prescribed by doctors as antidepressants such as Dexedrine Sulfate (dextro-amphetamine sulfate), Methedrine (methamphetamine hydrochloride), Ritalin Hydrochloride (methylphenidate hydrochloride), Tofranil (imipramine hydrochloride), and, of course, Benzedrine (amphetamine sulfate). Again, these were potent drugs that were valuable in combating depressive disorders, but circulating on the inmate black market, they created serious problems for prison administrators (as, indeed, they did outside the walls).

In the 1970s lithium carbonate was introduced to control recurrent violent behavior by inmates. The first experimental subjects included patients in California, New York, Connecticut, and North Carolina with such varied diagnoses as brain injury, schizophrenia, sociopathy, epilepsy, and manic-depressive psychosis. The use of lithium as a therapeutic agent dates back to 1859 when it was recommended for gout and kidney stones,[4] but as a treatment for psychiatric and behavioral disorders it was new. Experimenters at the California Medical Facility at Vacaville said that prisoners who were given lithium carbonate reported a decrease in aggressive feelings; either an increasing capacity to reflect on the consequences of their actions, or an increased capacity to control anger, or diminished anger. (Unfortunately, some also showed paranoid

population was on some kind of tranquilizer. Court testimony following two destructive riots at the Ohio Penitentiary in 1968 revealed that virtually all the prisoners in the rebellious maximum-security C & D block were on tranquilizers that summer—some of them on two or three different ataraxics, prescribed (unknown to each other) by different prison physicians. Unfortunately for the institution, the tranquilizers seemed not to have been sufficiently calming.

thought disorders and auditory hallucinations, and four of the subjects stopped taking lithium altogether because they thought that in their new, less aggressive frame of mind, they might be unable to defend themselves against other prisoners.)[5] The mechanism by which lithium acted was not entirely understood, but the chemical was known to enhance the metabolism of serotonin. (The lowering of serotonin has been shown to enhance the release of aggressive behavior in animals' brains.)[6] Lithium was best established as a treatment for manic-depressive psychosis, but as a group of New York experimenters observed (1972), "The mood stabilizing effect of lithium carbonate in emotionally unstable character disorder may be considered further evidence that this diagnosis is closely related to affective illness."[7]

Experiments with various psychotropic drugs proceeded on all fronts, each year finding new additions to the pharmacopoeia, so that any statement on the subject was almost out of date before it was published. Female hormones, too, were tried on sex and violent offenders because of the evidence of the role of androgens in the male aggressive and sexual behavior. Experiments showed that compounds with progesterone-like activity could suppress plasma testosterone in most normal male adults. Tests were accordingly conducted to inject the synthetic hormone Provera into sex deviates and epileptics with previously intractable outbursts of angry aggressiveness. Some experimenters reported that the hormone seemed to have a quieting effect.[8] (A similar rationale was used in the fifties and sixties by Dr. Georg K. Stürup at Herstedvester in Denmark to castrate psychopaths as a cure for their delinquency, an experiment for which he claimed success, but which was later abandoned.)[9]

While American prisoners were being used as guinea pigs for drug experiments, another form of experimental treatment was beginning to be tried on them with the sudden rise to popularity of behavior modification. "Behavior mod," as it was called, had its philosophical roots in hedonism and utilitarianism, its methodological roots in the animal learning and conditioning experiments of the Russian neuropathologist Vladimir Bekhterev (1857-1927), the Russian physiologist Ivan Pavlov (1849-1936), and the American psychologist Edward L. Thorndike (1874-1949). These pioneer investigators, of whom Pavlov was perhaps the most famous, provided a systematic basis for conceptualizing the behavioral interactions between organism and environment.[10] The pioneer American behaviorist was the psychologist John Broadus Watson (1878-1958) of the Johns Hopkins University, who focused attention on the implications for human psychology of the animal studies then under way in the United States.

Behaviorism, in effect, rejected the Freudians and, indeed, all subjective and introspective psychology. In his famous experiments, Pavlov had shown that he could cause a discrete stimulus (a bell) to elicit the same response in a dog as the original stimulus (food), so that after hearing bells and seeing food together, his dogs would begin to salivate at the sound of the bell alone. Pavlov was also able to reverse this behavior. Applied to people, this discovery meant that conditioning may be reinforced or extinguished. It did not, of course, imply that nothing *else* goes on in the human mind. But Watson was prepared to take this leap. To him, all adult behavior was the result of a series of stimuli and responses which, over a period of time, *conditioned* one to behave in a certain way. He believed that "given the relatively simple list of embryological responses which are fairly uniform in infants," he could build "any infant along any specified line—into rich man, poor man, beggar man, thief."[1]

During the 1920s millions of American infants were reared by behaviorist methods. If they cried, they were not picked up or loved; if they wanted food outside their strict four-hour schedules, they were not fed. Only if they smiled, were well behaved, and did what their parents wanted were they rewarded with food and affection. In the 1930s, however, behaviorism rather faded from the scene, as Freudian psychology came into the full flower of its popularity.

Nevertheless, animal laboratory experiments continued, and over the next twenty years experiments by B.F. Skinner and others added another and potentially more interesting string to the behaviorist bow: It was called *operant conditioning*. In operant conditioning, behavior is either strengthened or weakened by its consequences (rather than, as in Pavlov's classical conditioning experiments, by its antecedents). Thus the rat, pressing a lever, might get food (positive reinforcement) or an electric shock (negative reinforcement). Operant conditioning was, of course, not new. Animal trainers had for years been training seals, pigs, and dogs for circuses and sideshows by rewarding them if they performed their tasks right. But as a systematic theory and demonstrated method, operant conditioning is associated with Skinner.

Behaviorists now had three methods to apply to human beings. First was the classical conditioning of Pavlov; second was the operant conditioning of Skinner; and third was aversion therapy, the attempt to associate an undesirable behavior pattern with unpleasant stimulation—the layman would call it punishment. They had also the example of the Chinese, who had used these and other techniques in brainwashing American prisoners of war. By the 1960s the thought was occurring to a number of psychologists: Why not try them on those most intractable of human casualties, our criminals?

In a 1962 seminar of prison wardens and psychologists chaired by James V. Bennett, then director of the U.S. Bureau of Prisons, Dr. Edgar H. Schein, associate professor of psychology at the Massachusetts Institute of Technology, told the assembled wardens that the same brainwashing techniques used on American GIs would be quite acceptable if applied to criminals: "I would like to have you think of brainwashing not in terms of politics, ethics, and morals," he said, "but in terms of the deliberate changing of human behavior and attitudes by a group of men who have relatively complete control over the environment in which the captive population lives." He suggested such techniques as social disorganization and the creation of mutual mistrust, spying on the prisoners, and withholding mail from home. "If one wants to produce behavior inconsistent with the person's standard of conduct, first disorganize the group which supports those standards, then undermine his other emotional supports, then put him into a new and ambiguous situation for which the standards are unclear, and then put pressure on him."[12]

Listening to this advice, the wardens must have felt like Molière's *Bourgeois Gentleman,* who, upon being told the meaning of the word "prose," exclaimed: "Good heavens! Here I've been talking prose for forty years and didn't know it!" From time immemorial wardens had dealt with refractory prisoners by moving them around, withholding their mail, spying on them, and throwing them into solitary confinement (known as "the hole"); and now it appeared that these were, in reality, the very latest techniques of behavior modification. One panelist, when he was asked about the management of the unruly inmate, observed: "To some extent where we formerly had isolation as a controlling technique, we now have drugs, so that drugs in a sense become a new kind of restraint. The restraint is, therefore, biochemical, but it is restraint, nevertheless."[13] This answer must have pleased the wardens, whose interest in chemotherapy had from the beginning been more managerial than therapeutic.[c]

The more "progressive" American prison systems, like those of California and the Federal Bureau of Prisons, embraced behavior modification. So did many mental health systems, which instituted token economies as a reward for patients who behaved well. At the Patuxent Institution for Defective Delinquents in Jessup, Maryland, inmates were positively reinforced by being allowed to move upwards through a four-step graded tier system if they behaved well, and negatively reinforced by being moved down into "the hole" if they did not. Sometimes these "defective delinquents" were confined for months in dimly lighted, filthy isolation cells. In a class-action suit brought by Patuxent inmates (*McCrary* v. *Maryland*), associate director and psychologist Arthur Kandel explained that these cells did not constitute cruel and unusual punishment as alleged by the plaintiffs; rather, they were "negative reinforcers . . . used as positive treatment conditions."[d,14]

---

[c]Wardens have never been rewarded for curing their criminals; but they know very well that they will be punished if they allow them to get out of line. Or to use behaviorist terminology, they are given no positive reinforcement for any efforts at therapy, while getting negative reinforcement when they fail to keep order. Under the circumstances their priorities are understandable.

[d]The two-man court disagreed, ruling that the physical conditions in the segregation units constituted cruel and unusual punishment and said, "These conditions are contrary to the rehabilitation of the inmates and serve no therapeutic value of any kind." They ordered Patuxent to put a fifteen-day limit on "negative reinforcement," and mandated changes in virtually every aspect of institutional life. The graded tier system (except for its more flagrant abuses) was still permitted, and psychotherapy was included in the program as the "treatment of choice." All commitments to Patuxent were indeterminate, until the patient was cured or was able to sham a cure. Said one member of the staff, "If a man can sham well enough to make it in society, I have no objections. It means he's developed the internal controls that are necessary." [Sharland Trotter, "Patuxent: 'therapeutic prison faces test," in *APA Monitor* 6:5 (May 1975):1.]

California therapists tried a number of innovative experiments in behavior modification, including the Anectine suffocation treatments described in a previous chapter, which were carried out at Vacaville, Atascadero, and the California Institution for Women (CIW). Only at CIW were the experiments reported to the Food and Drug Administration; the other two did not report them on the grounds that the use of Anectine (succinylcholine chloride) was not experimental. Atascadero did not even bother to get consent before injecting the drug to stop the prisoners' breathing: One official reasoned that since Anectine was a standard adjunct to shock treatment, its use was not experimental because the prison staff, in this case, merely *omitted the shock*.[15]

Atascadero's enthusiasm for behavior modification did not visibly diminish despite the storm of public reaction to the Anectine program. Saying that "Psychotherapy is a dud," the director of research, Dr. Michael Serber, described plans for the establishment of the Physiological Laboratory for Behavior Studies. In 1971 he told interviewers of an experiment for curing sex deviates by first showing them erotic pictures and then, when they had an erection, administering electric shocks to them. This experiment he called "the errorless extinction of penile responses."[16] Dr. Serber was subsequently promoted to be director of the Atascadero State Hospital.

The Federal Bureau of Prisons, too, adopted behavior-modification techniques for its more recalcitrant inmates, described as those who, "in terms of personality characteristics shall be aggressive, manipulative, resistive to authority, etc."[17] Behavior-modification programs were instituted at Marion, Illinois; Leavenworth, Kansas; and El Reno, Oklahoma. In the Control Unit Treatment Program at Marion, fifty-one inmates were confined in unit segregation for up to sixteen months because they took part in a food and work strike in 1972; thirty-two of them were not released until a court order was obtained. The Government Accounting Office recommended to the attorney-general that the Bureau act to determine how long-term segregation programs were being conducted, but according to Congressman Ralph H. Metcalfe, who wanted the programs closed down, no such evaluation was ever undertaken.[18] Instead, the federal government went ahead with an ambitious plan to set up the Special Treatment and Rehabilitative Training project (START), to be housed in a new 13.5-million-dollar institution, the Behavioral Research Center at Butner, North Carolina. It is perhaps significant that in the first group designated for the program, fewer than half had been convicted of violent crimes; the majority were inmates who were considered "troublemakers" in prison. The stated purpose of the START program, which began experimentally at Marion and was supposed to be transferred later to Butner, was "to promote behavioral and attitudinal change in that element of the prison institution which has chronically demonstrated inability to effectuate adherence to established regulations." It would change such behaviors as "are maladaptive to living in a prison environment, as well as society," and, like Patuxent, it would work through a status system with three stages, or tiers, subdivided into nine levels. The prisoner on the bottom level would have only a bed, mattress, and pillow. He would eat in his cell and be allowed two showers a week—no visitors, reading material, radio, commissary, or cigarettes. By behaving well, he could work himself up in the system. Describing START for *The Prison Journal* (1974), James G. Holland drily observed, "Blessed are the meek, for they shall be promoted to Level Two."[19]

Behavior-modification programs were now going on in mental hospitals and prisons throughout the country. The most commonly used was probably a mark, point, or token system to reward inmates for docile behavior. Alcoholics were treated by giving them emetics (the unconditioned stimulus) and just before the onset of nausea, requiring them to taste, smell, or look at their favorite beverage.[e] In other, more drastic experiments, alcoholics were given Anectine or another brand of succinylcholine chloride, administered just before the patient took a drink, and producing near suffocation. Electric shocks were administered to alcoholics, homosexuals, and other patients in need of a "cure." Aversive suppression was also used: punishment, either in the form of an aversive stimulus after the fact (positive punishment) or the removal of positive reinforcements such as the deprivation of goodies (negative punishment). In one experiment a transvestite was placed on an electric grid and, while dressed in women's clothes, was given 200 shocks in eight days.[20] Behavior therapists treating transvestites at the Veterans' Hospital in Brecksville, Ohio, wrote a helpful article for *Behavior Therapy* in which they instructed their fellow professionals on how to make an inexpensive, quickly built shock grid for less than five dollars. (The relay-switching unit would, they added, cost an additional six.)[21]

Clearly, a new day had dawned in society's long efforts to control criminals. Writing in *Psychology Today* (1970), Professor James V. McConnell of the University of Michigan said, "Somehow we've got to *force* people to love one another, to *force* them to want to behave properly." To achieve this, he thought, punishment had to be used as precisely and dispassionately as a surgeon's scalpel. McConnell had spent years training flatworms, which may have accounted for his enthusiasm. He had had no trouble whatever training the worms, he said, but admitted having "one hell of a time" training new laboratory assistants. McConnell evidently considered criminals more like flatworms than like lab assistants, because he saw no problem in reforming *them.* In fact, by combining sensory deprivation with drugs, hypnosis, and an astute use of rewards and punishments, he thought, it was now possible to gain almost absolute control over an individual's behavior.

For misdemeanors, he would administer brief, painless punishment. Felons would be sent to a rehabilitation center to undergo "positive brainwashing." In their case it might be necessary to restructure their entire personalities. The

[e]This is a very old treatment, and in the nineteenth century, was the basis for the famous Keeley cure for alcoholics.

old-fashioned belief that we build up our personalities logically and by free will be dismissed as no more correct than the belief that the world is flat. No one, he said, owns his own personality. Our egos are forced on us by our genetic constitution and by society. Having had no say about what kind of personality he has acquired, there is no reason to believe that the antisocial individual has any right to refuse to acquire a better one. The techniques of behavioral control, McConnell concluded, "make even the hydrogen bomb look like a child's toy." He called behavioral psychologists "the architects and engineers of the Brave New World."[22]

Alas, even as Dr. McConnell limned this prospect, a storm was gathering over his "brave new world" of drug experiments and behavior modification. The first sounds of protest, by the experimental subjects themselves, were at first muted by the high walls of prisons and mental hospitals. But increasingly, questions were raised in professional journals by lawyers, psychologists, and psychiatrists. As reports of these experiments found their way into the newspapers, legislators also began to ask questions. Investigations were begun, lawsuits were filed. Soon the architects and engineers of the brave new world found themselves the center of a controversy more violent than anything they had ever known, one of such hurricane force as to threaten, not only their glorious blueprints for the future, but the very structure and design of research on human beings.

28

The "Brave New World" is Challenged

The mind-bending experiments on American prisoners that began in the 1950s with the ataraxic drugs and expanded in the 1960s into ambitious programs of behavior modification represented a triumph for the positivist view that criminality inheres, not in the shortcomings of society, but in the individual himself. As envisioned by the "architects and engineers" of the new order, these treatment modalities provided the ultimate weapons of social defense. Everything else, they thought, had proven ineffectual: the classic notions of punishment and deterrence; the liberal reformers' efforts to humanize prisons through education, group counseling, and more decent institutions; the diversion of offenders from the criminal justice system; work furlough and community-based corrections. Now, however, *at last,* the criminal could be changed by acting directly on his brain and central nervous system so that he would no longer *will* to do wrong.

The whole concept of free will, so dear, not only to Catholic tradition, but to Anglo-American jurisprudence, was in any case dismissed by the behaviorists as irrelevant—no more than a picturesque figment of the popular imagination, rather like the unicorn or the mermaid. Nobody's will is free, they said. We are all, from earliest childhood, conditioned by our experiences to respond and behave in certain ways, some of which may be good, some of which may be personally or socially harmful. The task of behavior modification is to change those responses that have turned the criminal into a lawbreaker. We can literally *make him over,* and it would be both irresponsible and an unkindness to him not to do so.

But as luck would have it, the more ambitious American experiments on prisoners were taking place in a social climate that by the late sixties and early seventies had become increasingly turbulent. Outside the walls, civil rights and anti-war protesters had sent mobs of blacks and young people into the streets, shouting revolutionary slogans and defying the public authorities. Behind the walls prisoners, too, were feeling restive and resentful. There were prison disturbances in states as widely separated as Florida, Ohio, California, Arizona, and New York.[1] After strikes and riots at several Ohio prisons in 1968 (two bloody and massively destructive ones at the Ohio Penitentiary), Commissioner of Correction Maury Koblentz explained darkly, "Outside influences stir things up," a comment for which he was given the Flying Fickle Finger of Fate Award by the popular television comedy show, *Laugh-In.* Warden R.W. Meier of the McNeil Island Federal Penitentiary expressed the same view to the 1969

203

Congress of the American Correctional Association. He blamed much of the revolutionary militancy behind the walls on war "resisters, draft dodgers, professional agitators, Communists, hippies and revolutionaries. . . . Former prisoners, militants, far-out liberals, subversives, and even a few clergymen, educators, and social workers on the outside seem to delight in fomenting unrest in prisons," he said.[2]

The new militancy did not provide a propitious climate for experimental programs in behavior modification. Critics inside and out rejected the very premise underlying such treatment. There was nothing wrong with *prisoners,* they asserted; prisoners were the victims of a society that callously deprived millions of the barest necessities of life, then punished the few among them who had the courage to rebel. It was not the people behind bars who needed behavior modification, it was society. This view was forcibly expressed by a group of radical young criminologists at the School of Criminology of the University of California. It was, of course, not a new point of view. Various changes had been rung on the same theme by Holbach and Brissot de Warville in the eighteenth century, by Engels, Turati, and Loria in the nineteenth, and by Bonger and his successors in the twentieth. But the radicals among the Berkeley criminologists went beyond an expression of philosophy and became active with the New Left in the political battles and street demonstrations of the day. The School of Criminology became so controversial that in 1974 the chancellor decided to close it down, a process which, in spite of violent student demonstrations, was finally completed in 1976.[a]

The philosophical debates that divided criminologists were not at first related to the peculiar experiments in behavior modification: the issues were much broader than that, embracing not only political philosophy but the whole concept of the nature of man and society. Yet it was inevitable that sooner or later, behavior modification would become an issue—perhaps *the* issue—in the argument over what should be done about criminals. At first there was little public awareness of what was happening at places like Vacaville and Atascadero. The earliest reports appeared in the so-called underground newspapers, that is, papers of radical views, uncertain financing, and sometimes irregular publication which proliferated during the Viet Nam war. These delighted in printing stories ignored by the great metropolitan dailies. Because California had been in the forefront of experimental behavior modification, it bore the brunt of their exposés. In 1970 the American Civil Liberties Union, which had become active in prison litigation, asked author Jessica Mitford, who lived in Oakland, if she would do an article on the civil rights of prisoners for a national magazine.

The ACLU had picked a woman of unusual wit, energy, and determination.

[a]The controversy was not limited to the putative radicalism of some of the faculty but also involved accusations by other university departments that its academic standards were low—a charge that had been leveled for a decade and provided an additional excuse for the decision.

The Honorable Jessica Freeman-Mitford (as she was known to *Burke's Peerage*) was one of the six beautiful daughters of Baron Redesdale. All of them were striking individualists, none more so than Jessica[b] who had become a well-known author and investigative reporter, best remembered for the 1963 best-seller, *The American Way of Death*, an exposé that made her the scourge of the funeral industry. When the ACLU approached her to do a study on prisoners' rights, she explained that she knew nothing about the subject. Nevertheless, her investigative instincts aroused, she accepted. When she told a criminologist that her topic was to be "prisoners' rights," he told her, "That's an easy assignment. Just turn in a sheaf of blank papers—they *haven't* any rights."[3]

It was not long before Jessica Mitford discovered the drug and behavior-modification experiments then going on in American prisons and was able to document from their own mouths the grandiose dreams of the behaviorists. She publicized the use of prisoners by pharmaceutical companies to test new drugs, and she described the immemorial brutality and degradation of prison life. These descriptions she juxtaposed with the high statements of principles that had for a century been the staple fare of correctional congresses. Her book on American prisons, which appeared in 1973, she called *Kind and Usual Punishment.* Written with dry understatement, it gave embarrassing and detailed publicity to the use of prisoners as pharmaceutical guinea pigs, and to the "brave new world" of personality reconstruction through drugs, brainwashing, and torture.

The professionals were particularly pained by it—not only the wardens, who now felt about her much as funeral directors once felt, but the mental health professionals, psychologists, and psychiatrists, who were forced to confront the issues posed by these experiments, and confront them where they least wanted to, in the public arena. The federal government, the American Medical Association, and the American Psychological Association all had ethical guidelines that were clearly violated by the experiments Jessica Mitford had so vividly described. The 1972 statement of principles of the American Psychological Association said, "The ethical investigator protects participants from physical and mental discomfort, harm and danger," adding that the subject must at all times have freedom to decline to participate in the research.[4] Then there were the federal guidelines for research on human subjects that governed the grants and contracts in which subjects might be at risk. The Department of Health,

[b]At the age of nineteen, Jessica Mitford had made headlines by running away to the Spanish Civil War, hoping to become a guerrilla fighter on the side of the Loyalists. (Her plan was spoiled when, at Lord Redesdale's insistence, the British government sent a destroyer to Bilbao to bring her home.) Another daughter, Nancy, became a well-known British novelist. Unity Valkyrie, celebrated by Hitler as "the most perfect Nordic beauty in the world," shot herself in Munich when England declared war on Germany and was returned to her family by the fuehrer in a special hospital train in 1940. Still another daughter, Diana, married the Fascist leader Sir Oswald Mosley and defiantly spent the war years in the women's prison at Holloway. Small wonder that Lady Redesdale once wistfully remarked, "Whenever I see the words 'Peer's Daughter' in a headline, I know it's going to be something about one of you girls."

Education and Welfare's *Institutional Guide to DHEW Policy on Protection of Human Subjects* (1971) stated that "an individual is considered to be 'at risk' if he may be exposed to the possibility of harm—physical, psychological, sociological, or other—as a consequence of any activity which goes beyond the application of those established and accepted methods necessary to meet his needs." The *Guide* required a careful review of such projects by a professional committee not involved in the research and the fullest explanation to the subject of all the procedures, discomforts, and risks involved. The subject was to be free not to participate or to withdraw at any time once the experiment was in progress. One clause would clearly have outlawed the Anectine experiments at Atascadero, which, it will be recalled, were not reported on the grounds that Anectine was an established drug in shock therapy. The clause read: "Even if considered established and accepted, the method may place the subject at risk if it is being employed *for purposes other than to meet the needs of the subject*" (emphasis added).[5]

Jessica Mitford's was not the first voice to have been raised in public protest. Enforced therapy was already the subject of considerable criticism—and some lawsuits—from those true believers in free will, the legal fraternity. In 1971 Nicholas Kittrie, a professor of law at American University, published *The Right to be Different: Deviance and Enforced Therapy.* What was to prevent the state, he asked, under the therapeutic aegis, from compelling changes in the education, job training, residence, or marital condition of anyone who might in the future become harmful to society? Under such a future therapeutic ideal, the criminal process might be abandoned altogether in favor of environmental manipulation and control. Where once the heretic was burned if he did not embrace orthodoxy and the aristocrat was beheaded to create a classless society, in the future the ideal might be to be social, orderly, cooperative, and "normal." Then all who were eccentric, asocial, or antisocial would be forced to undergo treatment.

For Enrico Ferri and his disciples, said Kittrie, the therapeutic state derived its justification from social defense. In America it claimed its ancestry in the doctrine of *parens patriae* and in welfare considerations. Currently there are no absolute limits on the exercise of these therapeutic powers; their moral problems are concealed because once the individual is treated, he may be incapable of objecting to it, being now pleasant and happy, with no recollection of his prior condition. "But where has the old 'soul' or personality gone, with its hangups, tensions, prejudices, bias, problems, dreams, talents, and individuality?" Kittrie demanded. "Has it not in a very real way been executed?"[6]

In a 1972 article ("Conditioning and Other Technologies Used to 'Treat?' 'Rehabilitate?' 'Demolish?' Prisoners and Mental Patients"), Roy G. Spece, Jr., one of the editors of the *Southern California Law Review,* considered not only the "right to treatment"—then being extensively litigated—but the right to be left alone. "Just as the courts have found a right to privacy of the marital bed, and a right to view obscenity in the privacy of one's home," he said, "so should they find an analogous right to privacy or freedom of the mind when a prisoner or mental patient is threatened with the application of therapies that drastically intrude into his person and engender gross changes in his behavior and thought patterns. Such a right would seem to be at the core of any notion of privacy and freedom because if one is not guarded in his thoughts, behavior, personality, and, ultimately, in his identity, then these concepts will become meaningless."[7]

In "The Ethics of Behavior Control" (1973), Perry London, a professor of psychology at the University of Southern California, noted that in the past, society always assumed that both social deviance and social responsibility were the chosen behavior styles of individuals in control of themselves at the deepest level of awareness, their desires. Now behavior technology was challenging the utility of such concepts by making it possible to populate utopia with human automata—people free at every level of behavior *except* desire. The real danger of this was not that "a few tyrannical rogues" would seize power and then "scramble our brains" to keep it. Rather, it was that such power, even when benevolently used, ran the risk of eroding freedom whenever it took place by the decision of someone other than the person on whom it was used—and even against the subject's wishes.

Our Western ideology of freedom, said London, has been well served by the myths of English history, the American and French revolutions, the Periclean Greeks, and the ancient Jews. No matter what limits society places on the expression of passions or the fulfillment of desires, "individual freedom always exists in the one domain where nobody can be hurt by its expression and nobody can question its inviolability—the human mind. . . ." The message of behavioral technology is that "will is ultimately not free, nor is ideology, nor man." It is this threat to our pet mythologies that so frightens us, he believed. Even the greatest tyrants of history have never had such power over other men, the power to make them do what others want them to do. London argued that *awareness* was the only ethical instrument of social control and that it must operate through education, not coercion, persuasion, rather than law. Behavior control should be vested internally, not in other people's hands. On the other hand, London thought that "informational and coercive methods" are both useful for expanding awareness and, to that extent, should be used. He concluded, "The more clear it is that will is, in absolute terms, a fiction, the more important it is to protect the individual whose rights have hitherto been borne upon that myth. For he is the same creature, with the same endowments, sentiments and intellect, whether he is guided by soft machinery or an immortal soul."[8]

Even if Jessica Mitford was not the first to protest behavior control in prisons, she was the first to expose the practice in embarrassing, sometimes grisly, detail and to shame the professional societies and agencies of government into taking action. In late 1973 the Health Subcommittee of the Senate

Committee on Labor and Public Welfare began hearings on research involving prisoners and asked Jessica Mitford to testify on the use of prisoners for testing drugs. On November 16, 1973, the Department of Health, Education and Welfare published a set of proposed new rules to provide protection for human research subjects; for the first time these contained special provisions for the protection of prisoners. On July 12, 1974, the National Research Act was signed into law, creating the National Commission for the Protection of Human Subjects of Biomedical and Behavioral Research. Eight states and the Federal Bureau of Prisons moved to abandon all research, including drug testing, in prisons. The secretary of HEW issued more and more guidelines for research involving departmental grants in May and August 1974, March 1975, and June 1976.[9] As one restriction followed another, alarm was expressed by those engaged in biomedical and behavioral research that the federal government was in danger of throwing out the baby with the bathwater. Were rules becoming, in fact, so strict as to outlaw all research on institutionalized subjects? If that was so, how would new drugs be tested on human subjects? (Jessica Mitford had suggested, only half in jest, that the stockholders of pharmaceutical companies be appointed guinea pigs for testing drugs, a suggestion the manufacturers could not have found amusing.)

It was striking that *Kind and Usual Punishment*, which also recounted the gross day-to-day degradation and brutalities of ordinary prison life, had no effect whatever on *these* immemorial abuses. Public attention (and apprehension) seemed centered on those invasions of human autonomy that posed a threat to free will. John P. Conrad in "What Happened to Stephen Nash? The Really Important Questions About Dangerousness" (1976) called attention to this anomaly:

We have all been properly horrified by *A Clockwork Orange*,[c] and Jessica Mitford has regaled us with the gothic treatments once administered, it seems, by some California correctional clinicians. We must be careful, but in our fear of error and abuse, we must still think clearly. For generations we have operated and continue to operate Adjustment Centers, punitive isolation, administrative segregation units, and Alabama doghouses[d] with some outcry, but not nearly as much as we get when we try to replace them with behavior modification programs, token economies, pharmacological interventions, or psychosurgery. Is it the case that there must be an absolute prohibition of any such intervention, but that our consciences can tolerate the daily confrontation of keeper with the kept at a constant level of threatened violence?[10]

---

[c]Anthony Burgess's 1962 novel, *A Clockwork Orange*, described an imaginary program for changing the behavior of criminals in some unspecified technological future. Unfortunately, in this case life imitated art; by the time the book was made into a movie (1971), the practices it recounted were already in use in California.

[d]"Adjustment Center" was the euphemistic name for the California prison system's most stringent security units. "Alabama doghouses" refers to a segregation unit at Draper, outside the main prison, and shaped like a doghouse, where prisoners were kept crowded together in total darkness. John Conrad, a former director of research for both the California and federal prison systems, was an expert witness for the court in a 1976 civil-rights case brought by inmates against the State of Alabama.

The answer appeared to be yes. Prisoners and public alike saw something new, something uniquely threatening in this technology that promised to control them, not only in their bodies, but in the innermost core of their personalities. In the federal prisons, there was a furore over the plans for Butner, and eventually they were abandoned.[e] In Maryland, legislation was introduced to close down Patuxent. The adjustment centers, the Alabama doghouses, even the ancient whipping post, did not look so fearsome to their potential victims as the threat of being turned into zombies. Even the general public, punitive though it had always been, recoiled before the prospects. In their minds there arose the ancient question, *Quis custodiet ipsos custodes?* Who was going to control these controllers? Was it to be a case of today the prisons—tomorrow the whole world?

In January 1977 the National Commission for the Protection of Human Subjects of Biomedical and Behavioral Research, which had been studying the issues involving prison inmates, published their report in the Federal Register. "... Innovative practices in prisons," they said, "intended to rehabilitate or treat prisoners, often have many attributes of behavioral research but are seldom introduced as such. The major controversy over participation of prisoners surrounds their use as subjects of biomedical research not related to their health or well-being and their unwilling involvement in experimental treatment or rehabilitative programs." They mentioned as examples so-called therapeutic communities, structured tier systems, token economies, aversive conditioning, castration and even psychosurgery, adding that "rehabilitative practices have not always been based upon prior scientific design and evaluation ... despite the fact that there are few, if any, approaches to the treatment or rehabilitation of prisoners for which effectiveness has been clearly demonstrated."[11]

The report acknowledged that there was much disagreement among professionals on the usefulness and desirability of such treatment. In a paper prepared for the commission, Martin Groder, M.D., the former warden-designate at Butner, had argued that *only* therapeutic psychosocial research directly addresses "the promise of rehabilitation." Offenders, he said, as wards of the state, have a right to treatment that will be abridged if correctional research is stifled through overregulation. A ban on such research, he told the commission, will ensure that no correctional innovations will be developed.

On the other hand, lawyers from Boston University's Center for Law and Health Sciences warned that medical treatment generally constitutes a battery if the patient has not consented to it. Although one jurisdiction has not applied this rule in cases involving convicts, they said, others have held that imprisonment does not deprive a person of the capacity to decide whether or not to consent to health care. The latter rule has been applied in cases dealing with physically invasive behavior-modification techniques, although there is no such holding on noninvasive techniques.[12]

---

[e]After much criticism and a number of court challenges, the entire START program was ended. Butner finally opened in May 1976, offering only the usual vocational and academic courses and counseling.

The commission noted that twenty-one states permitted biomedical research and twenty-three states behavioral research but that studies were now being conducted in only seven and five, respectively. Of five states doing behavioral research, four called it "therapeutic," and one claimed it was *both* therapeutic and nontherapeutic. The report recommended permission for "research on practices, both innovative and accepted, which have the intent and reasonable probability of improving the health or well-being of the individual prisoner," provided certain conditions be met (see below). But they warned:

The committees that review all research involving prisoners[f] should analyze carefully any claims that research projects are designed to improve the health or well-being of subjects and should be particularly cautious with regard to research in which the principal purpose of the practice under study is to enforce conformity with behavioral norms established by prison officials or even by society. *Such conformity cannot be assumed to improve the condition of the individual prisoner.*[13] (Emphasis added.)

For research on prisoners to be acceptable, said the commission, it must (1) fulfill an important social and scientific need; (2) the involvement of prisoners must satisfy conditions of equity; and (3) the participation of the subjects *must be voluntary*. The prisoners must be permitted to communicate with outside persons, attorneys, and review committees on a privileged, confidential basis. And, finally, (4) the living conditions in the prison must comply with seventeen enumerated standards. Those standards were so high that it was doubtful any prison in the United States could meet them.[g]

Thus by 1977 the issue of biomedical and behavioral experiments with prisoners was very much in doubt. Between threatened lawsuits, unfavorable publicity, and increasingly stringent research guidelines, that glorious world of behavior modification, where people could be *forced* to love each other and criminals, to embrace the professed standards (but not the pocketbooks) of the

[f]All research involving prisoners was to be reviewed by at least one human-subjects review committee or institutional review board composed of women and men of diverse racial and cultural backgrounds that included among its members prisoners or prisoner advocates, community representatives, behavioral scientists, and medical personnel not connected with either the research or the institution. In fact, such committees had already been set up by HEW directives for research involving grants from that department. However, the commission had been mandated by Congress to make recommendations for *all* research supported by the federal government or conducted in federal prisons.

[g]Among some of the requirements were that the prison population not exceed designed capacity, that there be single-occupancy cells for all who wanted them, that there be segregation of offenders by age, degree of violence, prior criminal record, and physical and mental health. The commission also required that there be good-quality medical facilities, adequately staffed and equipped and accredited by an outside accrediting organization; that there be adequate opportunity for prisoners who so desired to work for pay comparable to that of the research subjects; that the racial composition of staff be reasonably concordant with that of the prisoners; that inmates be permitted to lock their own cells, etc. Virtually any one of these requirements would have eliminated federal research grants to American prisons.

better classes, seemed to be receding once again to rainbow's end. John P. Conrad expressed the feelings of many when in 1976 he told the American Society of Criminology:

All of us are safer when we set firm limits on what we allow the state to do to any of us. Once we allow unrestrained pragmatism to govern our decisions, even in the disposition of the unworthiest of men, we generate an ethical cancer which will destroy the vitality of free institutions and the security of free men. Let us hope that when the day comes that science offers criminal justice a foolproof drug or surgical procedure to stop criminal behavior we will be principled enough to reject it.[14]

29 Some Reflections on the Mind of the Dangerous Offender

If the preceding chapters seem curiously schizophrenic, it is because we have looked at the mind of the offender from conflicting perspectives. Not only are psychiatry and the law frequently at odds here; so are ethics and expediency, individual rights and social defense. Even within the disciplines of psychology and psychiatry there are differing opinions about the etiology and treatment of deviant behavior. A glance at the second edition of the *Diagnostic and Statistical Manual of Mental Disorders* (DSM-II) shows that the criticism leveled by Szasz and Wertham at the first edition (DSM-I) still stands. While it is a useful glossary of psychiatric terms, the nosology does indeed seem eclectic, if not chaotic. In this omnium gatherum may be found such totally disparate concepts as schizophrenia, endocrine disorders, senile dementia, fetishism, acute alcohol intoxication, congenital syphilis, and passive-aggressive personality.[a]

An individual who commits a crime may be described by a psychiatrist as suffering from paranoid schizophrenia, acute alcohol intoxication, dyssocial behavior, or explosive, antisocial or passive-aggressive personality; but which of these terms, under the law, should excuse him from punishment?[b] On the other hand, which of these types is likely to be improved or deterred by legal sanctions? These are not frivolous questions. The law has wrestled long with them, like Jacob wrestling with the angel, and like Jacob, it hath prevailed not.

At the heart of the problem is the concept of responsibility. If an offender is not responsible, how can he be guilty? And if he is not guilty, why should he be punished? The answer appears to be: *as a measure of social defense.* It is an answer at odds with traditional Anglo-Saxon jurisprudence, and the law had designed elaborate obfuscations to confuse the matter further, as witness the

---

[a]As of the present writing (1977), DSM-III is in preparation. The first draft suggests that it has been totally reorganized to meet the criticism leveled at DSM-I and -II, of "chaotic nosology."

[b]In 1969 I attended the trial of an Ohio Penitentiary inmate who was charged with prison riot (a felony) and was found not guilty by reason of insanity after a defense psychologist testified he suffered from "passive-aggressive personality." DSM-II describes this disorder as follows: "This behavior pattern is characterized by both passivity and aggressiveness. The aggressiveness may be expressed passively, for example by obstructionism, pouting, procrastination, intentional inefficiency, or stubborness [sic]. This behavior commonly reflects hostility which the individual feels he dare not express openly. Often the behavior is one expression of the patient's resentment at failing to find gratification in a relationship with an individual or institution upon which he is over-dependent." After this verdict, the prisoner was shipped to the Lima State Hospital, an institution with which he may or may not have achieved a more gratifying relationship than he had with the penitentiary.

various statutes for the commitment of psychopaths, so-called defective delinquents, the mentally ill, and those found not guilty by reason of insanity. There
are few more terrible verdicts than not guilty by reason of insanity: it could
mean incarceration for the rest of one's natural life.

But if one leaves aside the legal questions and looks only at the medical,
important problems remain. How much validity is there to the concepts
subsumed under "neuroses" or "personality disorders"?[c] They certainly describe
the way some people behave, but what do they mean? To explain "personality
disorder" by saying it is "characterized by deeply ingrained maladaptive patterns
of behavior," and is sometimes determined by "malfunctioning of the brain" is
like explaining rain by saying it is characterized by falling water and is
sometimes determined by the malfunctioning of clouds.

Some day we may discover what malign influences underlie personality
disorders, whether they be social, biological, or demonic. In our present
rudimentary stage of knowledge, it is best to acknowledge that we do not know.
Some criminals, mad or not, seem to have spontaneous remissions; others
respond to the salvational efforts of chaplains, social workers, or mental health
professionals. And then there are those who wake up from a mystical experience, embracing God. Most, however, remain obdurately unresponsive to
anything but their own selfish appetites. That is why "rehabilitation," like all
the healing arts, continues to be something of a mystery, even to its practitioners.

What, then, about the remaining questions, those of ethics, individual rights
and social defense? Does an admittedly unjust society have the right to legalize
the predatory practices of its richest members while punishing the malefactions
of the poor even by taking over their minds and personalities? The poor, through
the years, seem to have been resigned to the ordinary indignities of the penal
system—adjustment centers, Alabama doghouses, and the rest. But the awesome
possibilities of behavior modification, especially when combined with psychoactive chemical agents, have aroused a spirit of rebellion, even in these perennial
losers. Prisoners through the ages have submitted to the dungeon, the lash, the
chain-gang and the gallows; what they fear most in these new treatment
modalities is the annihilation of the human spirit.

You ask, does not society have the right of self-defense? The answer is, of
course. A society, to survive, must defend itself. In fact, a society is defined by
its willingness to defend its members and by the feeling that an attack on one is
an attack on all. If it lacks that power, that will, and that feeling, it cannot call
itself a society.

---

[c]DSM-II lists the following neuroses: anxiety, hysterical (including conversion and dissocia-
tive types), phobic, obsessive compulsive, depressive, neurasthenic, depersonalization,
hypochondriacal, and others. Personality disorders include paranoid, cyclothymic, schizoid,
explosive, obsessive-compulsive, hysterical, asthenic, passive-aggressive, inadequate, and
others.

Yet there is one autonomy that the social contract cannot sign away. That is the autonomy of the soul—the freedom to be wise or foolish, generous or mean-spirited, brave or cowardly, good or evil. If free will is an illusion of Western society, it nevertheless remains its most cherished illusion. In the interests of social peace, man has little by little given up the power to do what he pleases. He will not willingly relinquish the power to *think* what he pleases.

We have accepted punishment because it assumes that we are morally responsible human beings. What we cannot accept is the attempt to meddle with our minds and personalities, even when—perhaps especially when—it is done with benevolent intentions. Commenting long ago (1949) on "The Humanitarian Theory of Punishment," English author C.S. Lewis had this to say:

Of all tyrannies a tyranny sincerely exercised for the good of its victims may be the most oppressive. It may be better to live under robber barons than under omnipotent moral busybodies. The robber baron's cruelty may sometimes sleep, his cupidity may at some point be satiated; but those who torment us for our own good will torment us without end, for they do so with the approval of their own conscience. They may be more likely to go to Heaven, yet at the same time, likelier to make a Hell of earth. Their very kindness stings with intolerable insult. To be "cured" against one's will and cured of states which we may not regard as disease is to be put on a level with those who have not yet reached the age of reason or who never will; to be classed with infants, imbeciles, and domestic animals. But to be punished, however severely, because we have deserved it, because "we ought to have known better," is to be treated as a human person made in God's image.[1]

**Part V
Physiology and Crime:
The Return of the Born
Criminal**

30 The Anatomy of Crime

Ever since the phrenology of Franz Josef Gall and Johann Gaspar Spurzheim in the early nineteenth century, people have been fascinated by the thought that the shape of the body determines the bent of the character. Gall read the destiny of the individual in the configurations of his skull; Lombroso identified his "born criminals" by such stigmata as jug ears, enormous frontal sinuses and jaws, a low forehead, a square and projecting chin, and broad cheekbones. Despite Charles Goring's assertion that *"there is no such thing as a physical criminal type"*—an assertion hotly disputed by Harvard anthropologist Earnest A. Hooton—the belief has persisted among some criminologists that, as Freud once put it, "anatomy is destiny."[a]

In 1939 Hooton published what was to have been the first volume of *The American Criminal: An Anthropological Study*, dealing in this case with *The Native White Criminal of Native Parentage*. Although dismissing Lombroso's notion of atavism, Hooton nevertheless agreed with the Italian criminologist that criminals have distinctive physical characteristics. He had made elaborate measurements on 17,077 individuals, including college students, convicts, firemen, policemen, and mental patients, and concluded that in nineteen out of thirty-three measurements, there was a significant difference between criminals and civilians. Criminals, he claimed, had low foreheads, high pinched nasal roots, crooked noses, compressed faces, and narrow jaws; they also had small (rather than jug) ears, long necks, and sloping shoulders. Physical inferiority is significant, he said, because it is associated with *mental* inferiority. Crime is the result of the impact of the environment on a low-grade human organism, and it will never be eliminated, Hooton thought, until we extirpate the mentally, physically, and morally unfit.[1]

Another version of the idea that anatomy is destiny is to be found in the body type (somatotype) theories which, in their modern form, originated with the German psychiatrist Ernst Kretschmer of the University of Tübingen. In his *Physique and Character* (1921), Kretschmer revived an ancient trichotomy of constitutional types, the asthenic (lean and long-limbed with underdeveloped muscles); the athletic, with strongly developed skeleton and musculature; and the short, rotund pyknic type. In addition, there was a category he called "dysplastic," which represented an incompatible mixture of types often characterized by glandular or other organic disturbances. Although Kretschmer was

---

[a]Freud was thinking, of course, not of the differences between criminals and noncriminals but of those between men and women.

primarily interested in the relationship between body type and mental disease,[b] in the later editions he applied his findings to criminality. He believed that criminals show roughly the same proportional distribution of constitutional types as are found in the general population—that is, about 20 percent pyknics, 40-50 percent asthenics and athletics, 5-10 percent dysplastics, and less than 30 percent mixed types—except that there are somewhat fewer pyknics among the criminals. The criminality of asthenics (whom he dubbed "leptosomes") tends to peak at a very early age, that of pyknics at a very late one. Athletics show a stable degree of criminality up to age 55. Leptosomes, said Kretschmer, are strongly represented among thieves and swindlers, athletics among those who commit crimes against the person. Pyknics are attracted to fraud, and dysplastics to sexual offenses.[2]

Somatotype theories had a wide following in Europe and were introduced to the United States by William H. Sheldon of the University of Chicago (later of the College of Physicians and Surgeons at Columbia University). Sheldon, who held doctorates in both psychology and medicine, was personally acquainted with Freud and Kretschmer. He was a proponent of what he called constitutional psychology and psychiatry, terming it "the precise reversal of the Freudian method," which starts with what is most subjective and most remote from the bodily reality, and then attempts to proceed toward what is relatively objective, the body. This, said Sheldon dismissively, is "like aiming for the South Pole by swimming North." The constitutionalists looked first at the organism and its body structure, in order to understand the temperament and psychological makeup of the individual. This was not a new approach, dating as it did from the time of Hippocrates. But Sheldon had worked out a scale that for the first time made it possible to type individuals with the same precision that a judge uses in awarding points at an animal show. His own interest in the subject he attributed to his father, a breeder of poultry and dogs, who had trained him to judge animals according to the point system.

"By the age of 15," he said, "I had attended many different kinds of livestock exhibits, and was probably as competent a judge at most of them as I could ever expect to become." It had never occurred to anyone to wonder how judges could agree almost perfectly in the use of such simple quantitative devices, and it did not now occur to Sheldon to question the application of a point scale to human beings. The term *thoroughbred* had an essentially quantitative meaning, he thought, whether "applied to roosters or to men." The "*t* component," as he called thoroughbredness, was really nothing but "*aesthetic pleasingness.*" But aesthetically pleasing to whom? Sheldon admitted that the West Coast African might have defensibly different standards from those of the Chinese or Swedes, just as Rhode Island Reds and Partridge Cochins are always

[b]He found a strong positive correlation between the asthenic and athletic types, and schizophrenia. He also found a correlation between the pyknic type and manic-depressive psychosis.

judged separately. As for the mongrels, the mixed types (which means most human types), one had to judge by strength, efficiency, intelligence, muscular coordination, and bodily harmony. Some blends are good, some are not.

In working out this quantitative scale for humans, Sheldon began with Kretschmer's basic somatotypes, to which he gave different names. The pyknics he called "endomorphs": these were fat people, with great development of the digestive viscera. The athletics he called "mesomorphs" (muscular individuals, with a predominance of bone, muscle, and connective tissue). And the asthenics he called "ectomorphs" (tall and thin, with relatively little body mass in relation to skin and nerves). With respect to these three components, each individual was rated on a scale of 1 to 7. The first numeral referred to endomorphy, the second to mesomorphy, and the third to ectomorphy. Thus a 7-1-1 was an extreme endomorph, and a 1-1-7 an extreme ectomorph. The somatotype 4-4-4 fell at the midpoint of the scale with respect to all three components.

Related to these bodily types were three basic temperaments. Endomorphs, said Sheldon, are viscerotonic: they love food, relaxation, and physical comfort, and are amiable and even tempered. Mesomorphs are somatotonic: assertive, energetic, dominant, and ruthless. Ectomorphs are cerebrotonic: restrained, controlled, cerebral, and hypersensitive. In a comparison between two hundred delinquent boys at the Hayden Goodwill Inn in Boston and a group of two hundred controls, Sheldon found that mesomorphy predominated but that almost half of the delinquents also showed unusual muscular weakness for their body type. Sheldon wondered whether this sort of inconsistency—it was, after all, anomalous that a muscular mesomorph should be lacking in muscle!—were not an underlying factor in delinquency.[3]

Sheldon's system of measurement was widely adopted, and in the late forties it was applied by Eleanor and Sheldon Glueck to a study of five hundred persistently delinquent boys with whom they matched five hundred nondelinquents on the basis of age, intelligence, ethnic origins, and type of neighborhood. In *Unraveling Juvenile Delinquency* (1950), the Gluecks reported that some 60 percent of the delinquent group were mesomorphs, as against 30 percent of the nondelinquents. Temperamentally, they were restless, energetic, impulsive, and destructive, sometimes to the point of sadism, and their attitudes tended toward hostility and defiance. They also came from bad homes and neighborhoods. Delinquency, the Gluecks thought, while it might be accounted for by any one of these factors, was probably the result, in most cases, of the interplay among them.[4]

This was not an unduly deterministic conclusion, but then, the Gluecks were not physicians. It should be noted here that outside of Calvinism the most deterministic views of criminality have had their origins in the medical sciences. Gall, Spurzheim, Lombroso, Lange, Kretschmer, and Sheldon were all physicians, trained to look at their subjects from the inside out. The physician understands human behavior as a reflection of physiological functioning, determined by body structure and chemistry, and affected by disease process and impairments. Thus *point of view*, in the most literal sense, becomes important here. Every discipline that has dealt with the criminal, whether it be religion, medicine, law, psychology, anthropology, or sociology, has looked at him from a different perspective—so much so that when taken all together, their divergent conclusions sound like nothing so much as the blind men describing the elephant. Not only do these disciplines explain the same phenomena differently, but they are quick to criticize each other's perspective because they are not trained to share it.

Sheldon did not hesitate to conclude that delinquent youths were "of extraordinarily poor stock and of low *t*."[5] The social criminologists, on the other hand, reject the view that some people are constitutionally inferior. Commenting on somatotyping, Sutherland and Cressey said that Sheldon and the Gluecks "have adopted a system characterized by a noted physical anthropologist as a 'new phrenology in which the bumps of the buttocks take the place of the bumps on the skull.' "[6] George B. Vold pointed out that theories of constitutional inferiority have a special methodological pitfall in that the clinical observer is prepared in advance to find in offenders the special symptoms he has in mind. Thus the characteristics Hooton found in criminals were used to indicate inferiority, and inferiority was assumed on the basis of these characteristics—a perfect example of circular reasoning. One wonders, said Vold, whether results might be different if clinicians and caseworkers had no previous knowledge of who was delinquent and who was not.[7]

At the heart of all theories of constitutional inferiority lies a question that, in Sheldon's words, "cannot long be ignored by any political group that desires to survive." In his view, "a projected social science which waives the question of the physical quality of its human material must remain either a precipitate of revolutionary opportunism or just a waste of time."[8] But what exactly did the constitutionalists have in mind? Hooton spoke darkly of the need to *extirpate* the mentally, morally, and physically unfit, a concept that could imply anything from selective breeding to gas ovens. To those who held this view, the logic was inescapable. If certain individuals are born to be bad, condemned by accident of birth to lives of nightmare and destruction, then the way to be rid of crime is to be rid of them *and their progeny*. This was the eugenic view that found its classical statement in *Buck* v. *Bell*: "three generations of imbeciles," thought Justice Holmes, "are enough." To Hooton and Sheldon (and, no doubt, could he have been resurrected, to R.L. Dugdale), three generations of criminals were also enough.

But after the Second World War, both eugenics and somatotypes went into popular eclipse. American criminologists, who were sociologically trained, had never, unlike the Europeans, taken either Kretschmer or Sheldon very seriously. The question of constitutional inferiority and its effect on crime was not to be revived until the 1960s with the discovery of an extra sex chromosome in some criminal populations. This was the XYY karyotype, widely publicized as "the chromosome of criminality," a subject to be discussed in the next chapter.

31 The Aberrant Chromosome

Until 1956 it was thought that humans had forty-eight chromosomes. The discovery that there were, in fact, only forty-six was made possible when a technique was introduced for differentiating between the nuclei of male and female cells by the examination of buccal mucosa smears (taken by scraping the inside of the cheek). In 1960 another technique was introduced for culturing white blood cells to obtain cell arrest in the metaphase stage of cell division. Because this would arrest the chromosomes in the process of meiosis and mitosis, it now became possible to count and analyze them as each pair separated. Within a year it was discovered that some people have extra sex chromosomes.[1]

The normal female carries two X (female) chromosomes, one from each parent. The normal male carries one X chromosome, inherited from his mother, and one Y (male) chromosome, inherited from his father. Blood samples from a man, therefore, should show the XY karyotype, or chromosomal characteristics. But to the astonishment of medical researchers, it was discovered that some men have three or four sex chromosomes, either XYY or XXY (the latter denominated Klinefelter's syndrome) or even XXYY. In 1965 Dr. Patricia Jacobs and two associates, Muriel Brunton and Marie M. Melville, reported on a survey in the Scottish Special Hospital at Carstairs of mentally subnormal male patients with dangerous, violent, or criminal propensities. Blood samples taken in a routine examination showed that twelve patients out of 197 had some chromosomal abnormality: seven had 47 chromosomes with an XYY constitution, one had 48 with an XXYY constitution, and one was XY XYY mosaic. The remaining three had structural abnormalities of the autosomes (non-sex chromosomes). The most important finding, the researchers thought, was that eight, or 3.5 percent, had the extra Y, or male, chromosome. By contrast, a sample of 1,709 randomly selected adult males and 266 randomly selected newborn babies had turned up not a single male with an XYY constitution.[2]

The Jacobs report, which appeared in the British journal *Nature,* galvanized the medical community. Because the report said that in this hospitalized sample of violent patients, a man more than six feet tall had one chance in two of being an XYY and that the mean height of XYY patients was six feet one inch, a survey began around the world in prisons, mental hospitals, and institutions for the criminally insane to see whether among the tall inmates there were any with the XYY configuration. The reasons for confining the survey to tall inmates of prisons and hospitals were that (1) short ones did not seem to suffer this

223

abnormality, (2) neither did many noninstitutionalized adults, and (3) karyo-typing was extremely expensive.

The journals now became filled with reports of XYYs around the world, and these were picked up by the newspapers, which hailed a breakthrough in criminology with the discovery of the "supermale" and the "chromosome of criminality." One survey in a large London prison (which disclosed 9 XYYs among 355 tall males) reported that compared to a control group, the nine had the following characteristics: a past history of mental illness, usually designated as psychopathy; decreased intelligence; lower achievement than father or brothers; more convictions than the controls but not more total offenses [i.e., they were at least unluckier, if not more ill-behaved]; increased height, in comparison to father or brothers; a criminal history of property offenses; an asocial personality; parental alcoholism; and homosexuality—covert rather than overt.[3] Other early studies variously described the typical XYY as having one or more physical or physiological abnormalities, being unusually tall, unintelligent, impulsive, and hyperaggressive. Although there seemed often to be no predispos-ing family history to account for his actions, his criminal activities began at an early age. In maximum-security institutions, these studies said, his numbers exceeded by as much as twentyfold the incidence of XYY males in the newborn population, and therefore he was at considerably higher-than-average risk of coming into conflict with the law.[4]

The extra Y chromosome made headlines in 1968 when Daniel Hugon was tried in Paris for murder. His defense attorney claimed that his client was an XYY and hence not responsible for his crime. After trial and conviction, Hugon was given a reduced sentence, presumably in consideration of his physiological defect. At about the same time, in Melbourne, Australia, Lawrence E. Hannell, on trial for murder, was acquitted by reason of insanity after testimony by the defense that he had an XYY constitution. (There had also been testimony about his mental deficiency, abnormal electroencephalogram, and temporal lobe epilepsy, so it is unclear how much weight was given to the chromosomal defect alone.)

During the late 1960s there were more than 160 articles in medical and professional journals on the XYY anomaly.[5] As is so often the case, the more studies that were done (on normal and institutionalized populations), the more questions arose, and the less certain the answers became. For example, in these early studies, no case of the extra Y chromosome was found among blacks. Did this mean that only white violence could be accounted for by the XYY chromosomes? Why was the XYY apparently associated with criminally violent behavior in some cases but not in the great majority?[6] There was even a strong disagreement about the actual character of XYY individuals. Although some studies described them as being exceptionally masculine and aggressive,[7] others said they were timid, reserved, and passive.[8] Research seemed to show an abnormally high incidence of XYYs among mentally ill or retarded criminals—1.9 percent as opposed to 0.15 percent in the population at large—but they were not much more common in ordinary prisons than they were outside.[9] And then there was the greatest question of all. If there were really 1.5 XYYs per thousand in England, France, the United States and elsewhere, where were they all? In the United Kingdom, only seventy had been found.[10] In France, as one writer pointed out, there should be about 30,000 such males; yet most had never gotten into trouble.[11] About the only thing really clear in the statistical picture was that XYY males were tall, and that they were more common in criminal mental institutions than they were outside; but even in such institutions, they constituted less than 2 percent of the population.

Because of the numerous articles on the subject and the striking disagreement among the findings, the Center for Studies of Crime and Delinquency in the National Institutes of Mental Health called together a small group of scientists and researchers from the field of genetics, medicine, psychiatry, psychology, sociology, and law to discuss the subject. In 1970 this group rendered a Scotch verdict of "not proven." "The demonstration of the XYY karyotype in an individual does not, in our present state of knowledge, permit any definite conclusions to be drawn about the presence of mental disease or defect in that individual," they said. "A great deal of further scientific evidence is needed." They pointed out that institutionalized offenders represent a select, recidivist, and handicapped subgroup and that XYY males may be less adept at evading arrest. Furthermore, various other types of chromosomal abnormalities (XXY, for example) equaled or exceeded the number of XYYs in institutionalized populations. What was needed was more research on XYY men on the outside before concluding that an extra Y chromosome "in some way compulsively drives a person to deviant and aggressive behavior. . . ."[12]

By this time the question of XYYs in the general population seemed to be the key to the many questions that remained unresolved. At Harvard Medical School, Dr. Stanley Walzer, a psychiatrist, and Dr. Park Gerald, a geneticist, set up a long-term project to detect chromosomal aberrations in the newborn and to determine what effects, if any, these might have on their later development.[13] At the same time a study was begun in Denmark in which chromosomal tests were performed on a sample of all males who had been born to residents of Copenhagen from 1944 through 1947. The sample consisted of those who were more than 184 centimeters tall, and of this group, the researchers were able to test 90.8 percent. A search of the Danish penal registers showed that 41.7 percent of the XYYs (five out of twelve) had been convicted of one or more criminal offenses, compared to 9.3 percent of the control group of normal XYs, a significant difference in rate. The XYYs had lower scores on the army selection intelligence test and in the educational level attained, leading the researchers to conclude that intellectual functioning was implicated as an important mediating variable but not necessarily the only one. Said the researchers, "People of lower intelligence may be less adept at escaping detection and so be likely to have a higher representation in a classificatory system based on registered crimes. The elevated crime rate found in our XYY group may therefore reflect a higher detection rate rather than simply a higher rate of commission of crimes." As for the supposed aggressiveness of the XYY, they found no evidence of this whatever. Most of the offenses committed by the group were nonviolent property crimes; among all the XYY criminals there was only a single instance of an aggressive act against another person, and the most serious sentence in the lot was for less than a year.[14] Thus was laid to rest the myth of the aggressive XYY supermale, without, however, resolving the questions: What does the extra Y chromosome do to the individual who carries it? Should anything be done for him, and if so, what?

In their prospective study, the Harvard researchers hoped to find out. But alas for scientific intentions! Walzer and Gerald, like the behaviorists, were to discover that important social and political implications may be read into the most innocently intended research, particularly if, as in this case, the university contains a vocal contingent of social activists. As the testing of baby boys progressed during the early 1970s, a group which called itself "Science for the People" and which included microbial biogeneticists Jonathan Beckwith of Harvard and Jonathan King of MIT, filed a formal complaint with the administration of the medical school. They also held a press conference and public meetings in the city of Cambridge in an effort to stop the project. Walzer and his family received about twenty abusive and threatening telephone calls.

Among 15,000 baby boys tested over a period of six years by the Harvard researchers, 45 had been found to have either the XXY or the XYY configuration. The parents had been told about the extra chromosomes; they were also told that as yet no one knew what the possible effects might be. The families were offered several visits a year by a psychiatrist and additional visits by a trained observer. There was a dual purpose in this: to compare the child's behavioral development with the norms for the general population and to try to help with any problems that might arise. But to critics of the project, this amounted to social stigmatization with every danger of a self-fulfilling prophecy.[15] In an article for *Harvard Magazine,* Beckwith and a young colleague, Larry Miller (also of Science for the People), argued that the XYY studies are not solely an academic issue, of concern only to scientists: they had already affected many lives, and even, to some extent, influenced social policy. "The myth that XYY individuals are unusually aggressive has reinforced a model held by some—that social problems can be attributed to genetic defects in individuals rather than to conditions of social and economic deprivation." Behavioral research can be dangerous, they said, when social assumptions are incorporated without acknowledging that they *are* social assumptions.[16]

In the same issue of *Harvard Magazine,* Professor Bernard D. Davis deplored the behavior of Science for the People. The interest of this group, he said, was not primarily a concern for the innocent children; it was rather the conviction that any attention to genetic factors might, like Social Darwinism and the eugenics movement, have reactionary social consequences.[17]

The protests of Beckwith and his Young Turks were rejected by the Harvard Medical School, whose final review committee concluded that the study had been properly evaluated and approved by the various school and hospital committees and did not violate any ethical principles. Beckwith appealed the rejection to the faculty and was defeated by a vote of 199 to 35. For several months there was no further attack on the XYY study. Then the Children's Defense Fund, an organization of public-interest lawyers, sent a representative to visit Dr. Stanley Walzer to ask that the study be terminated. Walzer, who had survived professional attacks, press conferences, abusive phone calls, and protest meetings, agreed finally to give up all further screening. He said, however, that he would continue with the patients already under study. Davis was dismayed by this outcome. He observed:

Perhaps our institutions, while tolerating dissent, might set limits on its style. For we must recognize that we are dealing not simply with legitimate dissent. Just as Lysenko destroyed all of genetics in the Soviet Union from 1935 to 1969, Science for the People aims to destroy the field of human behavioral genetics. . . .
    The layman finds the risks of harm from research highly visible, while the consequences of ignorance are likely to be seen as acts of God. . . . The layman also is inclined to take for granted the benefits of present knowledge, while the professional knows that we had to take risks to expand it.[18]

But Miller and Beckwith retorted that research of this type is too important to be left to peer committees, whose primary purpose, they said, is often the legitimization of research rather than the protection of subjects.

Those who cry "academic freedom" or "freedom of inquiry" often seek to stifle public discussion rather than to promote *informed* discussion. Instead of being brought into an issue long after its inception, as occurred in the XYY case, the public must be involved from the start. Science, like politics, is too important to be controlled only by its practitioners.[19]

The arguments over genetic and social factors were not new—the debate was at least a hundred years old—but the forum had changed, and so had the manners involved. The battles once fought with the pen in the discreet pages of obscure academic journals had taken to the press, the air waves, and the courts. The issues *were* important, but it seemed to many scientists that a new and disquieting note had been injected which involved far more than a question of academic bad manners: What was increasingly at stake, they thought, was the right of free inquiry in areas with profound political or social implications. Critics now claimed the license, not merely to argue with research they disapproved of, but to shout it down and drive it from the ideological marketplace. Scientists had lost their innocence at Hiroshima and had forfeited public trust and esteem through a generation of well-publicized, sometimes nasty, experiments on their fellow human beings; now they were being asked to pay the price. For them and their work, it seemed, there were to be no longer any ivory towers, not even at Harvard.

32 Brain Control and the Violent Offender

Harold Franklin Benson was a mild-mannered computer scientist who was injured in an auto accident on the Los Angeles Freeway. Thereafter, he suffered seizures of psychomotor epilepsy, during which he committed acts of terrifying and brutal violence that he could not afterwards remember. At the suggestion of a neurosurgeon, Dr. John Ellis, an electrode was planted in Benson's brain and attached to a power-pack computer in his shoulder so that his seizures could be aborted by delivery of an electric shock. Benson, *The Terminal Man,* was the 1972 creation of an adroit science-fiction writer Michael Crichton, a 1969 graduate of Harvard Medical School and a postdoctoral fellow at the Salk Institute. Like the hero of *A Clockwork Orange, Terminal Man* Benson was only one jump ahead of reality. Harvard already had its model for Dr. Ellis in the person of a neurosurgeon, Dr. Vernon H. Mark, who, together with two colleagues, Dr. Frank R. Ervin and Dr. William Sweet, formed the Neuro Research Foundation. The National Institutes of Mental Health had given them $500,000 to further their work on the implantation of electrodes in patients with brain pathology. A Senate subcommittee was so impressed by Dr. Sweet's testimony about their work that it ordered one million dollars for research in this area to be added to the budget of the National Institute for Neurological Diseases and Stroke. Moreover, the Foundation was given a grant from the Law Enforcement Assistance Administration to test procedures for screening habitually violent prison inmates for brain damage.[1]

Scientists had long been fascinated by the thought that there is something different about the criminal brain. Lombroso, it will be remembered, announced flatly that all born criminals are epileptics (although not all epileptics are criminals).[2] But although he had found, or thought he had found, that there was something anomalous about the configurations of the criminal skull, a century of postmortem examinations on aggressive criminals have revealed few abnormalities inside the brain that could be detected by any methods now available to medicine. On the other hand, a growing body of research since the 1940s has produced evidence of functional, as opposed to structural, defects in the brains of individuals with patterns of persistently aggressive criminal behavior.[3] These defects were discovered in electroencephalograms of their brain-wave patterns.

According to a 1972 report, twelve out of fourteen studies of the relationship between EEGs and psychopathic behavior indicated that between 47 percent and 58 percent of individuals diagnosed as "psychopaths" had abnormal EEGs. The abnormality most commonly detected was a so-called theta rhythm[a] known as the "14- and 6-per-second positive spike."[4] Theta activity is the principal component in normal children between two and six years of age,[5] but in adolescents and adults it often—not always—signals severe personality disorders. In their pioneering study of normal and psychopathic patients in British military hospitals (1942), Denis Hill and Donald Watterson found that 65 percent of their sample of aggressive psychopaths had EEGs similar to those of young children; among those who were also epileptic, 82 percent had abnormal electroencephalograms. Hill and Watterson concluded on the basis of their evidence that "an abnormal EEG constitutes for its possessor a handicap in the business of biological adaptation, failure of which may show itself . . . in undesirable, asocial behaviour."[6]

There were many subsequent EEG studies, some of delinquent children, some of adolescents, some of adult prisoners and mental patients. Among the characteristics reported for those showing the 6- and 14-per-second positive spiking were destructive behavior, temper tantrums, nightmares, hyperactivity, impulsivity, the inability to establish controls, a failure in awareness or memory of behavior, violent action without demonstrable feeling tone, and the inability to change the direction of an act until it was completed. Among the acts characteristic of these individuals were cruelty to children and animals without any showing of remorse; near-panic reactions, accompanied by extreme destructiveness; impulsive running away from home or school; larceny; fire setting; attempted suicide or aggressive behavior without adequate motivation; and sexual misbehavior accompanied by violence. Among their relatives there were histories of such difficulties as migraine headaches, violent temper, emotional problems, psychoses, epilepsy, psychopathic personality, alcoholism, criminality, and such family problems as divorce, child abuse, and abandonment. The medical histories of those with abnormal EEGs sometimes showed brain damage from injuries or a record of such diseases as chorea, encephalitis, meningitis, illnesses accompanied by a high fever, and *asphyxia livida* from a difficult birth. In other cases, however, their medical histories appeared to be normal.[7]

Because the EEGs of aggressive psychopaths often resemble those of young children, one of the first hypotheses advanced was that there is a failure of maturation involved—that somehow, in persons with severe personality disorders, the central nervous system has not developed normally.[b,8] As Alexander Shapiro put it (1968), "the behaviour patterns typical of psychopathy—egocentricity, low frustration tolerance, explosive attacks of aggressive behaviour, and mood swings—are not so much abnormal as characteristic of the

---

[a]The term "theta rhythms" is used to distinguish components at 4-7 c/s from those of delta frequency (below 4 c/s). [See W. Grey Walter, "Electroencephalography," in G.W.T.H. Fleming, ed., *Recent Progress in Psychiatry*, 2nd ed., (London: J. & A. Churchill, n.d.), p. 80.]

[b]The term "aggressive psychopath" is used in these studies to indicate a violent individual who shows no anxiety or remorse; who is impulsive and unpredictable; and who can neither be reformed nor deterred from his aberrant behavior.

behaviour of the young child in the 'tantrum stage' of its personality develop-ment."[9] But others suggested other hypotheses: that cortical influences may produce autonomic or endocrine effects, either directly or through biochemical means; or that structural brain damage or biochemical dysfunction, whether hereditary or acquired, may interfere with normal central nervous function.[10]

An important question raised by these studies was whether or not the symptoms of behavior disorder and autonomic dysfunctions commonly seen in patients with positive spikes were epileptiform in character. A 1965 study by John R. Hughes of over 1,900 patients with positive spikes showed an average incidence of convulsion of over 41 percent. The most common type of attack was grand-mal epilepsy, but there were also psychomotor attacks, petit mal and Jacksonian seizures.[11] This would seem consistent with the observations of Lombroso that there was some connection between epilepsy and the type he called the "born criminal." It did not answer the question of etiology, which continued to be a subject of debate. Was this spike phenomenon inherited or acquired? The evidence was very mixed. On the one hand, the medical histories of many individuals with the spike phenomenon showed a history of head injury or disease. Some studies showed, however, that where there was a family history of psychosis, maladjusted personality, alcoholism, or epilepsy, there was a greater probability that the EEG of the patient would be abnormal. Further-more, where the parents had abnormal electroencephalograms, there was a skew away from the normal in the distribution of EEG types in the children. In short, the scattered evidence suggested either maturation *or* acquired *or* inherited neurophysiological activity, but no one was quite sure which.[12] Hughes thought that because of the "complicated interplay between organic and psychiatric factors, psychologically oriented investigators will likely have great difficulty in explaining this disordered behavior solely on psychiatric grounds, while neuro-logically oriented investigators will usually have similar difficulty explaining the behavior solely on organic grounds."[13]

Most researchers thought that the locus of the positive spikes was within the thalamic or hypothalamic region of the brain. Others suggested the hippo-campus. Still others thought they might originate in the amygdala or the medulla oblongata. In short, nobody really knew. As for the abnormal EEGs, they were symptomatic only. One would have to go inside the head, inside that complex, convoluted organ called the brain, to be really sure what these tracings might mean.

Until the twentieth century the only portion of the brain that had been extensively investigated was the cerebral cortex, primarily because of its relative accessibility. But, according to some recent theories, human beings seem to have inherited three brains. One is the primitive, reptilian brain, which includes the hypothalamus, midbrain, and basal ganglia, and which organizes behavior in a stereotyped way, as though imprinted with ancestral lore. The second is a brain that appears to be inherited from the lower mammals and is often referred to as the limbic system because most of it is contained in the large limbic lobe which surrounds the brain stem. The limbic lobe is present in all mammals, and in both animal and man, operates at the animalistic level. The third and newest human brain is the neomammalian; it contains the neocortex, which surrounds the limbic structures and gives man his unique power of rational thought and symbolic communication.[14]

It is the paleomammalian limbic brain that most concerns those who study the physiology of violence. This part of the brain takes its name from *limbus,* which is Latin for "border," since it outlines the inner surface of each cerebral hemisphere in a C-shaped border. The top of the *C* is called the cingulum ("girdle" or "belt"). The bottom is known as the hippocampus ("seahorse") because it curls upon itself. The limbic brain includes the upper part of the brain stem as well as the deep structures of the cerebrum. The upper brain stem is called the thalamus (inner bridal chamber), the roof of this chamber the epithalamus, and the floor the hypothalamus. Other parts of the brain associated with functions of the limbic brain are the basal ganglia, the septal nuclei, the undersurface of the frontal lobe, the midbrain (middle portion of the stem), and the amygdala, an almond-shaped nucleus in front of the temporal lobe. The amygdala has extensive connections to many portions of the limbic system, especially the hypothalamus, and exerts important modulating influence over the emotions. Anatomists have defined from nine to fourteen different anatomical areas within the amygdala, each with a possibly different function. Alterations in the amygdala seem to produce changes in behavior. The emotional or limbic brain has a wide variety of functions, including the modulation and control of fight-or-flight behavior.[15]

The portion of the cortex associated with the limbic system is especially vulnerable to disease and injury.[16] Uncontrolled violent behavior is known to be one of the symptoms of structural brain damage due to lack of oxygen, head injury, viral infection, and tumors. Head injuries may damage the undersurface of the frontal lobe and the tips of the temporal lobe, parts of the brain lying closest to the skull bones; patients who have suffered such injuries may later be combative, showing signs of limbic dysfunction. After World War I the victims of encephalitis lethargica showed many behavioral symptoms, including violent and antisocial actions and difficulty in controlling impulses.[17]

According to Vernon H. Mark and Frank R. Ervin (*Violence and the Brain,* 1970), the subject of violence is poorly understood. It was long ascribed to a faulty genetic inheritance, they said—more recently to poverty, discrimination, or personal isolation in an increasingly fragmented society. But "the brain is the storehouse of all human experience—social, cultural, and educational—and the generator of all human behavior, both peaceful and violent." All behavior eventually must filter through the central nervous system. "...We believe, therefore, that studying the relationship between the brain and violence is the best way to understand the mechanisms of violent behavior.... If we can only learn to identify those people within our society who have a low threshold for impulsive violence because they suffer from brain malfunction, we will have taken the first step toward treating these individuals; and what is more important from the public view, toward preventing their violent behavior."[18]

What are the symptoms of limbic brain disease? According to Mark and Ervin, these include (1) a history of physical assault, especially wife and child beating; (2) a problem with alcohol such that even a small amount triggers acts of senseless brutality; (3) a history of impulsive sexual behavior that includes assaults; and (4) a history of reckless driving and serious accidents. This set of symptoms the authors call "the dyscontrol syndrome." In Great Britain, they said, there is a chance of nearly one in three that a motorist guilty of a serious driving offense will already be known to the police as a person suspected of some crime or will actually have a criminal record.[19]

Mark and Ervin claimed that bilateral temporal lobe abnormalities can be treated by stereotaxic surgery[c] in which electrodes are implanted in the brain and used to destroy a very small number of cells in a precisely determined area. According to them, once electrodes have been inserted they can be left without any harm to the patient until the surgeon is sure which cells are firing abnormally. Surgeons, they claimed, can both initiate and stop violent behavior in patients with temporal lobe disease by stimulating different points in the amygdala and hippocampus.[20] It was this claim, of course, that helped win them such large grants from the federal government, which was at that time much concerned with urban rioting. Mark, Sweet, and Ervin suggested (in a 1967 letter to the American Medical Association) that these disturbances might be the work of persons with "low violence thresholds" who needed to have their abnormalities pinpointed, diagnosed, and treated. In February 1973, *Ebony* magazine printed an article, "New Threat to Blacks: Brain Surgery to Control Behavior."[21]

But brain surgery on violent individuals was not a new threat. After experiments at Yale University in the 1930s in which the prefrontal area of the cerebral cortex was destroyed in monkeys and chimpanzees, it was discovered that these animals no longer showed rage reactions. It was as if the animals had joined the "happiness cult of the Elder Micheaux," the researchers reported. After hearing about these Yale experiments at the Second International Neurology Congress in London (1935), a Portuguese neuropsychiatrist, Dr. Egas Moniz persuaded Dr. Almeida Lima, a neurosurgeon, to operate on certain patients who had severe mental disorders and had proved refractory to other methods of treatment. The operation which was developed was called a prefrontal lobotomy. A small cutting apparatus, called a leucotome, was used to cut cores from the frontal cortex. The total number of cases operated on under

[c]This is surgery in which the tip of an instrument is directed in three planes in an attempt to reach a predetermined locus in the brain. The first stereotaxic device was developed in 1908 by British neurosurgeon Dr. Victor Horsley and his associate R.H. Clarke.

the direction of Dr. Moniz was about a hundred, and in 1949 he won the Nobel Prize for medicine. Unfortunately, by that time he was not in the best physical shape himself, having been turned into a hemiplegic by a lobotomized patient who shot him in the spine.[22]

This unfortunate outcome did not deter other surgeons, however, and lobotomies now became fashionable. In the United States, Dr. Walter Freeman and James Watts of the George Washington University introduced a new lobotomy technique to sever predetermined areas of the frontal lobes and their underlying connections. Freeman eventually performed or supervised operations on over 3,500 people. Some 40,000 operations were performed in the United States alone, but there were so many reports of gross personality deterioration in lobotomized patients that the operation, by the 1950s, had fallen into general disfavor, particularly since many of the calming effects from this irreversible procedure could be as well accomplished by the newly developed psychoactive drugs.

Among the first to use other surgical procedures on a large scale to cure behavior problems was a Japanese neurosurgeon, Dr. Hirataro Narabayashi, who, in collaboration with Dr. Y. Uchimura, initiated human stereotaxic surgery in Japan in 1951. At the Neurological Clinic in Tokyo these two researchers used a procedure that produced destruction of an area in the amygdala approximately ten millimeters in diameter. This was done by drilling a small burr hole in the skull and injecting a mixture of oil and wax to which lipiodol (an iodine-poppy-seed oil mixture) had been added. Many of the patients, although not all, were suffering from temporal lobe epilepsy, hyperkinesis, and aggressive symptoms. The doctors reported that after the operation the patients were quiet, obedient, and cooperative. Between 1958 and 1972, Dr. Narabayashi averaged about ten cases a year, of whom two thirds were markedly improved (the procedure worked best, he said, on the younger patients). He told the Third World Congress of Psychosurgery, meeting in Cambridge, England, in 1972, however, that he no longer operated on hyperactive or aggressive patients unless there was evidence of epilepsy.[23]

The same World Congress of Psychosurgery heard a report from Dr. Yong Kie Kim, who worked with Dr. W. Umbach at the Free University of Berlin. Kim said they had noted an increased sexual libido and food appetite in patients following the destruction of the basolateral amygdala. (Presumably this would be an unwise procedure to perform on sex criminals or patients with a weight problem.) Dr. V. Balasubramanian of the General Hospital in Madras also reported on the results of stereotaxic amygdalectomy in which he destroyed most of the amygdala in 115 patients. Referring to the operation as "sedative neurosurgery," he claimed that it made his patients quiet and manageable. A different part of the brain was involved in a calming operation done by Dr. Keiji Sano at the University of Tokyo. Sano destroyed a portion of the hypothalamus by passing an electric current through an electrode. According to him, patients who had been epileptic, violent, and uncontrollable before the operation became calm, passive, and tractable afterwards.[24]

By now there was considerable interest in some medical circles in the possibility of pinpointing those areas in the brain that trigger violent behavior, and either excising them, injecting some suitable substance, or implanting electrodes. It seemed like a shortcut to the millennium. There was no need to reform society, or worry about differential association, or even to apply draconian eugenics to the incurably violent, dangerous offender. The problem could be approached and solved directly—through the brain. Some day there might be hundreds or thousands or even millions of Harold Franklin Bensons walking the streets of our cities, not with a gun, but with a calming electrode implanted in their skulls—in short, not merely a Terminal Man, but an entire Terminal Society.

Was it really true that there are certain spots in the brain that trigger violence and that these can be detected, as Mark and Ervin claimed, by implanting electrodes? Dr. Elliot S. Valenstein, a behavioral physiologist at the University of Michigan, argued that the matter was much more complex than Mark and Ervin were prepared to admit. In *Brain Control* (1973), he pointed out that although William Chapman of the Massachusetts General Hospital reported being able to reproduce some clinical features of temporal lobe epilepsy by electrical stimulation of the amygdaloid nuclear region, the one feature of their illness that could not be reproduced was assaultive behavior. "In no instance," Chapman had reported, "was any subjective or behavioral response evoked that remotely resembled aggressiveness. This finding was disconcerting, as the major reason for selecting these patients for the electrical coagulation was intractable assaultiveness." Furthermore, in other stimulation studies, Kim and Umbach reported that stimulation at a number of spots in the amygdala produces aggressive responses, but *only in violent patients.* This suggests, said Valenstein, that the response produced by stimulation may be a reflection, not of some specific function in the area stimulated, but *of the patient's basic personality.* Animal studies too, he said, had shown that the temperament of the experimental subject may be a better predictor of its reaction to brain stimulation than the anatomical site of the electrode. He thought there was a lot of hit-and-miss planting of electrodes: "Taking the evidence as a whole," said Valenstein, "there is hardly justification for the enthusiasm Mark and Ervin attempt to generate in the broad applicability of their procedure."

The possibility of developing a means to detect persons with poor control over dangerous impulses may be "appealing" when considered in a social vacuum, but there is a very dangerous precedent inherent in the suggestion of combatting "the violent-triggering mechanisms of the brains of the nondiseased."

The suggestion by a neurosurgically oriented team that it would be desirable to screen people in order to prevent violence appears to be a poorly conceived plan as well as a potentially dangerous precedent.[25]

But others disagreed. The weapons for curing the hard-core violent offender were here: Why not try them? Too much time had been and was being wasted. Dr. M. Hunter Brown, a California neurosurgeon, called the curative efforts with prisoners at Vacaville "well-intentioned but timid efforts with inadequate tools," and said: "When this current effort fails, as it will, the state will turn to professionals for well-designed comprehensive programs including chromosome classification, activated electroencephalography, psychological testing, trials of newer medications that show promise, and finally neurosurgical intervention to specific target areas as indicated. Until then, humanity must mark time."[26]

In 1973 the Hastings Center convened a conference to discuss the question of "Physical Manipulation of the Brain." Among those present was Dr. José Delgado, a professor of neurophysiology at Yale, who had done some of the basic early work in stimulating the brains of animals. Delgado pointed out that there are three main types of brain control—the mechanical (surgery), the electrical (brain stimulation), and the chemical (placing drugs directly into the brain). There is also a fourth type, he said: the effect of the environment on the electrical and chemical activity of the brain. Experimental research may change the classical question of philosophy from "What is man?" to "What kind of a man are we going to construct?" By education and information, Delgado thought, "we are *forming* the individual, we are constructing his brain."

But Professor Rudolph Ehrensing of the Louisana State Medical Center asked him what happens to the concept of informed consent when we ask what kind of man *we* want to construct. Is there validity, or indeed any future, for the ideal of freedom (defining "freedom," broadly, as self-determination)? Delgado replied that Ehrensing had the wrong notion: "I would like to redefine freedom as the use of our intelligence within frames of reference given by culture and by experience."

Dr. Herbert G. Vaughan, professor of neurology at Albert Einstein College of Medicine, objected that the infant is not just a *tabula rasa,* whose brain has a genetically determined structure and capacities. We go too far, he said, in asking what kind of a man we want to construct. Professor William S. Sweet of Harvard explained to the group that he was willing to implant electrodes *only* when a human is in a serious, even a desperate situation with pain or behavioral manifestations. But Perry London of USC was not at all sure it is preferable to program man than to have the present randomly and chaotically programmed inputs, both genetic and informational. We need a definition of health, he thought, so we can make changes in a person's nature to a more valuable state. This problem, he said, is distinct from controlling behavior for society's sake. London thought we must apply three kinds of criteria: efficiency (does the technique work?), social costs, and respect for the persons to be controlled. Delgado was not impressed: "The inviolability of the brain," he claimed, "is only a social construct, like nudity."[27]

Thus went the debate over brain control within the medical profession. But, as so often happens, the legal profession was about to take a hand, throwing into doubt the entire future of brain surgery, electrodes, and other invasive techniques in the United States. The case involved was that of *Kaimowitz* v. *the Department of Mental Health* (1973). A certain John Doe—his name was never revealed in the litigation—had been confined as a "criminal sexual psychopath" after the murder and rape of a student nurse at the Kalamazoo State Hospital in Michigan where he was a mental patient. Doe was transferred as a suitable research subject to the Lafayette Clinic in 1973 for a study of uncontrollable aggression. There, twenty-four criminal sexual psychopaths were to undergo an experiment to test which was better: to treat the patient with the drug cyproterone acetate (which was supposed to reduce the male hormone flow and therefore reduce aggression) or to operate on the amygdaloid portion of the limbic system in order to achieve the same effect. Only one suitable subject was found, the aforesaid "John Doe," who had signed a form giving "informed consent" to become an experimental subject. His parents too had granted "informed consent," but testified later that they had agreed only to the insertion of depth electrodes.

In its decision the three-judge circuit court for Wayne County ruled that an amygdalotomy[d] on a patient committed under Michigan's Criminal Sexual Psychopath Law would be unlawful even though the subject at one time gave purported consent. "The court finds it impossible to give a truly competent, informed, and voluntary consent—not only because of the lack of capacity through illness and the inherent pressures of institutionalization, but also because the confined person naturally wants to do anything in order to get out," the decision said.

The court also sees in any nonconsensual psychosurgery a clear violation of the First Amendment right to have ideas and be able to express them. The well-known history of lobotomy shows the almost certain destruction or diminution of a patient's ability to exercise this right. The court also finds it plain that the constitutional right of privacy, including the sanctity of the body, must necessarily include the sanctity of the brain and the mind. The state has demonstrated no legitimate interest sufficient to override the First Amendment and privacy rights of the patient when these competing considerations are balanced.

The judges found that though extensive psychosurgery had been performed in the United States and throughout the world in recent years in an attempt to change objectionable behavior, "there is no medically recognized syndrome for aggression and objectionable behavior associated with *nonorganic* brain abnormality . . ." (emphasis added). "Absent a clearly defined medical syndrome, nothing pinpoints the exact location in the brain of the cause of undesirable

---

[d]The difference between an amygdalotomy and an amygdalectomy is that "otomy" means a cutting into, and "ectomy" means a cutting out of, the organ in question.

behavior so as to enable a surgeon to make a lesion, remove that portion of the brain, and thus affect undesirable behavior. . . . To advance scientific knowledge, it is true that doctors may desire to experiment on human beings, but the need for scientific inquiry must be reconciled with the inviolability which our society provides for a person's mind and body."

The court found three issues of informed consent: first, *the capacity to consent* (Doe lacked such a capacity because of his mental condition, the deprivation stemming from involuntary confinement, and the effects of institutionalization); second, *knowledge of the risk involved* (the outcome in this case was profoundly uncertain); and, finally, *voluntariness* ("The involuntarily detained mental patient is in an inherently coercive atmosphere even though no direct pressures may be placed upon him"). The decision concluded:

When the state of medical knowledge develops to the extent that the type of psychosurgical intervention proposed here becomes an accepted neurosurgical procedure and is no longer experimental, it is possible, with appropriate review mechanisms, that involuntarily detained mental patients could consent to such an operation. Second, we specifically hold that an involuntarily detained mental patient today *can* give adequate consent to *accepted* neurosurgical procedures.[28] (Emphasis added.)

Even though it was rendered in a Michigan court and was not binding outside its jurisdiction, the *Kaimowitz* decision sent tremors through the field of psychosurgery. Its reasoning cast doubt, not only on the future of such experimental surgery, but on many kinds of experiments that had been performed on institutionalized populations. The three standards of informed consent the court proposed—capacity to consent, knowledge of the risk involved, and voluntariness—would disqualify most experimental programs in mental hospitals. Two of the three standards would also disqualify prisoners. Yet brain research for the alleviation of violence, or, indeed, any mental illness, clearly required test subjects. Where were they to be found, if not in mental hospitals? Here, again, was a case where the rule of law and the requirements of medical progress had reached an impasse, with no solution easily apparent. The question involved, of course, was ultimately neither legal nor medical, but ethical. What are the rights of an individual whom society wishes to sacrifice for the common good? History is replete with such sacrifices, most of them unwilling: the virgin, murdered to appease some vengeful primitive god; Jonah tossed overboard by his shipmates; witches burned, murderers hanged, soldiers drafted into the army. Medicine too has had its sacrificial victims, from Walter Reed, who let himself be bitten by an infected mosquito, to the thousands of prison volunteers in drug-testing programs. Some come through unharmed, some become very ill, some die. The ethical dilemmas are not difficult when the victim has freely and knowingly made himself a guinea pig for the good of others. Nor do they pose any difficulty in the Nuremberg cases, where the lives of concentration camp inmates were sacrificed to the callous curiosity of German medicine. The difficulties begin when no harm is intended but the subjects are under the control of others, like prisoners, or, like mental patients, do not even know what is proposed to be done to them. It is frequently the case that a mental patient is too ill to understand some proposed experimental therapy which, if successful, could make him well again. Which should weigh more—the potential risk or the potential cure? Who is to decide, and on what grounds?

In *The Right to Be Different: Deviance and Enforced Therapy,* Nicholas Kittrie suggested that the greatest problem with these therapeutic efforts lies in what he called their "shaky philosophical underpinnings." We can see their origins in humanism and paternalism, he said, but their third parent, utilitarian determinism, goes unrecognized. We are prone to point to the fact that the alternative to therapy is the punishment, often barbarous, of those who cannot control their behavior. What we leave out of discussion is the social-defense argument, which was historically the foundation of the therapeutic order.[29]

But is psychosurgery a legitimate weapon of social defense? By the time Kittrie's book appeared in 1971, this issue had begun to arouse particular concern in the United States. A number of articles by Dr. Peter Breggin, a Washington psychiatrist, warning of its dangers, appeared in popular and scientific publications and in 1972 were reprinted in the *Congressional Record.* Crichton's *Terminal Man* added to the general anxiety, as did reports that three prisoners at Vacaville had undergone psychosurgery, and that the Justice Department was supporting research that might involve further operations on California inmates. Clearly, the dangers, if they existed, were not chimerical; the techniques were here, they were known, they were being used. Accordingly, Senator Sam Ervin, chairman of the Subcommittee on Constitutional Rights of the Sentate Judiciary Committee, in the fall of 1972 initiated a correspondence with officials in the Department of Health, Education and Welfare and with the Law Enforcement Assistance Administration (LEAA), seeking to learn the nature and extent of federal involvement in behavior modification and psycho-surgery.[30]

In July 1973 came the Kaimowitz decision in Michigan. In September of that year, during the debate over the National Research Act, Senator Glenn Beall offered an amendment providing for a two-year moratorium on psychosurgery in facilities that received federal funds until the subject could be thoroughly studied by the National Commission for the Protection of Human Subjects of Biomedical and Behavioral Research. During the debate, the moratorium provision was deleted, but the study itself was mandated by the new law; in the meantime, LEAA moved to end its support of research involving psychosurgery, which was terminated the following February. In 1973 the state of Oregon enacted the first comprehensive legislation for the regulation of psychosurgery, and Oregon was followed in 1974 and 1976 by California. The California legislation, unlike that of Oregon, did not recognize proxy or guardian consent to psychosurgery; rather, it forbade psychosurgery on individuals who lacked the capacity for informed consent. The prohibition extended to minors under the age of eighteen. For prisoners, it required not only informed consent but independent medical *and* judicial review.[31]

Meantime the National Commission for the Protection of Human Subjects was undertaking two studies of psychosurgery. The first was a review of the literature, under the direction of Dr. Elliot Valenstein, to discover the nature and purposes of the psychosurgery performed in recent years in the United States. The second was an evaluation of a group of patients who had undergone such surgery, to be conducted by a team of psychologists, psychiatrists, neurologists, and social workers. This team was directed by two neuropsychologists from Boston University, Dr. Allan F. Mirsky and Dr. Maressa H. Orzack.

Dr. Valenstein's study yielded some disquieting facts. Approximately a quarter of the psychosurgical operations performed in the United States, he found, were performed by surgeons doing no more than three operations a year; many surgeons averaged only one a year. This clearly raised questions about their ability to maintain adequate skills. In 1973, 48 percent of all such procedures were performed by just four surgeons. Valenstein found further that only 27 percent of neurosurgeons publish their results. Of those reports that had been published, Valenstein evaluated each for scientific design and use of data, and rated them on a scale of one to six. (One represented the best design and use of data, and six, a report presenting only descriptive information, and lacking comparison groups.) On this scale, almost 90 percent of American articles on psychosurgery rated no better than a four, and 41 percent were given the lowest rating of six.[e,32]

In view of the wide public concern expressed for prisoners and minorities, it is interesting to note that the Valenstein study found most psychosurgical patients were white, middle-class women. A 1974 review of six hundred cases by Dr. M. Hunter Brown had revealed only one black patient, two oriental Americans, and six Hispanic Americans. Valenstein found no specific reports on prisoners except for the three at Vacaville. His data, he said, yielded no reliable information on what proportion of psychosurgical patients are institutionalized.[33]

In June 1976 the commission held a public hearing to elicit the opinions of professional organizations, public-interest groups, and individuals. Speaking for the Task Force on Psychosurgery of the American Psychiatric Association, Dr. John Donnelly reported that in the three years 1971 through 1973, approximately five hundred psychosurgical procedures were performed in the

---

[e]The other commission study evaluating surgical outcome reported on a small group of patients who had undergone stereotaxic surgery for intractable pain and various psychiatric disorders such as obsessive-compulsive behavior. Since these problems are not of concern here, it is sufficient to say that in cases of that type, the outcome was mildly to highly favorable in 78 percent of the cases, with the best results being achieved in operations for the relief of pain.

United States. He said there was no evidence of intentional misuse of psycho-surgery for social or political purposes, or of the disproportionate involvement of minority groups or women.[f] The extent to which violent behavior is a sign of psychiatric illness (rather than a manifestation of political or social action), remains unknown, said Donnelly, but it is a treatment of last resort that should be performed only by a team of highly qualified specialists after screening by peer review committees. For the present, psychosurgery should not be performed on minors, nor should it be performed on prisoners if the purpose is to alter criminal behavior. Violent patients with recognized psychiatric disorders, he said, should be evaluated as surgical candidates *only in the context of their illness.*[34]

Dr. Charles A. Fager, speaking for the American Association of Neurological Surgeons, said that there is an international consensus that psychosurgery should be restricted to small, intracerebral structures. It should be used for disabling emotional and neurotic conditions, not for psychosis, and it should be considered only after other methods have failed, and only for the relief of suffering—*never for social and political purposes.* Dr. Richard W. Doty, representing the Society for Neuroscience, said that a poll of its membership showed that 89 percent of those responding thought psychosurgery should never be used to solve social problems except when certain recognized, incapacitating mental disorders are present. The society, he said, viewed psychosurgery as a treatment of last resort.[35]

After considering this and much other testimony, as well as their own studies, the National Commission for the Protection of Human Subjects of Biomedical and Behavioral Research in May 1977, issued their own report on psychosurgery. They recommended (1) that until the safety and efficacy of any procedure have been demonstrated, it should be performed only by competent surgeons at an institution with an institutional review board and never for any purpose other than medical treatment. (2) It may, with appropriate safeguards, be performed on voluntary mental patients. (3) It should not be performed on involuntary patients or prisoners unless a national advisory board has determined it has demonstrable benefit *for the treatment of a psychiatric symptom or disorder,* and then only under stringent safeguards, including the permission of a court. The commission further asked for the establishment of some "mechanism" for compiling and assessing information on psychosurgical procedures and outcomes, and it recommended that the secretary of Health, Education and Welfare support studies in this area.[36]

Thus in the six years between Kittrie's *Right to be Different* and the issuance of the commission's study, a remarkable consensus had developed in the United States. Kittrie's work did not, of course, speak to the issue of

[f]Valenstein reported that about 56 percent of psychosurgical patients were women. Since psychosurgery is most often indicated for affective (emotional) disorders, which afflict more women than men, this proportion is not unreasonable.

psychosurgery as such; its ambit was much broader and dealt with the whole range of ethical and legal questions involved in the treatment of mental illness. But in the most controversial areas of research and psychosurgical intervention, professionals and laymen alike had arrived at an agreement to treat people for their own good and not as a measure of "social defense," however defined. It is probable that the extraordinary speed with which this consensus was reached reflects the deepest fears in each of us that others may seek to control our minds and personalities. It is the same instinctive revulsion that greeted behavior modification, and before that, the draconian proposals of the eugenics movement. Most people would be willing to sacrifice a limb—and perhaps accept psychosurgery—to restore normal health and function. But given an informed choice, it is doubtful that any would sacrifice a portion of their brains in the interests of social defense. Where there are no constitutional barriers, as there are in the United States, the state could, of course, impose such a sacrifice. Whether it *should* or not is, in the last analysis, a philosophical and moral question. The answer—in this country, at least—has been agreed upon, and it is no.

33 Alcohol and Crime

Ever since crime statistics began to be studied in the early nineteenth century, there has been a consistent record of an association between alcohol and crimes of violence. At first the association seemed to be related to the price of bread: during hard times, as the price of bread grains rose (rye in Germany, wheat in France), there was an increase in property crimes; during good times, as grain prices fell and bread became cheaper, crimes of violence increased.[1] Statisticians had no trouble making the association between hard times and theft; but why should violence increase when times were prosperous? The reason seemed to be that the poorest classes, who in those days lived close to the level of starvation, had more disposable income then to spend on wine and spirits, and they often spent it in taverns, where brawls commonly led to assaults and homicides. Describing the Jacksonian era in the United States, Roger Lane commented in 1976 that the frequent riots, robberies, assaults, and murders of those days involved "boozy young men, as quick to take advantage as offense"—an observation which would be no less apt today. "Then, as now," he said, "violence often came in bottles. And the historian can almost smell the fumes arising from the record." That the times seemed so turbulent does not seem surprising when one considers that in Boston in the 1820s about one in every sixty-five inhabitants was engaged in selling liquor.[2]

At the turn of the century, Gustav Aschaffenburg, Willem Bonger, and Joseph Van Kan all noted the association between alcohol and crimes of violence. In Germany after 1882, said Aschaffenburg, there was a steady increase in crimes associated with drunkenness, such as aiding prisoners to escape, resisting an officer, breach of the peace, assault and battery, and malicious mischief. This growth corresponded, he said, to a steady increase in the consumption of alcohol (in Germany, not liquor, but beer).[3] Van Kan thought that material well-being exalted the vital instincts, increased alcohol consumption, and thereby increased crimes against morals.[4] Bonger noted from nineteenth-century statistics that in Germany between a fifth and a quarter of rapists were alcoholics, and that in France more than half were alcoholics.

Since these early studies, evidence has continued to accumulate of an association, not only between alcohol and crimes of violence, but between chronic alcoholism and career criminality. So persistent is this evidential thread, running as it does through studies of homicide, rape, genetic abnormalities, and the family history of psychopaths and mentally disordered offenders, that it must be considered the one factor in crime that can be neither argued down nor dismissed. One may laugh at Lombroso's criminal physiognomy, quarrel with Marxist economic determinism, ignore Kretschmer and Sheldon, and disbelieve those who think criminality is inherited; but alcohol has to be taken seriously, if not as a cause, then as a persistent, sometimes puzzling, factor in the criminal equation. There is no burking the evidence; it is too overwhelming.

The simplest observed relationship has been between drunkenness and crime. This, of course, is no mystery, since drunks are notoriously quarrelsome and lacking in internal controls. One of the major studies, Marvin Wolfgang's *Patterns in Criminal Homicide* (1958), analyzed all homicides committed in Philadelphia from 1948 through 1952. Wolfgang found that alcohol was present in either the victim or the offender in 63.6 percent of all homicides. In 43.5 percent of cases it was present in *both* the victim and his killer. Homicides were most frequent on Saturdays and least frequent on Tuesdays; similarly, alcohol was present in 73 percent of Saturday homicides, and only 42 percent of homicides that occurred on Tuesdays. Approximately 60 percent of all offenders who committed violent homicide had been drinking before the crime, while of those who killed nonviolently, half had been drinking.[5]

The same sort of results were obtained in a study of all criminal homicides occurring in Memphis and Shelby County, Tennessee, over an eight-year period. The file comprised 372 cases. Of the victims, 278, or 74.7 percent had been drinking at the time of their death. Of the fifty offenders whose drinking status was immediately examined, 43, or 86 percent, had been drinking at the time of the homicide. Reporting on these findings (1974), W. Slater Hollis observed that since a maximum of no more than 35 percent of the relevant total population would be drinking at any one time in the general geographical area, there was less than one possibility in a hundred that these differences could have occurred by chance.[6]

Similar evidence of a statistical relationship between crime and alcohol was found in a study by the Columbus, Ohio, Police Department of 882 persons picked up during or immediately after the commission of a felony in the period from March 1951 to March 1953. Just under 73 percent of these individuals showed alcohol in the bloodstream. Among those with readings of 0.10 percent or more were 45 percent of those accused of rape, 43 percent of those charged with felonious assault, 88 percent of those involved in cuttings, 67 percent of those charged with murder, 79 percent of the shooting cases, 60 percent of those arrested for robbery, 64 percent of those accused of burglary, 65 percent of the larceny cases, 59 percent of those charged with auto theft, and 60 percent of those accused of forgery. The forgery cases were probably understated, the department thought, because few forgers are arrested at the scene of the crime.[7]

The Columbus study was unusual in relating alcohol to so many different kinds of offenses. In most cases the studies have been related only to cases involving the death of the victim, and here the evidence has been quite consistent. According to Donald W. Goodwin (1973), in at least fifteen studies in English-speaking countries since 1940, an association has been noted between drinking and homicide. J.M. MacDonald, in *The Murderer and His Victim* (1961), did a survey of ten of these studies and found that the proportion of murderers who had been drinking prior to their crimes ranged from 19 percent to 83 percent, with a median of 54 percent.[8] In a 1958 study of the deaths by homicide, the Metropolitan Life Insurance Company reported that in almost 50 percent of these cases, the killer, the victim, or both had been drinking, and that in some instances, "no apparent motive for the slaying was demonstrated except that the slayer was crazed with liquor."[9]

The fact that violence occurs most frequently among close acquaintances complicates the analysis of the relationship between violence and the use of alcohol, since violence itself most frequently occurs among close acquaintances or members of the same family. Jared W. Tinklenberg observed in 1973 that the association between violence and alcohol involves the interplay of three factors: the pharmacological effects of alcohol, the personality of the drinker, and the psychosocial factors involved. Yet in all cultures that use alcohol, folk wisdom assumes that a relationship does exist between alcohol and violence, and that it is causal. Cultures that forbid drinking do so because of its effects on behavior. Tinklenberg described a Muslim tradition that at the first planting of grapes, Satan watered the ground with peacock's blood, then sprinkled the leaves with ape's blood, and finally drenched the grapes first with the blood of lions, and then with the blood of swine. That is why the first taste of wine makes a man strut like a peacock, lively and vivacious, and why later he is gay and playful like an ape. When he is drunk, he is like a lion, says the legend—ferocious and assaultive. And at last, when he is extremely intoxicated, he grovels like a swine and falls asleep.[10] There are few Christians, drinkers or not, who would deny the aptness of this Muslim metaphor.

Thus far we have considered only the relationship between alcohol and the criminal act. But what of the relationship between alcoholism and criminality? To what extent does the inability to handle alcohol contribute to a criminal career? Samuel B. Guze and his associates in the Department of Psychiatry of the Washington University School of Medicine in Saint Louis studied 223 male offenders consecutively released from Missouri prisons and reformatories from November 1960 through April 1961. Most of the individuals, the authors said, "would generally be regarded as sociopaths"[a] because of their early onset of delinquency, school misbehavior, frequent fighting, poor job histories, poor

---

[a]The "sociopath" is, broadly speaking, the same individual whom the nineteenth century called the "moral imbecile," the early twentieth called the "psychopath," and the American Psychiatric Association calls the "antisocial personality." The difference in nomenclature appears to be related to whether one looks at his malefactions from the moral, psychological, or social point of view. But the individual involved is hedonistic, callous, and antisocial, exhibiting few symptoms of anxiety and even fewer of guilt. (Lombroso considered that all of his "born criminals" were "moral imbeciles," although not all moral imbeciles were born criminals.) The type will be discussed at some length in the next chapter.

marital adjustments, excessive drinking and drug use, and recurrent trouble with the police. To be diagnosed as alcoholics, these men had to show symptoms in at least three out of five groups of drinking problems, as follows:

Group 1: Delirium tremens or cirrhosis; impotence associated with drinking; alcoholic blackouts; binges.

Group 2: Daily drinking; consuming the equivalent of over fifty-four ounces of whiskey a week; evasiveness about the amount of alcohol consumed.

Group 3: Being unable to stop drinking; trying to control it by allowing a drink only at certain times or under certain circumstances; drinking before breakfast; drinking nonbeverage forms of alcohol.

Group 4: A history of arrests for drinking; traffic offenses involving alcohol; trouble at work because of drinking; fighting associated with drinking.

Group 5: A feeling by the subject that he drank too much; feelings of guilt; family objections to his drinking; a loss of friends because of drinking.

Using these criteria of alcoholism, the authors reported (1962) that 43 percent of the males released from Missouri prisons and reformatories were unquestionably alcoholics, and another 11 percent were possibly so.

Of all the releasees they studied, 41 percent had a family history of alcoholism—50 percent of the alcoholics as compared to 33 percent of the nonalcoholics.[11] In a 1968 follow-up on the same group of ex-offenders, Guze and his fellow researchers reported that they had interviewed 260 first-degree relatives of these criminals and had found that half the male relatives had a history of school delinquency, 41 percent had a history of non-traffic arrests, and 31 percent had been jailed. (The correlations were greatest for fathers and brothers.) They also now raised their estimate of the percentage of alcoholics in the group of offenders to 64 percent, adding that "it is apparent that alcoholism is the single most important problem associated with criminal behavior aside from the fundamental issue of sociopathy."[12] An almost identical figure was found in a 1973 study of Ohio parolees by the Ohio State University Center for the Study of Crime and Delinquency. The researchers found that 66 percent of the parolees had a history of alcohol problems.[13]

It appears, then, that the relationship between alcohol and crime is not a simple one in which an individual has too much to drink and as a result of lowered inhibitions and impaired judgment, commits a criminal act. Such occasions certainly arise, but they are not the only—perhaps not even the major—problem. The relationship is more complex and more obscure, involving as it does the nature of the individual, the kind of family he comes from, the environment in which he lives, and the possible influences on his behavior of his genetic inheritance. All the arguments that have raged around the subject of criminal causation have been fought over alcohol, with results that are just as inconclusive. Nobody can *prove* anything, but opinions abound.

In 1966 Lee N. Robins published a thirty-year follow-up of children who were initially observed in a child-guidance center. Children who had been diagnosed as normal or neurotic grew up for the most part to lead normal lives, the study found, whereas the children who were diagnosed as antisocial had a significantly greater probability of remaining sociopathic. Of this latter group, 62 percent had, by the time of the follow-up, developed serious alcohol problems. Among the severely antisocial children who had alcoholic fathers, more than half were diagnosed thirty years later as sociopathic adults.[14]

Tinklenberg has asked whether assaultive offenders use more alcohol than nonassaultive ones with similar psychosocial characteristics and wondered whether individuals who commit assault are more likely to be under the influence of alcohol during their rare violent episodes than during their much more frequent nonviolent moments. "Or does alcohol," he asked, "with its central nervous system depressant effects reduce assaultive tendencies which otherwise would be manifested more frequently in violence-prone individuals?" The use of alcohol, he suggested, may merely increase the chances of getting caught after a violent act.[15] But the view that alcohol might reduce assaultive tendencies is distinctly in the minority. The more usual is that expressed by Gene L. Usdin (1967), that "basically the alcoholic who is homicidally dangerous to others is not dangerous because he is an alcoholic, but because of the removal of the barriers to impulses he can customarily inhibit." The other problem, Usdin pointed out, is that alcohol so affects motor coordination that the alcoholic becomes very dangerous behind the wheel of a car. "A person may commit murder while under the influence of alcohol, but much more significant are the negligent homicides committed while under the effects of alcohol."[16]

Unlike the association between alcohol and other violent crimes, the association between alcohol and vehicular homicide is all too well understood. If the United States is really as concerned about dangerous offenders as it pretends to be, why are so many people anxious to lock away for life those who rob or murder while under the influence of alcohol but are seemingly unwilling to remove those who present no less hazard to life and limb, but do so from a driver's seat? John R. Lion and Manoel Penna comment on this anomaly in "The Study of Human Aggression" (1974). "Dangerous drivers," they write, "are not yet perceived by society as violent in the same sense as an armed robber is, even though a group of dangerous recidivist drivers could probably be identified if we put our minds to it." They attribute our inconsistency to the fact that aggression is rooted in the origins of American culture: "We own guns, we drive cars, we drink."[17] That their analysis makes sense must be acknowledged when the practice of other countries is considered, both with respect to the possession of firearms and the use of alcohol by those who operate motor vehicles. In Sweden, the penalty for driving while under the influence is an automatic jail term, and the law is enforced. Could Americans be less serious about "dangerous of-fenders" than the citizens of other countries? Or is it that here, as in so many offenses, we are more likely to condone the ones we commit, and detest the ones we do not? Many of us drive after we have been drinking, but, drunk or sober, most of us do not commit homicides or armed robberies.

The law certainly does not excuse us if we do. In Anglo-Saxon jurispru-dence, drunkenness is viewed as voluntary, so that even if an intoxicated robber may not, in the strictest sense, be *compos mentis* at the time, he is still considered to have a guilty mind and be responsible for his crime. In *People* v. *Guillett,* a Michigan court expressed the view of the common law:

A man who puts himself in a position to have no control over his actions must be held to intend the consequences. The safety of the community requires this rule. Intoxication is so easily counterfeited, and, when real, is so often resorted to as a means of nerving up a man to the commission of some deliberate act, and withal it is so inexcusable in itself, that the law has never recognized it as an excuse for crime.

Another problem, said a Maine court (*State* v. *Arsenault,* 1956), is that "all that the crafty criminal would require for a well-planned murder, would be a revolver in one hand to commit the deed, and a quart of intoxicating liquor in the other with which to build his excusable defense."[18]

In recent years the tendency to view alcoholism as a disease has given rise to a certain judicial inconsistency. In *Driver* v. *Hinnant* (1966), the Fourth Circuit Court of Appeals considered the case of a defendant who was sentenced to two years' imprisonment for public intoxication. The record showed that he had been convicted of the same offense more than two hundred times. The court held in *Driver* that chronic alcoholism is an *involuntary* act and that conse-quently the defendant did not have a criminal intent (*mens rea*). Chronic alcoholism "has destroyed the power of his will to resist the constant, excessive consumption of alcohol; his appearance in public in that condition is not his volition but a compulsion symptomatic of the disease; and to stigmatize him as a criminal for this act is cruel and unusual punishment." The *Driver* decision was adopted later that same year by the Circuit Court for the District of Columbia in *Easter* v. *D.C.* Both decisions refer to the responsibility of a chronic alcoholic, not of someone who commits a crime while drunk.[19] Nor would they excuse defendants who had, while under the influence of alcohol, committed some offense other than public intoxication.[b] This position seems logically inconsis-tent, but it is understandable.

It seems clear that in confronting the relationship of alcohol to crime, as in

[b]However, in Columbus, Ohio in 1977 a jury found a chronic alcoholic not guilty of a crime spree committed when he was drunk, after the judge instructed them to decide whether he had *intended* the crimes. The man was a chronic recidivist with a long criminal record. After the verdict, the defendant burst into tears (and so, no doubt, did the prosecutor)!

so many other areas, we have failed signally not only to find solutions but even to recognize that the problem exists. The statistics that associate crime with alcohol are almost overwhelming. What we do not know is whether the drunken criminal commits a crime because of the alcohol, or because of a "bad" character that has been uncorked by the alcohol, or because of a physiological or psychological aberration that led him to drink in the first place. It does appear from evidence going back at least to the Jukes, that hard drinking and sociopathy are often found in the same families. But as Marc A. Schuckit has pointed out (1973), if all alcoholics with antisocial problems are called sociopaths or all sociopaths with drinking difficulties are classified as alcoholics, no distinct family patterns are ever likely to be uncovered. When the two are more clearly defined and separated, the degree of familial overlap between the two problems may become less striking. The strong apparent relationship may occur, he says, either because many alcoholics are sociopaths, or because there is a third factor, X underlying both alcoholism and sociopathy, or because many sociopaths abuse alcohol as a part of their antisocial behavior.[20]

And this, of course, brings us to a problem that we have thus far skirted. Who or what is the individual who has gone by so many titles in the last century and a half, the moral imbecile/psychopath/sociopath/antisocial personality? Does he really exist? Or are these just labels we pin on someone who behaves in unpleasant and destructive ways, while eluding our best efforts to socialize him? Like so many other questions in criminology, these have been the subjects of long and acrimonious debate among the biological, behavioral, and social sciences. It is time now, therefore, to look at the whole phenomenon of the antisocial personality, and to consider the role of psychopathy in the criminal equation.

34 Who Is the Psychopath?

The first question to address is, why should chapters on the psychopath be included under "Physiology and the Dangerous Offender"? Why not under "The Mind of the Dangerous Offender," or "Society and the Dangerous Offender"? To this perfectly reasonable question, the answer has to be, because the phenomenon ought to be discussed, and nobody is sure *where* it belongs. Opinions are not lacking, certainly: The sociologists tend to view psychopathy as social, while doctors with a physiological bent view it as physiological in origin; psychiatrists, on the whole, throw up their hands. No discipline has yet demonstrated a treatment that will cure psychopathy, and the question remains open: We simply do not know how to categorize this phenomenon.

The answer to the original question, then, is that the psychopath/sociopath/ antisocial personality is included in the section on physiology because there is as much reason to include him here as anywhere else. If this answer seems unsatisfactory, one can only plead that everything about the subject is unsatisfactory, beginning with the very first issue that arises—namely, does the psychopath really exist? Kittrie claimed that the term "appears to be an open-ended concept of convenience, drawn to accommodate social and administrative purposes, and used to group together disparate types of deviants identifiable only by their nonconformity with the standards of conduct established by a given community at a given historical period—the psychiatric purse seine for any person who indulges in antisocial conduct." The psychopath he termed a "Kafka-esque character . . . to whom no clear-cut social standards are applicable."[1] Barbara Wootton (1959) thought that the volume of literature on the subject was exceeded only by the confusion in which it was steeped. The so-called psychopath is, par excellence, "the model of the circular process by which mental abnormality is inferred from anti-social behaviour while anti-social behaviour is explained by mental abnormality." The attempt to turn psychopathy into a form of mental illness has the paradoxical effect "that if you are consistently (in old-fashioned language) wicked enough, you may hope to be excused from responsibility for your misdeeds; but if your wickedness is only moderate, or if you show occasional signs of repentance or reform, then you must expect to take the blame for what you do and perhaps also to be punished for it."[2]

But if there are those who are skeptical of the entire concept of psychopathy, prison wardens and those who run mental hospitals are not among them. Marion J. Koloski, who served as warden of three Ohio prisons, once said of this type of person that "everything he touches turns to mud."[3] Definitions may be difficult, but as one psychiatrist said, "I know an elephant when I see one, but damned if I can define one."[4] However, defined, and by whatever name, the psychopath is uniquely troublesome, whether in the bosom of his family, in a school, in a prison, or in a mental hospital. He repeatedly does things that frankly make no sense, often surprising even himself.[a] Yet he sounds rational. His cognitive faculties seem undisturbed, and he makes a convincing show of understanding right from wrong *at the verbal level.* In short, as Hervey Cleckley said in his classic study of psychopathy which he called *The Mask of Sanity* (1941), only very slowly do we realize that "we are dealing here not with a complete man at all but with something that suggests a subtly constructed reflex machine which can mimic the human personality perfectly."[5]

The type has been known for a very long time—in fact, since Hippocrates. Thomas Abercromby, the physician to James II, spoke in his *Treatise of the Mind* (1656) of a condition "in which all the upright sentiments are eliminated, while the intelligence presents no disorders." By the nineteenth century, the problem became widely recognized by physicians who dealt with mental disorders. The French psychiatrist, Jules Baillarger (1809-1890), described the syndrome as "insanity with consciousness," and as we saw in chapter 10, various clinicians called it by a variety of names: "mania without delirium" (Pinel), "instinctive monomania" (Esquirol), and "moral insanity" (Prichard). To these must be added the descriptive term of the French surgeon and alienist, Ulysse Trélat (1795-1879), who in 1861 published a book under the title *La folie lucide,* or "The Lucid Madness." Probably the best nineteenth-century clinical description was that by the Victorian alienist Henry Maudsley in 1874 (see p. 70). Even a century later, it remains a model of clarity and succinctness.

Emil Kraepelin (1856-1926) was the first psychiatrist to divide mental diseases into the dementia-praecox and manic-depressive groups. In his textbook on *Clinical Psychiatry* (1902), the German psychiatrist described "moral imbecility" as being characterized "by the absence or weakness of those feelings which inhibit the development of marked selfishness. The intellect as regards matters of practical life is moderately developed; patients apprehend well, are able to accumulate more or less knowledge which they utilize for their own advantage, possess a good memory, and show no defects in the process of thought." Kraepelin gave the following summary of typical case histories:

Morally, their lack of sympathy is manifested from youth up in their cruelty toward animals, the tendency to tease and use roughly playmates and an inaccessibility to moral influences. From this they develop the most pronounced selfishness, lack of sense of honor, and of affection for parents and relatives. It is impossible to train them because of the absence of love and ambition. They tell falsehoods, become crafty, deceitful, and stubborn. The egotism becomes more

[a]One prisoner of my acquaintance whose wit and intelligence were both of the highest order, who was as well read in criminology as most criminologists, and in psychology as most psychologists, once said to me: "You know, I have no trouble analyzing and understanding other people. The only person I have never been able to understand is myself."

and more evident in their great conceit, bragging and wilfulness, their inordinate desire for enjoyment, their indolence and dissipation. They are incapable of resisting temptation, and give way to sudden impulses and emotional outbursts, while the susceptibility to alcohol is especially prominent.

Very many professional criminals present the symptoms of moral imbecility to a marked degree. In these cases there is no doubt but that a scanty and defective training and education under circumstances unfavorable to a healthy moral development are of equal importance with the defective heredity. . . .[6]

The term "psychopath," which was in the beginning very loosely employed, was derived from the term "psychopathic inferiorities." It was first introduced by J.L.A. Koch in his 1891 monograph *Die Psychopathischen Minderwertig-keiten,* and further clarified by Adolf Meyer (1905), who referred to the state as "constitutional psychopathic inferiority,"[7] a term which, designated in American hospitals by the initials CPI (or CPS for "constitutional psychopathic state"), was to be employed by psychiatrists for half a century.[8]

Although judges have often been skeptical, viewing psychopathy as due, not to uncontrollable conduct, "but to conduct which is not controlled,"[9] a vast number of psychiatrists have agreed on the existence of this syndrome. A 1902 textbook on insanity speaks of "persons who indulge in vice with such persistence at a cost of punishment so heavy, so certain and so prompt, who incur their punishment for the sake of pleasure so trifling and so transient that they are by common consent considered insane although they exhibit no other indication of insanity."[10] In his 1939 study, *Psychopathic States,* the Scottish psychiatrist Sir David K. Henderson reviewed the various terms such as "defective delinquents," "emotionally constitutional inferiorities," and so forth,[b] and explained his own preferred term of "psychopathic state":

... the term psychopathic state is the name we apply to those individuals who conform to a certain intellectual standard, sometimes high, sometimes approaching the realm of defect but yet not amounting to it, who throughout their lives, or from a comparatively early age, have exhibited disorders of conduct of an antisocial or asocial nature, usually of a recurrent or episodic type, which, in many instances, have proved difficult to influence by methods of social, penal and medical care and treatment and for whom we have no adequate provision of a preventive or curative nature. The inadequacy or deviation or failure to adjust to ordinary social life is not a mere willfulness or badness which can be threatened or thrashed out of the individual so involved, but constitutes a true illness for which we have no specific explanation.

Psychopaths have no more power to control their behavior, he thought, "than the epileptic his fit or the malarial patient his ague."[11]

Perhaps the most complete clinical description of the psychopath/sociopath/antisocial personality was given by Cleckley in *The Mask of Sanity.* Hervey Cleckley, who was a professor of psychiatry and neurology at the Medical College of Georgia, had dealt with many persons of this type during his years as a psychiatrist with the United States Veterans Administration. In his clinical profile, he described sixteen characteristics he had noted in his practice.

[b]A study by H. Cason in the *Journal of Criminal Psychopathology* 4 (1943):522, found 202 technical terms denoting psychopaths.

1. The psychopath is charming and of good intelligence. "More often than not, such a person will seem particularly agreeable. . . ." He often scores high on intelligence tests. "Everything about him is likely to suggest desirable and superior human qualities, a robust mental health."
2. He is not delusional or irrational.
3. There is an absence of nervousness or psychoneurotic manifestations. He is poised and serene, even under circumstances that would upset another person.
4. The psychopath is unreliable. "Though he is likely to give an impression of being a thoroughly reliable person, it will soon be found that on many occasions he shows no sense of responsibility whatever." However, he may function with apparent responsibility for weeks or even months, long enough to win a scholarship, be acclaimed a top salesman, or be elected president of a club or a school honor society. Then suddenly he will do something dishonest or outlandish and for no apparent reason. His failures and disloyalties will continue, but at unpredictable times, so that he shows "not even a consistency in inconsistency but an inconsistency in inconsistency."
5. He is insincere, and he is a liar who can be trusted no more in his accounts of the past than in his promises for the future.
6. He is lacking in either shame or remorse. "His career is always full of exploits, any one of which would wither even a rather callous specimen of the ordinary man. Yet he does not, despite his able protestations, show the slightest evidence of major humiliation or regret."
7. His antisocial behavior is inadequately motivated. He will commit all kinds of misdeeds for astonishingly small stakes, and sometimes for no reason at all.[c]
8. His judgment is poor, and he never learns from experience. He will repeat over and over again patterns of self-defeating behavior. He will, for example, work hard to win release from a mental hospital, which he has thoroughly detested, then go out at once, get extremely drunk, and create enough disorder to get himself readmitted. Yet despite his poor judgment in actual living experiences, he may show excellent judgment in appraising theoretical situations. The advice he gives others is often sound.
9. He is pathologically egocentric and has no real capacity for love, although he often simulates affection or parental devotion. When the test of action comes, however, he is quite indifferent to the sufferings—financial, social, physical, and emotional—that he visits on his family.

---

[c]One felon of my acquaintance, after his release from prison, set up an elaborate underground scheme for smuggling out information embarrassing to the warden. He then sent the warden an anonymous letter, mailed from a nearby state, revealing to the warden who the courier was that was bringing out the information. This was an almost classic example of the self-defeating nature of psychopathic behavior.

10. His emotions are shallow. He feels neither real grief, nor deep indignation, nor true joy, nor great pride—though often he may put on a show of doing so. The conviction eventually dawns on those who have observed him for some time that what is involved is a readiness of expression rather than a strength of feeling.
11. The psychopath lacks insight to a degree usually found only in the most serious mental disorders. He has no capacity to see himself as others see him or to feel as others feel, being worse in this respect than the schizophrenic.
12. He does not respond to consideration, kindness, or trust. The axiom that one good turn deserves another, "a principle sometimes honored by cannibals and uncommonly callous assassins," is something he can cite verbally, but is unable to follow. While sometimes outwardly gracious in small things, in the big ones he is callous and unheeding.
13. Drunk or sober, but especially when drunk, he is guilty of fantastic and uninviting behavior. Psychopaths, even after very little alcohol, will create situations so bizarre and preposterous that they would be inconceivable to the ordinary person, drunk *or* sober.
14. Psychopaths often threaten suicide but almost never carry it out. The rarity of suicide among people of this type is remarkable, since they are so often in situations that would drive another person to take his own life.
15. The psychopath's sex life is impersonal, trivial, and poorly integrated.
16. The psychopath shows a consistent inability to make or follow any sort of life plan. Summing up, Cleckley said,

When one further considers that all this skein of apparent madness has been woven by a person of (technically) unimpaired and superior intellectual powers and universally regarded as sane, the surmise intrudes that some unconscious purpose to fail may be active, some unrecognized drive at social and spiritual self-destruction. Not merely a surmise but a strong conviction arises that this apparent sanity is a sanity in name only. . . . We find instead a spectacle that suggests madness in excelsis.[12]

The psychopath, by whichever of his 202 names he is called, has presented a baffling problem to families, public agencies, courts, mental hospitals, and prisons. Cleckley reported that in a 1935-1937 study in a federal psychiatric hospital of 857 new admissions, 236 cases, or more than a quarter of the total, represented character inadequacy and personality disorder of the type discussed.[d,13] Considering the behavior that is often involved, it may be a toss-up whether such an individual ends up in a prison or a mental hospital. A 1967-1968 study of 1,375 consecutive admissions to the Ohio State Peni-

---

dAmong the diagnoses listed by the staff were 102 of psychopathic personality, 60 of chronic alcoholism, 41 of chronic alcoholism with deterioration, 14 of acute alcoholic hallucinosis, 8 of psychopathic personality with psychotic episodes, 3 of acute alcoholism, and 8 of drug addiction.

tentiary, the Ohio reception center for adult male felons over the age of thirty, suggested that about one quarter of all admissions could be clinically described as psychopaths.[e],[14] If these two studies are at all indicative, personality disorders are a major public problem, whether looked at from the perspective of law or psychiatry. If the psychopath does not, as some experts aver, really exist, he remains a singularly troublesome nonentity. Henderson called him "the most disruptive element in society," all the more so because, while delinquents, the insane, and the retarded are usually cared for in institutions, most psychopaths function well enough to be at large.[15]

Despite what has been said here, most psychopaths are not found in institutions, although if their behavior is sufficiently disruptive, and their families cannot buy their way out of trouble, many of them end up there. It might be thought, particularly from the case histories recited by Cleckley, that few persons of this type can remain long at large. But it should be remembered that the examples observed by Cleckley had found their way into a mental hospital, and that like so many other psychopathologies, this one, too, is a matter of degree. In *The Psychopathic Delinquent and Criminal* (1953), George N. Thompson, a professor of neurology and psychiatry at the University of Southern California, presented a scale of personality in the shape of a bell curve. In the middle lay the theoretical range of normality, to the near right and left, an area of borderline symptoms, and then at the far left, the "psychoneurotic personality," and at the far right, the "psychopathic personality," two types Thompson considered incompatible. The psychopath, he said, has no regard for self, and but little concept of time as it relates to himself, whereas the psychoneurotic has little regard for anyone *but* himself, is extremely concerned with his past, is fearful of the present, and dreads the future.

The psychopathic personality is lacking in discretion, judgment, and wisdom. The psychoneurotic has an excess of all these, said Thompson—an extremely overdeveloped censor function, a magnified superego. The psychopath seeks momentary gratification, the psychoneurotic does not. The conditioned-reflex system of the psychoneurotic personality is easily conditioned and easily desensitized, whereas the conditioning mechanism in psychopaths is all but nonexistent. That is why, Thompson said, the patient with a psychopathic personality does not profit from experience and tends to repeat acts that have repeatedly led to failure. Thompson disagreed profoundly with the view that psychopathy is a diagnosis possible only in a complex modern society. He cited Australian aborigines described by Daisy Bates in her book *The Passing of the Aborigines* (1938). Although they were cannibals who in times of food shortage often cooked and ate their babies, this behavior (which civilized society would

---

[e]The diagnosis was made on the basis of various psychological tests such as the Lykken Activity Preference Questionnaire and the Minnesota Multiphasic Personality Inventory (MMPI). Researchers also used the Cleckley criteria and checked the individuals' records of arrests after the age of eighteen.

certainly consider psychopathic) was in that culture normal and customary. On the other hand, there were psychopaths even among these very primitive people. Miss Bates described a man who had always been different from other members of his tribe, given to ferocious outburst of emotion. As he grew older, he broke a tribal rule and occasionally killed a member of the tribe, but because he was so powerful, he was not molested. He wasted precious food: instead of eating all the edible parts, he dined on the delicacies such as liver (which he particularly liked), and left the rest of the carcass untouched. Here, thought Thompson, was an example of a psychopath, unable to adjust to the social standards, even of a cannibalistic society.[16]

A Danish study suggests that about 3 percent of the population may become sociopaths.[17] Such an estimate raises the same problem as the study of the XYY chromosomal abnormality: Where are they all? The opinion has been expressed that perhaps many of them are in politics or the selling of used cars, a suggestion that says more about the popular view of these professions than about the whereabouts of the individuals concerned. It is very probable that if their number is indeed this large, they are to be found among the myriad alcoholics, drug addicts, vagrants, ne'er-do-wells, and misfits of society. The classic black sheep from a good family is an example of the psychopath who often eludes both the law and the mental health systems because his relatives can pay for the damage he does, and for the private psychiatric treatment that will accomplish little good but may serve to pacify the court when he is caught red-handed in the commission of a crime ("My son is under psychiatric care. He did not know what he was doing").

Lewis A. Lindner has observed (1970) that some psychopaths "may have learned that they can stay out of mental hospitals on legal grounds and out of prison on psychiatric grounds." Those sociopaths who end up in prison could have avoided prolonged incarceration, he thought, had they voluntarily committed themselves to a mental hospital "and, thereby, obtained a psychiatric label."[18] The psychopathic patient seen by a private practitioner is not labeled as such, however, but is usually given some less onerous diagnosis like "intermittent hypomanic disorder." A poor sociopath is locked up as an "antisocial personality": a rich one is "hypomanic" and remains at large.

It is a fact that many people of this type, with good families and enough money, manage to elude the criminal justice system all their lives. This has led to some skepticism about the entire concept of psychopathy. After relating a rather long-winded definition by the Royal Medico-Psychological Association, Barbara Wootton concluded, "In simpler language still, psychopaths are extremely selfish persons and nobody knows what makes them so."[19] The matter, however, is actually a bit more complicated. The psychopath is not the ordinary kind of criminal, motivated by selfishness or greed. If he were, he would not be so difficult to deal with; the utilitarian calculus of hedonism could be applied to him, and he could be deterred from his malefactions by making them unprofitable. What makes the psychopath uniquely troublesome is that what is involved in his behavior is not self-interest, but self-destruction.

The problem of the psychopath is more complex even than that of the psychotic criminal, because the psychotic may be sent to a mental hospital and, with or without treatment, get well. Most mental hospitals will not willingly admit patients with a diagnosis of psychopathy: Long experience has taught them that treatment is of no use and that individuals of this type cause serious management problems. In prison, of course, psychopaths are equally troublesome. It is very probable that without the necessity for dealing with them, most prisons would be rather different from what they are. Yet, left to his own devices in society, this antisocial personality is not only obnoxious and troublesome, he is often dangerous. Psychopaths are to be found among assaultive drunks, homicidal drivers, sex offenders, and criminals of all types, from forgers to bank robbers. If such individuals are really sick, in any meaningful psychiatric or physiological sense, it is time that the nature of their problem were ascertained and a treatment discovered. There has been a considerable amount of research that points, in fact, to an underlying neurophysiologic disturbance in many psychopaths. We have already mentioned electroencephalographic abnormalities, but there is considerable other evidence also, much of it fascinating and suggestive. What it is, and where it seems to be pointing, will be the subject of the next chapter.

35 The Neurophysiology of Psychopathic Behavior

The explanations for psychopathy for the most part parallel the explanations for criminal behavior in general. Antisocial personality disorder has been attributed to such causes as poor heredity, bad neighborhoods, early separation from parents, parental abuse, brain injuries, viral diseases, and an unresolved Oedipal conflict—the list is long. Many of the studies of criminality that were cited in previous chapters undoubtedly involved such personalities, even though no effort was made to distinguish psychopaths from other delinquents or criminals. Lombroso claimed that his "born criminals" fitted Maudsley's category of "moral imbeciles." If one may judge from the record, so did R.L. Dugdale's infamous Jukes; indeed, they were a kind of mythic paradigm of the type. The various genetic studies of criminal twins undoubtedly involved persons who fitted this syndrome, although, again, they were not specifically distinguished in the research from other kinds of malefactors.

One problem with the subject has been the variability in definitions of psychopathy. During the nineteenth century there was a tendency to confuse this problem with other affective disorders like manic-depressive psychosis. Even as distinguished an authority as Sir David K. Henderson, in his *Psychopathic States* (1939), divided psychopaths into three types, the predominantly violent, aggressive individual, the predominantly passive or inadequate type, and what he called the "creative psychopath." Among the latter he included Joan of Arc and Lawrence of Arabia. All three varieties, he claimed, "the aggressive criminal, the inadequate psychoneurotic, the creative genius . . . are confined by an instability, queerness, explosiveness, intuitiveness and egocentricity which form the picture of psychopathic states."[1] As recently as 1959, Harry L. Kozol also included creative genius in this syndrome, saying of the psychopath that "he is, at one and the same time, the blessing and the bane of society. Without him there would be little if any art, literature, music or science—or crime. One does not *have* to be a psychopath to be a creator or a criminal, but it helps."[2]

Obviously, if one is going to equate the antisocial behavior of the criminal with the creativity of the artist and scientist and the insights of the saint, a rational consideration of the subject is ruled out. In fact, many creative geniuses are indeed egocentric and unstable. There is, however, an important difference. The creative person is single-minded; he has a purpose in life that he pursues diligently and at almost any cost. The psychopath is as aimless as he is lazy and unstable. The genius creates order—the psychopath, total anarchy. In the psychopath, as one writer put it, "the lid is off the Id."[3] No one should be labeled a psychopath unless he is guiltless, loveless, and aimless. T.E. Lawrence, one of the most guilt-ridden of modern men, would not qualify under any of these rubrics. As for Saint Joan, we know very little about her, but one thing is sure: No one in history had a better-defined purpose in life or showed more determination in pursuing it.

Let us leave the psychopathic label, then, to the antisocial personalities of the kind we have previously described and proceed to the question of etiology. We have already discussed the curious relationship between alcoholism and sociopathy (Chapter 3) and the problem of distinguishing one from the other. We have also mentioned the abnormal electroencephalograms found in patients diagnosed as sociopaths. There is a growing number of medical studies aimed at finding a physiological explanation for the extreme impulsivity that character-izes such individuals and for their seeming lack of moral sensitivity and emotional affect. Lombroso believed that his "born criminals" resembled "moral imbeciles" in their tactile insensibility, vascular reactions, and poverty of emotional response. They have "a physical insensibility greater than amongst most men, an insensibility like that which is encountered in some insane persons and especially in violent lunatics," he said, and it includes a dullness in the senses of taste, touch, and smell.

In general, in criminal man, the moral insensibility is as great as the physical insensibility; undoubtedly the one is the effect of the other. It is not that in him the voice of sentiment is entirely silent, as some literary men of inferior ability suppose; but it is certain that the passions which make the heart of the normal man beat with the greatest force are very feeble in him. The first sentiment which is extinguished in these beings is that of pity for the suffering of another, and this happens just because they themselves are insensible to suffering.[4]

Lombroso seems to have been the first to attribute the moral insensibility of the psychopath to defective neurological functioning—to this inability, literally, to feel what others feel, taste what they taste, smell what they smell. This is an interesting concept, but it was to be nearly a century before it was to be revived, and then not by criminologists but by medical researchers. In 1944 H. Krey reported administering a psychostimulant, benzedrine sulfate, to psychopathic and neurotic juvenile delinquents[a] and finding that their behavior improved, and in 1966 Eisenberg et al. reported improved behavioral ratings of twenty severely delinquent adolescents in a training school after the administration of d-amphet-amine.[5] These studies seem to have been an outgrowth of the interest in troublesome or hyperactive children, who were shown to respond favorably to the administration of psychostimulants. A number of researchers had noted that

---

[a]It should be noted here—and the same comment applies to all the research studies considered in this chapter—that the psychopath/sociopath is defined differently from one study to another (if, indeed he is defined at all), and this makes a comparison of results very difficult.

children who were hyperactive sometimes grew up to be sociopathic adults. Indeed, the behavior of both groups was, in some respects, rather similar. They were impulsive and difficult to condition, and they reacted in bizarre, unpredictable ways to stimuli in the environment. The question was, why?

From the medical (as opposed to the sociological) point of view, there came to be a number of hypotheses. Those who studied the EEGs of violent psychopathic delinquents and mental patients thought the answer was to be found in the brain, in some malfunction of the limbic system which might have resulted from hereditary or environmental factors (see Chapter 32). Another possibility was that psychopaths may have an abnormally low level of autonomic or cortical arousal. Still another suggestion was denervation supersensitivity in the sympathetic nervous system.

In 1949 D.H. Funkenstein et al. administered epinephrine (adrenalin) to a sample of fifteen sociopaths, along with groups of psychotics, neurotics, and normal individuals, and found an abnormal blood-pressure reactivity in thirteen of the sociopaths. In 1955 D.T. Lykken, a University of Minnesota psychologist, reported on the performance of nineteen felons who were "primary" sociopaths,[b] in comparison with fifteen noninstitutionalized student controls, on eight assorted psychological tests. On two tests that measured autonomic function, the sociopaths performed differently. They had a lower ability to learn a maze under stress, and they showed a diminished galvanic skin response (GSR) when lying. Since GSR is one of the measures used in polygraph (lie-detector) tests, the comparative impassivity of the psychopath makes it easy for him to confuse the tester; he lacks the anxiety under stress that is shown by normal or neurotic subjects. As Lykken himself noted, the psychopath is likely to view experimental situations as more of a challenge than a threat. One of Lykken's subjects, for example, noted that he had beaten the polygraph by digging one thumbnail under the other to produce responses to the wrong answers.[6][c]

It is the inability of psychopaths to feel anxiety in situations that arouse apprehension in other people that led Lykken to develop his Activity Preference Questionnaire, consisting of thirty-three forced-choice items, in which the test subject is asked which of two unpleasant activities he would prefer. One of each pair is designed to be boring, the other, for most people, arouses anxiety, e.g., having to cancel your vacation, or standing on the ledge of the twenty-fifth floor of a building; spending an evening with some boring people, or being seen naked by a neighbor. Psychopaths generally show a preference for the item that would

[b]Various investigators have at one time or another distinguished between different types of psychopaths, including the primary and the secondary, the idiopathic and the symptomatic, the aggressive and the inadequate, the hostile and the simple. "Primary" in this case means a true psychopath, as opposed to a neurotic with symptoms that make him sometimes appear psychopathic.

[c]One convict of my acquaintance claimed he could get an inconclusive reading from the polygraph by rubbing soap onto the palms of his hands, and that he had beaten the machine by doing so.

make most people apprehensive, and an avoidance of anything that suggests boredom. This is not surprising if, in fact, it takes a great deal to arouse them. Tests tend to show that it does. In fact, researchers have found that in nonstressful test situations, psychopaths are very likely to doze off. Both J. Schoenherr (1964) and R.D. Hare (1968) showed that psychopaths have a higher shock-detection threshold than do normal people. On the other hand, while psychopaths do not detect light shocks as easily, their maximum tolerance of pain from strong shocks is generally no different from those of nonpsychopaths. Perhaps, thought Hare, this is because the psychopath is unlikely to accept any more pain than necessary—it may be that the subjects *could* have tolerated more shock, but preferred not to.[7]

In his *Psychopathy: Theory and Research* (1970) Hare suggested that psychopathy may be related to a general tendency to attenuate sensory input. Since many of the cues necessary for adequate social functioning are subtle, the psychopath may simply not perceive them. Further, in an attempt to obtain higher arousal, the psychopath is likely to seek excitement. Hare believed that psychopaths should be naturally attracted to psychostimulants, like the amphetamines, which increase cortical arousal, and be inclined to avoid opiates and barbiturates, which reduce it.[8] This leaves unresolved the problem of alcohol, which is a central nervous system depressant. Theoretically, psychopaths should avoid alcohol, but the record, on the contrary, shows that many psychopaths have a major alcohol problem (although others, as expected, tend to be only light drinkers). The obnoxious alcoholic sociopath so vividly described by Cleckley may in fact not be so much a *heavy* drinker as one who has a poor tolerance for alcohol. The bizarre behavior that characterizes his drinking may be the result of a further decreased sensitivity to normal social stimuli in one whose sensitivity is already far too low.

——But the arousal theory is not the only one that has been advanced, and it does not seem to explain the psychopath's abnormally exaggerated response to adrenalin. We have already noted the experiment of Funkenstein in 1949. In 1964 S. Schacter and B. Latané reported that fifteen imprisoned male sociopaths showed a greater increase in pulse rate when injected with epinephrine than did control subjects. A similar test was performed in 1967-1968 by Lewis A. Lindner, Harry Allen, Harold Goldman, and Simon Dinitz on a group of Ohio Penitentiary inmates. These researchers screened 1,375 consecutive admissions, using the Cleckley criteria of sociopathy. They retained as potential subjects all inmates between the ages of twenty-one and thirty-five with an IQ greater than 100 and with fewer than five, or more than eleven, sociopathic characteristics. After eliminating prisoners with chronic medical disorders, they administered a battery of tests to the remaining forty-three, who were then categorized as nineteen sociopaths, ten mixed, and fourteen nonsociopaths. The subjects were given anxiety-producing tasks and injections of either a placebo or epinephrine, and, on a double-blind basis, were tested for heart rate and skin resistance.

Epinephrine seemed to elevate the heart rate and skin resistance more in the sociopath than in the nonsociopath, but on the average, not to the point of statistical significance. Some of the group reacted very much like normal individuals; others reacted in an erratic fashion. Could it be that the researchers were dealing with two distinct types of individuals?

The literature in this field suggested that there are, in fact, different kinds of psychopaths. Henderson spoke of the aggressives and the inadequates, distinguishing them by personality and behavior. Other writers had spoken of the primary or idiopathic psychopath, whose psychopathy was the core of his personality, and the secondary or symptomatic psychopath, who was not a true psychopath, even though he behaved like one. In the case of the secondary or symptomatic psychopath, the genesis of the illness was always apparent; in the case of the primary or idiopathic psychopath, it was not. Neither disease, nor trauma, nor early childhood experience seemed to explain the primary psychopath.

To clarify this question, the Ohio Penitentiary researchers separated their group into two classes, according to whether they showed high or low anxiety on the Lykken scale. The individuals with low anxiety scores they labeled "simple" sociopaths, the ones with high anxiety scores were labeled "hostiles." The high cardiovascular responsivity, they found, was characteristic only of the simple sociopaths, who most resembled the type described by Cleckley—impulsive, ingratiating, with much charm and superficial plausability. The hostiles were generally violent, hostile, and not at all charming. There was much evidence that the hostiles came from pathological family and environmental situations, whereas the simple sociopaths seemed to come from good family backgrounds of higher education and social status. The differences between them led the researchers to conclude that "whatever sociopathy may be, it is not a single entity. Much of the confusion concerning sociopathy stems from the failure to recognize this nosological difficulty."[9] They suggested that both the abnormal autonomic and the abnormal social behavior of the simple sociopath results from "a diminished function (partial or total) of catecholamine-secreting nerve endings including those involved with sensory receptors."[10] The paradoxical effect is to make him supersensitive to any catecholamine available from other sources—for example, the adrenal glands—and results in his inability to make graded autonomic responses to emotion-laden situations. The psychopath's nervous system works rather like an electric light switch: it is either totally off or totally on, and, in the presence of even small amounts of circulating catecholamine, he will pass from one state to the other with lightning rapidity. Thus although the psychopath is hard to arouse, when once he *is* aroused, his responses may be wildly exaggerated.

It is impossible in this short space to summarize the many studies which have been done on the physiologic responses of psychopathic subjects. Hare in his *Psychopathy: Theory and Research* brilliantly summarized the work that had been done before 1970, and in 1977 A.R. and Carol D. Mawson brought the research up to date in an article on "Psychopathy and Arousal" in which they suggested a related but different hypothesis to those that had gone before. They suggested that psychopaths may oscillate between states of high adrenergic and high cholinergic activation, and that the oscillations may be abnormal in two respects. First, the *magnitude* of the oscillations may be greater in psychopaths, resulting in excessive motor activity during arousal and in deeper levels of inhibition and slow-wave sleep during their "off" phase. Second, their rate of change may be faster, resulting in impulsive behavior.[11]

On the whole, this area of medical research has been largely ignored or dismissed by sociological criminologists, who do not believe that criminals of the type called "sociopathic" are biologically different from other people. Sociologists (and psychologists also) tend to explain psychopathy in terms of social pathology, whether bad homes, bad neighborhoods, parental abuse, or whatever, and it is deeply offensive to them to be told, in effect, that Lombroso might have been right—that some criminals *are* biologically different. The fight over sociopathy may be paralleling that over the hyperactive child, with one group of contestants arguing that something is wrong with the child's neurological functioning, and another, that what is at fault is the child's relationship to his family.

Those who take this medical research seriously argue that biological and environmental causes are not mutually exclusive. A number of things may impair the neurological functioning of an individual, they say, from viral infections and injuries to dietary deficiencies and inadequate childhood environment. The mechanisms by which these changes may be induced is not yet fully understood. But animal studies have produced some dramatic evidence that the brain can be permanently altered during pregnancy and postnatal development. Rats which, before a critical age, are allowed to see only horizontal lines, can never thereafter see vertical ones.[12] Should this impairment be blamed on neurological causes, they ask, or on environmental? What of monkeys who are deprived of mothering and grow up unable to feel affection for others? We know, in fact, that all animals, and not least man, are profoundly and lastingly affected by their life experiences and that these effects are manifested not only psychologically but somatically. We are imprinted with them, by means which we are only just beginning to understand.

Although these areas of research are still on the frontiers of science, to those working in them, the old debate over nature and nurture seems meaningless. Man, they argue, is both a biological entity and a social being. His social experience is reflected in his biological functioning, and his biological nature is reflected in his social functioning. Why waste time in sterile arguments over dogma when so much remains to be learned?

36 Some Reflections on the Search for Criminal Man

Are some people born to be bad? This is a question we have confronted over and over in the last hundred years. The medical evidence is mixed, but tantalizing. It is like a faint trail running through a tangled undergrowth, emerging now in one place, now in another, only to disappear again as one seeks to follow it. There are those who believe medical research has pursued a red herring through the underbrush. They not only reject the Lombrosian doctrine, they are so repelled by its implications they will not consider the evidence that biological factors may sometimes be implicated in violent and antisocial behavior. For some criminologists, like the Marxists, the objection may be primarily ideological. For others, it may involve questions of professional viewpoint and training. But in all, there is a natural reluctance to condemn other human beings for a putative biological and genetic inferiority. It is less repugnant simply to reject the evidence itself.

The rejection is made easier by the naiveté, the ethnocentricity, and the primitive, not to say careless, research that marked the early formulations of biological criminology. Lombroso, with his criminal type, is an easy man to make fun of—Dugdale, no less so. We shake our heads at the extraordinary assumption that criminals are closer to the lower animals than criminologists, or that one race, color, nationality, is better than another; we are indignant at Hooton's willingness to "extirpate" the unfit. But much evidence has accumulated since Aschaffenburg suggested that the inheritance of certain people—the children, he said, of drunkards, insane persons, and epileptics—"consists of physical and mental inferiority." The evidence is disquieting to say the least. It has been attacked, explained away, argued with, dismissed, and buried; but it keeps returning to haunt us. It is not even a stately ghost, but more like a poltergeist, tilting tables and hurling inkwells in the councils of criminologists.

True, the evidence is inconclusive; but where human behavior is concerned, *it will always be inconclusive.* The human organism is too complex, its environmental influences too diverse, for simple causative explanations. For every etiological study designed and carried out, critics are quick to advance a dozen alternative explanations to that offered by the researchers. Nowhere is this more true than in the hundred-year-old effort to separate nature from nurture. Maybe the time has come to acknowledge that they cannot be separated—that the battle of the academic disciplines over the causes of criminal behavior, in which so much ink has been spilled and paper consumed, is ultimately an exercise in futility.

For a century now we have asked ourselves an unanswerable question: What makes people become criminals? Let us suppose we had spent a comparable amount of time, money, and research to answer the question: What makes people become doctors? The anthropologists might have made a study of tribal shamans to see how they compared with members of the American Medical Association. Lombroso could have measured the skulls of Italian doctors and tested their reflexes and physical sensitivity. Eugenicists might have looked at the racial stock of the average medical population, and Hooton might have suggested the extirpation of certain genetic strains. Doctors could be karyotyped to see if they carried an unusual number of chromosomes, and their family histories might be taken, to determine whether graduates of medical schools were common among their relatives. Thus we might learn whether the practice of medicine is an inherited characteristic, or whether a child exposed from infancy to stethoscopes and Bandaids would be naturally influenced to enter medical school.

It is unnecessary, I think, to pursue the analogy. This is not an attempt to belittle the long and painstaking research that has gone into the study of criminology, but rather to suggest a truce in the ideological wars that have too long bloodied the pages of academic journals. Forest reserves are after all limited; why waste more paper to score debating points?

It seems clear to this observer that, like it or not, we are going to have to deal with crime without fully understanding Criminal Man. This is not to say that all our research has been wasted. If we find, for example, that physiological defects, inherited or acquired, make it more difficult for some people to live in society, and if those defects can be corrected early, without a gross transgression of human rights, then by all means let medical science do what it decently can. If inequalities of income and mass unemployment provide incentives for a criminal career, it seems only sensible to make serious efforts to correct them. It is wrong for people to be hungry and without work; it would be wrong even if crime were not so serious a problem. The real question we face is how to make intelligent use of the knowledge we have—about society, about economics, about human behavior—to take measures that are neither futile nor self-defeating and which do not violate the ethical standards of a decent society. If we can achieve *that*, then perhaps the long search for Criminal Man will not have been in vain.

**Part VI
Afterthoughts: Some
Policy Questions**

37

Bringing the Dangerous to Heel: The Search for Criminal Justice

One of Adlai Stevenson's favorite stories was of a little girl whose mother found her busily drawing a portrait with her crayons and asked her whose picture she was drawing. "God's," the child replied. "But honey," said her mother, "nobody knows what God looks like!" "They will when I get through with him," said the little girl.

For more than a century, people have been drawing the portrait of Criminal Man in the hopes that when they are done, we shall all know what he looks like. There have been many artists at work, and the portraits show a startling dissimilarity. Lately the artists have taken up their sketch pads to draw another figure whom they call the "Dangerous Offender." Each one's Dangerous Offender looks rather like his Criminal Man, but longer in the tooth and more ferocious—a somewhat degenerate relative from the bad side of the family. As creative endeavors, these portraits have a certain interest, even though they tell more about the artist than about the subject. We would get as true a likeness if we propped a mirror before us on the dressing table, looked squarely into it, and said: "*There* is Criminal Man."

Bernard Shaw once expressed a similar view: "The first prison I ever saw had inscribed on it 'Cease to Do Evil: Learn to Do Well'; but as the inscription was on the outside, the prisoners could not read it. It should have been addressed to the self-righteous free spectator in the street, and should have run 'All Have Sinned, and Fallen Short of the Glory of God.' "[1] These are good words to remember when, carried away by an excess of righteous zeal, we contemplate the measures by which we shall bring the dangerous to heel.

The fact is that it is not merely *homo delinquens* who is dangerous, it is homo sapiens also. One may ascribe this to Original Sin or to the paleomammalian brain and its limbic lobe. But as a biological species, we are designed to defend ourselves from perceived attack, to reproduce, to gratify our wants, and to defend our turf. This behavior, which is innate, has not only helped the species survive and overcome its enemies, it has also caused us trouble. For man is not only selfish, he is a social animal with a strong instinct for cooperation. One need not argue teleology—whether God or Nature *intended* him so, or he is merely the product of blind evolution. The fact is that cooperation, too, has survival value. The great ethical systems deal with that wavering boundary where innate selfishness must yield to social responsibility. So does the law, which must not only set the limits but enforce them. This has proven very difficult to do.

269

It is not necessary to posit some mythic Criminal Man or Dangerous Offender to explain gross selfishness, dishonesty, or violence. For centuries our ancestors thought Original Sin was explanation enough. (As someone has said—I cannot now remember who—Original Sin is the only theological doctrine for which there is the slightest objective evidence.) It would, in fact, be much more difficult to explain how this bipedal primate animal, who has but lately learned to walk upright and fashion tools, developed so large a capacity for compassion, altruism, and cooperation. Social Man is at least as mysterious as Criminal Man. They are not really two individuals, however; they are two aspects of the human personality. Each one of us embodies something of the one and something of the other. Robert Louis Stevenson personified this duality in his *Dr. Jekyll and Mr. Hyde.* Our religious commandments, our ethical precepts, and our laws are all designed to keep Hyde tethered, but like Houdini, he is an escape artist.

We have run into a great deal of trouble when we have tried to project criminality and dangerousness outward onto others—other races, other classes, other people—and have then waged ferocious war against them, as though by punishing the devil without, we could exorcize the demon within. We have never lacked for zeal in the war against crime, but we have often lacked for common sense.

This is not a war that will ever be won. As Norval Morris has so wisely observed, "there are no more causes of crime than there are causes of human behavior. Or, perhaps put more accurately, the causes of human behavior are the causes of crime."[2] The psychologists may, with great difficulty and even greater luck, change the behavior of a single individual with respect to a single character trait. A totalitarian society may, with the aid of secret police, firing squads, and reeducation camps, terrorize an entire community into submission—for a time, at least. It may be possible, through social reform, to make crime less attractive. But unless we are willing to put a policeman on every doorstep or an electrode in every head, human nature will reassert itself. As Quételet observed a hundred and fifty years ago, every social state supposes a certain number and order of crimes, and these are constantly reproduced. A libertarian society is very likely to be a society with many criminals, because when people are free to be themselves, they are free to misbehave. Free competitive enterprise was never limited to good works.

It is time we gave a decent burial to the concept of Criminal Man. In the grave next to him we should inter the Dangerous Offender. These are not ideas whose time has come, but whose time has gone. This is not to say we should give up on crime—only that we can deal with it more sensibly than by personifying an abstraction and then hacking it to death. Crime is real enough, but it is also an artifact. It is an artifact in the sense that crimes are defined, and the penalties prescribed, by law. It is a reality in that laws are constantly broken. We know how few criminals—i.e., lawbreakers—ever pay the penalty. When a Roman legion misbehaved, its commander lined up the troops and selected every tenth man for execution (hence the term "decimate"). In the United States, the number of felonies that are punished is fewer than one in a hundred, which means that a modern criminal's chances of getting off are better than a Roman legionary's. Little wonder that we have been tempted to forget the grubby realities of daily lawbreaking and pursue instead the chimera of the Dangerous Offender, as though by selecting him out of the herd and locking him away *before* he commits his offenses, we could magically solve the crime problem. As the late Mayor Richard Daley of Chicago was wont to say, "That is unreasonable reasoning."

Implicit in the long history of humanity's attempt to deal with criminals is the duality of our objectives. We want on the one hand to do justice, and on the other, to prevent crime. Neither objective has proved easily attainable—the second even less so than the first. There was a long period, from the breakdown of the Middle Ages to the end of the eighteenth century, when societies felt that the proper response to increasing social disorder was to make the severity of punishments keep pace with the rising crime rate. The greater the hordes of the hungry, homeless, and vagrant, the more draconian the statutes, as though by punishing the victims of that disorder, one could cure the ailment itself. As Richard Korn has observed, that is like trying to eradicate malaria by swatting mosquitoes instead of draining the marshes where they breed. We can get a bigger swatter and redouble the ferocity with which we strike—crushing mosquitos may even afford a certain emotional satisfaction. It does nothing to combat malaria.

Whenever society perceives that certain crimes are increasing, the expedient followed has been to make punishments more severe. Never mind that this has no visible deterrent effect. The most dreadful punishments have been inflicted since the beginning of time, and their only result has been the general degradation of society. Lombroso put this very well: "Our predecessors," he wrote, "cut off nose and ears, quartered, boiled in water and in oil, and poured melted lead down the throat. But they succeeded only in multiplying crimes and making them more horrible, for the frequency and ferocity of the punishments hardened men; in the time of Robespierre, even the children played at guillotining."[3]

The historical record is clear on this point: Increasing the severity of punishment has served neither of our two presumed objectives—to do justice and to prevent crime. The time came in England, by the eighteenth century, when there were so many capital crimes that law enforcement broke down altogether. Neither judges nor juries would convict—for who could in good conscience hang a man for cutting down a cherry tree? Even after the criminal law reforms of the nineteenth century, punishments were still barbarous enough. When the English poet and dramatist, Oscar Wilde, was a prisoner in Reading Gaol in 1896, there were three little children serving sentences for snaring rabbits. Like the most hardened felons awaiting trial, they slept on plank beds in cells with solid iron doors; they were crying with hunger. A kindly warder gave the smallest child a few biscuits, and for this was dismissed from his post. The children had been imprisoned because their parents were too poor to pay their fines. They were released only when Wilde paid them himself.[4]

No punishment should outrage our sense of justice. As Sir William Blackstone observed, though the end of punishment is to deter men from offending, it does not follow that it is lawful to deter them at any rate and by any means. Montesquieu observed that the reason for human "laxness" was not the moderation of penalties, but impunity for crimes. No matter how severe the statutes may be, he who is not caught is not punished. Most felons believe they will not be caught, and in this, they are quite right. For many offenses, the chances of going to prison are not much better than the chances of being struck by lightning. This is why the great objective of criminal deterrence has eluded us: incapacitation eludes us for the same reason. To enact harsher laws may seem politically expedient, but it only ensures that the few we catch may be the more barbarously punished. Do we really wish to go back to the time when "even the children played at guillotining"?

As Sir James Fitzjames Stephen pointed out, under the system of "*Timor in omnes, poena in paucos*"—fear for all, punishment for few—a convicted prisoner is looked on as a victim, chosen more or less by chance to be offered up for the crimes of society. There is no evidence that such a system deters anyone, and it violates our sense of justice. Not the least of its disadvantages is that it may lull us into the belief that we are dealing seriously with crime, when all we are doing is venting our frustrations.

The positivists took another tack altogether. Forget the crime, they said, and look at the criminal. Ask yourself, *is this man dangerous*? If he is, put him away—not as punishment, but as social defense. Even if his offense is small or he has committed no offense at all, if his physical stigmata reveal that he was born to do harm, he should be removed from society. In the century since this idea was first launched, there have been many efforts to select those who will commit tomorrow's crimes. Lombroso thought he could look at a man and read the signs of his feral nature: the enormous jaws, high cheek bones, jug ears, and solitary lines of the palm that manifested an "irresistible craving for evil for its own sake, the desire not only to extinguish life in the victim, but to mutilate the corpse, tear its flesh, and drink its blood."[5] Since Lombroso's time, the "born criminal" has been derided, he has changed his supposed stigmata, but he has never quite disappeared. The signs of criminality we once read in the ears we now read in the chromosomes. It may be that, in the effort to preselect the dangerous, we have merely progressed from crystal balls to tea leaves.

Should we even bother to punish? There are those who think we should not—that criminal sanctions are only vengeance, thinly disguised, and as such, unworthy of a civilized society. Karl Menninger calls punishment a "crime" and says that "the idea of punishment as the law interprets it seems to be that inasmuch as a man has offended society, society must officially offend him."[6] On the other hand, Sir James Fitzjames Stephen thought that "reluctance to punish when punishment is needed seems to me to be not benevolent but cowardice, and I think that the proper attitude of mind towards criminals is not long-suffering charity but open enmity; for the object of the criminal law is to overcome evil with evil."[7] He was not alone in this opinion; indeed, it takes little discernment to see that most of the public share this feeling.

Society is not ready to forego its pound of flesh. For this, if for no other reason, punishment must be accepted as a part of criminal justice. As Cicero put it, "*A natura hominis discenda est natura juris*": the nature of law must be founded on the nature of man. But there is no point in deluding ourselves about what our sanctions accomplish. The most they can hope for is to lend our criminal statutes a measure of credibility. Justice Holmes put it this way: "the law establishes certain minima of social conduct that a man must conform to at his peril. . . . If I were having a philosophical talk with a man I was going to have hanged (or electrocuted), I should say, I don't doubt that your act was inevitable for you but to make it more avoidable by others we propose to sacrifice you to the common good. You may regard yourself as a soldier dying for your country if you like. But the law must keep its promises."[8]

So the law keeps its promises—sometimes. Perhaps this is as much as can be expected of it. Perhaps in the centuries that we have dealt with criminals, we have burdened it with too many expectations. Criminal statutes are not some magical recipe for the abolition of crime. If they deter at all, which is doubtful, they clearly do not deter the people we fear most. If they keep malefactors off the streets, they do not keep enough of them off enough streets. A law by itself does not guarantee either arrest, conviction, or punishment. The Spanish have a saying about crazy people that applies equally well to criminals: *No son los que están, sino los que van*—it's not those who are locked up, it's those who are at large. Most of our criminals are at large.

Anyone who has read this book must be struck by the way our theories resemble styles in clothing—adopted one day, derided the next, then redis-covered and adopted once again, as though there had been no yesterdays. This recycling of fashions does not matter where only the length of a woman's skirt is at stake. It *does* matter when we are dealing with the lives of people and the safety of society. Criminology is too serious a science to be left to the faddists and the sadists. There is nothing more disconcerting than the realization that what is being proposed now for the better management of crime and criminals—to get tough, to increase sentences and make them mandatory, and to kill more killers—has been tried over and over again and abandoned as unworkable. It is sad but true that the reformation of criminals through education, psycho-therapy, and prayer has not worked either. As for that great rallying-cry of the positivists, the individualization of punishment, its chief, if not its only, effect has been an unconscionable disparity in judicial sentences. Thus we are left to contemplate the evidence that we have for centuries been going in circles.

In the mental storehouse where penologists keep their theories, there should be a sign clearly posted above each storage bin. It should read: WARNING: THIS IDEA WAS TRIED IN THE ____TH, ____TH, AND ____TH CENTURIES, AND DID NOT WORK. Perhaps this would not discourage any one for long, but it would at least put the burden of proof on the advocates to show that their ideas would work better this time.

The problem with recycling theories is that it leads to the taking of positions rather than the solving of problems. Today there is an angry polarization between those who would punish more harshly and those who would work harder to reform the fallen. It is clearly easier to punish than to reform (as any parent will tell you). But we could never outdo our ancestors in the administration of punitive sanctions, and if *they* did not succeed with the aid of rack, thumbscrew, and whipping post, what makes us imagine a mandatory fixed sentence will do the trick?

Perhaps we have been working at the wrong solutions after all. Perhaps crime is only another aspect of our society, like commerce. Quételet saw a disconcerting statistical regularity in the commission of crimes, a budget we meet with frightful regularity—"that of prisons, dungeons, and scaffolds." He showed that one can predict annually "how many individuals will stain their hands with the blood of their fellow-men, how many will be forgers, how many will deal in poison. . . ."[9] Engels put it somewhat differently: "Society creates a demand for crime which is met by a corresponding supply. . . ."[10] But many of the nineteenth-century writers on the subject thought that while one society may be more criminogenic than another, for any given country at any moment in history, crimes are as predictable as births, deaths, and taxes. Their evidence is worth thinking about.

It is certainly true that there are societies more disciplined than ours that have less crime. There are societies without the racial problem that have less crime, and societies with tighter family structures, less youthful unemployment, or more rural populations that have less, also. The Marxists teach that crime is a natural concomitant of capitalism—that man is naturally virtuous, only The System is vile. Communist societies may or may not have fewer thieves than we do; they certainly have less that is worth stealing. In any case, crusades against crime seldom take the form of crusades for the improvement of the social system. The reason is quite plain: It is easier to change laws than to change our culture, family structures, economic relationships, and ways of doing things. Passing harsh laws is politically popular, and it is emotionally satisfying.

We might all save ourselves much vexation if we decided that the proper end of criminal justice is simply that: criminal justice. Not the prevention or cure of criminality, or the abolition of crime, or the attainment of Utopia, but simple justice. Then we will all know what we are arguing about. Then we can ask ourselves the right questions: Is this the wisest use of our resources? Is it fair? Is it decent? Is it worthy of a civilized society? These questions are hard enough, without asking the unanswerable. As for our brother, Criminal Man, whom we have so long regarded—and treated—as a pariah, it might be well to remember the words of the nineteenth-century French criminologist, Armand Corre. "Criminals," he said, "must not be regarded as the refuse of society. They are a part of it—as a wound is a part of the body."[11]

Notes

Introduction

1. Willie Sutton's remarks are from an interview with syndicated column-ist Bob Greene, The Columbus *Citizen-Journal,* 9 March 1977. Weill's were jotted down from a now-forgotten source in a notebook which I keep.

2. 1929 interview in George Seldes, *The Great Quotations* (New York: Lyle Stuart, 1966), p. 140.

3. American Law Institute, *Model Penal Code* (Philadelphia, 1962), pp. 109-110.

4. Council of Judges, National Council on Crime and Delinquency, "Model Sentencing Act," *Crime and Delinquency* 18:4 (1972):348.

5. David Levine, "The Concept of Dangerousness: Criticism and Compro-mise." Paper presented at the National Criminology Conference, Institute of Criminology, University of Cambridge, 9 July 1975. Mimeographed.

6. Harry Kozol, *et al.,* "The Diagnosis and Treatment of Dangerousness." Reprinted by permission of the National Council on Crime and Delinquency from *Crime and Delinquency* 18:4 (1972):379.

7. Gunnar Myrdal, *Against the Stream: Critical Essays on Economics* (New York: Random House, 1975), pp. 1-3. Copyright © 1972, 1973 by Gunnar Myrdal. Reprinted by permission of Pantheon Books, a Division of Random House, Inc.

8. Ellen Glasgow, address to the Modern Language Association, 1936. Quoted in Bartlett.

9. Theodore R. Sarbin, "The Dangerous Individual: An Outcome of Social Identity Transformations," *Brit. J. Crim.* 7:3 (July 1967):285.

10. Etienne Gilson, lecture at the Ohio State University College of Law, 12 December 1966.

11. I am indebted for this anecdote to Geneva Stephenson of Columbus, Ohio, who interviewed the individual quoted here.

Chapter 1
The Dangerous Classes

1. H.A. Frégier, *Des classes dangereuses de la population dans les grandes villes et des moyens de les rendre meilleures,* 2 vols. (Paris, 1840), vol. 1, p. v.,

2. Ibid., pp. 6-7.

3. Charles Loring Brace, *The Dangerous Classes of New York and Twenty Years' Work among Them* (New York: Wynkoop, 1872), pp. i-iii.

4. P.H.D. d'Holbach, *Système social* (London, 1773); quoted in William

Adrian Bonger, *Criminality and Economic Conditions* (Boston: Little, Brown, 1916), p. 13.

5. Jean de la Bruyère, *Les charactères*. Quoted in Tryon Edwards, ed., *The New Dictionary of Thoughts* (Standard Book Company, 1965), p. 121.

6. Carl Ludwig von Bar, *A History of Continental Criminal Law* (London: J. Murray, 1916), pp. 31-37, 47.

7. David Hume, *History of England* (London, 1782), v. 2, p. 493, quoted in Sir George A. Nicholls, *A History of the English Poor Laws* (New York: Putnam, 1898), vol. 1, p. 46.

8. William Blackstone, *Commentaries on the Laws of England*, vol. IV: *Of Public Wrongs* (Boston: Beacon Press, 1962), pp. 432-435.

9. Sir James Fitzjames Stephen, *A History of the Criminal Law of England* (New York: Burt Franklin, n.d.), vol. 3, pp. 108-109.

10. The Statute of Labourers, 23 Edward III; quoted in Nicholls, op. cit., p. 36.

11. 34 Edward III, quoted in Nicholls, op. cit., p. 42.

12. Statute of Winchester, 13 Edward I, in Nicholls, op. cit., p. 34.

13. Hume, op. cit., vol. 2, p. 369; quoted in Nicholls, op. cit., p. 47.

14. 25 Henry VIII c. 14, in Nicholls, op. cit., p. 112.

15. Sir Thomas More, *Utopia,* (New York: Classics Club, 1947), pp. 33-34, 37.

16. 22 Henry VIII c. 12, quoted in Nicholls, op. cit., pp. 115-118.

17. Georg Rusche and Otto Kirchheimer, *Punishment and Social Structure* (New York: Columbia University Press, 1939), p. 19; Jerome Hall, *Theft, Law and Society* (Indianapolis: Bobbs-Merrill, 1952), p. 116.

18. Rusche and Kirchheimer, op. cit., p. 19.

19. Nicholls, op. cit., pp. 181-182, 186.

20. Christian Paultre, *De la répréssion de la mendicité et du vagabondage en France sous l'ancien régime.* Reprint of the 1906 edition. (Geneva: Slatkine-Megariotis Reprints, 1975), p. 16.

21. Jean Bodin, *Les six livres de la République* (Paris, 1577), p. 587; quoted in Paultre, op. cit., p. 56.

22. Guillebert de Metz, *Description de Paris sous Charles VI* (Paris, 1867), p. 232; quoted in Paultre, op. cit., p. 232.

23. Paultre, op. cit., p. 120.

24. Rusche and Kirchheimer, op. cit., pp. 20-22.

25. F. von Holtzendorff, *Das Verbrechen des Mordes und die Todesstrafe* (Berlin, 1875), p. 211; quoted in Rusche and Kirchheimer, op. cit., p. 22.

26. Rusche and Kirchheimer, op. cit., pp. 17, 19.

27. Nicholas N. Kittrie, *The Right to be Different: Deviance and Enforced Therapy* (Baltimore and London: Johns Hopkins Press, 1971), pp. 16-18.

28. Leon Radzinowicz, *A History of English Criminal Law and Its Administration from 1750* (London: Stevens, 1948), vol., 1, pp. 3, 35.

29. Stephen, op. cit., vol. 2, p. 179.

30. J.J. Rousseau, *Discours sur l'origine et les fondements de l'inégalité parmi les hommes* (Paris: Editions Sociales, 1965), p. 108.

31. Holbach, op. cit., p. 13.

32. J.P. Brissot de Warville, *Théorie des loix criminelles* (Utrecht, 1781), pp. 37, 333; quoted in Bonger, op. cit., pp. 15, 17-18.

Chapter 2
Changing Concepts of Crime and Punishment

1. Leon Radzinowicz, *Ideology and Crime* (New York: Columbia University Press, 1966), p. 2.

2. Edward Gibbon, *The Decline and Fall of the Roman Empire* (New York: Modern Library Edition, n.d.), vol. 1, p. 465.

3. Tacitus, *Annales* XV, 44, quoted in Gibbon, op. cit., p. 457.

4. Quoted in Alan Kors, *Witchcraft in Europe, 1100-1700* (Philadelphia: University of Pennsylvania Press, 1972), p. 132.

5. Ibid., p. 215.

6. Carl L. Becker, *The Heavenly City of the Eighteenth-century Philosophers* (New Haven, Conn.: Yale University Press, 1961), pp. 30-31.

7. Charles-Louis de Secondat, Baron de Montesquieu, *De l'esprit des lois* (Paris, 1868), bk. VI, ch. 12, p. 82; ch. 16, p. 87.

8. Jerome Hall, *Theft, Law and Society* (Indianapolis: Bobbs-Merrill, 1952), pp. 118, 127.

9. M. Cottu, *On the Administration of Criminal Justice in England* (London, 1822); quoted in Sir James Fitzjames Stephen, *A History of the Criminal Law of England* (New York: Burt Franklin, n.d.), vol. I, p. 439. (London: Macmillan, 1883.)

10. Stephen, op. cit., p. 439.

11. Hall, op. cit., p. 132.

12. Radzinowicz, op. cit., p. 25.

13. Leon Radzinowicz, *A History of English Criminal Law and Its Administration from 1750* (London: Stevens, 1948), vol. 1, p. 330.

14. Radzinowicz, *Ideology and Crime*, pp. 8-9.

15. Cesare di Beccaria, *An Essay on Crimes and Punishments* (London, 1785), p. 6.

16. Ibid., pp. 10, 14, 16.

17. Beccaria, op. cit., pp. 31-33.

18. Ibid., p. 23.

19. Ibid., p. 14.

20. Ibid., pp. 2, 9.

21. Ibid., pp. 98, 110-111.

22. Ibid., pp. 103, 107, 112.

23. Ibid., p. 179.

Chapter 3
The Ends of Punishment: A Classical View

1. William Blackstone, *Commentaries on the Laws of England*, vol. 4, *Of Public Wrongs.* Adapted by Robert Malcolm Kerr. (Boston: Beacon Press, 1962), pp. 8-9.

2. Ibid., pp. 9-10.

3. Sir James Fitzjames Stephen, *A History of the Criminal Law in England* (London: Macmillan, 1883), vol. 2, p. 80.

4. Gerhard O.W. Mueller, "Punishment, Corrections and the Law," 45 *Nebraska Law Rev.* (1966), p. 70.

5. Blackstone, op. cit., p. 298.

6. Quoted in James Heath, *Eighteenth Century Penal Theory* (London: Oxford University Press, 1963), pp. 98-99, 101-102.

7. Ibid., p. 102.

8. Jeremy Bentham, *An Introduction to the Principles of Morals and Legislation.* A reprint of the 1823 edition. (New York: Hafner Publishing Co., 1948), p. 1.

9. Ibid., p. 70.

10. Ibid., pp. 170-171.

11. Ibid., p. 171.

12. Ibid., pp. 178-182.

13. Leon Radzinowicz, *Ideology and Crime* (New York: Columbia University Press, 1966), p. 12.

14. Carl Ludwig von Bar, *A History of Continental Criminal Law* (London: J. Murray, 1916), p. 319.

15. Ibid., p. 320.

16. Ibid., pp. 320-321.

17. Nicholas N. Kittrie, *The Right to be Different: Deviance and Enforced Therapy* (Baltimore and London: Johns Hopkins Press, 1971).

18. Immanuel Kant, *Philosophy of Law* (Clifton, N.J., 1887), pp. 195-196, in Alan M. Dershowitz, "Criminal Sentencing in the United States: An Historical and Conceptual Overview," *Annals of the American Association of Political and Social Sciences* 423 (1976):120.

19. John Rawls, "Two Concepts of Rules," in H.B. Acton, ed., *The Philosophy of Punishment* (London: Macmillan, 1969), pp. 107-108.

20. Anthony M. Quinton, "On Punishment," in Acton, op. cit., p. 54.

Chapter 4
Political Deviants as "Dangerous Offenders"

1. Friedrich Engels, preface to the English translation of *The Communist Manifesto,* 30 January 1888, in Friedrich Engels and Karl Marx, *The Communist Manifesto* (Great Books edition, 1955), p. 1.

2. Ibid., pp. 7-9.

3. Ibid., pp. 1-2.

4. Bertram D. Wolfe, *Three Who Made a Revolution* (Boston: Beacon Press, 1961), p. 58.

5. See Wolfe, op. cit., ch. 16, for a fascinating account of the operation of police double agents under the Tsar.

6. Ibid., ch. 31.

7. Georges Sorel, *Reflections On Violence* (New York: Collier, 1961), pp. 171-172.

8. Webster's *New Collegiate Dictionary,* 1975.

9. Bernard le Bovier de Fontenelle, quoted in Carl L. Becker, *The Heavenly City of the Eighteenth-century Philosophers* (New Haven, Conn.: Yale University Press, 1961), p. 135.

10. Becker, op. cit., p. 43.

Chapter 5
Crime and Determinism

1. Constantin-François de Chasseboeuf, Comte de Volney, *Ouvres* (2d ed.), vol. 1, p. 249; in Carl L. Becker, *The Heavenly City of the Eighteenth-century Philosophers* (New Haven, Conn.: Yale University Press, 1961), p. 45.

2. Daniel Defoe, *An Essay on the Regulation of the Press,* London, 7 January 1704, in Luttrell Reprints (Oxford, 1948). Quoted by George Seldes, *The Great Quotations* (New York: Lyle Stuart, 1966), p. 198.

3. M.G. Kendall, "Statistics: The History of Statistical Methods," in the *International Encyclopedia of the Social Sciences* (1968), vol. 15, pp. 224-226.

4. Anne-Louise-Germaine, Baronne de Staël-Holstein, *On the Influence of the Passions on the Happiness of Men and Nations,* in *Oeuvres complètes* (Paris, 1820), vol. 3, p. 11. Quoted in Solomon Diamond's introduction to L.A.J. Quételet, *A Treatise on Man and the Development of his Faculties* (Gainesville, Fla.: Scholars' Facsimiles and Reprints, 1969), p. x.

5. Quételet, op. cit., pp. 95-96.

6. A.M. Guerry, *Statistique morale de l'Angleterre comparée avec la statistique morale de la France* (1864), pp. xlvi and lvii, in Leon Radzinowicz, *Ideology and Crime* (New York: Columbia University Press, 1969), p. 36.

7. David Landau and Paul F. Lazarsfeld, "Quetelet," in *The International Encyclopedia of the Social Sciences* (1968), vol. 13, p. 251.

8. Quételet, op. cit., p. viii.

9. L.A.J. Quételet, *Letter Addressed to H.R.H., the Grand Duke of Saxe-Coburg, on the Theory of Probabilities as Applied to the Moral and Political Sciences* (London, 1849), p. 86, in Landau, op. cit., p. 252.

10. Quételet, op. cit., p. 6.

11. Ibid., p. 6.

12. Ibid., pp. 95-96.

13. Thomas Henry Buckle, *The History of Civilization,* quoted in George Seldes, *The Great Quotations* (New York: Lyle Stuart, 1966), p. 125.

Chapter 6
Bread and Danger in the Nineteenth Century

1. Oliver Wendell Holmes, speech on "Learning and Science" to the Harvard Law School Association, 25 June 1895, in *The Mind and Faith of Justice Holmes* (Modern Library ed., 1954), p. 34. Holmes claimed to be quoting an old saying.

2. John V. Grauman, "Population Growth," *International Encyclopedia of the Social Sciences* (1968), vol. 9, p. 379.

3. Louis Blanc, *Organisation du travail,* 5th ed. (Paris, 1847), p. 71.

4. Leon Radzinowicz, *Ideology and Crime* (New York: Columbia University Press, 1966), pp. 38-39.

5. Eugène Buret, *De la misère des classes laborieuses en Angleterre et en France* (Paris, 1840), vol. 2, pp. 1-2.

6. Edouard Ducpetiaux, *Mémoire sur le paupérisme dans les Flandres* (Brussels, 1850), p. 39. Quoted in William Adrian Bonger, *Criminality and Economic Conditions* (Boston: Little, Brown, 1916), p. 34.

7. Victor Hugo, *Les Miserables* (Modern Library ed.), p. 719.

8. Quoted in Louis Chevalier, *Laboring Classes and Dangerous Classes in Paris during the First Half of the Nineteenth Century* (New York: H. Fertig, 1973), p. 449, note 4.

9. Ibid., pp. 1-2.

10. Vicomte de Launay, *Lettres Parisiennes,* 21 December 1843, in Chevalier, op. cit., p. 3.

11. Heinrich Heine, *De la France,* (Paris, 1873), pp. 101-102.

12. Hugo, op. cit., pp. 78-79.

13. Ibid., pp. 79, 82.

14. Chevalier, op. cit., pp. 314-315.

15. Buret, op. cit., quoted in Chevalier, op. cit., p. 360. No page numbers are given for Buret.

16. George Rudé, *The Crowd in the French Revolution* (New York: Oxford University Press, 1959) appendix on bread prices.

17. Hugo, op. cit., p. 719.

18. Chevalier, op. cit., p. 371.

19. Ibid., pp. 262-263.

20. Georg von Mayr, *Statistik der Gerichtlichen Polizei im Königreiche Bayern und in einigen anderen Ländern* (Munich, 1867); quoted in Gustav Aschaffenburg, *Crime and Its Repression* (Boston: Little, Brown, 1913), p. 106.

21. William Adrian Bonger, *Criminality and Economic Conditions* (Boston: Little, Brown, 1916), pp. 53, 62.

22. Ibid., pp. 43-44.

23. Joseph Van Kan, *Les causes économiques de la criminalité* (Paris, 1903), pp. 478-479, in Thorsten Sellin, *Research Memorandum on Crime in the Depression*, (New York: Social Science Research Council, 1937), p. 24.

24. Aschaffenburg, op. cit., pp. 109, 115, 119, 123.

25. Blanc, op. cit., p. 30.

Chapter 7
Crime and Class Conflict: A Marxist View

1. Lorenz von Stein, "Der Sozialismus in Deutschland," 1852; quoted in Thilo Ramm, "Friedrich Engels," *International Encyclopedia of the Social Sciences* (1968), vol. 5, p. 66.

2. Friedrich Engels, "To the Working Classes of Great Britain," introduction to *The Condition of the Working-class in England,* Marx and Engels, *Collected Works* (New York: International Publishing Co., 1975), vol. 4, p. 298.

3. Engels, *The Condition of the Working Class in England in 1844* (London, 1892), p. 24.

4. Ibid., p. 26.

5. Ibid., p. 27.

6. *The Artisan,* October 1843, quoted in Engels, *The Condition of the Working Class in England in 1844*, p. 35.

7. J.C. Symons, *Arts and Artisans at Home and Abroad* (Edinburgh, 1839), p. 116 et seq., quoted in Engels, *The Condition of the Working Class in England in 1844,* p. 38.

8. Ibid., p. 115.

9. Ibid., pp. 130-131.

10. Ibid., pp. 213-214.

11. Friedrich Engels, *Outlines of a Critique of Political Economy* (1844); in Marx and Engels, op. cit., vol. 3, pp. 440, 442.

12. Friedrich Engels, speech in Elberfeld, 8 February 1845, in Marx and Engels, op. cit., vol. 4, p. 248.

13. "To the Working Classes of Great Britain," in Marx and Engels, op. cit., vol. 4, p. 302.

14. V.I. Lenin, *Collected Works,* vol. 2, p. 22; quoted in Preface to Marx and Engels, op. cit., vol. 4, pp. xx-xxi.

15. Alfred G. Meyer, "Marxism," *International Encyclopedia of the Social Sciences* (1968), vol. 10, p. 42.

16. This summary of the economic causation theory is by Raffaele Garofalo, who, however, disagreed heartily with it. See his *Criminology* (Montclair, N.J.: Patterson, Smith, 1968), p. 143.

Chapter 8
Some Reflections on Eighteen Hundred Years of Danger

1. *The Book of Common Prayer,* Articles of Religion IX and XVII.

2. Article on "Predestination" in F.L. Cross, ed., *The Oxford Dictionary of the Christian Church* (London: Oxford University Press, 1958), p. 1099.

3. I Corinthians XV, 22.

Chapter 9
The Ladder of Perfection

1. Introduction by L.J. Rather in Rudolf Virchow, *Disease, Life and Man* (Stanford, Calif.: Stanford University Press, 1958), p. 12.

2. Rudolf Virchow, "On the Mechanistic Interpretation of Life," (1858) in Virchow, op. cit., p. 102.

3. Joseph Addison, *The Spectator* no. 519, in Loren Eiseley, *Darwin's Century: Evolution and the Men Who Discovered It* (New York: Doubleday Anchor Books, 1961), p. 259.

4. For a summary of these Darwinian precursors, see Jacques Barzun, *Darwin, Marx, Wagner: Critique of a Heritage* (New York: Doubleday Anchor Books, 1958), pp. 40-43.

5. J.C. Lavater, *Essays on Physiognomy,* 3 vols. (London, 1789), commentary to Plate 36, vol. 3; in Richard Hunter and Ida Macalpine, *Three Hundred Years of Psychiatry, 1535-1860* (London and New York: Oxford University Press, 1963), p. 521.

6. Hubert Lauvergne, *Les forçats considérés sous le rapport physique, morale et intellectuel observés au bagne de Toulon* (Paris, 1844), quoted in Constancio Bernaldo de Quirós, *Modern Theories of Criminality* (Boston: Little, Brown, 1912), p. 3.

7. Carl Gustav Carus, *Grundzüge einter neuen und wissenschaftlichen Kranioscopie* (Stuttgart, 1840), quoted in Bernaldo de Quirós, op. cit., p. 3.

8. Augustin-Benoit Morel, *Traité des dégénérescences physiques, intellectuelles et morales de l'espèce humaine* (1857), quoted in Bernaldo de Quirós, op. cit., p. 7.

9. Robert Chambers, *Vestiges of the Natural History of Creation,* 5th ed. (London, 1846), pp. 364, 368. (This book appeared first in 1844.)

10. Ibid., pp. 369-372.

11. Ibid., pp. 407, 409.

12. J.W. Dawson, "On the Antiquity of Man," *Edinburgh New Philosophical Journal* (1864), 19:53; quoted in Eiseley, op. cit., p. 274.

13. Eiseley, op. cit., p. 275.

14. Barzun, op. cit., pp. 30-31.

15. From *Social Statics,* 1851. In Herbert Spencer, *Herbert Spencer on Social Evolution. Selected Writings* (Chicago and London: University of Chicago Press, 1972), pp. 18-19.

16. Barzun, op. cit., p. 26.

17. Benjamin Disraeli, speech at Oxford Diocesan Conference, 25 November 1864.

18. *The Galaxy* (1867), vol. 4, p. 1881; quoted in Eiseley, op. cit., p. 264.

19. Carl Vogt, *Lectures on Man* (London, 1864), p. 198, in Eiseley, op. cit., p. 268.

20. Charles Darwin, letter to Sir Charles Lyell, quoted in Eiseley, op. cit., p. 261.

21. Quoted in Eiseley, op. cit., p. 269.

22. Hans Kurella, *Cesare Lombroso, A Modern Man of Science* (London: Rebman, 1911), p. 12.

23. Henry Piddington, writing in the *Journal of the Asiatic Society of Bengal,* 1855; quoted in Eiseley, op. cit., p. 262.

24. G. Pouchet, *The Plurality of the Human Race,* (London, 1864), p. 15; quoted in Eiseley, op. cit., p. 262.

25. Ibid., p. 141.

26. Herbert Spencer, "Progress: Its Law and Cause;" in Spencer, op. cit., p. 41.

27. Barzun, op. cit., p. 95.

Chapter 10
The Positivist Revolution

1. Cesare Lombroso, speech to the opening of the Sixth Congress of Criminal Anthropology, Turin, 1906; in introduction by Maurice Parmelee to Cesare Lombroso, *Crime: Its Causes and Remedies* (Boston: Little, Brown, 1918), p. xv.

2. Cesare Lombroso, introduction to Gina Lombroso Ferrero, *Criminal*

Man According to the Classification of Cesare Lombroso (New York and London: Putnam, 1911), p. xv.

3. Richard Hunter and Ida Macalpine, *Three Hundred Years of Psychiatry, 1535-1860* (London and New York: Oxford University Press, 1963), p. 712.

4. Kurella, Hans, *Cesare Lombroso, A Modern Man of Science* (London: Rebman, 1911), p. 5.

5. Philippe Pinel, *A Treatise on Insanity* (New York: Hafner Publishing Co., 1962), par. 4, 61, 62-64.

6. J.H. Cox, *Practical Observations on Insanity* (London, 1806); quoted in Walter Bromberg, *The Mold of Murder: A Psychiatric Study of Homicide* (New York and London: Grune & Stratton, 1961), p. 59.

7. James Cowles Prichard, *A Treatise on Insanity and Other Disorders Affecting the Mind* (London, 1835); quoted in Hunter and Macalpine, op. cit., pp. 840-841.

8. J.E.D. Esquirol, *Mental Maladies: A Treatise on Insanity.* A facsimile of the English 1845 edition. (New York and London: Hafner Publishing Co., 1965), pp. 320-321.

9. Kurella, op. cit., pp. 19-20.

10. Lombroso, speech to the Sixth Congress of Criminal Anthropology, Turin, 1906; quoted in introduction by Maurice Parmelee to Cesare Lombroso, *Crime: Its Causes and Remedies* (Boston: Little, Brown, 1918), p. xiv.

11. Lombroso, *Crime, Its Causes and Remedies,* p. 5.

12. Ibid., pp. xviii-xix.

13. Henry Maudsley, *Responsibility in Mental Disease* (London, 1874), pp. 58, 171-172 in Lombroso, *Crime, Its Causes and Remedies,* pp. 21-22.

14. Lombroso, *Crime, Its Causes and Remedies,* p. 8.

15. Ibid., pp. 7-9.

16. Introduction by Cesare Lombroso to Gina Lombroso Ferrero, *Criminal Man,* p. xx.

17. Published in 1878 in enlarged form as *La negazione de libero arbitrio e la teorica dell' imputabilità.* See Hermann Mannheim, *Comparative Criminology,* 2 vols. (London: Routledge, 1965), vol. 1, p. 219.

18. Enrico Ferri, *Criminal Sociology* (New York, 1898), p. 11.

19. Ibid., p. 165.

20. Raffaele Garofalo, *Criminology* (Montclair, N.J.: Patterson Smith, 1968), p. 406.

21. Ibid., p. 273.

22. Ibid., p. 275.

23. Ibid., p. 298.

24. Ibid., p. 300.

25. Ibid., p. 305.

26. Ibid., pp. 411-412.

27. Ibid., p. 307.

28. Ibid., p. 308.

29. Enrico Ferri, quoted in Gustav Aschaffenburg, *Crime and Its Repression* (Boston: Little, Brown, 1913), p. 129.

30. Enrico Ferri, quoted in Marc Ancel, *Social Defence: A Modern Approach to Criminal Problems* (London: Routledge, 1965), p. 45.

31. Aschaffenburg, op. cit., p. 249.

32. Lombroso, op. cit., passim.

33. Charles B. Goring, *The English Convict* (London, 1913), p. 145; quoted in Mannheim, op. cit., vol. 1, p. 218.

34. Goring, op. cit., pp. 24-25, in Earnest A. Hooton, *The American Criminal* (Cambridge, Mass.: Harvard University Press, 1939), p. 16.

35. Aschaffenburg, op. cit., p. 241.

36. Ancel, op. cit., pp. 56, 59.

37. Ferri, op. cit., p. 255.

38. Raymond Saleilles, *The Individualization of Punishment* (Boston: Little, Brown, 1911), p. 123.

Chapter 11
The Jukes and the Kallikaks, or The Dangers of Being Ill-bred

1. R.L. Dugdale, *"The Jukes": A Study in Crime, Pauperism, Disease and Heredity*, 5th ed. (New York: Putnam, 1895), p. 8.

2. Ibid.

3. Samuel Hopkins Adams, "The Juke Myth," *Saturday Review*, 2 April 1955, p. 13.

4. Dugdale, op. cit., p. 49.

5. Ibid., pp. 18-19.

6. A.H. Estabrook, *The Jukes in 1915* (Washington: Carnegie Institution, 1916).

7. Edwin H. Sutherland and Donald R. Cressey, *Criminology*, 8th ed. (Philadelphia/New York/Toronto: Lippincott, 1970), p. 114.

8. Dugdale, op. cit., pp. 55-58.

9. Francis Galton, *Inquiries into Human Faculty and Its Development*, 2d ed. (New York: Dutton, 1907), p. 44.

10. Raffaele Garofalo, *Criminology* (Montclair, N.J.: Patterson Smith, 1968), p. 92.

11. Adams, op. cit., p. 49.

12. Henry H. Goddard, *The Kallikak Family. A Study in the Heredity of Feeble-mindedness* (New York: Macmillan, 1912), p. 50.

13. Henry H. Goddard, *The Criminal Imbecile* (New York: Macmillan, 1916), pp. 106-107.

14. *Buck v. Bell*, 274 U.S. 200, 207 (1927).

Chapter 12
Is Criminality Inherited?

1. Walter Bagehot, *Physics and Politics*, vol. IV: *Nation-making*; quoted in Raffaele Garofalo, *Criminology* (Montclair, N.J.: Patterson Smith, 1968), p. 108.

2. Garofalo, *Criminology*, p. 108.

3. Ibid., p. 3.

4. Ibid., p. 110.

5. Thomas Henry Huxley, Prolegomena to "Evolution and Ethics" (1894), in *Selections from the Essays of T.H. Huxley* (New York: Crofts, 1948), p. 115.

6. Gustav Aschaffenburg, *Crime and Its Repression* (Boston: Little, Brown, 1913), p. 129.

7. Havelock Ellis, *The Criminal* (Montclair, N.J.: Patterson Smith, 1973), pp. 103-104.

8. Ibid., pp. xxii-xxiii.

9. Ibid., pp. 23 and 430.

10. *Buck* v. *Bell*, 274 U.S. 200, 207 (1927); quoted in Oliver Wendell Holmes, Jr., *The Mind and Faith of Justice Holmes* (New York: Random House, The Modern Library, 1954), p. 358.

11. Ibid., p. 356.

12. Oliver Wendell Holmes, Jr., *The Common Law*, in Holmes, op. cit., pp. 58, 61.

13. Oliver Wendell Holmes, Jr., "Learning and Science," speech to Harvard Law School Ass'n, 25 June 1895. In Holmes, op. cit., p. 35.

14. Oliver Wendell Holmes, Jr., "The Path of the Law," address to the Boston University School of Law, 8 January 1897, in Holmes, op. cit., p. 85. The quotation is from Havelock Ellis, citing Garofalo.

15. Holmes, *The Common Law*, pp. 51-52.

16. Travis Hirschi and David Rudiskill, "The Great American Search: Causes of Crime 1876-1976," in *The Annals of the American Academy of Political and Social Science* 423 (1976):17.

17. Carl Murchison, *Criminal Intelligence* (Worcester, Mass., 1926); cited in Hermann Mannheim, *Comparative Criminology* (London: Routledge, 1965), vol. 1, p. 276.

18. Johannes Lange, *Crime as Destiny* (London: Allen & Unwin, 1931), pp. 35, 28.

19. Ibid., p. 41.

20. J.B.S. Haldane, "Scientific Calvinism," *Harper's* 159 (October 1929):554-555. Copyright © 1929 by Harper's Magazine. © renewed 1956 by Harper's Magazine. All rights reserved. Reprinted with permission.

21. Karl O. Christiansen, "Threshold of Tolerance in Various Population Groups Illustrated by Results from Danish Criminological Twin Study." In

A.V.S. de Reuck and Ruth Porter, eds., *The Mentally Abnormal Offender* (Boston: Little, Brown, 1968), pp. 107-120.

22. Odd Steffen Dalgard and Einar Kringlen, "A Norwegian Twin Study of Criminality," in *Brit. J. Criminology* 16:3 (1976):223, 226.

23. Sarnoff A. Mednick, "Considerations Regarding the Role of Biological Factors in the Etiology of Criminality," *Proceedings of the II International Symposium on Criminology* (São Paulo, 1975), pp. 13-16.

Chapter 13
Some Reflections on "Science" and the Dangerous Offender

1. Eric Sevareid, *This is Eric Sevareid* (New York: McGraw, Hill, 1964), p. 13.

2. Jules-Henri Poincaré, *Science and Hypothesis* (Chicago: Great Books, 1962), p. 36.

3. Bertrand Russell, "Philosophy for Laymen," in *Unpopular Essays* (New York: Simon and Schuster, 1950), p. 29.

4. J. Wallace Sterling, *The Stanford Observer* (June 1968), p. 5.

5. William James, *Pragmatism* (New York: Longmans Green, 1914), p. 78.

6. *Webster's New Collegiate Dictionary* (Springfield, Mass.: G. & C. Merriam Co., 1975).

7. I am indebted for this anecdote to the late historian Edward Maslin Hulme, who was at Stanford during Dr. Jordan's tenure.

8. Barbara Wootton, *Social Science and Social Pathology* (London: Allen & Unwin, 1959), p. 327.

Chapter 14
Darwinism, Socialism, and Crime: The Great Debate

1. Constancio Bernaldo de Quirós, *Modern Theories of Criminality* (Boston: Little, Brown, 1912), pp. 70-71.

2. F. Turati, *Il delitto e la questione sociale* (Milan, 1883), quoted in Raffaele Garofalo, *Criminology* (Montclair, N.J.: Patterson Smith, 1968), p. 144.

3. Garofalo, op. cit., p. 144.

4. Bernaldo de Quirós, op. cit., pp. 67-69.

5. Ibid., p. 70.

6. Garofalo, op. cit., pp. 145-147.

7. Bernaldo de Quirós, op. cit., p. 71.

8. Achille Loria, *The Economic Foundations of Society* (New York: Scribner's, 1899), pp. 45-46; John Stuart Mill, *On Liberty* (Chicago: The Great Books Foundation, 1955), p. 8.

9. Loria, op. cit., pp. 48, 69.

10. Ibid., pp. 107-108.

11. Ibid., pp. 108-110.

12. Ibid., pp. 110, 111, 114.

13. Enrico Ferri, *Socialismo e scienza positiva,* quoted in Bernaldo de Quirós, op. cit., p. 69.

14. Bernaldo de Quirós, op. cit., p. 71.

15. Ibid., p. 72.

16. Gabriel Tarde, *Penal Philosophy* (Montclair, N.J.: Patterson Smith, 1968), pp. 49-50.

17. *Actes du Premier Congres International d' Anthropologie Criminelle, Biologie et Sociologie, Rome, 1885* (1886-7), p. 167; quoted in Leon Radzinowicz, *Ideology and Crime* (New York: Columbia University Press, 1966), p. 45. What Lacassagne said was, "les sociétés ont les criminels qu'elles méritent."

18. Tarde, op. cit., p. 50.

Chapter 15
Crime and Social Progress

1. Raffaele Garofalo, *Criminology* (Montclair, N.J.: Patterson Smith, 1968), p. 162.

2. Cesare Lombroso, *Crime: Its Causes and Remedies* (Boston: Little, Brown, 1918), pp. 43, 51.

3. Quoted in Garofalo, op. cit., p. 167.

4. Leon Radzinowicz, "Economic Pressures," in Radzinowicz and Marvin E. Wolfgang, *Crime and Justice,* vol. 1, *The Criminal in Society* (New York and London: Basic Books, 1971), p. 435.

5. Garofalo, op. cit., p. 167.

6. Filippo Poletti, *Del sentimento nella scienza del diritto penale* (Undine, 1882), ch. 8; in Garofalo, op. cit., p. 170.

7. Gabriel Tarde, *La criminalité comparée* (Paris, 1886), p. 73; quoted in Garofalo, op. cit., pp. 171-172.

8. Garofalo, op. cit., p. 171.

9. Ibid., p. 172.

10. Emile Durkheim, "Crime as a Normal Phenomenon," from *Rules of Sociological Method* (Glencoe: The Free Press, 1958), pp. 65-73; in Radzinowicz and Wolfgang, op. cit., p. 391.

11. Durkheim, in Radzinowicz and Wolfgang, op. cit., pp. 392-394.

12. Ibid., p. 394.

13. Arthur Cleveland Hall, *Crime in Its Relation to Social Progress,* quoted in Leon Radzinowicz, *Ideology and Crime* (New York: Columbia University Press, 1966), pp. 86-87.

14. Durkheim, in Radzinowicz and Wolfgang, op. cit., p. 395.

Chapter 16
Economics and Criminality in the Twentieth Century

1. Austin T. Turk in his introduction to Willem Bonger, *Criminality and Economic Conditions,* (Bloomington and London: University of Indiana Press, 1969), p. 4.

2. Bonger, op. cit., p. 22.

3. Ibid., pp. 23-45.

4. Ibid., p. 86.

5. Enrico Ferri, *Criminal Sociology* (New York: Appleton, 1898), p. 56. He repeats essentially the same argument in *The Positive School of Criminology* (Chicago: C.H. Kerr and Co., 1906), p. 60.

6. Bonger, op. cit., pp. 87-89.

7. Ibid., pp. 93-96.

8. Ibid., pp. 103-110.

9. Ibid., pp. 126-127.

10. Ibid., pp. 135-139.

11. Ibid., pp. 141-153.

12. Ibid., p. 200.

13. George R. Davies, "Social Aspects of the Business Cycle," *Quarterly Journal of the University of North Dakota* 12 (January 1922):107-121. Cited in Thorsten Sellin, *Research Memorandum on Crime in the Depression* (New York: Social Science Research Council, 1938), p. 31.

14. William F. Ogburn and Dorothy S. Thomas, "The Influence of the Business Cycle on Certain Social Conditions," *J. of American Statistical Association* 18 (September 1922):324-340. In Sellin, op. cit., p. 31.

15. Sellin, op. cit., pp. 31-38.

16. George B. Vold, *Theoretical Criminology* (New York: Oxford University Press, 1958), p. 173.

17. Sellin, op. cit., pp. 600-662.

18. Vold, op. cit., pp. 180-181.

19. From the introduction by Max Horkheimer to Georg Rusche and Otto Kirchheimer, *Punishment and Social Structure* (New York: Columbia University Press, 1939).

20. Ibid., p. 207.

Chapter 17
Familial Neglect and Criminal Association

1. David J. Rothman, *The Discovery of the Asylum: Social Order and Disorder in the New Republic* (Boston: Little, Brown, 1971), p. 66.

2. *First Annual Report* of the New York Prison Association (New York, 1845), pp. 30-31. Cited in Rothman, op. cit., p. 73.

3. R.L. Dugdale, *"The Jukes": A Study in Crime, Pauperism, Disease and Heredity,* 5th ed. (New York: Putnam, 1895), p. 13.

4. Ibid., p. 58.

5. Charles Loring Brace, *The Dangerous Classes of New York and Twenty Years' Work Among Them* (New York: Wynkoop, 1872), p. ii.

6. Quoted in William Adrian Bonger, *Criminality and Economic Conditions* (Boston: Little, Brown, 1916), p. 612.

7. Gustav Aschaffenburg, *Crime and Its Repression* (Boston: Little, Brown, 1913), p. 127.

8. Ibid., pp. 132-134.

9. Gabriel Tarde, *Penal Philosophy* (Boston: Little, Brown, 1912), p. 252.

10. Ibid., p. 327.

11. Gabriel Tarde, *The Laws of Imitation* (Gloucester, Mass.: Peter Smith, 1962), pp. 215, 224.

12. Tarde, *Penal Philosophy,* pp. 331-341.

13. Ibid., pp. 362, 377.

14. Ibid., p. 393.

15. Edwin H. Sutherland and Donald R. Cressey, *Criminology,* 8th ed. (Philadelphia/New York/Toronto: Lippincott, 1970), pp. 75-76.

16. Ibid., pp. 77-79.

17. Donald R. Cressey, "The Differential Association Theory and Compulsive Crimes," in *J. Crim. Law, Criminology and Police Science* 45 (1954):29.

Chapter 18
Social Disorganization

1. Brinley Thomas, "Migration: Economic Aspects," in *International Encyclopedia of the Social Sciences,* v. 10 (1968), p. 296.

2. W.I. Thomas and Florian Znaniecki, *The Polish Peasant in Europe and America,* vol. 4 (Boston: R.G. Badger, 1920); in Stuart H. Traub and Craig B. Little, eds., *Theories of Deviance* (Itasca, Ill.: Peacock Publishers, 1975), pp. 35-36.

3. Ibid., pp. 36-37.

4. See Sophonisba P. Breckinridge and Edith Abbott, *The Delinquent Child and the Home* (New York: Charities Publication Committee, 1912); Robert E. Park, Ernest W. Burgess, and Roderick D. McKenzie, *The City* (Chicago: University of Chicago Press, 1925); Clifford R. Shaw, *Delinquency Areas* (Chicago: University of Chicago Press, 1929); and Clifford R. Shaw and Henry D. McKay, "Social Factors in Juvenile Delinquency," in National Commission on Law Observance and Enforcement, *Report on the Causes of Crime,* vol. 2 (Washington, D.C., 1931).

5. Clifford R. Shaw and Henry D. McKay, *Juvenile Delinquency and Urban*

Areas (Chicago: University of Chicago Press, 1942), in Leon Radzinowicz and Marvin E. Wolfgang, eds., *Crime and Justice,* vol. 1 (New York and London: Basic Books, 1971), pp. 406-409; and Shaw and McKay, op. cit., p. 375.

    6. Radzinowicz and Wolfgang, op. cit., p. 417.

    7. Ibid., pp. 411-412, 414.

    8. Ibid., pp. 417-418.

Chapter 19
Cultures, Subcultures, and Anomie

    1. Dugald Stewart, *Philosophy of the Human Mind,* vol. 1; quoted in Thorsten Sellin, *Culture Conflict and Crime. A Report of the Subcommittee on Delinquency of the Committee on Personality and Culture* (New York: Social Science Research Council, 1938), p. 18.

    2. Sellin, op. cit., p. 18.

    3. Ibid., pp. 20-24.

    4. Ibid., pp. 25-26.

    5. Ibid., pp. 28-30, 39-41.

    6. Ibid., pp. 58-60, 68. The quotation by Whitehead is from his *Adventures of Ideas,* cited in Shlomo Shoham, *Crime and Social Deviation* (Chicago: University of Chicago Press, 1966), p. 42.

    7. Sellin specifically cited the works of William Healy, *Mental Conflict and Misconduct* (Boston: Little, Brown, 1917) and William A. White (*Crimes and Criminals,* New York: Farrar, Rinehart, 1933). See Sellin, op. cit., p. 68.

    8. Sellin, op. cit., p. 83.

    9. Webster's *New Collegiate Dictionary,* 1975.

    10. Emile Durkheim, *Suicide,* in Stuart H. Traub and Craig B. Little, eds., *Theories of Deviance* (Itasca, Ill.: Peacock Publishers, 1975), pp. 63-68.

    11. Robert K. Merton, *Social Theory and Social Structure* (Glencoe, Ill.: Free Press, 1949), pp. 128-129.

    12. Albert K. Cohen, *Delinquent Boys: the Culture of the Gang* (Glencoe, Ill.: Free Press, 1955), quoted in Marvin E. Wolfgang, Leonard Savitz, and Norman Johnston, eds., *The Sociology of Crime and Delinquency* (New York: Wiley, 1970), pp. 286-288.

    13. Richard A. Cloward and Lloyd E. Ohlin, *Delinquency and Opportunity* (London: Routledge & Kegan Paul, 1961), p. 7; quoted in Leon Radzinowicz and Marvin E. Wolfgang, eds.: *Crime and Justice,* vol. 1, *The Criminal in Society* (New York and London: Basic Books, 1971), p. 480.

    14. Marvin E. Wolfgang and Franco Ferracuti, *The Subculture of Violence* (New York: Barnes and Noble, 1967), pp. 99-101, 104, 153-155.

    15. Ibid., pp. 158-161.

Chapter 20
Societal Reactions and Self-concept

1. Edwin M. Lemert, "Social Structure, Social Control, and Deviation." In Lemert, *Human Deviance, Social Problems, and Social Control* (Englewood Cliffs, N.J.: Prentice-Hall, 1967), p. 17.

2. William Lecky, *History of European Morals* (New York: Braziller, 1955), pp. 282-286; quoted in Edwin M. Lemert, "The Concept of Secondary Deviation," in Lemert, op. cit., p. 42.

3. Lemert, "The Concept of Secondary Deviation," p. 44.

4. Howard S. Becker, *Outsiders: Studies in the Sociology of Deviance* (New York: Free Press, 1963), p. 9; quoted in Sue Titus Reid, *Crime and Criminology* (Hinsdale, Ill.: Dryden Press, 1976), p. 232.

5. Shlomo Shoham, *Crime and Social Deviation* (Chicago: University of Chicago Press, 1966), pp. 38-40.

6. Theodore R. Sarbin, "The Dangerous Individual: An Outcome of Social Identity Transformations," *Brit. J. of Criminology* 7:3 (July 1967):286-294.

7. Robert K. Merton, *Social Theory and Social Structure* (Glencoe, Ill.: Free Press, 1949), pp. 179-183.

8. Simon Dinitz, Frank R. Scarpitti, and Walter C. Reckless, "Delinquency Vulnerability: A Cross Group and Longitudinal Analysis," *Am. Soc. Rev.* 27:4 (August 1962):517; in Walter C. Reckless, *The Crime Problem* (New York: Appleton-Century-Crofts, 1967), p. 445.

9. Ibid., p. 446.

Chapter 21
Crime, Power, and Conflict

1. Dennis H. Wrong, "Power in America," in G. William Domhoff and Hoyt B. Ballard, eds., *C. Wright Mills and the Power Elite* (Boston: Beacon Press, 1968), p. 88.

2. Philip Rieff, "Socialism and Sociology," in Domhoff, op. cit., pp. 167-168.

3. Robert S. Lynd, "Power in the United States," in Domhoff, op. cit., p. 105.

4. Paul M. Sweezy, "Power Elite or Ruling Class?", in Domhoff, op. cit., p. 116.

5. C. Wright Mills, "The Professional Ideology of Social Pathologists," *Am. J. Soc.* 49:2 (September 1943); in C. Wright Mills, *Power, Politics and People* (New York: Oxford University Press, 1963), pp. 531-534.

6. Ibid., pp. 528, 535-540.

7. Ibid., pp. 549-550.

8. Thomas H. Marshall, "Sociology at the Crossroads," inaugural lecture at the London School of Economics, 21 February 1946; in Thomas H. Marshall, *Class, Citizenship, and Social Development* (New York: Doubleday, 1964), pp. 12-14.

9. See introduction by Seymour Martin Lipset in Marshall, op. cit., p. vi.

10. Ralf Dahrendorf, *Class and Class Conflict in Industrial Society* (Stanford, Calif.: Stanford University Press, 1959), pp. 157-158. The quotation from *Das Kapital* is found on p. 9.

11. Ibid., pp. 159-167.

12. George B. Vold, *Theoretical Criminology* (New York: Oxford University Press, 1958), pp. 208, 209, 211, 214-219.

13. Austin T. Turk, "Law as a Weapon in Social Conflict," *Social Problems* 23:3 (February 1976), pp. 276, 282.

14. Richard Quinney, *The Social Reality of Crime* (Boston: Little, Brown, 1970), pp. 15-23.

15. Barry Krisberg, *Crime and Privilege: Toward a New Criminology* Englewood Cliffs, N.J.: Prentice-Hall, 1975), pp. 20, 34, 40, 55.

16. See *Struggle for Justice: A Report on Crime and Punishment in America. Prepared for the American Friends' Service Committee* (New York: Hill and Wang, 1971).

17. *New York Times*, 2 September 1969, p. 44.

Chapter 22
Some Reflections on the Social Science of Criminology

1. Mortimer J. Adler, *Art and Prudence* (New York and Toronto: Longmans, 1937), pp. 252-254.

2. Ibid., pp. 254-255.

3. Ibid., pp. 255-259.

Chapter 23
Psychoanalysis: The Search for Motive

1. A.A. Brill, Introduction to *The Basic Writings of Sigmund Freud* (New York: Modern Library, 1938), pp. 5-6.

2. Ibid., pp. 6-8.

3. Edwin I. Megargee, "A Critical Review of Theories of Violence," in Donald J. Mulvihill and Melvin M. Tumin, eds., *Crimes of Violence,* vol. 13 (Washington, D.C.: Government Printing Office, 1969), p. 1070.

4. Quoted in Brill, op. cit., p. 7.

5. Sigmund, Freud, *The Ego and the Id* (New York: The Norton Library, 1962), pp. 15, 28; *idem.,* "New Introductory Lectures on Psychoanalysis," in

Great Books of the Western World, vol. 34 (Chicago: Encyclopedia Brittanica, 1952), pp. 831, 834, 839; *idem.,* "Psychoanalysis," in *Encyclopedia Brittanica* 1955, vol. 18, p. 667P; and Hermann Mannheim, *Comparative Criminology,* vol. 1 (London: Routledge, 1965), p. 313.

6. S.H. Foulkes, *Psycho-analysis and Crime* (Cambridge: The Cambridge University Faculty of Law, 1944), quoted in Mannheim, op. cit., p. 314.

7. Franz Alexander and Hugo Staub, *The Criminal, the Judge and the Public: A Psychological Analysis* (New York: Macmillan, 1931), p. 33.

8. Ibid., pp. 34-36.

9. Ibid., pp. 4-5, 8.

10. Ibid., pp. 9-10, 3-5.

11. Ibid., pp. 10, 13.

12. Ibid., 53-54.

13. Ibid., pp. 56, 59, 63, 68.

14. Ibid., pp. 113-114, 120, 130.

15. William Healy, *Mental Conflicts and Misconduct* (Boston: Little, Brown, 1926), p. 16.

16. Ibid., pp. 31-32.

17. Henri Bergson, *Creative Evolution,* 1911, p. 4; in Healy, op. cit., pp. 24-25. (The work was published as *L'evolution créatrice* in 1907.)

18. Karl Menninger, *The Crime of Punishment* (New York: Viking, 1968), p. 174.

19. Karl Menninger, *Whatever Became of Sin?* (New York: Hawthorne, 1973), p. 88.

20. Menninger, *The Crime of Punishment,* pp. 178, 181-184.

21. George B. Vold, *Theoretical Criminology* (New York: Oxford University Press, 1958), p. 125.

22. James W.L. Park, "What Is a Political Prisoner?", *American Journal of Correction* (November-December 1972):22. Reprinted with permission.

Chapter 24
Mad or Bad? The Issue of the "Guilty Mind"

1. Aristotle, Nicomachaean Ethics, Book 3, ch. 1, and J.W. Jones, *The Law and Legal Theory of the Greeks* (Oxford: Clarendon Press, 1956), cited in Laurence B. Tancredi, Julian Lieb, and Andrew E. Slaby, *Legal Issues in Psychiatric Care* (Hagerstown, Md.: Harper & Row, 1975), p. 2.

2. Nigel Walker, *Crime and Insanity in England,* vol. 1 (Edinburgh: Edinburgh University Press, 1968), pp. 17, 19-23.

3. Alan M. Dershowitz, "Indeterminate Confinement: Letting the Therapy Fit the Harm," in 123 *U. Penna. Law Rev.* 297, 306 (1974).

4. Isaac Ray, *A Treatise on the Medical Jurisprudence of Insanity*

297

(Cambridge, Mass.: Harvard University Press, 1962), p. 22. (First published in 1838.)

5. Walker, op. cit., pp. 55-57.

6. Sir Matthew Hale, *Pleas of the Crown* (London: 1678), cited in Ray, op. cit., p. 20.

7. Ray, op. cit., p. 29.

8. Walker, op. cit., pp. 78-79.

9. Ibid., pp. 78, 81.

10. Ibid., pp. 81, 90.

11. Ray, op. cit., p. 27.

12. Ibid., p. 29.

13. Ibid., p. 32.

14. Ibid., pp. 33-34.

15. Ibid., pp. 39-40.

16. Ibid., pp. 42-47.

17. Ibid., Appendix 1 from the 1871 edition, pp. 349-350.

18. Walker, op. cit., pp. 90-91.

19. Ibid., pp. 92-95. The quotation from Isaac Ray is found in Ray, op. cit., p. 21.

20. 10 Cl. & Fin. 200, in Ray, op. cit., pp. 97-102.

21. Francis Temple Grey and Charles H. Tuttle, "Insanity in Law," in *The Encyclopedia Brittanica* 1955, vol. 12, pp. 392-393.

22. Ray, op. cit., p. 344.

23. 49 N.H. 399 (1870), in Ray, op. cit., p. 345.

24. Ray, op. cit., pp. 4, 5, footnote. The statement was made by Judge Bazelon in "The Future of Reform in the Administration of Criminal Justice," the Edward Douglas White Lectures in Law, 1964.

25. Andrew S. Watson, "Durham Plus Five Years: Development of the Law of Criminal Responsibility in the District of Columbia," *Am. J. of Psychiatry* 116:4 (October 1959):289-297.

26. Jerome Hall, *Studies in Jurisprudence and Criminal Theory* (New York: Oceana Publications, 1958), note 2, p. 282; cited in Sol Rubin, *Psychiatry and Criminal Law: Illusions, Fictions, and Myths* (Dobbs Ferry, N.Y.: Oceana, 1965), pp. 7-8.

27. David L. Bazelon, "Equal Justice for the Unequal," Isaac Ray Lectureship Award Series of the American Psychiatric Association, University of Chicago, 1961, lec. 2, p. 2, cited in Rubin, op. cit., p. 9.

28. Ibid., pp. 9-10, and Clarence Ray Jeffery, *Criminal Responsibility and Mental Disease* (Springfield, Ill.: C.C. Thomas, 1967), pp. 292-293.

29. Jeffery, op. cit., p. 290.

30. Ibid., pp. 292-293.

31. Walker, op. cit., p. 150.

Chapter 25
The Insane Dilemma of the United States

1. William Blackstone, *Commentaries on the Laws of England,* vol. 4, *Of Public Wrongs* (Boston: Beacon Press, 1962), pp. 21-22.

2. From her Memorial to the Legislature of Massachusetts, quoted in Francis Tiffany, *Life of Dorothea Lynde Dix* (Ann Arbor, Mich.: Gale, 1971), p. 76. (This work was originally written in 1890.)

3. From a letter by Dr. Daniel Hack Tuke to Francis Tiffany, August 1888, describing the visit of Dorothea Dix to England in 1855; in Tiffany, op. cit., p. 242.

4. Henry M. Hurd, William F. Drewry, Richard Dewey, Charles W. Pilgrim, G. Alder Blumer, and T.J.W. Burgess, *The Institutional Care of the Insane in the United States and Canada* (Baltimore: Johns Hopkins Press, 1916), p. 348.

5. Ibid., p. 349, and Albert Deutsch, *The Mentally Ill in America* (New York: Columbia University Press, 1949), p. 412.

6. Nigel Walker, *Crime and Insanity in England,* vol. 1 (Edinburgh: Edinburgh University Press, 1968), p. 95, and Home Office, Department of Health and Social Security, *Report of the Committee on Mentally Abnormal Offenders* (London, HMSO 1975), p. 13.

7. Alan A. Stone, *Mental Health and Law: A System in Transition* (Rockville, Md.: National Institute of Mental Health, 1975), p. 203.

8. John H. Hess, Jr., and Herbert E. Thomas, "Incompetency to Stand Trial: Procedures, Results and Problems," *Am. J. Psych.* 119:8 (1963):713-720.

9. Interview by Ysabel Rennie with program coordinator at Atascadero State Hospital, 4 August 1971. Although my notes show the name and ward of this staff member, they are being omitted for his protection. I have no reason to doubt his account; he was, in fact, very proud of his treatment methods.

10. Interview by Ysabel Rennie with Dr. Henry Luidens, former superintendent of the Lima State Hospital, 3 March 1969.

11. Interviews of former Lima patients by Ysabel Rennie in 1971; visit of inspection to the Lima State Hospital and interviews with staff, November 1972.

12. Visit to the California Medical Facility by Ysabel Rennie, August 1971. Statement was made 2 August 1971 by Dr. Stephen Sheppard. I visited both S-Wing and the Intensive Treatment Unit and observed the conditions here described.

13. *The Anvil* (Sacramento, July 1971), p. 12.

14. Jessica Mitford, *Kind and Usual Punishment: The Prison Business* (New York: Knopf, 1973), pp. 127-128.

15. *U.S. ex rel. Schuster* v. *Herold,* 410 F. 2d 1071 at 1075, 1076 (2d. Cir., 1969), cert. den., 396 U.S. 847 (1969); and *U.S. ex rel. Schuster* v. *Vincent* 524 F. 2d 153 (2d Cir., 1975).

16. *Matthews* v. *Hardy,* 420 F. 2d 607 at 610, 611 (D.C. Cir., 1969), cert. den., 397 U.S. 1010 (1970).

17. Herbert Fingarette, *The Meaning of Criminal Insanity* (Berkeley: University of California Press, 1972), p. 3.

18. David Levine, "Criminal Behavior and Mental Institutionalization," *Journ. Clin. Psychol.* 26:3 (1970):279-284.

19. David Levine, "Crime, Mental Illness, and Political Dissent," 1975. Mimeographed.

20. Henry R. Rollin, *The Mentally Abnormal Offender and the Law* (Oxford: Pergamon, 1969), pp. 3, 123.

21. Thomas S. Szasz, *Law, Liberty, and Psychiatry* (New York: Macmillan, 1963), pp. 144-145.

22. Levine, "Crime, Mental Illness, and Political Dissent."

23. Szasz, op. cit., p. 48.

24. Fingarette, op. cit., pp. 25-28.

25. Thoreau's remarks on the telegraph, and his little anecdote, are found in ch. 1 of *Walden.*

Chapter 26
The Psychiatric Diagnosis of Dangerousness

1. Hans Toch, *Violent Men: An Inquiry into the Psychology of Violence* (Chicago: Aldine, 1969), p. 214.

2. Fredric Wertham, *A Sign for Cain: An Exploration of Human Violence* (New York: Macmillan, 1966), pp. 231, 243.

3. Ibid., p. 254, 264.

4. Thomas Szasz, *Law, Liberty, and Psychiatry* (New York: Macmillan, 1963), pp. 33, 35, 46.

5. Thomas Szasz, "On Involuntary Psychology," *New York Times,* 4 August 1975, p. 19.

6. American Psychiatric Association, Task Force on Clinical Aspects of the Violent Individual, *Clinical Aspects of the Violent Individual.* Task Force Report 8 (July 1974), pp. 1-2.

7. Ibid., pp. 11-13.

8. Ibid., pp. 15-17, 23.

9. Ibid., pp. 23-25.

10. Ibid., pp. 25-26, 33.

11. John R. Lion and Russell R. Monroe, "Clinical Research of the Violent Individual," *J. Nerv. and Mental Disease* 160:2 (1975):75.

12. John R. Lion and Manoel Penna, "The Study of Human Aggression." In Richard E. Whalen, ed., *The Neuropsychology of Aggression* (New York and London: Plenum: 1974), pp. 168-170, 173.

13. Home Office, Department of Health and Social Security, *Report of the Committee on Mentally Abnormal Offenders,* Cmnd. 6244 (London, 1975), p. 58.

14. Harry L. Kozol, Richard J. Boucher, and Ralph Garofalo, "The Diagnosis and Treatment of Dangerousness," *Crime and Delinquency,* 18:4 (October 1972):371.

15. John Monahan, "Dangerous Offenders. A Critique of Kozol et al.," *Crime and Delinquency* 19:3 (July 1973), pp. 418-419.

16. George B. Vold, *Theoretical Criminology* (New York: Oxford University Press, 1958), p. 302.

17. "Psychiatrist Calls Prison 'Warehouse for Mentally Ill,'" Sacramento *Bee,* 25 April 1971.

18. Interview with Ysabel Rennie, 28 July 1971. Robison, a former unit research director for the California Department of Corrections, was author of *The California Prison, Parole and Probation System, Technical Supplement No. 2* (Sacramento, 1969).

Chapter 27
Treating the Intractable: The Experimental
Sixties and Seventies

1. "John Irwin, Ph.D., Ex-con," *Christian Science Monitor,* 19 July 1971, p. 11.

2. Information on these and other drugs from the *Physicians' Desk Reference to Pharmaceutical Specialties and Biologicals* (Oradell, N.J.: Medical Economics, 1977), *Idem,* 1965.

3. Jessica Mitford, *Kind and Usual Punishment: The Prison Business* (New York: Knopf, 1973), p. 129.

4. S.D. Morrison, C.W. Erwin, D.T. Gianturco, and C.J. Gerber, "Effect of Lithium on Combative Behavior in Humans," *Dis. Nerv. Syst.* 34 (1973):186.

5. Joe P. Tupin, David B. Smith, T.L. Clanon, L.I. Kim, A. Nugent, and A. Groupe, "The Long-term Use of Lithium in Aggressive Prisoners," *Comp. Psychiat.* 14:4 (1973):311-317.

6. Michael H. Sheard, "Effect of Lithium on Human Aggression," *Nature* 230 (12 March 1971):114.

7. Arthur Rifkin, Frederick Quitkin, Carlos Carrillo, Arnold G. Blumberg, and Donald F. Klein, "Lithium Carbonate in Emotionally Unstable Character Disorder," *Arch. Gen. Psychiat.* 27 (1972):523.

8. Dietrich Blumer and Claude Migeon, "Hormone and Hormonal Agents in the Treatment of Aggression," *J. Nerv. Ment. Dis.* 160:2 (1975):127-137.

9. John P. Conrad, *Crime and Its Correction: An International Survey of Attitudes and Practices* (Berkeley and Los Angeles: University of California

Press, 1965), pp. 235-236; G.K. Stürup, "Sex Offenses: The Scandinavian Experience," *Law and Contemp. Prob.* 25:2 (1960):361-375.

10. American Psychiatric Association, Task Force on Behavior Therapy, *Behavior Therapy in Psychiatry* (New York, 1974), p. 4.

11. John B. Watson, quoted in Walter Samuel Hunter, "Behaviourism," *Encyclopedia Brittanica,* 1955, vol. 3, p. 328.

12. Edgar H. Schein, "Man Against Brainwashing," *Corrective Psychiatry and Journal of Social Change* 8:2 (1962); quoted in Mitford, op. cit., p. 121.

13. Mitford, op. cit., p. 122.

14. Sharland Trotter, "Patuxent 'therapeutic' prison faces test," *APA Monitor* 6:5 (May 1975):4.

15. Roy G. Spece, Jr., "Conditioning and Other Technologies Used to 'Treat'? 'Rehabilitate'? 'Demolish'? Prisoners and Mental Patients." 45 *S. Cal. L. Rev.* 616, 617-618 (1972).

16. Interview of Michael Serber with Ysabel Rennie, 4 August 1971.

17. Confidential Federal Bureau of Prisons Memorandum, quoted in Mitford, op. cit., p. 124.

18. *Fortune News,* September 1975, p. 7.

19. James G. Holland, "Behavior Modification for Prisoners, Patients, and Other People," *The Prison Journal* 54:1 (1974):25-26.

20. Ralph K. Schwitzgebel, *Development and Legal Regulation of Coercive Behavior Modification Techniques with Offenders* (Chevy Chase, Md.: National Institutes of Mental Health, 1971), pp. 10, 11, 14.

21. Fred L. Royer, Richard Rynearson, Warren Rice, and Denis Upper, "An Inexpensive, Quickly Built Shock Grid for Use with Humans," in *Behavior Therapy* 2 (1971):251-252.

22. James V. McConnell, "Criminals Can Be Brainwashed—Now," *Psychology Today* 3:11 (April 1970):14, 74.

Chapter 28
The "Brave New World" is Challenged

1. For an account of prisoner militancy in this period, see ch. 13, Prison Protest, in Jessica Mitford, *Kind and Usual Punishment: The Prison Business* (New York: Knopf, 1973), pp. 228-247.

2. American Correctional Association, *Congress of Corrections Proceedings,* 1969; quoted in Mitford, op. cit., p. 231.

3. Mitford, op. cit., p. 3.

4. Ethical Principles in the Conduct of Research with Human Participants. Adopted by the American Psychological Association, December 1972, Principles 5 and 7.

5. U.S. Department of Health, Education and Welfare, *The Institutional*

Guide to DHEW Policy on Protection of Human Subjects (Washington, D.C.: Government Printing Office, 1971), pp. 1-4.

6. Nicholas N. Kittrie, *The Right to be Different: Deviance and Enforced Therapy* (Baltimore and London: Johns Hopkins Press, 1971), pp. 350-351, 360, 388.

7. Roy G. Spece, Jr., "Conditioning and Other Technologies Used to 'Treat'? 'Rehabilitate'? 'Demolish'? Prisoners and Mental Patients," 45 *S. Cal. L. Rev.* 616, 663. Reprinted with permission.

8. Perry London, "The Ethics of Behavior Control," in R.W. Wertz, ed., *Readings on Ethical and Social Issues in Biomedicine* (Englewood Cliffs, N.J.: Prentice-Hall, 1973), pp. 174-176.

9. See *The Federal Register* 38:221 (16 November 1973) p. 31738; ibid. 39:105 (30 May 1974), pp. 18914-18920; ibid. 39:165 (23 August 1974), pp. 30648-30657; ibid. 40:50 (13 March 1975), pp. 11854-11858; and ibid. 41:125 (28 June 1976), pp. 26572-26573. See also *Public Law* 93-348, 1974.

10. John P. Conrad, "What Happened to Stephen Nash? The Really Important Questions about Dangerousness." Speech to the Western Division, American Society of Criminology, San Diego, Calif., 11 February 1976.

11. U.S. Department of Health, Education and Welfare, "Protection of Human Subjects: Research Involving Prisoners and Notice of Report and Recommendations of the National Commission for the Protection of Human Subjects of Biomedical and Behavioral Research." In *Federal Register* 42:10 (14 January 1977), pp. 3081, 3077.

12. Ibid., p. 3088.

13. Ibid., pp. 3082, 3080.

14. John P. Conrad, "Right, Wrong, and Sheer Indifference: Ethics for the Correctional Pragmatist." Paper presented to the American Society of Criminology, Tucson, Ariz., 4 November 1976.

Chapter 29
Some Reflections on the Mind of the Dangerous Offender

1. C.S. Lewis, "The Humanitarian Theory of Punishment," in *Res Judicatae* 6:2 (1953):228. This article was reprinted from the March 1949 issue of a now-defunct Australian journal, *Twentieth Century*.

Chapter 30
The Anatomy of Crime

1. Earnest Albert Hooton, *The American Criminal: An Anthropological Study,* vol. 1, *The Native White Criminal of Native Parentage* (Cambridge, Mass.:

Harvard University Press, 1939), pp. 242-247, 254, 275, 281, 283, 306-309.

2. Ernst Kretschmer, *Physique and Character* (New York: Harcourt, Brace, 1925). This is a translation of the second (1922) edition. Also Kretschmer, *Körperbau und Charakter,* 21st/22nd ed. (Hamburg, 1955), cited in Hermann Mannheim, *Comparative Criminology,* v. 1 (London: Routledge, 1965), pp. 236-239.

3. William H. Sheldon, *Varieties of Delinquent Youth: An Introduction to Constitutional Psychiatry* (New York: Harper, pp. 5, 14-15, 20-21, 26-27, 805.

4. Sheldon and Eleanor Glueck, *Unraveling Juvenile Delinquency* (New York: Commonwealth Fund, 1950), pp. 281-282, 343.

5. Sheldon, op. cit., p. 22.

6. Edwin H. Sutherland and Donald R. Cressey, *Criminology*, 8th ed. (Philadelphia/New York/Toronto: Lippincott, 1970), p. 120.

7. George B. Vold, *Theoretical Criminology* (New York: Oxford University Press, 1958), pp. 65-67.

8. Sheldon, op. cit., p. 22.

Chapter 31
The Aberrant Chromosome

1. T.K. Maclachlan, "Criminological Implications of Sex Chromosome Abnormalities," in D.J. West, ed., *Criminological Implications of Chromosome Abnormalities. Papers Presented to the Cropwood Round-table Conference,* December 1969 (Cambridge: University of Cambridge, 1969), pp. 9, 10.

2. Patricia A. Jacobs, Muriel Brunton, and Marie M. Melville, "Aggressive Behavior, Mental Subnormality and the XYY Male," *Nature* (25 December 1965):1351-1352.

3. A.W. Griffiths, et al., "An Investigation of a Group of XYY Prisoners," in West, op. cit., pp. 32-39.

4. Seymour Kessler and Rudolf H. Moos, "Phenotypic Characteristics of the XYY Male," *Comments on Contemp. Psychiat.* 1:4 (1972):107. Also Hans Forssman, "The Mental Implications of Sex Chromosome Aberrations," *Brit. J. Psychiat.,* 117:539 (1970):360.

5. National Institute of Mental Health, Center for Studies of Crime and Delinquency, *Report on the XYY Chromosomal Abnormality* (Chevy Case, Md.: NIMH, 1970), pp. 3-5.

6. Donald J. Mulvihill and Melvin M. Tumin, Codirectors, *Crimes of Violence: A Staff Report Submitted to the National Commission on the Causes and Prevention of Violence,* vol. 12 (Washington, D.C.: Government Printing Office, 1969), p. 421.

7. See, e.g., Forssman, op. cit., and Lissy F. Jarvik et al., "Human Aggression and the Extra Y Chromosome," *Am. Psychol.* 28:8 (1973):679-680.

8. See, e.g., Q. Debray, "L'apport de la génétique à la connaissance du criminel," *La Nouvelle Presse Médicale* 1:37 (1972):2474; and Seymour Kessler and Rudolf H. Moos, "Phenotypic Characteristics of the XYY Male," *Comments on Contemp. Psychiat.* 1:4 (1972):109.

9. Kessler, op. cit., p. 110; Jarvik, op. cit., p. 679.

10. Maclachlan, op. cit., p. 18.

11. Lise Moor, "Un gène de la délinquance. Mythe ou realité?" *Annales Médico-Psychologiques* 2:4 (1972):521.

12. NIMH *Report,* pp. 5, 14, 16.

13. Bernard D. Davis, "XYY: The dangers of regulating research by adverse publicity," in *Harvard Magazine* 79:2 (Oct. 1976), p. 26. Copyright © 1976, Harvard Magazine, Inc. Reprinted by permission.

14. Herman A. Witkin et al., "Criminality in XYY and XXY Men," *Science* 193:4253 (13 August 1976):547-553.

15. Davis, op. cit., pp. 26, 28.

16. Jonathan Beckwith and Larry Miller, "The XYY Male: The Making of a Myth," in *Harvard Magazine* 79:2 (October, 1976), pp. 30-33. Copyright © 1976, Harvard Magazine, Inc. Reprinted by permission.

17. Davis, op. cit., p. 30.

18. Ibid., pp. 29-30.

19. Beckwith and Miller, op. cit., p. 33.

Chapter 32
Brain Control and the Violent Offender

1. Elliot S. Valenstein, *Brain Control: A Critical Examination of Brain Stimulation and Psychosurgery* (New York: Wiley, 1973), pp. 240-241, 247-250.

2. Cesare Lombroso, *Crime: Its Causes and Remedies* (Boston: Little, Brown, 1918), p. xxiii.

3. Harold Goldman, "The Limits of Clockwork: The Neurobiology of Violent Behavior." Research monograph for the Dangerous Offender Project, the Academy for Contemporary Problems, 1977. Mimeographed.

4. B.D. Murdoch, "Electroencephalograms, Aggression and Emotional Maturity in Psychopathic and Non-psychopathic Prisoners," *Psychologia Africana* 14 (1972):216.

5. W. Grey Walter, "Electro-encephalography," in G.W.T.H. Fleming, ed., *Recent Progress in Psychiatry,* 2d ed. (London: J. & A. Churchill, n.d.), p. 80.

6. Denis Hill and Donald Watterson, "Electro-encephalographic Studies of Psychopathic Personalities," *J. Neur. & Psychiat.* 5 (1942):47-65.

7. Edward D. Schwade and Sara G. Geiger, "Abnormal Electro-encephalographic Findings in Severe Behavior Disorders," *Dis. Nerv. Syst.* 17:10 (1956):307-308; John R. Hughes, "A Review of the Positive Spike Phenome-

non," in William P. Wilson, ed., *Applications of Electroencephalography in Psychiatry* (Durham, N.C.: Duke University Press, 1965), p. 71.

8. Hill and Watterson, op. cit., p. 64.

9. Alexander Shapiro, "Delinquent and Disturbed Behavior within the Field of Mental Deficiency," in A.V.S. de Reuck and Ruth Porter, *The Mentally Abnormal Offender* (Boston: Little, Brown, 1968), p. 83.

10. Murdoch, op. cit., p. 217.

11. Hughes, op. cit., p. 80.

12. John R. Knott, "Electroencephalograms in Psychopathic Personality and in Murderers," in Wilson, op. cit., p. 24.

13. Hughes, op. cit., p. 73.

14. Goldman, op. cit.

15. Vernon H. Mark and Frank R. Ervin, eds., *Violence and the Brain* (New York: Harper & Row, 1970), pp. 21-24.

16. Goldman, op. cit.

17. Mark and Ervin, op. cit., pp. 56, 57.

18. Ibid., pp. 1-2.

19. Ibid., pp. 126-127.

20. Ibid., p. 70.

21. Valenstein, op. cit., p. 259.

22. Ibid., p. 55.

23. Ibid., pp. 54-55, 213-222.

24. Ibid., pp. 223-234.

25. Ibid., pp. 240-247, 253-254.

26. Ibid., p. 255.

27. "Physical Manipulation of the Brain." Hastings Center *Report,* special supplement, May 1973, pp. 1-11. Quoted by permission of the Institute of Society, Ethics and the Life Sciences, Hastings Center.

28. "Involuntarily Committed Inmate Can't Consent to Psychosurgery," 13 *Crim. Law Reporter* 2452 (22 August 1973).

29. Nicholas N. Kittrie, *The Right to Be Different: Deviance and Enforced Therapy* (Baltimore and London: Johns Hopkins Press, 1971), pp. 401-404.

30. U.S. Department of Health, Education and Welfare, Office of the Secretary, "Protection of Human Subjects. Use of Psychosurgery in Practice: Reports and Recommendations for Public Comment." In *Federal Register* 42:99 (23 May 1977), p. 26319.

31. Ibid., pp. 26319-26321.

32. Ibid., pp. 26323-26325.

33. Ibid., pp. 26324, 26328.

34. Ibid., p. 26326.

35. Ibid., pp. 26327, 26328.

36. Ibid., pp. 26329-26332.

Chapter 33
Alcohol and Crime

1. Gustav Aschaffenburg, *Crime and Its Repression* (Boston: Little, Brown, 1913), pp. 108-113, 119.

2. Roger Lane, "Criminal Violence in America," *The Annals* 423 (1976):12.

3. Aschaffenburg, op. cit., p. 119.

4. Joseph van Kan, *Les causes économiques de la criminalité* (Paris, 1903), pp. 478-479, quoted in Thorsten Sellin, *Research Memorandum on Crime in the Depression* (New York: Social Science Research Council, 1937), p. 24.

5. Marvin E. Wolfgang, *Patterns in Criminal Homicide* (Philadelphia: University of Pennsylvania Press, 1958), pp. 5, 136-138, 140, 144-153, 166.

6. W. Slater Hollis, "On the Etiology of Criminal Homicides—The Alcohol Factor," *J. Police Sci. & Admin.*, 2:1 (1974):50-51.

7. Lloyd M. Shupe, "Alcohol and Crime," *J. Crim. Law & Criminology* 44 (1954):661-663.

8. J.M. MacDonald, *The Murderer and His Victim* (Springfield, Ill.: C.C. Thomas, 1961), quoted in Donald W. Goodwin, "Alcohol in Suicide and Homicide," *Quarterly J. of Studies on Alcohol* 34:1 (March 1973):151.

9. *Statistical Bulletin of the Metropolitan Life Insurance Company*, September 1958; in Goodwin, op. cit., pp. 150-151.

10. Muslim tradition, cited in Jared R. Tinklenberg, "Alcohol and Violence," in Peter G. Bourne and Ruth Fox, eds., *Alcoholism: Progress in Research and Treatment* (New York and London: Academic, 1973), p. 203.

11. Samuel B. Guze, Vicente B. Tuason, Paul D. Gatfield, Mark A. Stewart, and Bruce Picken, "Psychiatric Illness and Crime with Particular Reference to Alcoholism: A Study of 223 Criminals," *J. Nerv. Ment. Disease* 134:6 (June 1962):512-521.

12. Samuel B. Guze, Edwin D. Wolfgram, Joe K. McKinney, and Dennis P. Cantwell, "Delinquency, Social Maladjustment and Crime: The Role of Alcoholism," *Dis. Nerv. System* 29:4 (April 1968):239-243.

13. Interview by Ysabel Rennie with Richard P. Seiter, Ohio State University Center for the Study of Crime and Delinquency, 20 August 1974.

14. L.N. Robins, *Deviant Children Grown Up: A Sociological and Psychiatric Study of Sociopathic Personality* (Baltimore: Williams & Wilkins, 1966), pp. 113, 295.

15. Tinklenberg, op. cit., pp. 206-207.

16. Gene L. Usdin, "Broader Aspects of Dangerousness," in Jonas R. Rappeport, ed., *The Clinical Evaluation of the Dangerousness of the Mentally Ill* (Springfield, Ill.: C.C. Thomas, 1967), p. 46.

17. John R. Lion and Manoel Penna, "The Study of Human Aggression," in Richard E. Whalen, ed., *The Neuropsychology of Aggression* (New York and London: Plenum, 1974), pp. 173, 179.

18. *People* v. *Guillett*, 343 Mich. 1, 69 N.W. 2d 140-141; and *State* v. *Arsenault*, 152 Me. 121, 124 A. 2d 741, 746. Quoted in Nicholas N. Kittrie, *The Right to be Different: Deviance and Enforced Therapy* (Baltimore and London: Johns Hopkins Press, 1971), pp. 268-269.

19. Laurence R. Tancredi, Julian Lieb, and Andrew E. Slaby, *Legal Issues in Psychiatric Care* (Hagerstown, Md.: Harper & Row, 1975), pp. 107-108. The decisions cited by the authors are *Driver* v. *Hinnant* (356 F. 2d 761) and *Easter* v. *D.C.* (361 F. 2d 50).

20. Marc A. Schuckit, "Alcoholism and Sociopathy: Diagnostic Confusion," *Quart. J. of Studies on Alcohol* 34:1 (March 1973):160-162.

Chapter 34
Who Is the Psychopath?

1. Nicholas N. Kittrie, *The Right to be Different: Deviance and Enforced Therapy* (Baltimore and London: Johns Hopkins Press, 1971), pp. 191, 193.

2. Barbara Wootton, *Social Science and Social Pathology* (London: Allen & Unwin, 1959), p. 250.

3. Conversation of Marion J. Koloski with Ysabel Rennie—date uncertain, but probably 1971. Koloski had served as superintendent of the Ohio State Reformatory at Mansfield and of the Chillicothe Correctional Institute, and, very briefly, as warden of the Ohio Penitentiary after the first 1968 riot. He was being interviewed about his recollections of the second 1968 riot when he made the quoted remark.

4. William and Joan McCord, *Psychopathy and Delinquency* (New York: Grune & Stratton, 1956), p. 2.

5. There have been many editions of Hervey Cleckley's *The Mask of Sanity,* which first appeared in 1941. This quotation is taken from the third edition (St. Louis: Mosby, 1955), p. 424.

6. Emil Kraepelin, *Clinical Psychiatry: A Textbook for Students and Physicians* (New York and London: Macmillan, 1902), pp. 403-404.

7. Walter Bromberg, *The Mold of Murder: A Psychiatric Study of Homicide* (New York and London: Grune & Stratton, 1961), p. 63.

8. Cleckley, op. cit., p. 28.

9. David K. Henderson, *Psychopathic States* (New York: Norton, 1939), p. 19. Henderson, however, did not agree with the judges' view.

10. C. Mercier, *Textbook of Insanity* (London: Allen & Unwin, 1902), quoted in Henderson, op. cit., pp. 19-20.

11. Henderson, op. cit., pp. 18, 20.

12. Cleckley, op. cit., pp. 382-417.

13. Ibid., pp. 547-548.

14. Lewis A. Lindner of the Department of Psychiatry, Ohio State

308

University Medical School, in a report to the seminar on the Ascherman Act sponsored by the Ohio Department of Mental Health and Mental Retardation, Grove City, Ohio, 27 October 1972.

15. Henderson, op. cit., p. 138.

16. George N. Thompson, *The Psychopathic Delinquent and Criminal* (Springfield, Ill.: C. C. Thomas, 1953), pp. 50-52, 43-44.

17. Study by K.H. Fremming (1951), cited in Ian Gregory, *Psychiatry, Biological and Social* (Philadelphia: Saunders, 1961), p. 459. This was a lifetime expectancy study for a Danish population.

18. Lewis A. Lindner, et al., "Antisocial Personality Type with Cardiac Lability," *Arch. Gen. Psychiat.* 23 (1970):261.

29. Wootton, op. cit., p. 249.

Chapter 35
The Neurophysiology of Psychopathic Behavior

1. David K. Henderson, *Psychopathic States* (New York: Norton, 1939), pp. 43, 113-119.

2. Harry L. Kozol, "The Psychopath Before the Law," *New England J. of Med.* 260:13 (1959):637.

3. J. Chornyak, 1941, quoted in William and Joan McCord, *Psychopathy and Delinquency* (New York: Grune & Stratton, 1956), p. 8.

4. Introduction by Maurice Parmelee to Cesare Lombroso, *Crime, Its Causes and Remedies* (Boston: Little, Brown, 1918), p. xxiii; and Lombroso, ibid., p. 5.

5. Richard P. Allen, Daniel Safer, and Lino Covi, "Effects of Psycho-stimulants on Aggression," *J. Nerv. Ment. Dis.* 160:2 (1975):142.

6. D.T. Lykken, *A Study of Anxiety in the Sociopathic Personality* (unpublished doctoral thesis, University of Minnesota, 1955). Cited in Lewis A. Lindner, et al., "Antisocial Personality Type with Cardiac Lability," *Arch. Gen. Psychiat.* 23 (1970):260; and Robert D. Hare, *Psychopathy: Theory and Research* (New York/London/Sydney/Toronto: Wiley, 1970), pp. 49-50.

7. Hare, op. cit., pp. 64-65.

8. Ibid., pp. 68-69.

9. Harry Allen, et al., "Hostile and Simple Sociopaths: An Empirical Typology," *Criminology* 9 (May 1971):45.

10. Lindner (1970), op. cit., pp. 264-265.

11. A.R. Mawson and Carol Deinhardt Mawson, "Psychopathy and Arousal: A New Interpretation of the Psychophysiological Literature," *Biological Psychiatry* 12:1 (1977):49-73.

12. Harold Goldman, speaking to a seminar on "The Neurobiology of Violence," The Academy for Contemporary Problems, 25 July 1975.

Chapter 37
Bringing the Dangerous to Heel: The Search for
Criminal Justice

1. George Bernard Shaw, *The Crime of Imprisonment* (New York: The Citadel Press, 1961), p. 70.

2. Norval Morris, *The Honest Politician's Guide to Crime Control* (Chicago: University of Chicago Press, 1970), p. 18.

3. Cesare Lombroso, *Crime, Its Causes and Remedies* (Boston: Little, Brown, 1918), p. 383.

4. See H. Montgomery Hyde, *Oscar Wilde: A Biography* (New York: Farrar, Straus & Giroux, 1975), pp. 315-317.

5. Cesare Lombroso, introduction to Gina Lombroso Ferrero, *Criminal Man According to the Classification of Cesare Lombroso* (New York: Putnam, 1911), p. xv.

6. Karl Menninger, *The Crime of Punishment* (New York: Viking, 1968), p. 71.

7. Sir James Fitzjames Stephen, *A History of the Criminal Law of England* (New York: Burt Franklin, n.d.) v. 2, p. 179.

8. Oliver Wendell Holmes, to Harold J. Laski, (12/17/25); in *Holmes-Laski Letters* (Cambridge: Harvard University Press, 1953), p. 806.

9. L.A.J. Quételet, *A Treatise on Man and the Development of his Faculties* (Gainesville, Fla.: Scholars' Facsimiles and Reprints, 1969), p. 6.

10. Friedrich Engels, *Outlines of a Critique of Political Economy,* in Marx and Engels, *Collected Works* (New York: International Publishers, 1975), v. 3, p. 442.

11. Armand Corre, *Essai sur la criminalité*, p. 76; quoted in Gustav Aschaffenburg, *Crime and Its Repression* (Boston: Little, Brown, 1913).

Bibliography

Acton, Harry Burrows, ed. *The Philosophy of Punishment.* London: Macmillan, 1969.

Adams, Samuel Hopkins. "The Juke Myth." *Saturday Review,* 2 April 1955, p. 13.

Adler, Mortimer J. *Art and Prudence.* New York and Toronto: Longmans, 1937.

Alexander, Franz, and Staub, Hugo. *The Criminal, the Judge and the Public: A Psychological Analysis.* New York: Macmillan, 1931.

Allen, Harry; Lindner, Lewis; Goldman, Harold; and Dinitz, Simon. "Hostile and Simple Sociopaths: An Empirical Typology." *Criminology* 9 (May 1971):27-47.

Allen, Harry E., and Gatz, Nick. "Abandoning the Medical Model in Corrections: Some Implications and Alternatives." *The Prison Journal* 54:2(1974):4-14.

Allen, Richard P.; Safer, Daniel; and Covi, Lino. "Effects of Psychostimulants on Aggression." *Journal of Nervous and Mental Disease* 160:2(1975):138-145.

American Law Institute. *Model Penal Code: Proposed Official Draft, July 30, 1962.* Philadelphia.

American Psychiatric Association, Task Force on Behavior Therapy. *Behavior Therapy in Psychiatry.* New York, 1974.

American Psychiatric Association, Task Force on Clinical Aspects of the Violent Individual. *Clinical Aspects of the Violent Individual.* Task Force Report 8, July 1974.

Ancel, Marc. *Social Defence: A Modern Approach to Criminal Problems.* Translated by J. Wilson. London: Routledge, 1965.

Armstrong, G.K. "The Retributivist Hits Back." In *The Philosophy of Punishment,* ed. H.B. Acton. London: Macmillan, 1969.

Aschaffenburg, Gustav. *Crime and Its Repression.* Translated by Adalbert Albrecht. Boston: Little, Brown, 1913.

Ashley—Montagu, M.F. "The Concept of Atavism." *Science* 87 (1938):462-463. (*See also* Montagu, Ashley.)

Azcarate, Carlos L. "Minor Tranquilizers in the Treatment of Aggression." *Journal of Nervous and Mental Disease* 160 (1975):100-107.

Bailey, William C.; Martin, J. David; and Gray, Louis N. "Crime and Deterrence: A Correlation Analysis." *Journal of Research in Crime and Delinquency* 11:7 (1974):124-143.

Bandura, Albert. *Aggression: A Social Learning Analysis.* Englewood Cliffs, N.J.: Prentice-Hall, 1973.

Bandura, Albert, and Walters, Richard H. "Dependency Conflicts in Aggressive Delinquents." *The Journal of Social Issues* 14:3(1958):52-65.

Banfield, Edward C. *The Unheavenly City Revisited.* Boston and Toronto: Little, Brown, 1974.

Bar, Carl Ludwig von. *A History of Continental Criminal Laws.* Translated by Thomas S. Bell. London: J. Murray, 1916.

Barzun, Jacques. *Darwin, Marx, Wagner: Critique of a Heritage.* New York: Doubleday Anchor Books, 1958.

[Beccaria, Cesare Bonesana di.] *An Essay on Crimes and Punishments. Translated from the Italian with a Commentary Attributed to Mons. de Voltaire, Translated from the French,* 4th ed. London, 1785.

Becker, Carl L. *The Heavenly City of the Eighteenth-century Philosophers.* New Haven, Conn.: Yale University Press, 1961.

Becker, Gary S., and Landes, William M., eds. *Essays in the Economics of Crime and Punishment.* New York and London: National Bureau of Economic Research, 1974.

Beckwith, Jonathan, and Miller, Larry. "The XYY Male: The Making of a Myth." *Harvard Magazine,* October 1976, pp. 30-33.

Bem, Daryl J., and Allen, Andrea. "On Predicting Some of the People Some of the Time: The Search for Cross-situational Consistencies." *Psychological Review* 81 (1974):506-520.

Bentham, Jeremy. *An Introduction to the Principles of Morals and Legislation.* A reprint of the 1823 edition. New York: Hafner Publishing Co., 1948.

Bernaldo de Quirós, Constancio. *Modern Theories of Criminality.* Translated by Alfonso de Salvio. Boston: Little, Brown, 1912.

Blackstone, William. *Commentaries on the Laws of England.* Vol. 4, *Of Public Wrongs.* Adapted by Robert Malcolm Kerr. Boston: Beacon Press, 1962.

Blanc, Louis. *Organisation du travail,* 5th ed. Paris, 1847.

Blumer, Dietrich, and Migeon, Claude. "Hormone and Hormonal Agents in the Treatment of Aggression." *Journal of Nervous and Mental Disease* 160(1975):127-137.

Boelkins, R. Charles and Heiser, Jon F. "Biological Bases of Aggression." In *Violence and the Struggle for Existence,* eds. David N. Daniels, Marshall F. Gilula, and Frank M. Ochberg. Boston: Little, Brown, 1970.

Bonger, Willem. *Criminality and Economic Conditions.* Abridged and with an introduction by Austin T. Turk. Bloomington and London: University of Indiana Press, 1969.

Bonger, William Adrian. *Criminality and Economic Conditions.* Translated by Henry P. Horton. Boston: Little, Brown, 1916.

Bourne, Peter G., and Fox, Ruth. *Alcoholism: Progress in Research and Treatment.* New York and London: Academic, 1973.

Brace, Charles Loring. *The Dangerous Classes of New York and Twenty Years' Work among Them.* New York: Wynkoop & Hallenbeck, 1872.

Bromberg, Walter. *The Mold of Murder: A Psychiatric Study of Homicide.* New York and London: Grune & Stratton, 1961.

Bromberg, Walter, and Cleckley, Hervey M. "The Medico-Legal Dilemma, A Suggested Solution." *Journal of Criminal Law and Criminology* 42 (1952):729-745.

Buret, Eugène. *De la misère des classes laborieuses en Angleterre et en France.* Paris, 1840.

Carney, Francis L. "The Indeterminate Sentence at Patuxent." *Crime and Delinquency* 20 (1974):135-143.

[Chambers, Robert.] *Vestiges of the Natural History of Creation.* 5th ed. London, 1846.

Chappell, Duncan, and Monahan, John. *Violence and Criminal Justice.* Lexington, Mass.: Lexington Books, 1975.

Chevalier, Louis. *Laboring Classes and Dangerous Classes in Paris during the First Half of the Nineteenth Century.* New York: H. Fertig, 1973.

Christiansen, Karl O. "Threshold of Tolerance in Various Population Groups Illustrated by Results from Danish Criminological Twin Study." In *The Mentally Abnormal Offender,* eds. A.V.S. de Reuck and Ruth Porter. Boston: Little, Brown, 1968.

Clark, Gerald R.; Telfer, Mary A.; Baker, David; and Rosen, Marvin. "Sex Chromosomes, Crime and Psychosis." *American Journal of Psychiatry* 126 (1970):1659-1662.

Cleckley, Hervey M. *The Mask of Sanity: An Attempt to Clarify Some Issues about the So-called Psychopathic Personality,* 3rd ed. Saint Louis: Mosby, 1955.

Cocozza, Joseph J., and Steadman, Henry J. "Some Refinements in the Measurement and Prediction of Dangerous Behavior." *American Journal of Psychiatry* 131 (1974):1012-1014.

Cohen, Albert K. "Multiple Factor Approaches." In *The Sociology of Crime and Delinquency,* eds. Marvin E. Wolfgang, Leonard Savitz, and Norman Johnston. New York: Wiley, 1970.

Coleman, Lee S. "Perspectives on the Medical Research of Violence." *American Journal of Orthopsychiatry* 44 (1974):675-685.

The Committee on Nomenclature and Statistics of the American Psychiatric Association. *Diagnostic and Statistical Manual: Mental Disorders,* 1st ed. Washington, D.C., 1952.

_____. *DSM-II: Diagnostic and Statistical Manual of Mental Disorders,* 2d ed. Washington, D.C., 1968.

Conrad, John P. "Right, Wrong, and Sheer Indifference: Ethics for the Correctional Pragmatist." Paper presented at the annual meeting of the American Society of Criminology, Tucson, Ariz., 4 November 1976. Mimeographed.

_____. "What Happened to Stephen Nash? The Really Important Questions about Dangerousness." Speech to the Western Division, American Society of Criminology, San Diego, Calif., 11 February 1976. Mimeographed.

Cooper, H.H.A. "Penal Policy and the Dangerous Offender: Remember the Poor Baker." *Chitty's Law Journal* 22:6 (1974):191-203.

Corson, Samuel A. "The Violent Society and Its Relation to Psychopathology in Children and Adolescents." In *Society, Stress and Disease,* vol. 2, ed. L. Levi. New York: Oxford University Press, 1976.

Council of Judges, National Council on Crime and Delinquency. *Guides to Sentencing the Dangerous Offender*. New York, 1969.

Council of Judges, National Council on Crime and Delinquency. "Model Sentencing Act. 2d edition." *Crime and Delinquency* 18:4(1972):344-368.

Cressey, Donald R. "The Differential Association Theory and Compulsive Crimes." *Journal of Criminal Law, Criminology and Police Science* 45 (1954):29-40.

Crockett, R. "Habituation to Criminal Behaviour." *British Journal of Criminology* 13 (1973):384-393.

Cross, Rupert. *Punishment, Prison and the Public*. London: Stevens and Sons, 1971.

Dahrendorf, Ralf. *Class and Class Conflict in Industrial Society*. Stanford, Calif.: Stanford University Press, 1959.

Dalgard, Odd Steffen, and Kringlen, Einar. "A Norwegian Twin Study of Criminality." *The British Journal of Criminology* 16 (1976):213-231.

Daniels, David N.; Gilula, Marshall F.; and Ochberg, Frank M., eds. *Violence and the Struggle for Existence*. Boston: Little, Brown, 1970.

David, F.N. "Francis Galton." In *The International Encyclopedia of the Social Sciences* 1968, vol. 6, pp. 48-53.

Davis, Bernard D. "XYY: The Dangers of Regulating Research Through Adverse Publicity." *Harvard Magazine*, October 1976, pp. 26-30.

Debray, Q. "L'apport de la génétique à la connaissance du criminel." *La Nouvelle Presse Médicale* 1:37 (1972):2473-2476.

Department of Health, Education and Welfare. *The Institutional Guide to DHEW Policy on Protection of Human Subjects*. Washington, D.C.: Government Printing Office, 1971.

Department of Health, Education and Welfare, Office of the Secretary. "Protection of Human Subjects." In *Federal Register* 42:10 (14 January 1977):3076-3091.

_____. "Protection of Human Subjects. Use of Psychosurgery in Practice and Research: Report and Recommendations for Public Comment." In *Federal Register* 42:99 (23 May 1977):26318-26332.

De Reuck, A.V.S., and Porter, Ruth, eds. *The Mentally Abnormal Offender*. Boston: Little, Brown, 1968.

Dershowitz, Alan M. "Criminal Sentencing in the United States: An Historical and Conceptual Overview." *The Annals of the American Academy of Political and Social Science* 423 (1976):117-132.

_____. "Imprisonment by Judicial Hunch: The Case Against Pretrial Preventive Detention." *The Prison Journal* 50 (1970):12-22.

_____. "Indeterminate Confinement: Letting the Therapy Fit the Harm." 123 *University of Pennsylvania Law Review* 297 (1974).

_____. "The Law of Dangerousness: Some Fictions about Predictions." *Journal of Legal Education* 23 (1970-1971):25-47.

_____. "Preventive Confinement: A Suggested Framework for Constitutional Analysis." 51 *Texas Law Review* 1278 (1973).

_____. "The Psychiatrist's Power in Civil Commitment." *Psychology Today,* February 1969, pp. 43-47.

Deutsch, Albert. *The Mentally Ill in America.* New York: Columbia University Press, 1949.

Dinitz, Simon; Goldman, Harold; Lindner, Lewis; and Foster, Tom. "Drug Treatment of the Sociopathic Offender." N.d. Mimeographed.

Dollard, John; Doob, Leonard W.; Miller, Neal E.; Mowrer, O.H.; and Sears, Robert R. *Frustration and Aggression.* New Haven, Conn.: Yale University Press, 1939.

Domhoff, G. William, and Ballard, Hoyt B., eds. *C. Wright Mills and the Power Elite.* Boston: Beacon Press, 1968.

Dugdale, R.L. *"The Jukes": A Study in Crime, Pauperism, Disease and Heredity,* 5th ed. New York: Putnam 1895.

Ehrlich, Isaac. "The Deterrent Effect of Criminal Law Enforcement." *Journal of Legal Studies* 1 (1972):259-275.

_____. "Participation in Illegitimate Activities: An Economic Analysis." In *Essays in the Economics of Crime and Punishment,* eds. Gary S. Becker and William M. Landes. New York and London: National Bureau of Economic Research, 1974.

Eiseley, Loren. *Darwin's Century: Evolution and the Men Who Discovered It.* New York: Doubleday Anchor Books, 1961.

Ellis, Havelock. *The Criminal.* Reprinted from the fifth edition with an introduction by Michael J. Hindelang. Montclair, N.J.: Patterson Smith, 1973.

Engels, Frederick. *The Condition of the Working Class in England in 1844.* London, 1892.

Ennis, Bruce J., and Litwack, Thomas W. "Psychiatry and the Presumption of Expertise: Flipping Coins in the Court Room." 62 *California Law Review* 694 (1974).

Esquirol, J.E.D. *Mental Maladies: A Treatise on Insanity.* A facsimile of the English 1845 edition. New York and London: Hafner Publishing Co., 1965.

Ferdinand, Theodore N. "The Criminal Patterns of Boston Since 1849." *American Journal of Sociology* 73 (1967):84-99.

Ferrero, Gina Lombroso. *Criminal Man According to the Classification of Cesare Lombroso.* Introduction by Cesare Lombroso. New York and London: Putnam, 1911.

Ferri, Enrico. *Criminal Sociology.* New York: Appleton, 1898.

_____. *The Positive School of Criminology.* Translated by Ernest Untermann. Chicago: C.H. Kerr and Co., 1906.

Fieve, Ronald R.; Rosenthal, David; and Brill, Henry. *Genetic Research in Psychiatry.* Baltimore and London: Johns Hopkins University Press, 1975.

Fingarette, Herbert. *The Meaning of Criminal Insanity.* Berkeley: University of California Press, 1972.

Foote, Caleb. "Preventive Detention—What Is The Issue?" *The Prison Journal* 50 (1970):3-11.

Forssman, Hans. "The Mental Implications of Sex Chromosome Aberrations." *The British Journal of Psychiatry* 117:539 (1970):353-363.

Frederick, Calvin J. "Dangerousness and Mentally Disturbed Persons." Paper presented before the Law and Socialization Committee of Division 9, American Psychological Association, 2 September 1974. Mimeographed.

Frégier, H.A. *Des classes dangereuses de la population dans les grandes villes et des moyens de les rendre meilleures.* 2 vols. Paris, 1840.

Freud, Sigmund. *The Basic Writings of Sigmund Freud.* Translated and edited by A.A. Brill. New York: Random House, The Modern Library, 1938.

_____. *The Ego and the Id.* New York: The Norton Library, 1962.

_____. "New Introductory Lectures on Psychoanalysis." In *Great Books of the Western World,* vol. 34. Chicago: Encyclopedia Brittanica, 1952.

_____. "Psychoanalysis." In *The Encyclopedia Brittanica* 1955, vol. 18, pp. 666P-668.

Galton, Francis. *Inquiries into Human Faculty and Its Development.* New York: Dutton, 1907.

Garofalo, Raffaele. *Criminology.* Translated by R.W. Millar from the Italian edition of 1905. Montclair, N.J.: Patterson Smith, 1968.

Geis, Gilbert. "Violence and Organized Crime." *The Annals of the American Academy of Political and Social Science* 364 (1966):86-91.

Gibbens, T.C.N.: Pond, D.A.; and Stafford-Clark, D. "A Follow-up Study of Criminal Psychopaths." *Journal of Mental Science* 105 (1959):108-115.

Glaser, Daniel; Kenelick, Donald; and O'Leary, Vincent. *The Violent Offender.* Washington, D.C.: Government Printing Office, 1966.

Glueck, Sheldon and Eleanor. *Unraveling Juvenile Delinquency.* New York: Commonwealth Fund, 1950.

Goddard, Henry H. *The Criminal Imbecile.* New York: Macmillan, 1916.

_____. *The Kallikak Family: A Study in the Heredity of Feeble-mindedness.* New York: Macmillan, 1912.

Goldman, Harold. "The Limits of Clockwork: The Neurobiology of Violent Behavior." Research monograph for the Dangerous Offender Project, The Academy for Contemporary Problems, 1977. Mimeographed.

Goldman, H.; Lindner, L.A.; Dinitz, S.; and Allen, H.E. "The Simple Sociopath: Physiologic and Sociologic Characteristics." *Biological Psychiatry* 3 (1971):77-83.

Goldstein, Joseph, and Katz, Jay. "Dangerousness and Mental Illness: Some Observations on the Decision to Release Persons Acquitted by Reason of Insanity." 70 *Yale Law Journal* 225 (1960).

Goodwin, Donald W. "Alcohol in Suicide and Homicide." *Quarterly Journal of Studies on Alcohol* 34:1 (1973):144-164.

Griffiths, A.W.; Richards, B.W.; Zaremba, J.; Abramowicz, T.; and Stewart, A. "An Investigation of a Group of XYY Prisoners." In *Criminological Implications of Chromosome Abnormalities*, ed. D.J. West. Cambridge: University of Cambridge, 1969.

Gunn, John. *Violence in Human Society*. Newton Abbot, Devon: David and Charles, 1973.

Guze, Samuel B. "A Study of Recidivism Based upon a Follow-up of 217 Consecutive Criminals." *Journal of Nervous and Mental Disease* 138 (1964):575-580.

Guze, Samuel B.; Wolfgram, Edwin D.; McKinney, Joe K.; and Cantwell, Dennis P. "Delinquency, Social Maladjustment and Crime: The Role of Alcoholism." *Diseases of the Nervous System* 29:4 (1968):239-243.

Guze, Samuel B.; Tuason, Vicente B.; Gatfield, Paul D.; Stewart, Mark A.; and Picken, Bruce. "Psychiatric Illness and Crime with Particular Reference to Alcoholism: A Study of 223 Criminals." *Journal of Nervous and Mental Disease* 134 (1962):512-521.

Häfner, H., and Böker, W. "Mentally Disordered Violent Offenders." *Social Psychiatry* 8 (1973):221-229.

Haldane, J.B.S. "Scientific Calvinism." *Harper's Magazine*, October 1929, pp. 551-558.

Hall, Jerome. "Mental Disease and Criminal Reponsibility—M'Naghten versus Durham and the American Law Institute's Tentative Draft." 33 *Indiana Law Journal* 212 (1958).

Hall, Jerome. *Studies in Jurisprudence and Criminal Theory*. New York: Oceana Publications, 1958.

———. *Theft, Law and Society*, 2d ed. Indianapolis: Bobbs-Merrill, 1952.

Halleck, Seymour L. "Legal and Ethical Aspects of Behavior Control." *American Journal of Psychiatry* 131 (1974):381-385.

———. "A Multidimensional Approach to Violence." In *Violence and Criminal Justice*, eds. Duncan Chappell and John Monahan. Lexington, Mass.: Lexington Books, 1975.

———. *Psychiatry and the Dilemmas of Crime*. New York: Harper & Row, 1967.

Haller, Mark H. "Theories of Criminal Violence and Their Impact on the Criminal Justice System." In *Crimes of Violence*, vol. 13, eds. Donald J. Mulvihill and Melvin M. Tumin. Washington, D.C.: Government Printing Office, 1969.

Hare, Robert D. *Psychopathy: Theory and Research*. New York/London/Sydney/Toronto: Wiley, 1970.

Hart, H.L.A. *Punishment and Responsibility: Essays in the Philosophy of Law*. New York and Oxford: The Clarendon Press, 1968.

Healy, William. *The Individual Delinquent*. Boston: Little, Brown, 1924.

———. *Mental Conflicts and Misconduct*. Boston: Little, Brown, 1926.

Heath, James. *Eighteenth Century Penal Theory*. London: Oxford University Press, 1963.

Heilbrun, A.B.; Knopf, I.J.; and Bruner, P. "Criminal Impulsivity and Violence and Subsequent Parole Outcome." *British Journal of Criminology* 16 (1976):367-377.

Heine, Heinrich. *De la France*. Paris, 1873.

Hellman, Daniel S., and Blackman, Nathan. "Enuresis, Firesetting and Cruelty to Animals: A Triad Predictive of Adult Crime." *American Journal of Psychiatry* 122 (1966):1431-1435.

Henderson, David K. *Psychopathic States*. New York: Norton, 1939.

Hess, John H., Jr., and Thomas, Herbert E. "Incompetency to Stand Trial: Procedures, Results and Problems." *American Journal of Psychiatry* 119 (1963):713-720.

Hill, Dennis, and Watterson, Donald. "Electro-encephalographic Studies of Psychopathic Personalities." *Journal of Neurology and Psychiatry* 5 (1942):47-65.

Hirschi, Travis, and Rudisill, David. "The Great American Search: Causes of Crime 1876-1976." *The Annals of the American Academy of Political and Social Science* 423 (1976):14-30.

Holland, James G. "Behavior Modification for Prisoners, Patients, and Other People as a Prescription for the Planned Society." *The Prison Journal* 54 (1974):23-37.

Hollis, W. Slater. "On the Etiology of Criminal Homicides—The Alcohol Factor." *Journal of Police Science and Administration* 2:1 (1974):50-53.

Holmes, Oliver Wendell, Jr. *The Mind and Faith of Justice Holmes: His Speeches, Essays, Letters and Judicial Opinions*. New York: Random House, The Modern Library, 1954.

Home Office, Department of Health and Social Security. *Report of the Committee on Mentally Abnormal Offenders*. Cmnd. 6244. London, 1975.

Hooton, Earnest A. *The American Criminal: An Anthropological Study*. Vol. 1: *The Native White Criminal of Native Parentage*. Cambridge, Mass.: Harvard University Press, 1939.

Hughes, John R. "A Review of the Positive Spike Phenomenon." In *Applications of Electroencephalography in Psychiatry*, ed. William P. Wilson. Durham, N.C.: Duke University Press, 1965.

Hunter, Richard, and Macalpine, Ida. *Three Hundred Years of Psychiatry, 1535-1860*. London and New York: Oxford University Press, 1963.

Hurd, Henry M.; Drewry, William F.; Dewey, Richard; Pilgrim, Charles W.; Blumer, G. Alder; and Burgess, T.J.W. *The Institutional Care of the Insane in the United States and Canada*. Baltimore: Johns Hopkins Press, 1916.

Huxley, Thomas Henry. *Selections from the Essays of T.H. Huxley*. Edited by Alburey Castell. New York: Crofts, 1948.

"Involuntarily Committed Inmate Can't Consent to Psychosurgery." 13 *Criminal Law Reporter* 2452 (1973).

Itil, Luran M., and Wadud, Abdul. "Treatment of Human Aggression with Major

Tranquilizers, Antidepressants and Newer Psychotropic Drugs." *Journal of Nervous and Mental Disease* 160 (1975):83-99.

Jacobs, Patricia A.; Brunton, Muriel; and Melville, Marie M. "Aggressive Behavior, Mental Subnormality and the XYY Male." *Nature* 5047 (25 December 1965):1351-1352.

Jarvik, Lissy F.; Klodin, Victor; and Matsuyama, Steven S. "Human Aggression and the Extra Y Chromosome. Fact or Fantasy?" *American Psychologist* 28 (1973):674-682.

Jeffery, Clarence Ray. *Criminal Responsibility and Mental Disease.* Springfield, Ill.: Charles C. Thomas, 1967.

_____. "The Historical Development of Criminology." In *Pioneers in Criminology*, edited Hermann Mannheim. Montclair, N.J.: Patterson Smith, 1972.

Jonas, Hans. "Philosophical Reflections on Experimenting with Human Subjects." In *Readings on Ethical and Social Issues in Biomedicine*, ed. R.H. Wertz. Englewood Cliffs, N.J.: Prentice-Hall, 1973.

Justice, Blair: Justice, Rita; and Kraft, Irvin A. "Early Warning Signs of Violence: Is a Triad Enough?" *American Journal of Psychiatry* 131 (1974):457-459.

Kasinsky, Renée Goldsmith. "The 'Mentally Disordered Offender': A Captive of the State?" Speech to the American Society of Criminology, Toronto, 30 October 1975. Mimeographed.

Kendall, M.G. "Statistics: The History of Statistical Methods." In *The International Encyclopedia of the Social Sciences* 1968, vol. 15, pp. 224-232.

Kessler, Seymour, and Moos, Rudolf H. "Phenotypic Characteristics of the XYY Male." *Comments on Contemporary Psychiatry* 1:4 (1972):105-112.

Kido, Matazo. "An EEG Study of Delinquent Adolescents with Reference to Recidivism and Murder." In *Folia Psychiatrica et Neurologica Japonica* 27 (1973):77-84.

Kittrie, Nicholas N. *The Right to be Different: Deviance and Enforced Therapy.* Baltimore and London: Johns Hopkins Press, 1971.

Knott, John R. "Electroencephalograms in Psychopathic Personality and in Murderers." In *Applications of Electroencephalography in Psychiatry,* ed. William P. Wilson. Durham, N.C.: Duke University Press, 1965.

Knott, John R., and Gottlieb, Jacques S. "The Electroencephalogram in Psychopathic Personality." *Psychosomatic Medicine* 5 (1943):139-142.

Kors, Alan. *Witchcraft in Europe, 1100-1700.* Philadelphia: University of Pennsylvania Press, 1972.

Kozol, Harry L. "The Psychopath Before the Law." *New England Journal of Medicine* 260:13 (1959):637-644.

Kozol, Harry L.; Boucher, Richard J.; and Garofalo, Ralph. "The Diagnosis and Treatment of Dangerousness." *Crime and Delinquency* 18:4 (1972):371-392.

Kraepelin, Emil. *Clinical Psychiatry: A Textbook for Students and Physieians.*

Abstracted and adapted from the sixth German edition of Kraepelin's *Lehrbuch der Psychiatrie* by A. Ross Defendorf, M.D. New York and London: Macmillan, 1902.

Kretschmer, Ernst. *Physique and Character: An Investigation of the Nature of Constitution and of the Theory of Temperament.* New York: Harcourt, Brace, 1925.

Kreuz, Leo E., and Rose, Robert M. "Assessment of Aggressive Behavior and Plasma Testosterone in a Young Criminal Population." *Psychosomatic Medicine* 34 (1972):321-332.

Krisberg, Barry. *Crime and Privilege: Toward a New Criminology.* Englewood Cliffs, N.J.: Prentice-Hall, 1975.

Kurella, Hans. *Cesare Lombroso, A Modern Man of Science.* London: Rebman, 1911.

Landau, David, and Lazarsfeld, Paul F. "Quetelet." In *The International Encyclopedia of the Social Sciences* 1968, vol. 13, pp. 247-255.

Landau, Simha F. "Pathologies among Homicide Offenders: Some Cultural Profiles." *The British Journal of Criminology* 15 (1975):157-166.

Lane, Roger. "Crime and Criminal Statistics in Nineteenth Century Massachusetts." *Journal of Social History,* Winter 1968, pp. 156-163.

_____. "Criminal Violence in America." In *The Annals of the American Academy of Political and Social Science* 423 (1976):1-13.

_____. "Urbanization and Criminal Violence in the Nineteenth Century: Massachusetts as a Test Case." In *The History of Violence in America: Historical and Comparative Perspectives. A Report Submitted to the National Commission on the Causes and Prevention of Violence,* eds. Hugh Davis Graham and Ted Robert Gurr. New York: Praeger, 1969.

Lange, Johannes. *Crime as Destiny.* London: Allen & Unwin, 1931.

Lemert, Edwin M. *Human Deviance, Social Problems, and Social Control.* Englewood Cliffs, N.J.: Prentice-Hall, 1967.

_____. *Social Pathology.* New York/Toronto/London: McGraw-Hill, 1951.

Levine, David. "The Concept of Dangerousness: Criticism and Compromise." Paper presented at the National Criminology Conference, Institute of Criminology, University of Cambridge, 9 July 1975. Mimeographed.

_____. "Crime, Mental Illness, and Political Dissent," 1975. Mimeographed.

_____. "Criminal Behavior and Mental Institutionalization." *Journal of Clinical Psychology* 26:3 (1970):279-284.

Lewis, C.S. "The Humanitarian Theory of Punishment." *Res Judicatae* 6:2 (1953):224-230. Reprinted from *Twentieth Century,* March 1949.

Lifton, Robert Jay. *Thought Reform and the Psychology of Totalism.* New York: Norton, 1961.

Lindner, Lewis A.; Goldman, Harold; Dinitz, Simon; and Allen, Harry E. "Antisocial Personality Type with Cardiac Lability." *Archives of General Psychiatry* 23 (1970):260-267.

Lion, John R. "Conceptual Issues in the Use of Drugs for the Treatment of Aggression in Man." *Journal of Nervous and Mental Disease* 160 (1975):76-82.

Lion, John R.; Bach-y-Rita, G.; and Ervin, F.R. "Enigmas of Violence." In *Violence and the Brain*, eds. Vernon H. Mark and Frank R. Ervin. New York: Harper & Row, 1970.

Lion, John R., and Monroe, Russell R. "Clinical Research of the Violent Individual." *Journal of Nervous and Mental Disease* 160:2 (1975):75.

Lion, John R., and Penna, Manoel. "The Study of Human Aggression." In *The Neuropsychology of Aggression.*, ed. Richard E. Whalen. New York and London: Plenum, 1974.

Liszt, Franz von. *Tratado de Derecho Penal [Lehrbuch des deutschen Strafrechts]*. Vol. 1. Translated from the 18th German edition by Quintiliano Saldaña. Madrid: Editorial Reus, 1926. Vol. 2. Translated from the 20th German edition by Luis Jiménez de Asúa. Madrid: Editorial Reus, 1927. Vol. 3. Translated from the 20th German edition by Luis Jiménez de Asúa, Madrid: Editorial Reus, 1929.

Lombroso, Cesare. *Crime: Its Causes and Remedies*. Translated from the French edition of 1899 by Henry P. Horton. Boston: Little, Brown, 1918.

London, Perry. "The Ethics of Behavior Control." In *Readings on Ethical and Social Issues in Biomedicine*, ed. Richard W. Wertz. Englewood Cliffs, N.J.: Prentice-Hall, 1973.

Loria, Achille. *The Economic Foundations of Society*. London and New York, 1899.

Mabbott, J.D. "Punishment." In *Justice and Social Policy*, ed. Frederick A. Olafson. Englewood Cliffs, N.J.: Prentice-Hall, 1961.

MacIver, Robert. "Social Causation." In *The Sociology of Crime and Delinquency*, eds. Marvin E. Wolfgang, Leonard Savitz, and Norman Johnston. New York: Wiley, 1970.

Maclachlan, T.K. "Criminological Implications of Sex Chromosome Abnormalities: A Review." In *Criminological Implications of Chromosome Abnormalities*, ed. D.J. West. Cambridge: University of Cambridge, 1969.

McClearn, Gerald E. "Behavioral Genetic Analyses of Aggression." In *The Neuropsychology of Aggression*, ed. Richard E. Whalen. New York and London: Plenum, 1974.

McConnell, James V. "Criminals Can Be Brainwashed—Now." *Psychology Today*, April 1970, p. 14.

McCord, William and Joan. "The Effects of Parental Role Model on Criminality." *The Journal of Social Issues* 14 (1958):66-75.

McCord, William and Joan. *Psycopathy and Delinquency*. New York: Grune & Stratton, 1956.

McGarry, A. Louis. "The Fate of Psychotic Offenders Returned for Trial." *American Journal of Psychiatry* 127 (1971):1181-1184.

Mannheim, Hermann. *Comparative Criminology.* 2 vols. London: Routledge, 1965.

————, ed. *Pioneers of Criminology.* Montclair, N.J.: Patterson Smith, 1972.

Mark, Vernon H., and Ervin, Frank R., eds. *Violence and the Brain.* New York: Harper & Row, 1970.

Marshall, Thomas H. *Class, Citizenship and Social Development.* New York: Doubleday, 1964.

Marx, Karl, and Engels, Frederick. *Collected Works.* Vols. 3 and 4. New York: International Publishing Co., 1975.

Marx, Karl, and Engels, Friedrich. *The Communist Manifesto.* Chicago: The Great Books Foundation, 1955.

Mawson, A.R., and Mawson, Carol Deinhardt. "Psychopathy and Arousal: A New Interpretation of the Psychophysiological Literature." *Biological Psychiatry* 12:1 (1977):49-73.

Mead, Margaret. "Cultural Factors in the Cause and Prevention of Pathological Homicide." *Bulletin of the Menninger Clinic* 28 (1964):11-22.

Mednick, Sarnoff A. "Considerations Regarding the Role of Biological Factors in the Etiology of Criminality." In *Proceedings of the II International Symposium on Criminology.* São Paulo, Brazil, 1975.

Megargee, Edwin I. "A Critical Review of Theories of Violence." In *Crimes of Violence: A Staff Report Submitted to the National Commission on the Causes and Prevention of Violence*, eds. Donald J. Mulvihill and Melvin M. Tumin. Vol. 13. Washington, D.C.: Government Printing Office, 1969.

Mendelson, Jack H., and Mello, Nancy K. "Alcohol, Aggression and Androgens." In *Aggression: Proceedings of the Association for Research in Nervous and Mental Diseases.* New York, 1972.

Menninger, Karl. *The Crime of Punishment.* New York: Viking, 1968.

————. *Whatever Became of Sin?* New York: Hawthorne, 1973.

Merton, Robert K. *Social Theory and Social Structure.* Glencoe, Ill.: Free Press, 1949.

Meyer, Alfred G. "Marxism," *International Encyclopedia of the Social Sciences* (1968), vol. 10, pp. 41-45.

Michael, Jerome, and Adler, Mortimer J. *Crime, Law and Social Science.* New York and London: Harcourt, Brace, 1933.

Miller, Walter B. "Violent Crimes in City Gangs." *The Annals of the American Academy of Political and Social Science* 364 (1966):96-112.

Mills, C. Wright. *Power, Politics, and People.* New York: Oxford University Press, 1963.

Mirsky, Allan F., and Harman, Nancy. "On Aggressive Behavior and Brain Disease—Some Questions and Possible Relationships Derived from the Study of Men and Monkeys." In *The Neuropsychology of Aggression*, ed. Richard E. Whalen. New York and London: Plenum, 1974.

Mitford, Jessica. *Kind and Usual Punishment: The Prison Business.* New York: Knopf, 1973.

Monahan, John. "Abolish the Insanity Defense?—Not Yet." 26 *Rutgers Law Review* 719 (1973).

———. "Dangerous Offenders: A Critique of Kozol *et al.*" *Crime and Delinquency* 19 (1973):418-420.

———. "Dangerousness and Civil Commitment." Testimony before the California Assembly Select Committee on Mentally Disordered Criminal Offenders, 13 December 1973. Mimeographed.

———. "The Prevention of Violence." In *Community Mental Health and the Criminal Justice System*, ed. John Monahan. New York: Pergamon, 1976.

Monahan, John, and Cummings, Lesley. "Social Implications of the Inability to Predict Violence." *Journal of Social Issues* 31 (1975):153-163.

Monroe, Russell R. "Anticonvulsants in the Treatment of Aggression." *Journal of Nervous and Mental Disease* 160 (1975):119-126.

Montagu, Ashley. "Aggression and the Evolution of Man." In *The Neuropsychology of Aggression*, ed. Richard E. Whalen. New York and London: Plenum, 1974. (*See also* Ashley-Montagu, M.F.)

Montesquieu, [Charles Louis de Secondat, Baron de la Brède et de]. *De l'esprit des lois*. Paris, 1868. (First published in 1748.)

Moor, Lise. "Un gène de la délinquance: Mythe ou réalité?" *Annales Médico-Psychologiques* 2:4 (1972):520-527.

More, Sir Thomas. *Utopia*. New York: Classics Club, 1947.

Morris, Norval. *The Honest Politician's Guide to Crime Control*. Chicago: University of Chicago Press, 1970.

———. *The Future of Imprisonment*. Chicago: University of Chicago Press, 1974.

Morrison, S.D.; Erwin, C.W.; Gianturco, D.T.; and Gerber, C.J. "Effect of Lithium on Combative Behavior in Humans." *Diseases of the Nervous System* 34 (1973):186-189.

Moyer, K.E. "The Physiology of Violence." *Psychology Today*, July 1973, pp. 35-38.

Mueller, Gerhard O.W. "Punishment, Corrections and the Law," 45 *Nebraska Law Review* 58 (1966).

Mulvihill, Donald J., and Tumin, Melvin M., Codirectors. *Crimes of Violence: A Staff Report Submitted to the National Commission on the Causes and Prevention of Violence*. Vols. 11, 12, and 13. Washington, D.C.: Government Printing Office, 1969.

Murdoch, B.D. "Electroencephalograms, Aggression and Emotional Maturity in Psychopathic and Non-psychopathic Prisoners." *Psychologia Africana* 14 (1972):216-231.

Murphy, Jeffrie G. "Criminal Punishment and Psychiatric Fallacies." 4 *Law and Society Review* 111 (1969-1970).

Nash, Donald J. "Genetic Aspects of Contemporary Violence." In *Contemporary Violence: A Multidisciplinary Examination*, ed. Charles G. Wilber. Springfield, Ill.: C.C. Thomas, 1975.

324

National Commission on Law Observance and Enforcement. *Report on the Causes of Crime*, vol. 1. Washington, D.C.: Government Printing Office, 1931.

National Institute of Mental Health, Center for Studies of Crime and Delinquency. *Report on the XYY Chromosomal Abnormality.* Chevy Chase, Md.: NIMH, 1970.

Nicholls, George A. *A History of the English Poor Laws in Connection with the State of the Country and the Condition of the People*, vol. 1, A.D. 924 to 1714. New York: Putnam, 1898. Vol. 2, A.D. 1714 to 1853. New York: Putnam, 1904.

Orenberg, Elaine K.; Renson, Jean; Elliott, Glen R.; Barchas, Jack D.; and Kessler, Seymour. "Genetic Determination of Aggressive Behavior and Brain Cyclic AMP." *Psychopharmacology Communications* 1 (1975):99-107.

Packer, Herbert L. *The Limits of the Criminal Sanction.* Stanford, Calif.: Stanford University Press, 1968.

Park, James W.L. "What Is a Political Prisoner?" *American Journal of Correction*, November-December 1972, p. 22.

Paultre, Christian. *De la répréssion de la mendicité et du vagabondage en France sous l'ancien régime.* Reprint of the 1906 edition. Geneva: Slatkine-Megariotis Reprints, 1975.

Pfohl, Stephen J. *Right to Treatment Litigation: A Consideration of Judicial Intervention into Mental Health Policy.* Ohio Department of Mental Health and Mental Retardation, December 1975. Mimeographed.

"Physical Manipulation of the Brain." *The Hastings Center Report*, Special Supplement, May 1973.

Pinel, Philippe. *A Treatise on Insanity.* Translated by D.D. Davis. New York: Hafner Publishing Co., 1962. (First published in 1806.)

Powell, Elwin H. "Crime as a Function of Anomie." *Journal of Criminal Law, Criminology and Police Science* 57 (1966):161-171.

"Psychiatrist Calls Prison 'Warehouse for Mentally Ill.' " *Sacramento Bee*, 25 April 1971.

Quételet, Lambert-Adolphe-Jacques. *A Treatise on Man and the Development of His Faculties.* Facsimile of the English translation of 1842, with an introduction by Solomon Diamond. Gainesville, Fla.: 1969.

Quinney, Richard. *The Social Reality of Crime.* Boston: Little, Brown, 1970.

Quinton, Anthony M. "On Punishment." In *The Philosophy of Punishment*, ed. H.B. Acton. London: Macmillan, 1969.

Radzinowicz, Leon. *A History of English Criminal Law and Its Administration from 1750*, vol. 1. London: Stevens, 1948.

_____. *Ideology and Crime.* New York: Columbia University Press, 1966.

Radzinowicz, Leon, and Wolfgang, Marvin E. *Crime and Justice.* Vol. 1. *The Criminal in Society.* New York and London: Basic Books, 1971.

Ramm, Thilo. "Friedrich Engels," *International Encyclopedia of the Social Sciences* (1968):, vol. 5, pp. 64-68.

Rappeport, Jonas R. *The Clinical Evaluation of the Dangerousness of the Mentally Ill.* Springfield, Ill.: C.C. Thomas, 1967.

Rappeport, Jonas R.; Lassen, George; and Hay, Nancy B. "A Review of the Literature on the Dangerousness of the Mentally Ill." In *The Clinical Evaluation of the Dangerousness of the Mentally Illl,* ed. Jonas R. Rappeport. Springfield, Ill.: C.C. Thomas, 1967.

Rawls, John. "Two Concepts of Rules." In *The Philosophy of Punishment,* ed. H.B. Acton. London: Macmillan, 1969.

Ray, Isaac. *A Treatise on the Medical Jurisprudence of Insanity.* Cambridge, Mass.: Harvard University Press, 1962. (First published in 1838.)

Rector, Milton. "Who Are the Dangerous?" *Bulletin of the American Academy of Psychiatry and the Law* 1 (1973):186-188.

Reid, Sue Titus. *Crime and Criminology.* Hinsdale, Ill.: Dryden Press, 1976.

Rifkin, Arthur; Quitkin, Frederick; Carrillo, Carlos; Blumberg, Arnold G.; and Klein, Donald F. "Lithium Carbonate in Emotionally Unstable Character Disorder." *Archives of General Psychiatry* 27 (1972):519-523.

Robins, Lee N. *Deviant Children Grown Up: A Sociological and Psychiatric Study of Sociopathic Personality.* Baltimore: Williams & Wilkins, 1966.

Rollin, Henry R. *The Mentally Abnormal Offender and the Law.* Oxford: Pergamon, 1969.

Rosen, Ephraim; Fox, Ronald E.; and Gregory, Ian. *Abnormal Psychology.* Philadelphia/London/Toronto: Saunders, 1972.

Roth, Martin. "Human Violence as Viewed from the Psychiatric Clinic." *American Journal of Psychiatry* 128 (1972):1043-1055.

Rothman, David J. *The Discovery of the Asylum: Social Order and Disorder in the New Republic.* Boston: Little, Brown, 1971.

Rousseau, J.J. *Discours sur l'origine et les fondements de l'inégalité parmi les hommes.* Paris: Editions Sociales, 1965.

Royer, Fred L.; Rynearson, Richard; Rice, Warren; and Upper, Denis. "An Inexpensive, Quickly Built Shock Grid for Use with Humans." *Behavior Therapy* 2 (1971):251-252.

Rubin, Sol. *Psychiatry and Criminal Law: Illusions, Fictions and Myths.* Dobbs Ferry, N.Y.: Oceana Publications, 1965.

Rudé, George. *The Crowd in the French Revolution.* New York: Oxford University Press, 1959.

Rusche, Georg, and Kirchheimer, Otto. *Punishment and Social Structure.* New York: Columbia University Press, 1939.

Saleilles, Raymond. *The Individualization of Punishment.* Boston: Little, Brown, 1911.

Sarbin, Theodore R. "The Dangerous Individual: An Outcome of Social Identity Transformations." *The British Journal of Criminology* 7:3 (July 1967):285-295.

Schmitt, Francis O.; Dev, Parvati; and Smith, Barry H. "Electronic Processing of Brain Cells." *Science* 193 (9 July 1976):114-193.

Schneider, Kurt. *Psychopathic Personalities*. Springfield, Ill.: C.C. Thomas, 1958.

Schrag, Clarence. *Crime and Justice: American Style*. Rockville, Md.: National Institute of Mental Health, 1971.

_____. "Critical Analysis of Sociological Theories." In *Crimes of Violence*, eds. Donald J. Mulvihill and Melvin M. Tumin. Washington, D.C.: Government Printing Office, 1969.

Schuckit, Marc A. "Alcoholism and Sociopathy: Diagnostic Confusion." *Quarterly Journal of Studies on Alcohol* 34:2 (1973):157-164.

Schwade, Edward D., and Geiger, Sara G. "Abnormal Electroencephalographic Findings in Severe Behavior Disorders." *Diseases of the Nervous System* 17 (1956):307-317.

Schwade, Edward D., and Geiger, Sara G. "Severe Behavior Disorders with Abnormal Electroencephalograms." *Diseases of the Nervous System* 21 (1960):616-620.

Schwitzgebel, Ralph K. *Development and Legal Regulation of Coercive Behavior Modification Techniques with Offenders*. Chevy Chase, Md.: National Institute of Mental Health, 1971.

Scott, John Paul. *Aggression*. Chicago and London: University of Chicago Press, 1958.

Sellin, Thorsten. *Culture Conflict and Crime: A Report of the Subcommittee on Delinquency of the Committee on Personality and Culture*. New York: Social Science Research Council, 1938.

_____. *Research Memorandum on Crime in the Depression*. New York: Social Science Research Council, 1937.

Shapiro, Alexander. "Delinquent and Disturbed Behavior within the Field of Mental Deficiency." In *The Mentally Abnormal Offender*, eds. A.V.S. de Reuck and Ruth Porter. Boston: Little, Brown, 1968.

Shaw, Clifford R., and McKay, Henry D. *Juvenile Delinquency and Urban Areas*, 2d ed. Chicago: University of Chicago Press, 1969.

Shaw, George Bernard. *The Crime of Imprisonment*. New York: The Citadel Press, 1961.

Sheard, Michael H. "Effect of Lithium on Human Aggression." *Nature* 230 (12 March 1971):113-114.

_____. "Lithium in the Treatment of Aggression." *Journal of Nervous and Mental Disease* 160 (1975):83-99.

Sheldon, William H. *Varieties of Delinquent Youth: An Introduction to Constitutional Psychiatry*. New York: Harper, 1949.

Shoham, Shlomo. *Crime and Social Deviation*. Chicago: University of Chicago Press, 1966.

Shore, Milton F. "Psychological Theories of the Causes of Anti-social Behavior." *Crime and Delinquency* 17 (1971):456-478.

Shupe, Lloyd M. "Alcohol and Crime." *Journal of Criminal Law and Criminology* 44 (1954):661-664.

Silverman, Daniel. "The Electroencephalogram of Criminals." *Archives of Neurology and Psychiatry* 52 (1944):38-42.

Snare, Annika. "Dialogue with Nils Christie." *Issues in Criminology* 10 (1975):35-47.

Sorel, Georges. *Reflections on Violence.* New York: Collier, 1961.

Spece, Roy G., Jr. "Conditioning and Other Technologies Used to 'Treat'? 'Rehabilitate'? 'Demolish'? Prisoners and Mental Patients." 45 *Southern California Law Review* 616 (1972).

Spencer, Herbert. *Justice: Being Part IV of the Principles of Ethics.* New York, 1892.

_____. *Herbert Spencer On Social Evolution. Selected Writings.* Edited and with an introduction by J.D.Y. Peel. Chicago and London: University of Chicago Press, 1972.

_____. *Social Statics, Abridged and Revised.* Reprint of the 1892 edition. Osnabrück, 1966.

Spielberger, Charles D., ed. *Current Topics in Clinical and Community Psychology.* New York and London: Academic, 1970.

Steadman, Henry J. "The Psychiatrist as a Conservative Agent of Social Control." *Social Problems* 20 (1972):263-271.

_____. "Some Evidence on the Inadequacy of the Concept of Dangerousness in Law and Psychiatry." *Journal of Psychiatry and Law* (Winter 1973):409-426.

Steadman, Henry J., and Keveles, Gary. "The Community Adjustment and Criminal Activity of the Baxstrom Patients: 1966-1970." *American Journal of Psychiatry* 129 (1972):305-310.

Steadman, Henry J., and Cocozza, J.J., "The Criminally Insane Patient: Who Gets Out?" *Social Psychiatry* 8 (1973):230-238.

Steadman, Henry J., and Cocozza, Joseph J. "Dangerousness among Incompetent Felony Defendants: A Tentative Assessment of Predictive Validity." Paper presented to the American Society of Criminology, Toronto, 30 October 1975.

Stephen, Sir James Fitzjames. *A History of the Criminal Law of England.* 3 vols. New York: Burt Franklin, n.d. *Idem.* London: Macmillan, 1883.

Stigler, George J. "The Optimum Enforcement of Laws." In *Essays in the Economics of Crime and Punishment*, eds. Gary S. Becker and William M. Landes. New York and London: National Bureau of Economic Research, 1974.

Stone, Alan A. *Mental Health and Law: A System in Transition.* Rockville, Md.: National Institute of Mental Health, 1975.

Struggle for Justice: A Report on Crime and Punishment in America Prepared for the American Friends Service Committee. New York: Hill and Wang, 1971.

Stürup, George K. "Will this Man be Dangerous?" In *The Mentally Abnormal Offender*, eds. A.V.S. de Reuck and Ruth Porter. Boston: Little, Brown, 1968.

Sutherland, Edwin H., and Cressey, Donald R. *Criminology*, 8th ed. Philadelphia/New York/Toronto: Lippincott, 1970.

Szasz, Thomas. *Law, Liberty and Psychiatry*. New York: Macmillan, 1963.

_____. "On Involuntary Psychiatry." *New York Times* 4 August 1975, p. 19.

Szurek, Stanislaus A. "Notes on the Genesis of Psychopathic Personality Trends." *Psychiatry* 5 (1942):1-6.

Tancredi, Laurence R.; Lieb, Julian; and Slaby, Andrew E. *Legal Issues in Psychiatric Care*. Hagerstown, Md.: Harper & Row, 1975.

Tarde, Gabriel. *The Laws of Imitation*. Gloucester, Mass.: Peter Smith, 1962. (First published in 1903.)

_____. *Penal Philosophy*. Boston: Little, Brown, 1912. *Idem.*, Montclair, N.J.: Patterson Smith, 1968.

Taylor, Ian; Walton, Paul; and Young, Jock. *The New Criminology: For a Social Theory of Deviance*. London and Boston: Routledge, 1973.

Thomas, W.I., and Znaniecki, Florian. *The Polish Peasant in Europe and America*, vol. 4. Boston: R.G. Badger, 1920.

Thompson, George N. *The Psychopathic Delinquent and Criminal*. Springfield, Ill.: C.C. Thomas, 1953.

Tiffany, Francis. *Life of Dorothea Lynde Dix*. Ann Arbor, Mich.: Gale, 1971.

Tinklenberg, Jared R. "Alcohol and Violence." In *Alcoholism: Progress in Research and Treatment*, eds. Peter G. Bourne and Ruth Fox. New York and London: Academic, 1973.

Tinklenberg, Jared R., and Woodrow, Kenneth M. "Drug Use among Youthful Assaultive and Sexual Offenders." In *Aggression: Proceedings of the Association for Research in Nervous and Mental Diseases*. New York, 1972.

Toch, Hans. *Violent Men: An Inquiry into the Psychology of Violence*. Chicago: Aldine, 1969.

Toomey, Beverly G.; Allen, Harry E.; and Simonsen, Clifford E. "The Right to Treatment: Professional Liabilities in the Criminal Justice and Mental Health Systems." *The Prison Journal* 54 (1974):43-56.

Townsend, Joseph. *A Dissertation on the Poor Laws by a Well-wisher to Mankind*. Berkeley/Los Angeles/London/: University of California Press, 1971. (Originally published in 1786.)

Traub, Stuart H., and Little, Craig B., eds. *Theories of Deviance*. Itasca, Ill.: Peacock Publishers, 1975.

Tupin, Joe P.; Smith, David B.; Clanon, T.L.; Kim, L.I.; Nugent, A.; and Groupe, A. "The Long-term Use of Lithium in Aggressive Prisoners." *Comprehensive Psychiatry* 14 (1973):311-317.

Turk, Austin T. "Law as a Weapon in Social Conflict." *Social Problems* 23:3 (February 1976):276-291.

Usdin, Gene L. "Broader Aspects of Dangerousness." In *The Clinical Evaluation of the Dangerousness of the Mentally Ill,* ed. Jonas R. Rappeport. Springfield, Ill.: C.C. Thomas, 1967.

Valenstein, Elliot S. *Brain Control: A Critical Examination of Brain Stimulation and Psychosurgery.* New York: Wiley, 1973.

Van den Haag, Ernest. *Punishing Criminals: Concerning a Very Old and Painful Question.* New York: Basic Books, 1975.

Villeneuve-Bargemont, Alban de. *Economie politique chrétienne, ou recherches sur la nature et les causes du paupérisme, en France et en Europe, et sur les moyens de le soulager et de le prévenir,* vol. 1. Paris, 1854.

Virchow, Rudolf. *Disease, Life and Man.* Stanford, Calif.: Stanford University Press, 1958.

Vold, George B. *Theoretical Criminology.* New York: Oxford University Press, 1958.

Von Hirsch, Andrew. *Doing Justice: The Choice of Punishments.* New York: Hill and Wang, 1975.

_____. "Prediction of Criminal Conduct and Preventive Confinement of Convicted Persons." 21 *Buffalo Law Review* 717 (1972).

Walker, Nigel. *Crime and Insanity in England.* Vol. 1: *The Historical Perspective.* Edinburgh: Edinburgh University Press, 1968.

Walter, W. Grey. "Electro-encephalography." In *Recent Progress in Psychiatry,* 2d ed., ed. G.W.T.H. Fleming. London: J. & A. Churchill, n.d.

Weihofen, Henry. *The Urge to Punish. New Approaches to the Problem of Mental Irresponsibility for Crime.* New York: Farrar, Strauss, 1956.

Wenk, Ernest A., and Halatyn, Thomas V. *An Analysis of Classification Factors for Young Adult Offenders.* Vol. 6: *Violence Factors.* Unpublished report by the Research Center, National Council on Crime and Delinquency. Davis, Calif., October 1974. Mimeographed.

Wenk, Ernest A.; Robison, James O.; and Smith, Gerald W. "Can Violence Be Predicted?" *Crime and Delinquency* 18 (1972):393-402.

Wertham, Fredric. *The Show of Violence.* New York: Doubleday, 1949.

_____. *A Sign for Cain: An Exploration of Human Violence.* New York: Macmillan, 1966.

Wertz, Richard W., ed. *Readings on Ethical and Social Issues in Biomedicine.* Englewood Cliffs, N.J.: Prentice-Hall, 1973.

West, D.J., ed. *Criminological Implications of Chromosome Abnormalities. Papers presented to the Cropwood Round-table Conference, December 1969.* Cambridge: University of Cambridge, 1969.

Wexler, David B. "Therapeutic Justice." 57 *Minnesota Law Review* 289 (1972).

Whalen, Richard E., ed. *The Neuropsychology of Aggression.* New York and London: Plenum, 1974.

Wilber, Charles G., ed. *Contemporary Violence: A Multidisciplinary Examination.* Springfield, Ill.: C.C. Thomas, 1975.

Wilkins, Leslie T. "Equity and Republican Justice." *The Annals of the American Academy of Political and Social Science* 423 (1976):152-161.

Witkin, Herman A.; Mednick, Sarnoff A.; Schulsinger, Fini; Bakkestrom, Eskild;

Christiansen, Karl O.; Goodenough, Donald R.; Hirschhorn, Kurt; Lundsteen, Claes; Owen, David R.; Philip, John; Rubin, Donald B.; and Stocking, Martha. "Criminality in XYY and XXY Men." *Science* 193 (13 August 1976):547-554.

Wolfe, Bertram D. *Three Who Made a Revolution.* Boston: Beacon Press, 1961.

Wolfgang, Marvin E. *Patterns in Criminal Homicide.* Philadelphia: University of Pennsylvania, 1958.

Wolfgang, Marvin E.; Figlio, Robert M.; and Sellin, Thorsten. *Delinquency in a Birth Cohort.* Chicago: University of Chicago Press, 1972.

Wolfgang, Marvin E.; Savitz, Leonard; and Johnston, Norman, eds., *The Sociology of Crime and Delinquency.* New York: Wiley, 1970.

Wolfgang, Marvin E., and Ferracuti, Franco. *The Subculture of Violence.* New York: Barnes and Noble, 1967.

Wootton, Barbara. *Social Science and Social Pathology.* London: Allen & Unwin, 1959.

Index

Abbott, Edith, 127
Abercromby, Thomas, 252
Académie des Sciences Morales et Politiques, 3
acquittal in insanity cases, 165, 166, 171, 178-179, 179n, 181
Adams, Samuel Hopkins, 80, 82
Addison, Joseph, 60
adjustment centers, 208, 208n
Adler, Mortimer J., 148
adoption studies of criminality, 91
adulteration of food, 114
age and crime, 35, 36
alcohol, 200; Aschaffenburg on, 243; and auto accidents, 247; and chances of arrest, 247; and child abuse, 189; consumption, Boston, 243; consumption, Germany, 243; consumption, Jacksonian era, 243; and crime, 37, 45, 105, 243-250; and dangerousness, 188; and EEGs, 231; effect on central nervous system, 247; and homicide, 243, 244-245, 247; and inhibitions, 247; and law, 247-248; Muslim views on, 245; and psychopathy, 245-246, 249, 254, 255; Van Kan on, 243; and violence, 243, 245
alcoholics, treatment for, 200
alcoholism, 246
Alexander, Franz, 155-157
Alexander III, 30
Alfonso XIII, 29
American Association of Neurological Surgeons, 241
American Civil Liberties Union, 204
American Law Institute, definition of dangerous person, xiv
American Medical Association, 205
American Psychological Association, 205
American Psychiatric Association, 188-190
American Psychiatric Association Task Force on Psychosurgery, 240-241

anarchism, 29
anatomy and crime, 69, 75-76, 102, 219-222
Anectine, 182-183, 199, 206
anomie, 133-134
anthropology, 60, 62-63, 64, 72, 95, 102, 104
Aristotle, 161
Arnold, Edward ("Mad Ned"), 162-163
arraignment, insanity at, 179
Artena, ecclesiastical state of, 121
Articles of Religion, 53
Aschaffenburg, Gustav, 45, 74-75, 85-86, 121, 265
Ashford, Daisy, 120
asphyxia livida, 230
assassinations of Alexander II, 29-30; Bogolepov, 30; Duc de Berry, 27; Empress Elizabeth, 29; Grand Duke Sergei, 30; Plehve, 30; President McKinley, 29; Sadi Carnot, 29; Sipyaghin, 30; Umberto I, 29
asthenic type, 219-220. *See also* ectomorphs
ataraxics, 194-195
Atascadero State Hospital, 180-181, 182n, 199, 204
atavism, 64, 67, 69, 85, 102
athletic type, 219-220. *See also* mesomorphs
Auburn Penitentiary, 119
Auburn State Lunatic Asylum, 178
aversive therapy, 197. *See also* behavior modification, brainwashing, conditioning
Azev, Yevno, 30-31

Bagehot, Walter, 85
Baillarger, Jules, 252
Balasubramanian, V., 234
Balzac, Honoré de, 41
Barzun, Jacques, 63, 64-65
Bates, Daisy, 256-257
Bazelon, Judge David L., 172, 173

331

Narabayashi, Hirataro, 234
Narodnaya Volya, 29-30
National Council on Crime and Delinquency, Model Sentencing Act, xiv-xv
nationalism, 27
Natural Law, 33
natural selection, 65; and criminality, 61; retrogressive, 61, 85
Nazis, 92, 116, 121
Neanderthal man, discovery of, 62
Nero, 11
neurotics, and crime, 157, 158; vs. psychopaths, 256
New Hampshire test for insanity, 166, 171. *See also* Durham test
New York State Criminal Procedure Law, definition of "dangerous incapacitated person," xv
norms of social behavior, 141
Nugent, Dr. Arthur G., 182-183

Oedipus complex, 155, 157
Oettingen, A. von, 44-45
Ogburn, William F., 115
Ohio Penitentiary, 194-195n, 203, 213n
Ohio Revised Code, definition of dangerous offender, xiv
Ohlin, Lloyd, 134-135
Okhrana, 30
opportunity and crime, 129, 135, 139
Organized Crime Control Act, definition of "dangerous," xv
Original Sin, 53, 54, 269
Orzack, Maressa H., 240
Owen, Robert, 51, 51n

Park, James W.L., 159
parole from mental hospitals, 181-182
Patuxent Institution, 198, 209
Paul, Saint, 54
Paul IV, Pope, 121
Paultre, Christian, 8
Pavlov, Ivan, 196
Peel, Sir Robert, 169
Penna, Manoel, 190-191, 247

People v. *Guillett,* 248
Perley, Chief Justice, 171
person, crimes against, 45
personality, tampering with, 206
personality disorders, 190, 213-214. *See also* diagnosis, psychiatric
philosophes, 13, 17
phrenology, 61, 67
physicians' view of criminality, 221-222
physiognomy, 61
physiology and crime, Ch. 30 (219-222)
physique and criminality. *See* anatomy, somatotype theories
Pike, State v., 171
Pilsudski, Bronislaw, 30, 30n
Pinel, Philippe, 68
pleasure principle, 156
Plehve, V.K., von, 30
Poincaré, Henri, 93
Poletti, Filippo, 106
political deviants, 27-32
polygraph (lie detector), 261
population, 40; growth, U.S., 125
positive spikes, 229-231
positivism, 59, 63, 67-78; and dangerousness, 272; and societal causation theories, 147-148
Positivist School of criminology, 65, 67-78. *See also* positivism
poverty, relationship to crime, 4-5, 37, 41, 45-46, 47, 54, 95-96, 113-114, 115, 134, 204
power, 145
power élite, 141
predestination, 53
prediction of dangerousness, 188, 189-190, 191-192
prehensory instinct, 113
prevention, 74
preventive detention, 77
Prichard, James C., 68
Priestley, Joseph, 21
Prins, Adolphe, 76-77
prisons, disturbances in US, 203-204; effect on dangerousness, 138-139;

341

standard for, 210, 210n
profession, influence on crime, 36
progress and crime, Durkheim on,
107-108; Ferri on, 107; Garofalo
on, 107; Hall on, 108; Lombroso
on, 105; Lucas on, 105-106; Poletti
on, 106; Tarde on, 106-107
proletariat, 39-40, 50, 95-96
propensity to crime, 35, 36-37
property crimes, 45, 49, 100, 113-116
Protection of Human Subjects, National Commission for, 209-211,
239-241
Proudhon, Pierre-Joseph, 29
psychiatry, 67, 69
psychoanalysis, 153-159, 186, 194
psychopaths, 68-69, 70-71, 167-168, 168n;
251-258, 259-264; aggressive, 230-
231; and alcohol, 245-246, 249,
254, 255; anxiety in, 261, 263;
arousal in, 263-264; Australian
aboriginal, 256-257; brain surgery
for, 237; charm, 254; Cleckley on,
252-255; and creativity, 259; description of, 68-70, 252-255, 257;
diagnosis, 257; EEGs in, 229-231;
egocentricity, 254; emotional shal-
lowness, 254; environmental causes,
264; and epinephrin, 261-263; galvanic skin response of, 261; hard to
condition, 256; Henderson on, 253,
259; and hyperactivity, 260-261;
insensitivity, 262; intelligence, 254,
255; Kittrie on, 251; Kozol on, 259;
Kraepelin on, 252; Lykken test,
261; and maturation, 229-230;
Maudsley on, 70; neurophysiology
of, 259-264; physical insensitivity,
260; numbers in population, 257;
in Ohio Penitentiary, 255-256, 263;
and polygraph test, 261; poor vs.
rich, 257; in prison, 255-256; in
psychiatric hospitals, 255; vs. psy-
choneurotics, 256; response to
stimulants, 260, 262; sexual, 237;
shamelessness, 254; treatment of,
useless, 258; types of, 259, 261n,

263; unreliability, 254; Wootton on,
251, 257
psychosurgery. *See* surgery
punishment, 15, 62; in Adjustment Centers, 208, 208n; in Alabama doghouses, 208, 208n; Beccaria on, 16-
17; in behavior modification, 200;
Blackstone on, 19, 20; Bonger on,
112; capital, 9, 17, 271; certainty
of, 16-17; Constituent Assembly
on, 24; for dangerous offenders, 77;
deterrent effects of, 13-14, 20;
differential, of rich and poor, 9-10;
Divine, 112; during reign of Elizabeth, 1, 6-7; ends of, 19-20; in England, 271-272; *estrapade*, 8; an evil,
17, 21; executions, 8; in French
criminal code of 1790, 23-24; Garofalo on, 74; Grotius on, 20; Holmes
on, 273; for incapacitation, 21;
individualization of, 74; of insane,
162-163, 165; Jaucourt on, 20; and
justice, 272; Kirchheimer on, 117;
and law, 16; Lombroso on, 271;
Luther on, 8; Menninger on, 272-
273; Middle Ages, 5-6; objectives
of, 21; ordained by God, 19; of
poor, 145-146; proportionality of,
14, 24, 72; and rehabilitation, 215;
in Rights of Man, 23; for rogues,
vagabonds and beggars, 7; in Rome,
4; Romilly on, 9; severity of, 17,
117, 271; and social class, 8-9, 17;
and Social Contract, 19; and therapy, 239; of thieves in reign of Henry VIII, 6; torture, Tudor period,
6-7; unconscious, 157; US, 208-
209; of vagrants, 5, 8-9; as vengeance, 21, 192, 272-273
pyknik type, 219-220. *See also* endomorphs

Quételet, Lambert-Adolphe-Jacques,
34-37
Quinney, Richard, 145
Quinton, Anthony, 25

Rackstraw, Ralph, xix

Whitehead, Alfred North, 133
"Wild Beast" test, 163, 163n
Wilde, Oscar, 271-272
willpower, 158; as check on criminality, 120
Winchester, Statute of, 5
witches, 12, 32
Wolfe, Bertram D., 30
Wolfgang, Marvin E., 135, 244
Wootton, Barbara (Barbara Frances

Wootton Wright, Baroness Wootton of Abinger), 95, 251, 257
Wrong, Dennis H., 141

XYY chromosome. *See* chromosomes

Zangwill, Israel, 126
Znaniecki, Florian, 125-126
Zoar, xix

About the Author

Ysabel Rennie received the B.A. and M.A. in history from Stanford University, where she was a member of Phi Beta Kappa. At Harvard she held the Longfellow Fellowship from Radcliffe College and was awarded the Agassiz Fellowship for further studies in Buenos Aires. While there, she wrote *The Argentine Republic* (Macmillan, 1945). Mrs. Rennie has served in government (The Office of Strategic Services and Department of State), has been a columnist for the *Washington Post,* and has written two novels, *The Blue Chip* (Harper's, 1954) and *Kingside* (Holt, Rinehart & Winston, 1963).

For the past decade she has been involved with prison problems in Ohio, where she has served on the Governor's Task Force on Corrections and on the Ethical Review Committee of the Department of Mental Health and Mental Retardation. In 1972 Mrs. Rennie was given the Ohio Governor's Award "for excellence of achievement benefiting mankind and improving the quality of life for all Ohioans."